Substance and the Fundamentality of the Familiar

Substance and the Fundamentality of the Familiar explicates and defends a novel neo-Aristotelian account of the structure of material objects. While there have been numerous treatments of properties, laws, causation, and modality in the neo-Aristotelian metaphysics literature, this book is one of the first full-length treatments of wholes and their parts. Another aim of the book is to further develop the newly revived area concerning the question of fundamental mereology, the question of whether wholes are metaphysically prior to their parts or vice versa. Inman develops a fundamental mereology with a grounding-based conception of the structure and unity of substances at its core, what he calls Substantial Priority, one that distinctively allows for the fundamentality of ordinary, medium-sized composite objects. He offers both empirical and philosophical considerations against the view that the parts of every composite object are metaphysically prior, in particular the view that ascribes ontological pride of place to the smallest microphysical parts of composite objects, which currently dominates debates in metaphysics, philosophy of science, and philosophy of mind. Ultimately, he demonstrates that Substantial Priority is well motivated in virtue of its offering a unified solution to a host of metaphysical problems involving material objects.

Ross D. Inman is Assistant Professor of Philosophy at Southwestern Baptist Theological Seminary, USA. He is a former Research Fellow at the University of Notre Dame, Center for Philosophy of Religion and Saint Louis University. He was awarded the 2014 Marc Sanders Prize in Philosophy of Religion. His research has appeared in *Philosophical Studies, Oxford Studies in Philosophy of Religion, Metaphysica,* and *Philosophia Christi.*

Routledge Studies in Metaphysics

For a full list of titles in this series, please visit www.routledge.com

1 **The Semantics and Metaphysics of Natural Kinds**
   Edited by Helen Beebee and Nigel Sabbarton-Leary

2 **The Metaphysics of Powers**
   Their Grounding and their Manifestations
   Edited by Anna Marmodoro

3 **Freedom of the Will**
   A Conditional Analysis
   Ferenc Huoranski

4 **The Future of the Philosophy of Time**
   Edited by Adrian Bardon

5 **Properties, Powers and Structures**
   Issues in the Metaphysics of Realism
   Edited by Alexander Bird, Brian Ellis, and Howard Sankey

6 **The Puzzle of Existence**
   Why Is There Something Rather than Nothing?
   Edited by Tyron Goldschmidt

7 **Neo-Davidsonian Metaphysics**
   From the True to the Good
   Samuel C. Wheeler III

8 **Neo-Aristotelian Perspectives in Metaphysics**
   Edited by Daniel D. Novotný and Lukáš Novák

9 **Nominalism about Properties**
   New Essays
   Edited by Ghislain Guigon and Gonzalo Rodriguez-Pereyra

10 **Substance and the Fundamentality of the Familiar**
    A Neo-Aristotelian Mereology
    Ross D. Inman

Substance and the Fundamentality of the Familiar
A Neo-Aristotelian Mereology

Ross D. Inman

NEW YORK AND LONDON

First published 2018
by Routledge
711 Third Avenue, New York, NY 10017

and by Routledge
2 Park Square, Milton Park, Abingdon, Oxon OX14 4RN

Routledge is an imprint of the Taylor & Francis Group, an informa business

 2018 Taylor & Francis

The right of Ross D. Inman to be identified as author of this work has been asserted by him in accordance with sections 77 and 78 of the Copyright, Designs and Patents Act 1988.

All rights reserved. No part of this book may be reprinted or reproduced or utilised in any form or by any electronic, mechanical, or other means, now known or hereafter invented, including photocopying and recording, or in any information storage or retrieval system, without permission in writing from the publishers.

Trademark Notice: Product or corporate names may be trademarks or registered trademarks, and are used only for identification and explanation without intent to infringe.

Library of Congress Cataloging-in-Publication Data
A catalog record for this book has been requested

ISBN: 978-1-138-06559-8 (hbk)
ISBN: 978-1-315-15960-7 (ebk)

Typeset in Sabon
by Apex CoVantage, LLC

To Suzanne,
my love,
whose "beauty awakens the soul to act."
—Dante Alighieri

Contents

List of figure   ix
Acknowledgments   xiii

    Introduction   1

1   Serious Essentialism   11

2   Grounding and Essence   53

3   Fundamental Mereology and the Priority of Substance   75

4   Against Part-Priority   115

5   Substantial Priority: Cats, Statues, and Lumps   159

6   Substantial Priority: Vagueness, the Many, and Overdetermination   183

7   Getting Personal: Substantial Priority and Personal Ontology   203

8   Substantial Priority: Counting the Cost   231

9   Substantial Priority and Empirical Inadequacy   257

    Conclusion   279

Bibliography   283
Index   301

Figure

3.1 Three-Atom Model   87

The most ancient opinions are often returned to as if new, and many delight in resurrecting them because—having been forgotten—they seem to say new and marvelous things. And so it is that the young listen to them with pleasure, because it is natural for what is new and marvelous to delight the senses.
—John Buridan, *In De an.* III.11

[O]ur moderns do not give enough credit to Saint Thomas and to the other great men of his time and that there is much more solidity than one imagines in the opinions of the Scholastic philosophers and theologians, provided that they are used appropriately and in their proper place. I am even convinced that, if some exact and thoughtful mind took the trouble to clarify and summarize their thoughts after the manner of the analytic geometers, he would find there a great treasure of extremely important and wholly demonstrative truths.
—Gottfried Wilhelm Leibniz, *Discourse on Metaphysics* 11

Acknowledgments

I'd first and foremost like to express my deepest gratitude to my wife, Suzanne, to whom this book is dedicated. Suzanne, your faithful love and support have been an unending source of strength in my life and throughout the duration of this project. I'm quite certain that I wouldn't be the person I am today without your friendship.

I'm especially indebted to my mentor and dear friend J. P. Moreland, at whose knee I first learned metaphysics and who continues to inspire me to be a better philosopher and a better human being.

I also want to express my appreciation to my doctoral supervisor, Peter Simons, for his incisive comments on a large portion of the book. His formal and technical philosophical acumen, combined with his sensitivity to the contours of the history of Western philosophy and science, helped make the book much more rigorous than it would have otherwise been.

I also would like to express my thanks to Jeff Brower, Rob Koons, Jonathan Lowe, and Jonathan Schaffer for their generous encouragement and willingness to offer helpful and perceptive feedback on the ideas to follow. I am particularly grateful for the influence of Jonathan Lowe, who served as an examiner on my doctoral dissertation (which this book is largely based on) just a few months before his death. True to form, Jonathan was encouraging and gracious and offered constructive feedback on the ideas in the pages to follow; the landscape of contemporary metaphysics is surely impoverished by his absence.

I'd also like to extend a warm thanks to Anna Marmodoro and the members of the Power Structuralism in Ancient Ontologies project at Oxford University. Many of the ideas presented here were given a preliminary hearing during the course of the 2012 academic year, part of which was spent in residence at Oxford University as a visiting graduate student. The congenial nature of the project members along with their knack for philosophical rigor made the 2012 Michaelmas term philosophically fruitful and immensely enjoyable. Lastly, I am grateful to the many friends along the way who gave of their time and resources to offer helpful comments on various parts of the manuscript. Thanks are in order to Caleb Cohoe, Matthew Frise, Paul Gould, Bradley Rettler, Phillip Swenson, and Craig Thompson.

Introduction

Amidst the widespread disagreement in contemporary metaphysics there has emerged roughly two general postures or stances regarding the nature of properties, modality, laws of nature, time, causation, persistence, mereology, and even metaphysical inquiry itself.[1] While the origins of these two postures toward traditional metaphysical disputes can be traced back to our ancient philosophical predecessors, their influence on analytic metaphysics in the second half of the twentieth century hardly needs emphasizing.

The first general metaphysical posture, what I will refer to as "neo-Aristotelianism," takes its cue from Aristotle and his medieval interpreters.[2] For the neo-Aristotelian, the denizens of spacetime belong to fundamental ontological and natural kinds as expressed by their existence, identity, and persistence conditions. Some of these spacetime occupants are metaphysically elite, fundamental, or basic in that their natures are such that they fail to depend on any distinct entity for their existence and identity. Hence the category of substance as a basic particular lies at the heart of a neo-Aristotelian ontology. Properties, whether particular or universal, are metaphysically posterior to their substantial bearers. Causation, it is argued, is best understood in light of the manifestation of the powers and liabilities of individual substances. Modal truths, according to many in this camp, are plausibly grounded in the powers, dispositions, or the natures of fundamental substances (and the relations between them).[3] Laws of nature, argue some, are derivative on the dispositional essences of the natural properties of substances.[4] A neo-Aristotelian metaphysic, then, is shot-through with necessary connections, particularly those that stem from the natures of fundamental substances. At bottom, the neo-Aristotelian considers the causal motor and cement of the universe to ultimately derive from propertied particulars that are metaphysically fundamental—that is, Aristotelian substances.

The second general metaphysical posture, what has gone under the label of "neo-Humeanism," has as its patron saint the Scottish Enlightenment philosopher David Hume. The widespread appeal and influence of neo-Humeanism in contemporary analytic metaphysics, however, is largely the product of the work of the late David Lewis.

Perhaps the central tenet of neo-Humeanism is the doctrine of *Independence*, the thesis that there are no necessary connections between distinct existences. According to Independence, the instantiation of a property at some point in spacetime does not entail or necessitate anything about any distinct point in spacetime. Accompanying Independence is the thesis of *Humean Supervenience*: the thesis that the world is an arrangement of instantaneous, point-sized instantiations of perfectly natural properties, a "vast mosaic of local matters of particular fact, just one little thing and then another . . . And that is all."[5] By Lewis's lights, the only fundamental relations that obtain between the occupants of spacetime are temporal or spatial relations, nothing more. While not all adherents to a neo-Humean metaphysic follow Lewis in countenancing such a sparse ontological base, the fact remains that the neo-Humean task is to account for the apparent causal, modal, and nomic riches of the actual world in terms of the spatiotemporal distribution of these point-sized qualities and the fundamental relations between them. On this view, the identity and qualitative nature of ordinary material objects composed of these point-sized masses such as trees, people, and poodles—*what* they are and *how* they are—are entirely dependent on the point-sized distribution of local matters of fact.

Yet an adherence to Independence makes this task a difficult one. The reason is clear: the distribution of qualities and the relations between them does not, by itself, entail anything about what *does* happen, what *would* happen, or what *must* happen at any distinct place in the arrangement. Be that as it may, Neo-Humeans have all but shied away from such a daunting task.

Properties, by the neo-Humean's lights, are intrinsically impotent in that they in no way entail or necessitate a particular outcome in the world. As such, in order to account for facts about ways the world *could* have been—i.e., modal facts, the neo-Humean must look beyond the rather dim resources of the actual world. The neo-Humean solution here is to increase the number of Humean mosaics that resemble the actual world so that there are enough of them to account for the plenitude of possibilities, that is, all of the ways things could have been. Possible worlds, at least for Lewis, are simply alternative concrete Humean mosaics and are just as real as the actual mosaic we find ourselves in. Thus to affirm that there could have been a talking donkey is to say that there exists a concrete (albeit isolated) spatiotemporal world that contains a talking donkey as a part (although even non-Lewisian varieties of neo-Humeanism "outsource" the truthmakers for modal claims as well, albeit to abstracta considered as either maximally consistent states of affairs or propositions); facts about what is necessary and possible, then, are best construed in terms of existential quantification over concrete possible worlds.

With this machinery in hand, the neo-Humean is able to ground ways the actual world *would* have been if certain circumstances had obtained—i.e., counterfactuals, in terms of ways things go in distinct possible worlds.

A counterfactual conditional $A\square\rightarrow C$ is true, for instance, just in case in the possible worlds most similar to the actual world where A is true, C is true as well. Causation, likewise, is analyzed in terms of counterfactual dependence: event a causes event b just in case a and b both occur and are distinct and were a not to occur, b would not have occurred. Finally, the laws of nature, as opposed to mere accidental regularities in nature, are those regularities that are theorems of an ideally simple and explanatorily strong description of the world. Employing only the resources of actual and possible local matters of fact devoid of intrinsic modal content, the neo-Humean offers a competing fundamental ontology of properties, modality, mereology, causation, and laws than that of the neo-Aristotelian.

Neo-Aristotelianism is on the rise in contemporary analytic metaphysics. But while those in the neo-Aristotelian camp have offered in-depth treatments of laws, causation, and modality in terms of irreducibly powerful properties, there has been, by comparison, less work devoted to considering what a neo-Aristotelian mereology might look like.[6] The exception of Fine (1994c; 1999; 2010), Koslicki (2007; 2008), and Lowe (1998) withstanding, such a gap in the neo-Aristotelian camp is peculiar indeed given the pride of place Aristotle and the medievals gave to the category of substance over property in fundamental ontology.

A central aim of this book is to help narrow this gap in the neo-Aristotelian literature. The current metaphysical climate, I believe, is ripe for reexamining a classical conception of substance. There are two contemporary factors that contribute to the timeliness of such a project. First, analytic metaphysics has seen a resurgence of interest in the notion of metaphysical grounding or priority in the very recent past. While the notion of metaphysical dependence or priority has been with the Western philosophical tradition from its inception, an increasing number of philosophers are beginning to appreciate the enduring value of this piece of metaphysical machinery.

Second, arguably one of the primary sub-areas of analytic metaphysics responsible for its triumphal return in the second half of the twentieth century has been the area of mereological metaphysics. Though its contemporary roots originate with the work of the Polish logician Stanisław Leśniewski, particularly his 1916 *Foundations of a General Theory of Manifolds* published in Polish, it wasn't until the arrival of Henry S. Leonard's and Nelson Goodman's *The Calculus of Individuals* in English in 1940 that formal mereology began to be a topic of interest in its own right in contemporary anglophone philosophy. And with the 1987 publication of Peter Simon's *Parts: A Study in Ontology* serving as the bridge linking issues in contemporary analytic metaphysics with formal mereology as well as the subsequent arrival of Peter van Inwagen's *Material Beings* in 1990, the sub-discipline of mereological metaphysics was underway. Today, it is difficult to think of any area of analytic metaphysics that remains untouched by the reach of mereology.

The philosophical study of parts and wholes (mereology) and the notion of metaphysical grounding naturally gives rise to the question of the priority relations that obtain between a whole and its parts, what Jonathan Schaffer has recently labeled *fundamental mereology*. Fundamental mereology has a rich and exciting historical pedigree spanning the work of Plato, Aristotle, Plotinus, Boethius, Abelard, Aquinas, Scotus, Spinoza, Leibniz, Husserl, Bradley (to name a few), and continues to provide the underlying framework for many of the debates at the heart of contemporary metaphysics, philosophy of science, and the philosophy of mind.

By Schaffer's lights there are two exhaustive and exclusive options in fundamental mereology, each formulated with reference to the cosmos, the maximal sum or fusion of all concrete material reality. A pluralistic fundamental mereology—*Pluralism* for short—claims that the proper parts of the cosmos are metaphysically prior to the whole. A monistic fundamental mereology—*Monism* for short—on the other hand, claims that the cosmos itself is fundamental and thus metaphysically prior to its many proper parts. Perhaps the predominant fundamental mereology endorsed by contemporary philosophers is a variant of Pluralism—what Schaffer calls *Atomism*—and takes the minimal microphysical parts of the cosmos to be metaphysically fundamental; every object composed out of microphysical entities is derivative or non-fundamental.

A common assumption shared by Pluralists and Monists alike is that the live options in fundamental mereology exclude views that assign metaphysical fundamentality to ordinary, medium-sized composite objects or a particular subset thereof; the metaphysically fundamental entities or substances (to use more traditional terminology) reside exclusively at either the top or bottom level of the hierarchy of composition. Conspicuously absent from recent discussions of fundamental mereology, then, is an explication and defense of the tenability of ascribing metaphysical fundamentality to at least some intermediate composite objects corresponding to ordinary, macrophysical composite objects like people, trees, and tigers. A central aim in this book is to carve out space for a heretofore neglected fundamental mereology, one that countenances fundamental intermediate composite objects, and attempt to show that such a view is defensible in light of recent opinion to the contrary.

A robust neo-Aristotelian fundamental mereology hinges on a host of assumptions in fundamental ontology that need to be examined in their own right. The first chapter is devoted to developing and defending my preferred fundamental ontology—serious essentialism—which holds that the fundamental joints in reality are constituted by primitive natures that defy reduction in terms of modal notions such as necessity and possibility. I aim to make a clean break with modal essentialism and offer a neo-Aristotelian account that situates the notion of essence within a robust categorial ontology.

In Chapter 2, I apply the aforementioned serious-essentialist framework to the notion of metaphysical grounding. Here I outline a host of guiding assumptions about metaphysical grounding and its formal and structural features. I attempt to motivate a view with historical roots in medieval Aristotelianism which takes the notion of grounding at work in mereological metaphysics, viz. ontological dependence, to obtain ultimately in virtue of the natures or essences of entities. On my view, only a species of essential grounding is best suited to carve out relations of metaphysical priority and posteriority between wholes and their parts.

I then turn in Chapter 3 to explicating the question of fundamental mereology in light of the recent work by Jonathan Schaffer. I explicate Schaffer's proposed constraints and options in fundamental mereology and argue for an alternative classification of views in terms of what I call *Minimal Fundamental Mereology* that does not run the risk of excluding ordinary composite objects such as tigers, trees, and people from being metaphysically fundamental and prior to their parts. I then begin to unpack my preferred fundamental mereology—*Substantial Priority*—which employs the classical Aristotelian insight that substances are metaphysically fundamental in the sense that they are not only metaphysically prior to each of their parts, but also ground the existence and identity of each of their parts. The heart of Substantial Priority is the view that some ordinary, composite objects fall within the category of *substance* understood in this sense. As such, not all ordinary composite objects are grounded either in the cosmos (as per Monism) or in microphysical reality (as per Atomism).

The primary aim of Chapter 4 is to critically engage what is, arguably, the predominant fundamental mereology at play in the contemporary literature, Part-Priority, in its most popular guise, *Priority Microphysicalism* (PM). According to Part-Priority, the proper parts of composite objects are prior to their wholes. PM is the view that the smallest, microphysical parts of composite objects are metaphysically prior to the objects of which they are a part. After considering several lines of evidence in favor of Part-Priority and PM, I examine two general arguments against these views. The first—*the argument from the possibility of gunk*—targets Part-Priority in particular and trades on both the metaphysical possibility of gunky worlds (worlds devoid of mereological simples) and the thesis that every (non-empty) grounding domain includes, of necessity, at least one metaphysically fundamental entity. The second argument—*the argument from the failure of whole-part supervenience*—sets its sights on both Part-Priority and PM and argues that a composite object's failing to supervene on its proper parts (and their basic arrangements) entails its failure to be grounded in its proper parts. I offer examples from quantum mechanics, chemistry, and systems biology that suggest a failure of whole-part supervenience for at least some mereological wholes; while Part-Priority may provide the correct grounding description for certain kinds of composite objects, it fails as a *global* fundamental mereology as it is ill-suited to account for plausible instances of mereological structure in the natural sciences.

I then turn in Chapters 5 and 6 to motivating Substantial Priority in particular by showing that the view lends a unified solution to a host of conundrums in contemporary metaphysics. In Chapter 5 I consider the problem of Tibbles the Cat and Goliath and Lumpl. In Chapter 6 I consider causal overdetermination, the Problem of the Many, and the Argument from Vagueness. I argue that Substantial Priority is theoretically fruitful in so far as it affords a unified solution to each of the earlier puzzles, while preserving important commonsense intuitions about the existence of ordinary composite substances, many of which play an integral role in our-best empirical theories.

In Chapter 7 I take up the task of exploring the relationship between Substantial Priority and personal ontology. I offer two additional arguments in favor of Substantial Priority, *the terminus argument* and *the tracking argument*, the latter of which turns on the notion that the nature and activity of human persons carves out genuinely non-redundant causal (libertarian free will) and qualitative (phenomenal consciousness) structure in the world. Substantial Priority offers a fundamental mereology that is favorable to those who come to the question of fundamental mereology with such antecedent commitments in the metaphysics of mind and free will. I then show how Substantial Priority offers a natural framework to account for certain unity-intuitions in the philosophy of mind, and how the view opens up important dialectical space concerning several important arguments against materialism and hylomorphism about human persons.

In the last two chapters I take up the task of defending Substantial Priority from what I consider to be the most formidable objections. Any respectable view in mereological metaphysics must carry its weight in light of impending objections, and Substantial Priority is no exception. While Substantial Priority is certainly not without its own theoretical costs, I argue that the view is worth taking seriously and deserves a place at the table as a viable yet underappreciated metaphysic of material objects.

A Brief (Partisan) Remark on Metaphysical Theorizing

Let me conclude with some remarks about how I approach metaphysical theorizing in general. Much of the theorizing in contemporary metaphysics proceeds by model-building.[7] Competing models aim to track the general structural features of reality and tend to be weighed according to their elegance, simplicity, and overall explanatory virtues. Models in mereological metaphysics, for example, are judged as more plausible than their rivals on the basis of offering the best overall fit with the agreed-upon data in need of explanation. Of course, the scope of the relevant data concerning material objects in need of explanation is a contentious matter in its own right.

In what follows, I aim to bring a host of data into reflective equilibrium to converge on a metaphysical model concerning the mereological and grounding structure of material objects.[8] Here I will briefly mention what I consider to be the most important data to be preserved in metaphysical theorizing: intuitive fit with pre-philosophical beliefs, empirical adequacy with respect to total science, and theoretical utility. Let's briefly look at each of these in turn.

I take seriously our pre-philosophical beliefs about what metaphysicians target in their theorizing: modality, mereology, causation, persistence, time, human persons, etc. In so far as possible, I think we should aim to preserve pre-philosophical beliefs about the structure of the world, what things there are or could be, and how they are characterized and behave. This, of course, applies to ordinary material objects—their existence, nature, structure, and causal activity. We take these beliefs "seriously" in our metaphysical theorizing by allowing them to serve as epistemic difference-makers;[9] pre-philosophical beliefs (or seemings) about the existence, nature, and causal activity of material objects constitutes defeasible justification on these matters. This is not, of course, to say that the pre-reflective beliefs we bring to our metaphysical theorizing are somehow closed-off from revision, only that they place prima facie constraints on our theorizing. Metaphysics should strive to reconstruct how the world appears in all its many-faceted splendor. I take this to include, in good Chisholmian fashion (1976: 15), obvious facts about ourselves such as our own basic awareness of ourselves as conscious, causal agents in the world.

With that said, however, it is important to recognize the limits of pre-philosophical beliefs and intuitions in metaphysical theorizing–what they can and cannot deliver concerning matters in fundamental ontology. We might say that such beliefs about matters metaphysical are good servants, but poor masters. We cannot, of course, simply "read off" views about the fundamental structure of reality from our pre-philosophical beliefs about a particular domain. Perhaps this is often due to the fact that pre-philosophical beliefs about a domain, say identity (whether synchronic or diachronic), are simply too course-grained to *decisively* settle matters on their own (e.g., "It sure seems that's the very same cat I saw hanging around here the other day . . . QED mereological essentialism is false"). Such beliefs do not wear their precise metaphysical commitments on their sleeve. In fact, pre-philosophical beliefs (e.g., "there are chairs," "I could have been a cobbler") are often minimally consistent with a variety of differing metaphysical semantics (metaphysical truth-conditions) regarding ordinary modal, mereological, causal, and temporal discourse. This is simply to say that the pre-philosophical beliefs we bring to our metapahysical theorizing are more often than not underdetermined by competing fundamental ontologies. This does not, however, warrant a swift rejection of a Moorean-methodology in metaphysics (applied to mereology, "Mereological Mooreanism") as some have suggested.[10]

Pre-philosophical beliefs about the world are thus worth preserving in our metaphysical models at great costs. Yet the metaphysician is in the market for more than a fundamental ontology that saves ordinary appearances and discourse. The metaphysician ought to be deeply concerned with constructing models that are informed and constrained by our best empirical theories about the world. Moreover, I'm of the opinion that metaphysical theorizing, especially in mereological metaphysics, should be constrained by what we know about the world from *total science*, physics as well as the special sciences (chemistry, biology, and psychology). If a model about the mereological structure of the natural world appears to be in tension with what we are reasonably justified in believing on the basis of total science, then this amounts to a significant strike against the model in my estimation.

The requirement that a model be empirically adequate with respect to total science deserves underscoring. When contemporary metaphysicians do aim to develop their views with an eye toward the best empirical theories on offer, they tend to march solely to the beat of fundamental physics. And this is certainly the case when it comes to contemporary mereological metaphysics.[11] This is quite understandable; fundamental physical theory has wielded remarkable predictive power and demands respect. But respect is one thing, sidelining well-entrenched empirical theories from other scientific domains in one's metaphysical theorizing is quite another. For what it's worth, my sympathies lie with those who lament the fact that contemporary mereological metaphysics has more often than not taken its cue more from formal, set-theoretic and algebraic systems rather than well-entrenched empirical theories about the unity of material objects in diverse empirical domains.[12]

What holds true regarding the limits of pre-philosophical beliefs for our metaphysical theorizing, I believe, holds true for theorizing in light of our best empirical theories about the natural world. Empirical theory does not on its own deliver fundamental ontology. Molecular biology, for example, does not decisively tell us that mereological nihilism is false; stage theory isn't fatally compromised by the deliverances of chemical theory; and we don't straightforwardly learn from fundamental physical theory (or its mathematical formalism) that fundamental ontology can do without tense, parthood, or individuals. While a view to the contrary would certainly make the metaphysician's task much easier (although it may just as well put us out of a job!), it fails to recognize that empirical theories often *presuppose* substantive views in fundamental ontology. So while the deliverances of total science ought to serve as an epistemic difference-maker in our metaphysical theorizing, they are in no way suited to unilaterally dictate fundamental ontology.

Lastly, metaphysical models should aim to be theoretically virtuous. We rightly prize metaphysical views that are elegant, theoretically simple, rich in explanatory scope and power, and ideologically and ontologically parsimonious (i.e., minimize primitives and ontological excess with respect to quantity and quality). While there will, of course, always be tradeoffs to some degree among these theoretical virtues, they ought to guide and govern theory-choice in metaphysics.

Bringing the earlier data—fit with pre-philosophical beliefs, empirical adequacy with total science, and theoretical utility—into reflective equilibrium is certainly no easy task as there will be many competing ways to evaluate a model's theoretical virtues alongside its accompanying costs (say its departing significantly from pre-philosophical beliefs). Some say so much the worse for metaphysics; I say all the more reason to proceed with the utmost care and humility.

Notes

1. Here I emphasize that these are very general postures as there are a wide variety of views that fall under both camps in contemporary metaphysics. See Koons and Pickavance (2017) for an excellent overview of these general postures in contemporary metaphysics (and more besides).
2. See the recent volumes by Tahko (2012) and Novák et al. (2012) for a sampling.
3. See Jacobs (2010).
4. See Bird (2007) and Freddoso (1986).
5. Lewis (1986b: ix).
6. For a sampling of this work see Bird (2007), Mumford and Anjum (2011), and Jacobs (2010), respectively.
7. See Paul (2012b).
8. Lewis (1983a: x).
9. I borrow "epistemic difference-maker" from Sider (2013).
10. Sider (2013).
11. See Dasgupta (2009) and Sider (2013) for a few representative examples.
12. Simons (1987, 2006) and Earley (2005) both underscore this very point about mereological metaphysics. Simons (2006: 613) is worth quoting: "It appears that most ontologists have been following the paradigm of abstract algebra when it would have been better to take a lead from sciences such as geology, botany, anatomy, physiology, engineering, which deal with the real."

1 Serious Essentialism

1.1 Essentialism: On Getting Serious

It is now commonplace in contemporary metaphysics to find the view that reality consists of objective *de re* modal structure. In our present philosophical context, "essentialism" is widely understood to be the view that (minimally) objects have some of their properties essentially or necessarily. Penelope Mackie (2006: 1), for instance, remarks that by essentialism about individuals she means "the view that individual things have essential properties, where an essential property of an object is a property that the object could not have existed without." For those who have embraced the reinstatement of *de re* necessity after its long demise at the hands of Quine and his positivistic forerunners, these defenses are a welcome sign indeed.

There has, however, been a relatively recent surge of suspicion regarding whether such a thin modal conception of essence is suited to capture many of our thick essentialist intuitions about reality. Here I join the chorus of those who espouse what has been called "genuine," "serious," or "real" essentialism, a modal ontology with a non-modal conception of essence at its core.[1] I take it for granted here and in what follows that reality does in fact exhibit modal structure of the metaphysical variety; I thereby leave the topic of modal conventionalism and deflationism to others. The joints that constitute the modal structure of the world are carved out by the natures of things as specified by their respective ontological category and natural kind (if they are empirically specifiable).

Broadly, my aim in this chapter is twofold. In the first section I set out to argue, following closely the work of Kit Fine (1994a), Michael Gorman (2005), David Oderberg (2007), and E. J. Lowe (2008b) that a modal gloss on essence is ill suited to capture what we take ourselves to be after in positing objective *de re* modal structure in the world—namely, the fundamental nature or identity of things. As useful as possible worlds are as a formal device for facilitating modal inferences, etc., they do little by way of elucidating the fundamental natures of things and the grounds of metaphysical necessity and possibility, or so I claim.

In the place of a modal account of essence, I develop in the second section a neo-Aristotelian alternative in terms of a robust notion of real definition. My own proposed neo-Aristotleian essentialism differs from Fine's in many respects, primarily with respect to its retention of the categorial and natural kind fundamental ontology in which the notion of real definition was first introduced.

1.1.1 Modal Essentialism

In its current guise, the predominant essentialist paradigm can be divided into two primary theses regarding the notion of essence, whose conjunction I will refer to as *modal essentialism*. Taking the operator "□" to stand for metaphysical necessity, we have the following tenets of modal essentialism:[2]

(ME) Modal Essentialism

ME1: x is essentially Φ iff $\Box(Ex \rightarrow \Phi x)$
ME2: the essence of x is the sum or collection of x's essential properties.

Read ME1 in the following manner: x is essentially Φ if and only if it is necessarily the case that if x exists, then it is Φ. ME1 and ME2 are standard fare for many contemporary metaphysicians who are congenial to essentialism in the metaphysics of modality.[3] ME1 captures the earlier notion that x's essential properties are those it has in every possible world in which it exists; that is, those that it modally requires for its existence. ME2, on the other hand, expresses the thesis that the essence of x *just is* the sum or collection of properties that x modally requires for its existence—i.e., its essential properties.

1.1.2 Modal Essentialism and the Asymmetry of Essentiality

I want to take issue with both ME1 and ME2 of modal essentialism. With the publication of his 1994 paper "Essence and Modality," Kit Fine has led the contemporary charge against a modal analysis of essence. Since Fine's groundbreaking work in this area, there has been a surge of interest in neo-Aristotelian-minded philosophers in highlighting the shortcomings of assimilating essence to modality as well as exploring alternative grounds for modal truths that are within the confines of the actual world.

Interestingly enough, the various critiques of modal essentialism offered by Fine and company have focused almost exclusively on ME1 of modal essentialism at the expense of ME2.[4] My aim is to show why *both* tenets of modal essentialism miss their mark in capturing a fine-grained notion of essence. This project is not a new one. The idea that natures or essences were the ground of modal truths and irreducible to properties was vigorously defended by many of the medieval scholastics.[5]

At its core, serious essentialism consists of both a positive and a negative project in the metaphysics of modality. Here I want to narrow in on the negative undercurrent of this particular strand of thinking against modal essentialism, and then turn to the positive project, viz. the development of a more fine-grained notion of essence, in the following section.

To begin, let us turn to ME1. ME1 states that x is essentially Φ if and only if it is necessarily the case that if x exists then it is Φ. First, note the force of the biconditional driving ME1: modal requirement for existence is both necessary *and* sufficient to capture a thing's essence. For an object to have a property essentially *just is* what it modally requires for its existence. Herein lies the first challenge put forward by Fine. While modal requirement for existence may be necessary for a thing's essence, it is certainly not sufficient. Objects that have properties essentially have them necessarily (i.e. it is no surprise that the fundamental identity of a thing tracks that thing in every world in which it exists), Fine argues that the converse of this is subject to several counterexamples which thereby render ME1 false.

The first counterexample involves Socrates (s) and his singleton {s}, the set whose sole member is Socrates. It is plausible, according to standard modal set theory, that necessarily, if Socrates exists, then he is a member of his singleton set (where, again, "E" denotes the existence predicate):

(a) $\Box(Es \rightarrow s \in \{s\})$.

This is precisely because {s} exists if and only if Socrates exists, that is, Socrates necessitates the existence of his singleton. Now, according to our first tenet of modal essentialism, ME1, (a) is equivalent to the following thesis, where the sentential operator with the subscript "$\Box_x$" is to be read as "it is part of the essence of x" or "x is essentially such that:"

(b) $\Box_s(s \in \{s\})$,

where (b) states that it is part of the essence of Socrates that he be a member of his singleton. But here, as Fine aptly points out, it is implausible to suggest that it is part of the essence or identity of Socrates that he be related to his singleton, or any set-theoretic entity for that matter, in this way. Surely Socrates is what he is without reference to *any* set-theoretic entity whatsoever. More generally, the problem is that there does not seem to be an essential connection between set-theoretic entities and the nature or essence of persons. As Fine (1994a) puts it, "There is nothing in the nature of a person, if I may put it this way, which demands that he belongs to this or that set or which demands, given that the person exists, that there even be any sets."

To state this a bit more precisely, there is a *modal symmetry* between Socrates belonging to his singleton and his singleton having Socrates as a member. It is necessary that whenever both Socrates and his singleton exist they stand in such relations to one another. However, there appears to be an *essential asymmetry* between Socrates and his singleton, that is, in terms of their respective essence or identity. While the identity of Socrates's singleton—its being *what* it is—involves reference to Socrates, this is not the case regarding Socrates and his being a member of his singleton. The crux of the objection here is that, intuitively, ME1—modal requirement for existence—seems to misconstrue the essence of Socrates by including features that fail to delimit his fundamental nature.

A second counterexample offered by serious essentialists relies on the notion of Socrates and his *life*.[6] Suppose we assume transworld identity as well as the plausible assumption that it is necessarily the case that in every world in which Socrates exists there exists a temporally extended event that is his life, S_L. Now consider all the worlds in which Socrates exists, $w_a \ldots w_n$, along with his respective lives in those worlds, $S_{La} \ldots S_{Ln}$. On one standard construal of the modal features of events, the existence and identity of $S_{La} \ldots S_{Ln}$ depends on the existence and identity of Socrates in $w_a \ldots w_n$. From this it follows that if it is one and the same Socrates that exists in $w_a \ldots w_n$ via transworld *identity*, then it is one and the same life that exists in those worlds as well. While $S_{La} \ldots S_{Ln}$ may differ from one another in a qualitative sense, they are numerically one and the same life, the life of Socrates.

If so, then we have another case of *modal symmetry* between Socrates and his life. In every world in which Socrates exists his life exists (and vice versa). However, like the case of Socrates and his singleton, there is a crucial *essential asymmetry* between Socrates and his life in that while $S_{La} \ldots S_{Ln}$ depend for their existence and identity on Socrates, the converse does not seem to be the case. As a result, ME1 does not have the resources to account for the essential asymmetry between Socrates and his life.

Lastly, for those who are less inclined toward sets and abstract objects in general, Fine provides a similar counterexample as the first to the sufficiency of ME1 without such machinery. He asks the reader to consider two seemingly unrelated objects, Socrates (s) and the Eiffel Tower (T). Now, from it necessarily being the case that if Socrates exists then he is numerically distinct from the Eiffel Tower,

(c) $\Box(Es \rightarrow s \neq T)$,

together with ME1, we get the following result:

(d) $\Box_s(s \neq T)$.

Since ME1 of modal essentialism construes the having of an essential property as being *equivalent* to modal requirement for existence, it follows that it belongs to the essence of Socrates that he be numerically distinct from the

Eiffel Tower. As before, Fine (1994: 5) argues, plausibly, that there is nothing in Socrates's nature or essence which relates him in any such way to the Eiffel Tower.

Here the modal essentialist might retort that the earlier counterexamples, far from undermining the reduction of essence to modal requirement for existence, demonstrates that a further condition must apply to the properties that are said to constitute Socrates's essence. More specifically, one might rejoin that the properties that constitute Socrates's essence must be *relevant* to Socrates in some sense or other. And, in the case of the aforementioned properties *being a member of {Socrates}* and *being numerically distinct from the Eiffel Tower*, such properties fail to exhibit the proper relevance to Socrates and thereby fail to qualify as parts of his essence.

However, this added condition of relevance to ME1 in order to account for the essential asymmetry that obtains between Socrates and his singleton faces a problem. As Fine points out, it is very difficult to account for such asymmetry in terms of the concept of relevance that does not already make reference to the essence of Socrates in some sense or other. For one, this line of thinking seems to be saying that the reason why it is not part of Socrates's essence that he be a member of his singleton is because the property *being a member of {Socrates}* does not exhibit the proper relevance to *what* Socrates is fundamentally, that is, his nature or essence. But again, the essence of Socrates appears to factor into the very notion of relevance used to adjudicate between those properties that are essentially connected to Socrates and those that are not. Consequently, such a notion of relevance cannot be used to ground the essential asymmetry between Socrates and his singleton.[7]

Consider one way of tightening up the relevant sorts of properties or features appealed to in ME1 that make up a Socrates's essence. Not just *any* properties that Socrates modally requires for his existence are privileged enough to be included in his essence. Della Roca (1996) has argued that Fine's counterexamples to modal essentialism rely heavily on what he calls "trivially necessary properties," properties that we can define as follows:

> A property P is a *trivially necessary property* of object x iff x necessarily has P and either (i) all objects necessarily have P or (ii) P is a logical consequence of some property G that all objects necessarily have.

Examples of trivially necessary properties that meet condition (i) would be *being a man if a bachelor, being self-identical, being either round or not round, or being temporally extended or not being temporally extended*. Such properties are necessarily exemplified by not only x but by every existing object whatsoever—i.e., they are universally necessary. Trivially necessary properties meeting condition (ii), on the other hand, are those that can be logically derived from a universally necessary property. The

16 *Serious Essentialism*

(impure) property *being identical to x*, for instance, can be derived from *x*'s exemplifying the property *being self-identical*, itself a trivially necessary property shared by every entity.

We can now contrast trivially necessary with non-trivially necessary properties and maintain that the essential properties of a thing are those non-trivially necessary properties that it modally requires for its existence. With this distinction in hand, the modal essentialist can go on to modify ME1 in the following manner (where "*x: Tx*" denotes the set of trivially necessary properties):

ME1*: *x* is essentially Φ iff $\Box(Ex \rightarrow \Phi x) \wedge \neg(\Phi \in x: Tx)$.

As it turns out, ME1* is the medicine that kills the metaphysical patient. As Nathan Wildman (2016) has pointed out, there are non-trivially necessary properties that ME1* construes as parts of the essence of Socrates that, intuitively, are not.

Wildman asks us to consider the following disjunctive property that lists every possible kind to which an object might belong, save the kind *electron*: *being either a human, or a mountain, or a zebra, or a centaur, or a hydrogen chloride (HCl) molecule, or a . . .*, call this property T. T is a non-trivially necessary property in so far as all objects fail to necessarily have T—all electrons, for instance, fail to exemplify T—and T is not a logical consequence of some property that all objects necessarily have. Yet Socrates exemplifies T in so far as he is essentially human. Consequently, it follows from ME1* that T is part of the essence of Socrates. But T seems just as (if not more) irrelevant to the nature of Socrates as the property originally appealed to in Fine's counterexample to ME1— namely, *being a member of {Socrates}*.

A second worry with ME1* is that it eliminates Socrates's essence altogether in that it implies that *all* necessary properties are trivially necessary properties.[8] To see this, suppose that Socrates is necessarily human—i.e., *being human* is a necessary property of Socrates. If *being human* is a necessary property of Socrates, it follows that every object (including Socrates) has the trivially necessary property *being Socrates and being human or not being Socrates*. From the supposition that Socrates is self-identical, it follows that *being Socrates and being human* is a trivially necessary property of Socrates. This, together with the application of the rule of simplification, it follows logically that *being human* is a trivially necessary property of Socrates. Since, by ME1*, no trivially necessary property can enter into the essence of a thing, it follows, implausibly, that *being human* is not an essential property of Socrates. In so far as this line of thinking can be generalized to any necessary property of a thing, ME1* threatens to dissolve the notion of essence entirely. As a result, ME1* is in no better position (it is, in fact, in a worse position) than ME1 to explicate the notion of essence.[9]

Consequently, modal essentialism does not appear to have the resources to account for the essential asymmetry between Socrates and the various entities in the earlier counterexamples. In fact, ME1 appears to get the order of explanation backward: it is precisely *because* of Socrates's essence–*what* he is–that he is essentially distinct from the Eiffel Tower in every possible world in which he exists, if there be possible worlds at all. Contrary to what many take to be the pride of contemporary essentialism, essence is unable to be reduced to modal requirement for existence in so far as the latter is inadequate to capture the fine-grained structure of essence.

1.2 Serious Essentialism

For many contemporary essentialists, modal essentialism is so ingrained in the current mindset that it is hard to imagine what an alternative essentialist framework might look like. Yet more and more philosophers with essentialist leanings are taking the "Finean-turn" away from modal essentialism to a more serious variety.[10] I want to join the chorus of contemporary philosophers who recommend that we take a page from Aristotle and the medieval scholastics (whether or not they know it!) in understanding necessity and possibility in terms of the notion of essence and not vice versa.[11]

In this section I develop an alternative essentialist framework, what has generally come to be called "serious" or "real essentialism." We must acknowledge at the outset, however, that the label "serious essentialism" has a broad semantic range and encompasses a wide variety of views in the metaphysics of modality. As I understand it here, the minimal unifying feature of serious essentialism in modal metaphysics is the conviction that essence is irreducible to modality. I put my particular version of serious essentialism, which falls much more in line with the Aristotelian and medieval Aristotelian tradition, forward as being one particular variant of serious essentialism in the literature.

Toward this aim, I begin by examining the positive undercurrent of Fine's work in modality that has led to the reinstatement of Aristotelian essentialism in contemporary metaphysics. I then turn to an explication of essence in terms of real definition. While I wholeheartedly agree with Fine in rejecting modal essentialism in favor of a more robust approach to the notion of essence in terms of real definition, I part company with Fine and other prominent serious essentialists in making a clean break with modal essentialism in its entirety.

1.2.1 Essence and Real Definition

We saw earlier that Fine's negative project was directed at undermining the sufficiency of modal requirement for existence in capturing the essence or identity of Socrates. Fine concludes from his negative project that the contemporary assimilation of essence to modality is fundamentally misguided and that, as a consequence, the corresponding conception of metaphysics should be given up . . . the notion of essence which is of central importance to the metaphysics of identity is not to be understood in modal terms or even to be regarded as extensionally equivalent to a modal notion.

(Fine 1994a: 3)

Thus, *any* modal account of essence that appeals to the prior concepts of necessity and possibility will fail to capture the requisite distinctions regarding the nature and identity of Socrates. We can, then, think of Fine's positive contribution to the reinstatement of an Aristotelian variety of essentialism as including (i) the explication of essence in terms of real definition and (ii) an account of the structure of essence in what he calls the "constitutive" and the "consequential" essence.

Let us begin with the first tenet of Fine's positive project that has helped reinstate serious essentialism in the metaphysics of modality. Fine suggests that instead of explicating essence in terms of metaphysical necessity—what an object requires of necessity in order for it to exist—he maintains that the source of metaphysical necessity lies in the nature or identity of things. On Fine's view, truths of necessity and possibility obtain in virtue of truths of essence, and not vice versa.[12]

As a result, modal truths are not explanatory basic truths of reality, not explanatory "bedrock" so to speak. Rather, "Necessity has its source in those objects which are the subject of the underlying essentialist claim . . . We should view metaphysical necessity as a special case of essence" (Fine 1994a: 9). Fine contends that various kinds of entities such as concepts (both *logical*, i.e., the concept of disjunction, and *non-logical*, i.e. the concept of bachelorhood), and individual objects give rise to their own domain of necessary truths that are true in virtue of the essence or nature of the entities in question. For a proposition to be metaphysically necessary, then, is for it to be true in virtue of the essence or nature of *all* objects whatsoever. Likewise, for a proposition to be logically and conceptually necessary is for it to be true in virtue of the essence of all logical concepts and true in virtue of the essence of all concepts, respectively. In general, it is because of what individual objects and concepts are that the relevant modal facts are true of them, and not vice versa. Contrary to modal essentialism (ME1), then, modal truths are true in virtue of the natures or essences of entities.

But how exactly are we to understand the notion of essence at work in the earlier account? We have seen that modal essentialism's inability to capture the structure of essence has led us to a more fine-grained notion of essence, one that does not include necessary features of Socrates that are seemingly unrelated to *what* he is in the most fundamental sense. What's more, the priority of essence over necessity requires that our requisite notion of essence needs to be unpacked in distinctively non-modal terms.

With Fine and other serious essentialists, I suggest that we return, once again, to the traditional Aristotelian and scholastic conception of *real definition* to elucidate a more fine-grained, non-modal account of essence.[13] Fine (1994a: 3) states,

> [T]he traditional assimilation of essence to definition is better suited to the task of explaining what essence is. It may not provide us with an analysis of the concept, but it does provide us with a good model of how the concept works. Thus my overall position is the reverse of the usual one. It sees real definition rather than de re modality as central to our understanding of the concept.
>
> (Fine 1994a: 3)

We do not, however, *analyze* essence in terms of real definition. Rather, the notion of essence itself ought to be taken as primitive and unanalyzable. Along these lines Fine (1995: 53) states, "Indeed, I doubt whether there exists any explanation of the notion in fundamentally different terms." This does not, however, consign us to silence when it comes to filling out what a non-modal conception of essence might look like.

In general, to define some object x or some linguistic item "n" is to set forth the limit of x or "n" "in such a way that one can distinguish it from all other things of a different kind."[14] A definition can be said to include both a *definiendum*, that which is defined, and a *definiens*, that which does the defining. Following philosophical tradition, Fine contends that definitions *per se* can be either *nominal* (i.e., linguistic) or *objectual* (i.e., pertaining to a thing, *res*). A *nominal definition* has as its definiendum a *word*, where the definiens takes the form of a sentence or collection of sentences. By providing a nominal definition of a word, *exculpate* for instance as "to show or declare that someone is not guilty of wrongdoing," one is setting certain limits or boundaries on a linguistic item that distinguishes that item from other non-synonymous terms in the language to which it belongs.

A *real definition*, on the other hand, has as its definiendum an object or entity, where the definiens takes the form of a proposition or collection of propositions that is true in virtue of the identity of the object being defined. Consequently, when we define some actual or possible entity we thereby specify its essence or fundamental kind, that is, the nature of that thing or what its nature *would* be if it existed.

More specifically, a real definition of a substance is a proposition or collection of propositions which signifies its identity (i.e. *what it is*) in the most fundamental sense, that is, what is directly *definitive* of the substance as determined by the fundamental substantial kind to which it belongs.[15] Moreover, by x's "identity" here I do not mean the relation of self-identity

($x = x$) which every entity bears to itself trivially. Rather, I have in mind what Bishop Butler (1914: 23) meant by the notion: "[E]verything is what it is, and not another thing." For every occupant of spacetime to have an identity, nature, or essence in this sense is simply the affirmation that spatiotemporal reality is not an amorphous lump; that various regions are occupied by *identifiable* and *definable* physical structures or "software" as the late James F. Ross aptly put it.[16]

For the most part, in what follows I will restrict my attention to the real definitions of substances that occupy regions of spacetime. It is, however, important at this point to briefly distinguish two different senses of essence in addition to real definition, *particular* essence and *individual* essence.

Consider a portion of gold, g. We have seen that the real definition of g states *what it is to be* gold, in this case, "to be gold is to be metal whose atomic constituents have atomic number 79." Real definitions express the fundamental substantial kind to which an individual substance belongs. We can also speak of the *particular essence* of gold in that g itself is a particularized instance of the substantial kind *gold*. As an instance of the kind *gold*, g is a substance that is the object of a substantial real definition, it is the concrete substance that we aim to define.[17]

More generally, the objects of substantial real definitions are particular instances of substantial kinds. When speaking of the particular essence of an individual substance, I use synonymously the locutions "the particular nature of x," "the particular essence of x," and "x as a particular kind of substance." Thus, one could, on my view, substitute "particular substantial nature" for "particular kind of individual substance" without loss of meaning or content. Contrary to some serious essentialists, an individual substance occupying a region of spacetime does not, strictly speaking, *have* an (particular) essence or nature in the same way it has a spatial location, a heart, or a certain mass at a time; rather, the substance simply *is* what we might call a "particularlized-nature," that is, a particular instance of a substantial kind.[18] In the same way, I'm inclined to think that the particular essence of a substance ought not be thought of as a constituent or proper part to which the substance is related, whether such a relation be construed in mereological or non-mereological terms.

In addition to real definition and particular essence, we can also speak more narrowly of g's *individual essence, what it is to be the instance of the kind* gold *that* g *is* (in contrast to some other instance). In other words, g's individual essence involves *which* particular instance of gold g is as opposed to any other particular instance of *gold*. Historically, the notion of individual essence factored in to the question of individuation, what it is that makes an entity the very entity that it is as opposed to any other entity. Some essentialists (both past and present) have argued that the individual essence of g, for instance, consists in its having a purely non-qualitative (and non-sharable) property such as *being identical to* g," a property that is often referred to as a "haecceity" (lit. "thisness").[19] Other essentialists have argued that instances of kinds (particular essences) are self-individuating in that they are not individuated by any distinct entity. There is, on this view, no need to introduce haecceities to play the individuating role of kind-membership itself.[20] While I will have a bit more to say in the following chapter on the question of individuation as it relates to a certain species of metaphysical grounding, I will set aside the precise nature of individuation at this point. Given the earlier distinct senses of essence, the locution "the essence of g" can refer to either the real definition, the particular essence, or the individual essence of g.

My own neo-Aristotelian ontology is in agreement with Lowe (2011) in claiming that the (particular) essence of g ought to be construed as either no entity at all or as being identical to g in the sense described earlier.[21] Where Lowe opts for the first route and refuses to reify essences in any sense, I take the second route and claim that the particular nature or essence of g *just is* g qua instance of the substantial kind *gold*.[22] Thus, consider the following real definition of gold: to be gold is to be a metal whose atomic constituents have atomic number 79. The real definition of gold expresses the substantial kinds *being a metal* and *having atomic number 79*. The particular essence of g, on the other hand, just is g qua particular instance of *gold*.

At the heart of the notion of real definition and serious essentialism in particular is the thesis that reality exhibits objective *categorial* and *naturally specifiable* joints. Nature's joints are "specifiable" in the sense that we commonly take our classificatory judgments about categorial structure to be both intelligible and more or less epistemically justified (although such justification is, of course, defeasible). For my purposes in this essay, I will assume without further argument that reality is in fact structured in this way, although I will have a bit more to say on this score in what follows.[23]

Real definitions, then, aim to track reality's categorial and naturally specifiable joints by answering the question: *what is it to be a thing of a particular category or kind*? We must not, however, presume that such a question has a *single* uniform answer in so far as every living being, for instance, falls under many distinct kinds thereby generating multiple answers to the question *what is it to be a thing of a particular kind, K*. For this reason, the serious essentialist has traditionally claimed that kinds, both categorial and natural, form a nested hierarchy with the more general being included in or implied by the more specific in the hierarchy. According to the serious essentialist, real definitions aim to capture the *fundamental* or lowest-level category or kind to which a thing belongs.

Take an individual tiger by way of example. For the serious essentialist, the real definition of a tiger (whatever it may in fact be) will seek to explicate *what it is to belong to the kind* Panthera Tigris, which will involve, at the very least, empirical inquiry into the distinguishing features, powers, and capacities that set tigers apart from every other living organism (category) as well as every other kind of carnivorous animal (natural kind). Thus, the real definition of a tiger will involve reference to *both* its fundamental ontological category as well as the fundamental natural kind to which it belongs.

A tiger's fundamental or "lowest" ontological category, for instance, is that of *living organism*. It is in virtue of being a member of a certain *category* of object—a substance—that tigers are capable of persisting through the replacement of their constituting matter (contra mere portions of stuff or aggregates for instance). Whether objects of the category of *substance* in particular are capable of persisting through time and change in such a manner is, on my view, a question to be settled by a priori philosophical reflection on the concept of a substance. More specifically, it is because a tiger is a certain *kind* of substance—a living organism—that it is capable of self-initiating and self-directing action as well as undergoing metabolic growth (contra non-living substances). Consequently, any entity that lacked the earlier features could not be a tiger in so far as such powers are inseparably tied to *what it is to be a tiger*.

As a tiger is a certain *kind* of living organism, reference to its fundamental ontological category only partly constitutes its nature; it hardly needs stating that the real definition of a tiger involves more than an appeal to the category *living organism*. Here we must appeal not only to categorial structure but also to the lowest *natural kind* that is definitive of individual tigers. A tiger is a certain kind of *animal*: a *vertebrate*, *mammal*, and *carnivore*. The real definition (whatever it may be in point of fact) of a tiger will denote the fundamental kind of thing a tiger is, which will inevitably point (to be elucidated next) to those features and dispositions that distinguish tigers from other members of the genus *Panthera Tigris*. The underlying point here is that a serious essentialist metaphysic is committed to the thesis that the real definition for *any* empirically specifiable entity will involve *both* categorial as well as natural kind classification. As a result, our knowledge of the real definitions of individual substances will inevitably involve integrating a robust engagement with the natural sciences with a well-developed fundamental ontology.[24]

It is important to note that real definitions may exhibit a certain degree of accuracy and completeness. The fact that some real definitions are more accurate and complete than others in no way casts doubt on their ability to track reality's joints in general. To illustrate this, consider the following proposed real definitions:

A. A circle is the locus of a point moving continuously in a plane at a fixed distance from a given point.[25]
B. Sand is a naturally occurring granular material composed of finely divided rock and mineral particles.[26]
C. Gold is a metal whose atomic constituents have atomic number 79.

Compare A, B, and C. In contrast to A and C, which seem to be accurate and complete real definitions of a circle and the element of gold respectively, B is not a *complete* real definition of sand in so far as it is not specific enough to distinguish it from other forms of granular material composed of finely divided rock and mineral particles such as silt and gravel (which would involve further specification of the required particle diameter range).

The view that essence is captured by real definition has a long and impressive historical pedigree. Arguably, the concept of real definition first appears in Plato's representation of Socrates's search for the nature of piety (*Euthyphro*), temperance (*Charmides*), justice (*Republic* I), courage (*Laches*), virtue (*Meno*), and beauty (*Hippias Major*). As Morrison (2006) notes, "In fact our concept 'essence' goes back historically to Socrates's quest for definitions: 'the essence of F' is whatever is given by a correct answer to the Socratic question, 'What is F?'" Aristotle (*Meta*. 1031a12), as is well known, himself upholds the connection between essence and real definition by saying, "clearly, then, definition is the formula of the essence."[27]

What's more, Aquinas relied heavily on the relationship between essence and real definition in his ontology. In addition to making the essentialist point that to "be circumscribed by essential limits belongs to all creatures" (*ST* 1.50.2), he holds that "it is clear that the essence of a thing is what its definition signifies" and "that by which a real thing is constituted in its proper genus or species is what is signified by the definition expressing what the real thing is, philosophers sometimes use the word 'quiddity' for the word 'essence.'"[28] For Aquinas in particular, a real definition of an object signifies those fundamental characteristics that are *constitutive* of that object—i.e., that serve to mark out its metaphysical limits or boundaries in the form of a lowest (*infima*) species and specific difference (which thereby constitutes the definiendum).

The notion of real definition has also been utilized in the work of Spinoza and Leibniz. Spinoza, in his *On the Improvement of the Understanding*, states "A definition, if it is to be called perfect, must explain the inmost essence of a thing."[29] Leibniz made an explicit distinction between nominal and real definitions, primarily in his critique of Hobbes's attempt to collapse all definition to the nominal variety. For Leibniz, a real definition of an entity is that "through which the possibility of a thing is ascertained."[30]

1.2.2 The Structure of Essence

We've examined several reasons for thinking that ME1 falls short in capturing the fine-grained structure of essence. At this point, I want to turn to the oft neglected second tenet of modal essentialism, ME2.

Recall that ME2 states that the essence of an entity, x, is the sum or collection of its essential properties, viz. those that it modally requires for its existence. On ME2, while x's essence or identity is restricted to the sum of those properties that satisfy the description Φ, it consists of nothing more than a sum, collection, or set of properties. Let us further divide ME2 into the following two claims:

ME2$_a$: The essence of x is identical to a *sum* or *collection*.
ME2$_b$: The essence of x consists entirely of *properties*.

One often finds both tenets of ME2 as part and parcel of the modal essentialist package concerning the nature and structure of essence. In this section I attempt to motivate a clean break from modal essentialism in arguing against ME2 in its entirety. While Fine is correct to challenge the current orthodoxy of ME2$_a$, he nonetheless retains much of the spirit of modal essentialism in his affirmation of ME2$_b$.

Regarding ME2$_a$, we have seen that the modal essentialist construes essences as sums or collections of necessary properties (recall the formulation in §2.1). To state an entity's essence E then is akin to listing the various members of a set or the parts of an arbitrary mereological sum. And since arbitrary sums and collections are what they are irrespective of the structure that obtains among their items, structure is inconsequential to conveying essence.

Suppose we take the essence of an entity to be construed along the lines of a set, E, whose individual members p and q are necessary properties. It is well known from set-theory that the structure or order of the individual members p and q of E is irrelevant to the identity of the set of which they are members, $\{p, q\}$. Where E = $\{p, q\}$, the task for the modal essentialist is to solve for p and q. This is precisely what we see in Plantinga (1974) with his search for the essence of Socrates, which he takes to include the necessary properties *being a non-number, being possibly snub-nosed* as well as Socrates's various world-indexed properties (*alpha* being the actual world) such as *being snub-nosed-in-alpha* and *being-the-husband-of-Xanthippe-in-alpha*. On this view, the necessary properties *being human, being identical to Socrates,* and *being-married-to-Xanthippe-in-alpha* all equally (albeit partially) capture the essence of Socrates.[31]

In contrast to the widespread modalist trend in treating the necessary properties (and hence the essence) of a thing as akin to unstructured set or mereological sum, serious essentialists argue that not all necessary features are on metaphysical par with one another (as we have seen in our counterexamples to ME1). Serious essentialism, both historically and in its current guise, maintains that a thing's necessary features are *structured* or ordered in such a way that not all of them are equally *definitive* of that thing in the most fundamental sense and thus be included in its real definition.

Call the sum total of the necessary features of an object, the features the object has in every possible world in which it exists, its *modal profile*. On the serious essentialist view that I will develop next, the modal profile of an object is better represented as roughly akin to an ordered n-tuple such as N = $\langle f_1 \ldots f_n \rangle$. Unlike sets, the structure of $f_1 \ldots f_n$ of the ordered *n*-tuple is vital to the identity of that ordered *n*-tuple. If modal profiles are understood more along the lines of an ordered *n*-tuple, then the items belonging to an object's modal profile stand in certain priority (whether logical or explanatory) relations to one another, where the precise nature of priority here varies among serious essentialists.

Fine's own way of capturing the ordered structure of an object's modal profile is to distinguish between an object's *constitutive* and *consequential* essence, a distinction he claims (roughly) mirrors the Aristotelian distinction between essence and propria (more on this distinction next). The basic idea here is that not all necessary properties are metaphysically on par with one another in that some carve their bearers at the joints more than others.

On Fine's view, a property *F* is part of the *constitutive essence* of an object *x* if *F* is not had in virtue of being a consequence of some more basic necessary property of *x*. Correlatively, something *G* is part of the *consequential essence* of *x* if *G* is not part of the constitutive essence of *x*. The notion of consequence employed by Fine here is one of *logical consequence*: where

> the property Q is a (logical) consequence of the properties $P_1, P_2, \ldots$, or that they (logically) imply Q, if it is a logical truth, for any object, that it has the property Q whenever it has the properties $P_1, P_2, \ldots$.[32]

Here the properties belonging to the constitutive and the consequential essence are subsets of the total set of the necessary properties of an object.

According to Fine (1995: 57), "the constitutive essence is directly definitive of the object, but the consequential essence is only definitive through its connection with other properties." To illustrate, Fine asks us to consider, once again, the example of Socrates. The constitutive essence of Socrates will include (at the very least) his *being a man*, that is, *being a man* is said to signify (at least in part) what he is in the most fundamental sense and thereby factor into the real definition of Socrates. Contrast this with the disjunctive property *being a man or a mountain* which is said to belong to the consequential essence of Socrates in virtue of being a logical consequence (via the rule of addition) of Socrates's *being a man*.[33] But intuitively, *being a man* and *being a man or a mountain* do not carve Socrates's essence in precisely the same manner; the former seems to be more fundamental to Socrates's identity than the latter. Consequently, contra ME2a, there is a hierarchical ordering between Socrates's necessary properties, those belonging to the constitutive essence being more closely "tied" to Socrates than those of the consequential essence. For this reason, the real definition of Socrates represents those properties of Socrates that belong solely to his constitutive essence.

The fundamental distinction between that which is directly definitive of a thing and that which is a consequence or follows from the former is one that I wholeheartedly accept. In fact, to some degree, I am in agreement with Fine's characterization of the constitutive essence as including the explanatorily basic items that make up an object's modal profile. However, one need not follow Fine in employing the machinery of logical consequence to explicate the notion that the items belonging to an object's modal profile are hierarchically ordered with respect to one another.

For one, it appears that Fine's appropriation of logical consequence runs the risk of excluding features of a thing that are, plausibly, said to follow from or are closely tied to its essence proper.[34] For instance, it seems to follow from the essence of a triangle that it has three sides. Yet the proposition "triangles have three sides" is not *logically* entailed by the proposition "triangles have three angles." A less abstract example is offered by Gorman (2005: 282):

> An atom's being prone to bond can legitimately be called a "consequence" of its having such a number of protons—its having such a number of protons is why it is prone to bond. But note that it is not a logical truth that an atom with such a number of protons is an atom that is prone to bond. Its proneness to bond follows from, is a consequence of, its having such a number of protons, but not in Fine's sense.

I will have much more to say next about my own understanding of the ordering that obtains between the items included in an object's modal profile (§2.4). The question as to what is directly definitive of an entity brings us our second tenet of ME2, ME2$_b$, the claim that essences consist entirely of properties.

While Fine explicitly rejects ME2$_a$, he nevertheless retains the view captured by ME2$_b$, that essences consist entirely of *properties*. Fine is not alone among those serious essentialists who gloss essences or natures as consisting of properties in particular.[35] Elsewhere, Fine reiterates his adherence to ME2$_b$ by saying,

> We have supposed that each object has a unique essence or definition, where this is something that may be identified either with the class of properties that it essentially has or with the class of propositions that are true in virtue of what it is.[36]

While Fine is surely right to part company with ME2a and thereby emphasize the fact that an entity's modal profile is structured to a certain degree, I am inclined to think that it is misguided to divorce the notion of real definition from an ontology of substantial kinds and contend that the modal profile of an object consist solely of *properties* that stand in certain logical relations to one another (Fine 1995: 66). On this point, Fine's view retains much more of the spirit of modal essentialism as per ME2 than he might like to admit. While I have no qualm with Fine's identification of the real definition with a proposition or collection of propositions, I do, however, want to take issue with the claim that that which is expressed by the real definition—namely, a substantial kind—*just is* a group of properties, strictly speaking. In rejecting tenet ME1 *and* ME2, we thereby make a clean break from modal essentialism in its entirety.

It is well known that Aristotle and medieval Aristotelians were of the opinion that the nature of a thing as expressed by its real definition—what it is fundamentally—is not only prior to the various modal truths it makes true but is also prior to its characterizing properties and thus (contra ME2b) cannot be identified with any of those properties.[37] Contrary to modal essentialism and Fine's own serious-essentialist metaphysic, I wholeheartedly accept this line of thinking.

But before I attempt to motivate this line of thinking, we need to get clear on what exactly is being proposed. In order to make the distinction between an object's essence and its properties more perspicuous we need to distinguish between two sorts of *predicables*, those that are *constitutive* of a thing and those that *characterize* a thing.[38] Constitutive predicables are those included in real definitions in so far as they delimit *what* a thing is fundamentally instead of *how* it is characterized. It is constitutive predicables that, strictly speaking, express the essence or nature of a thing.

Characterizing predicables, in contrast to their constitutive counterparts, characterize a particular and therefore specify *how* that particular is modified, including its relevant causal powers and capacities. Our turn to a more fine-grained notion of essence brings with it (following Aristotle and the scholastics) the distinction between two sorts of accidents that serve to characterize a particular, those that are *extraneous* and those that are *proper* to an object. Extraneous accidents largely correspond to what we would in contemporary parlance call accidental (non-essential) properties, properties a particular could lose and thereby continue to exist as such. Proper accidents, on the other hand, are those properties of a thing that necessarily characterize each member of a particular kind but are not, strictly speaking, part of the essence of a thing; proper accidents are not directly definitive of *what* the object is. Proper accidents (or *propria* as they are traditionally called) are necessary non-essential properties.

This distinction between necessary non-essential properties (*propria*) and that which constitutes the essence of a thing has been neglected due to the widespread influence of modal essentialism in contemporary metaphysics that construes every item in an object's modal profile as equally constitutive of its fundamental identity—i.e., *what* that thing is. Modal essentialism, as we have seen, collapses the distinction between the necessary and the essential, thereby making the category of a necessary non-essential property (proper accidents) a non-starter.

One particular reason for the widespread conflation of constitutive and characterizing predicables is due to the ambiguity of predications of the form "*x* is F." This ambiguity regarding different sorts of predicables in natural language was naturally transferred over into the canonization of first-order predicate logic as championed by Frege and Russell. As Lowe (2006) has pointed out, given the particular categorial ontology (one devoid of substantial kinds) of object and property in which modern first-order predicate logic was forged, it is no surprise that it is incapable of formally distinguishing between a proposition stating that a substance is a certain *kind* of thing and a proposition stating that a substance exemplifies a certain *property*. This is because on standard first-order predicate logic both statements are expressed as "x is F," or simply Fx.

Now, consider the case where x is a mammal, a polar bear for instance. While both are true predications of x, there is a grave ontological difference between saying "x is white" and "x is a mammal." The former involves a characterizing predicable of x—namely, *whiteness* (a property), which is said to characterize or modify x in some particular manner. The latter, on the other hand, involves a constitutive predicable of x—namely, *mammal* (a substantial kind), which is said to be constitutive of x and thereby (partly) enters into the real definition of a polar bear in a way that the property *whiteness* does not. While *being a mammal* can be predicated of x and rightly included as part of its essence, it would be imprecise to say that *being a mammal* is a *property* of x. This is precisely because, intuitively, *being a mammal* is not a *way* x is characterized but, rather, part of *what* x is; it is, to use our preferred terminology, a constitutive and not a characterizing predicable of x.[39]

But what exactly are the truthmakers for predications involving constitutive and characterizing predicables? Here I need to say a bit more about the overall categorial ontology that I will work from in the course of the essay. In general, I am inclined to endorse (but will not argue for) what Lowe (2006) calls a "four category ontology" that consists of the two fundamental categories of universals *substantial kind* and *property*, and the two fundamental categories of particulars, *substance* and *trope*.[40] These categories are fundamental, I claim, in the sense that entities in a given world which fall into these four categories are (collectively) necessary and sufficient as truthmakers for all basic or fundamental truths about that world. As was previously stated, I assume here that reality exhibits deep ontological and naturally specifiable joints. That is, there is an objective difference between an electron and an aardvark as well as an objective similarity between two members of the *Felinae* family. I am tentatively inclined to think that such joints are, at bottom, best explained in terms of the sharing of numerically identical, multiply exemplifiable substantial kind universals. It is in virtue of being instances of substantial kinds that particular substances "carve out" the objective natural joints in the world which account for the natural differences and similarities between things. Tropes, in like manner, are non-transferable particularized properties, both powerful and non-powerful, whose natural groupings are best explained by their being instances of one and the same property considered as a universal.

I endorse a truthmaker theory of predication which claims that all true predications, or at least all true predications of the form "x is F," are to be explained in terms of truthmakers. I take the truthmakers for the aforementioned constitutive and characterizing predications of the form "x is a mammal" and "x is white" (where x ranges over a concrete object) to correspond to individual substances and tropes, respectively.[41] Predications involving constitutive predicables such as "polar bears are mammals"—i.e., essential predications—are made true by a particular kind of substance, a polar bear. On the other hand, predications involving characterizing predicables such as "polar bears are white," have as their truthmakers non-transferable tropes or modes. If the characterizing predication involved a dispositional-attribution such as "polar bears are disposed to have fur," then its truthmaker would be a dispositional trope.

I take the distinction between constitutive and characterizing predicables to be both natural and intuitive. Along these lines, Lowe (2006: 92) gives the example of a rose,

> Being red is a way a flower may be, as is being tall or being delicate. But being a *rose* is not a way a flower may be: it is what certain flowers are, in the sense that they are particular instances of that kind of thing.

Similarly, Brian Ellis (2001: 92) hints at the distinction between constitutive and characterizing predicables in stating, "I say that an electron is an electron, not something that has the property of being an electron. In my view, there is no such property. There is no property of being a horse, either, and for the same sort of reason." Lastly, Heil (2003: 47) puts it succinctly as follows: "Thus, 'is a horse' is satisfied, not by properties possessed by particular objects, but by substances of particular *kinds*."[42] It is in this sense that I take statements involving constitutive predicables to track deepest the classificatory and natural joints in nature.

One could multiply examples here. On this line of thinking, *being a metal* is not, strictly speaking, a property of gold (as being of such-and-such hue would be) but rather partly constitutive of the essence of gold. *Having chemical composition H_2O* is not, strictly speaking, a property of water, but is nonetheless constitutive of it and thereby part of its essence.[43]

1.2.3 Essence, Explanation, and Property-Clustering

But here we might ask whether there is an argument that can be given in favor of the irreducibility of essence to properties beyond the earlier appeal to intuition? While I do not think there are knockdown arguments to be had here, I do believe that there is at least one plausible reason that supports such a thesis. Consider the following line of reasoning: if a thing's essence or nature were nothing more than properties along the

30 Serious Essentialism

lines of ME2b, then it raises the question of *why* such properties are uniformly co-instantiated in things of that particular kind.

That various kinds of substances exhibit a stable pattern of activity in virtue of their causal powers and qualities is a central datum of scientific explanation. Instances of the kind *living organism*, for instance, uniformly exhibit a certain stable set of causal powers and capacities. At the very least, part of the characteristic pattern of activity of living organisms involves the power to undergo metabolic growth and reproduction. Those who endorse ME2b (including Fine) and thus the reducibility of constitutive to characterizing predicables maintain that the natures of living organisms are nothing more than the sum of the aforementioned powers and capacities (where we can assume for illustration that such powers alone are sufficient to constitute its essence); the earlier powers and capacities suffice to constitute the essence of living organisms.

One rather prominent defender of this line of thinking is Armstrong:

> Suppose that a particular has all the properties which are required for something to be gold or an electron. Will it not be gold or be an electron? Why postulate some further universal which it must exemplify in order to be gold or an electron?
>
> (1978: 62)[44]

Armstrong's point is that when it comes to telling the deep ontological story concerning various kinds of individual substances, only properties need apply. An electron's possessing a privileged set of properties is sufficient to account for the classificatory difference between it and a photon, for instance. The objection can be traced back to the seventeenth century to Robert Boyle's (1991: 40) attempt to eliminate the scholastic notion of substantial form in favor of a cluster of accidents which serves to "stamp" or "essentially modify" a portion of matter and thereby distinguish it from other modified portions of matter.[45]

We have, however, already stated a general worry with collapsing essence to properties in this way. If the substantial kinds that constitute the essences of substances are reducible to mere collections of powers and properties one may plausibly ask for an explanation as to *why* the properties and powers in such a collection are systematically unified in substances of the same kind.[46] We can put this as a need to explain the following, where "$P_1 \ldots P_n$" denotes a range of essential properties that constitute a property cluster "C," and "Cs" represents the entities that exemplify C:

> CLUSTER: the essential properties, $P_1 \ldots P_n$ of a cluster, C, are systematically co-instantiated in the Cs.

That is: in virtue of *what* do $P_1 \ldots P_n$ systematically cluster to form an integral unity in the Cs? What, for instance, explains the uniform possession of the power to dissolve gold by particular bodies of aqua regia? Again, without appealing to the fact that various portions of gold (Cs) belong to one and the same irreducible substantial kind, what undergirds the uniform possession of the properties of *being malleable* and *having a high luster* by particular portions of gold?

Take two representative essential properties of an electron endorsed by the proponent of ME2b: *being a fundamental particle* (P1) and *having unit negative charge* (P2). Of these two properties we might ask: why are P1 and P2 systematically co-instantiated in electrons as opposed to some other particle? The demand for an explanation here is all the more pressing given that there is no necessary connection between P1 and P2; that is, the instantiation of one does not necessitate the instantiation of the other. There are particles that instantiate P1 and not P2 (photons) and particles that instantiate P2 and not P1 (chloride ions). If the nature of an electron were constituted solely by a cluster of properties that are modally separable from one another in such a way, then one is hard pressed to explain *why* individual electrons uniformly possess P1 and P2 in particular as opposed to those properties that constitute a photon or a chloride ion.[47]

One rather obvious retort is that that CLUSTER is simply a brute fact, one that is in no way in need of an explanation. I mention this view only to set it aside in so far as the predominant view in the literature assumes there to be an objective feature of reality that serves to explain CLUSTER.

A more promising route would be to offer a nomological explanation of CLUSTER, one that grounds an explanation of CLUSTER in the laws of nature.[48] This response can be generalized to all kinds of substances at various levels of reality (not just biological or chemical) and is capable of being subdivided according to (i) the modal or non-modal status of the laws which serve to explain CLUSTER and (ii) the relevant degree of modal strength ascribed to such laws.

One obvious candidate for an explanation of CLUSTER along these lines, one which seems to presuppose an intrinsically demodalized account of natural laws, is Richard Boyd's (1999) *homeostatic property cluster view*. For Boyd, natural kind joints *just are* sufficiently unified clusters of properties (phenotypic traits for biological kinds, which is his primary concern), where the unity of the relevant property set is explained by *homeostasis*.

Homeostasis between a range of properties (whether taken from physics, chemistry, or biology) occurs when a law-governed mechanism or group of mechanisms ensures that a cluster of properties hover within a confined (albeit indeterminate) range. That a certain structural chemical property such as *being composed of two parts hydrogen and one part oxygen* is uniformly accompanied by the further chemical properties *having a boiling point of 100 degrees celsius* and *having a freezing point of zero degrees celsius* is explained by the presence of a stable (law-governed) homeostatic causal mechanism operative at the chemical level.

Here I think the best route for this view is to appeal to the success of nomological explanations of property clustering in fundamental physics as support for their position. The phenomena of quark confinement within a hadron, for instance, can be explained nomologically by an appeal to the color force field generated by the exchange of gluons between quarks. One could argue that the strong nuclear force serves as the mechanism that regulates homeostasis between the quarks within the hadron, thereby providing an explanation of the clustering of quarks in strict nomological terms.

While Boyd claims that the co-occurrence of properties is more than mere "statistical artifact," he is clear that the clustering that results from homeostasis is a *contingent* matter. While this fact alone does not commit Boyd to a regularity view of the laws of nature, it does imply that the first-order relation governing homeostasis cannot be too strong so as to *necessitate* the clustering of a particular group of properties. Whatever glue holds property clusters together, it cannot be too strong. On the demodalized conception of laws undergirding Boyd's view, the clustering of the properties P1 and P2 is merely contingent: no heavyweight metaphysical machinery need apply in order to explain their systematic co-instantiation in individual electrons.

First, perhaps the most glaring shortcoming of a nomological explanation for CLUSTER in general is the prima facie absence of the purported laws that are claimed to do the explanatory work on this account.[49] Regarding P1 and P2, Oderberg (2011: 90–91) contends that there *is* no law relating *only* these properties (which would be required in order to explain why *those* properties are co-instantiated), thus the explanation of CLUSTER in terms of such a law is a non-starter. Further, to stipulate that P1 and P2 are, in fact, related *only in the electrons* (as opposed to photons) is to tacitly restate the explanandum. The very fact that needs explaining is why, apart from being explained in terms of being an irreducible *kind* of thing (i.e. an electron), a certain range of properties exhibit such uniformity *in electrons* (i.e., Ks). Consequently, to say that P1 and P2 cluster in electrons *because* there is an electron-specific law that relates P1 and P2 leaves something to be desired.

Second, to identify the natures of substances with clusters of properties and homeostatic mechanisms adds little explanatory value. When considering *which* homeostatic mechanisms govern the relevant property cluster C (as opposed to a distinct cluster), the cluster view responds by saying that it is those mechanisms that cause covarying similarity between the relevant properties in C. However, Boyd (1999) is clear that the properties that constitute C vary over time. If so, we may rightly ask which of these varying properties at any given time are those that constitute C instead of a distinct cluster, C*? After all, not just *any* covarying properties are sufficient to constitute C. In order to specify which properties are those that belong to C and not C* at any given time, the cluster proponent must quantify over a particular range of properties at the exclusion of others. But which properties make it into the domain? Here it would appear that the only avenue the cluster proponent has in specifying which properties belong to C (and not C*) is to appeal to those that are unified by the homeostatic mechanisms that belong to C. But this leaves us with our original question: which homeostatic mechanisms belong to C? Without recourse to some prior notion of a unifying ground in place that is distinct from characterizing properties, the cluster view is left in an explanatory circle.[50]

Third, in so far as the earlier appropriation of Boyd's homeostatic view relies on an intrinsically demodalized theory of laws, it falls prey to the very same objections that plague a Humean view of laws in general. Here I will not rehearse these objections as they are well-known to anyone familiar with the literature. I will only register my view that laws as mere reports or, at best, systematizations of nature (as important as these may be) as per the regularity theory fails to capture the deep explanatory structure undergirding the natural sciences.[51]

To explain CLUSTER in terms of the fact that P1 and P2 are regularly or contingently co-instantiated is to merely state what we intuitively are after in the first place: an explanation as to *why* P1 and P2 behave in precisely this manner. Here, I believe Denkel's (1996) remarks are on point:

> [I]f [properties] could exist independently, why should they, in actuality, exist in compresences everywhere? If such a possibility were granted, the fact that the world is inhabited by objects rather than scatterings and conglomerates of properties would need quite a bit of explaining.
> (1996: 31–2)[52]

If there is no constraint governing the clustering of properties, why think they would exhibit such a tight-knit unity at all? The sheer fact that property clustering on this first nomological explanation of CLUSTER is *contingent* as such renders it ill-suited in the eyes of many to play a predictive role in scientific explanation.

On the view that I am advocating, Denkel's demand for an explanation of the systematic co-instantiation of properties by various objects is accounted for in the following manner: the reason *why* P1 and P2 are uniformly co-instantiated in electrons (rather than in photons, say) is that they are grounded in and inseparably tied to one and the same irreducible substantial kind.

But perhaps a nomological explanation of CLUSTER can be salvaged by an appeal to a stronger theory of laws that can bear the weight of what we take ourselves to be after in the scientific enterprise. Here, David Armstrong's (1983) conception of laws as nomic necessitation relations between universals comes to mind.[53] Interestingly enough, Armstrong himself admits the need for an explanation of CLUSTER, one that involves a principle of unity with modal import. Toward satisfying this aim, he employs his theory of laws involving what he calls "nomic connections" between the properties required for the existence of some particular: "nomic connections between . . . [the] properties [of gold or of an electron] which bind the properties up into a unity."[54] Second-order nomic connections ground the *nomologically necessary* co-presence of first-order properties (e.g., it is because the universal *F-ness* necessitates the universal *G-ness* that they are copresent in certain particulars).

Here it is important to note that, for Armstrong, nomic necessitation is a metaphysically contingent relation; it is weaker than robust metaphysical necessity, but stronger than mere first-order regularity (but entails such regularity).[55] Thus, if something is negatively charged then it *must*, according to the laws of nature, repel another negatively charged entity. But the modal import explaining the co-presence of universals in certain particulars is explained entirely in terms of properties and the relation of nomic necessitation: irreducible kinds or natures are rendered superfluous on his view (cf. Armstrong 1978: 63).

Yet by Armstrong's own admission the relation of nomic necessitation is not sufficient to adequately explain CLUSTER. In addition to the relation of nomic necessitation, Armstrong introduces what he calls *the principle of particularization* to explain CLUSTER:

> Although Essentialist Realism has been rejected, it does seem that it has an element of truth . . . It is the truth that for each particular, there exists at least one monadic universal which makes that particular just one, and not more than one, instance of a certain sort. Such a universal will be a "particularlizing" universal, making that particular *one* of a kind. Without such a universal, the particular is not restricted to certain definite bounds, it is not "signed to a certain quantity," we do not have a "substance," we do not have *a* particular.
> (Armstrong 1978: 62)

This passage is revealing in its admission of precisely what the serious essentialist claims is required to adequately explain CLUSTER: both substantial kinds and their instances are irreducibly unified. Interestingly enough, with one hand Armstrong attempts to eliminate kinds altogether in favor of properties and relations of nomic necessitation. On the other hand, however, he countenances (under the guise of a "particularizing universal") a sort of universal which plays one of the roles traditionally assigned to substantial kinds. Here Michael Loux's maxim rings true (1974: 782): "Invariably, it turned out that they could reduce substance-concepts to the concepts of characteristics only if they illicitly smuggled in vestiges of the kind-concepts they were trying to eliminate." Armstrong grants that without a higher-order unifier underlying the instantiation of the various properties we find in the world, it is difficult to make sense of the claim that the particular with those properties is a *single* entity.

What we find in the natural world, however, are various instances of substantial kinds that exhibit a deep unity as well as uniform range of causal dispositions that are (for the most part) stable in the various causal contexts in which they operate. Particular kinds of substances, be they electrons, carbon atoms, or mammals, are *unified* and *stable* units of causal activity. Electrons uniformly spin and respond in certain ways to electromagnetic fields *in virtue* of their stable causal powers and properties. Consequently, Armstrong's admission of a higher-order unifier of the powers and properties of particulars concedes the point to the serious essentialist: there is something in virtue of which properties and their instances are intrinsically unified.

But suppose we strengthen the nomological explanation of CLUSTER one last time so that the laws are not merely nomologically necessary (and contingent) as per Armstrong, but metaphysically necessary as per dispositional essentialism. In its most general form, dispositional essentialism is the view that properties have dispositional essences.[56] When applied to natural laws the view states that laws supervene on the dispositional essences of properties. From these two theses it follows that laws are metaphysically necessary: if the essence of a disposition remains constant in every possible world in which it exists, and laws supervene on the essences of dispositional properties, then laws are metaphysically necessary.

In the concluding sections of his excellent book on the metaphysics of science, Bird (2007: 208–11) sets out to explain CLUSTER in terms of a dispositional essentialist gloss on Boyd's homeostatic property cluster view. Where Boyd's own law-governed explication of homeostasis was intrinsically demodalized, Bird has metaphysical modality in spades. Bird states,

> Thus it seems to me to be plausible that Boyd's homeostatic property cluster idea can be extended to all natural kinds. The laws will explain why there are certain clusters; they will also explain the natures of those clusters—the loose and vague clusters in biology, the partially precise clusters of chemistry and the perfectly precise clusters of particle physics. Boyd introduces his idea in order to provide an alternative to the essentialist view of natural kinds. However, if I am right, the homeostatic property cluster approach can be expanded to include the essentialist view in respect of the kinds to which it applies. The laws of nature will explain why—*necessarily*—there are no members of chemical and microphysical kinds that lack certain properties, why of necessity certain properties cluster together in a partially or fully precise manner.
> (Bird 2007: 210–11)

Apart from its being susceptible to the very same objections we noted earlier to nomological explanations of CLUSTER in general as well as homeostatic clustering in particular, the deeper problem regarding Bird's proposal stems from his own admission that laws are epiphenomenal: it is dispositional properties that do all the work in explaining *why* laws obtain (2007: 47). The order of explanation runs from dispositional properties to laws, not the other way around. It is a law of nature that everything possessing property P, under certain circumstances or stimulus S, yields a particular manifestation M, precisely *because* it is part of the nature of P to be disposed to yield M in S.

One is hard pressed, then, to interpret Bird's statement earlier that "laws will explain why there are certain clusters; they will also explain the natures of those clusters." Here Bird's view seems to be committed to a rather arbitrary asymmetry regarding the explanatory relationship between properties and laws (former explain the latter) and clusters of properties and laws (latter explain the former). What explains this asymmetry? After all, on this view, it is plausible to assume that natural laws regarding property clustering (if there be such laws) are just a subset of natural laws per se. If dispositional properties are the explanatory grounds for the laws of nature per se, then why wouldn't dispositional properties or clusters thereof also be the explanatory grounds for laws explaining the co-instantiation of properties?

There must, then, be something about the individual properties *themselves* (and not the laws which govern the homeostatic mechanism as per Bird's appropriation of Boyd) that play a role in explaining CLUSTER.[57] Perhaps Bird thinks that an explanation of CLUSTER lies in the fact that it is part of the individual dispositional essences of P1 and P2 that they be exclusively co-instantiated with one another. But this is clearly false. It cannot be part of the dispositional essence of *being a fundamental particle* that it be disposed to be co-instantiated solely with the dispositional essence of *having unit negative charge* for the simple reason that it de facto clusters with the dispositional essence *having zero charge* in photons. Likewise, as we have seen, *having unit negative charge* clusters not only with *being a fundamental particle* in electrons but also (in fact) with *being a non-fundamental particle* in chloride ions.[58]

Bird might be tempted to make the following revision: it is part of the individual dispositional essences of P1 and P2 that they be co-instantiated *only in electrons*. But as was stated before, to claim that the explanation for why P1 and P2 cluster and covary is that it is part of their dispositional essences to be co-instantiated *only in the electrons* is to once again restate the explanandum and not to explain it.

Consequently, I am inclined to think that reference to the substantial kinds expressed by the real definitions of substances are ineliminable when it comes to offering an ultimate explanation for CLUSTER. The deep causal uniformity and stability of property groupings we see in sodium chloride molecules, say, is best explained by the fact that they inseparably proceed from one and the same essence and thus are instances of a single, unified substantial kind. Irreducible natural kind structure, as Brian Ellis (2001: 285) points out, "guarantees that certain properties are uniquely clustered."

Note, however, that while law-governed homeostatic property-clusters may not be suited to provide the reductive basis for natural kind structure and therein an ultimate explanation for CLUSTER in terms of properties alone, this is not to say that such mechanisms are entirely irrelevant to property clustering in nature. It simply does not follow that if substantial kinds do not reduce to law-governed homeostatic property clusters that law-governed homeostatic mechanisms are therefore superfluous in factoring into the causal or empirical story as to how properties cluster in the natural world. Even if we grant that there were such law-governed homeostatic mechanisms at work in the clustering of the properties that characterize electrons, it is plausible to think that the presence of these mechanisms would be explained by the instantiation of the substantial kind *electron*.

To illustrate, take individual substances of the biological kind *Apodemus sylvaticus*—i.e., common wood mice. Along with other distinctive murine properties (e.g., having a unique molar pattern), individual wood mice will be, in virtue of being certain kinds of living organisms, disposed to exhibit a particular range of properties—e.g., a weight of 20g to 35g and a length of 7cm to 12cm.[59] We may well suppose that law-governed biological mechanisms are causally relevant in accounting for the stability and cohesion of the aforementioned properties exemplified by individual wood mice. But as was noted earlier, the presence of specific biological mechanisms that factor into the empirical story concerning the unity of the properties of wood mice is best explained by the fact that such mechanisms necessarily characterize instances of the substantial kind *Apodemus sylvaticus*. It is in virtue of being an instance of the substantial kind *Apodemus sylvaticus* that a wood mouse exhibits one *particular* range of properties and dispositions rather than another, whose cohesion is governed by distinct law-governed homeostatic mechanisms operative at the biological level.

1.2.4 The Explanatory Naturalness of Essence

While we have grounds to resist identifying a substance's nature with its characterizing properties, this is not to deny that there is an intimate relationship between the two. But how exactly are we to understand the connection between essence and properties or, to use our prescribed terminology, between constitutive and characterizing predicables? If we are to part company with Fine's explication of the structure of a thing's modal profile in terms of a logical ordering over properties per se, what are we to offer in its place?

In this section, I want to attempt to unpack an alternative account of the ordering that obtains among the items of an object's modal profile (what the modal essentialist refers to as its "essence"). As the primary actors on the world's stage, substances are dynamic and active. Passivism, the view held by many early modern philosophers that the occupants of spacetime are fundamentally inert and passive, is a world devoid of substances, by my lights.[60] Some of these powerful particulars undergo radio active decay, some spin, some dissolve in water, others engage in the philosophical

38 Serious Essentialism

enterprise, and others biological assimilation, all depending on the nature of substance in question.

Herein lies our first conception of the ordering that obtains among the items of an substance's modal profile. This ordering is summed up nicely in the medieval maxim *agere sequitur esse*—i.e., act follows being or *what* a thing is determines *how* it is.[61] A substance's being of a particular ontological category and natural kind determines not only its necessary causal powers and capacities, but also the full range of ways that it can be characterized or modified. For Aristotelians, an adequate explanation of CLUSTER resides in the fact that necessary properties, powers, and capacities are determined or fixed by *what* that substance is fundamentally.

A bit more carefully, let us refer to the range of causal activity a substance is disposed toward in every world in which it exists as its *causal profile*. The causal profile of a substance will be a proper subset of its modal profile. Driving the medieval maxim *agere sequitur esse* is the idea that the nature or essence of a substance necessitates its causal profile—*how* the substance qua member of a particular kind is disposed to behave. The medievals often referred to this ordering relationship between the nature of a substance and its causal profile (or in medieval Aristotelian parlance "propria") by saying that the latter was "caused by,"[62] "added onto,"[63] "follow from,"[64] "conjoined to,"[65] "rooted in,"[66] and "connaturally and inseparably inhere,"[67] in a thing's essence. Locke, in summarizing the view of many of his scholastic predecessors, stated the view nicely when he said,

> For, since the powers or qualities that are observable by us are not the real essence of that substance, but depend on it, and flow from it, any collection whatsoever of these qualities cannot be the real essence of that thing.[68]

More precisely, we can state this relationship between an individual substance of a particular kind and its respective causal profile as follows:

(KPC) *Kind-Power Connection*: for any particular substance of kind K, there is a causal profile P such that, necessarily, for any x, if x is a K then x has P.

Here we must tread carefully. KPC maintains that it is necessarily the case that a substance of kind K has a certain range of causal powers which dispose it toward a certain range of behaviors. Salt, on this view, is *disposed to dissolve in water* in every world in which it exists; there is a metaphysically necessary connection between the nature of salt and the causal power *being disposed to dissolve in water*.[69]

While the nature of a substance necessitates a particular range of dispositional properties as per KPC, it is important to note that it does not necessitate the *manifestation* of the various powers and liabilities that make up those profiles. Substances of the kind *salt* do not necessitate the *manifestation* of the disposition to dissolve in water such that they are the truth-maker for the occurant predication "salt dissolves in water." As the manifestation of a causal power is susceptible to finks, mask, preventers, etc., the having of a power does not *necessitate* its manifestation, rather, it *disposes* the bearer of the power toward that manifestation.[70] While various kinds of substances do not necessitate the manifestation of their causal profiles, they nevertheless necessitate the having of the dispositional properties that make up such profiles; substances of that kind *must* have that causal profile in every world in which they exist.

This view of the relationship between the nature of a substance and its respective causal powers is not without its contemporary proponents. Regarding substances as objects of scientific inquiry, Harré (1970) maintains,

> Within this view one may see their behavior as flowing from their natures or constitutions as consequences of what they *are*. So they must behave in the specified way, or not be the things they are. And so necessarily while they are the things they are, they behave in those ways or have a tendency to behave in those ways or are disposed to behave in those ways . . . [B]eing of the right nature endows a thing or material with the power to manifest itself in certain ways or to behave in certain ways in the appropriate circumstances.
> (Harré 1970: 88)

Moreover, while Loux (1974: 782) holds fast to the irreducibility of kinds to characterizing properties, he nevertheless maintains the intimate relationship between the two predicables:

> To deny, however, that kinds can be eliminated in favor of characteristics is not to deny the important connection between being a member of a kind and exhibiting certain characteristics. That such a connection exists and that it is more than merely contingent are both claims no one can doubt. Their indubitability likely lies at the bottom of many attempts to reduce substance-kinds to characteristics. But while granting the relevant connection, one can deny that predicating a kind of an object is merely ascribing a set of characteristics to it. This is what I am denying; and denying it, I am arguing, is plausible.
> (Loux 1974: 782)

On this view, it is metaphysically impossible for a substance to exist and thereby fail to have a causal profile; a substance's possessing a particular causal profile is no mere contingent matter.

Understanding KPC goes a long way toward dissolving many of the objections originating in the early modern period surrounding the distinction between the nature of a substance and its characterizing properties. The main thrust of the objections come in two stages, beginning with a metaphysical charge of bare particularity given the distinction between the substance qua member of a kind and its characterizing properties, and proceeding to an epistemological worry about our knowledge of the natures of substances so considered.

If members of substantial kinds are distinct from their characterizing properties, then does this not construe the former as "bare" substrata, mere featureless pincushions for properties?[71] The objection that substances are bare substrata goes roughly as follows: (i) a particular kind of substance, say Tibbles the cat, is characterized by various properties (shape, size, color, etc.); (ii) On an Aristotelian view, Tibbles is numerically distinct from the characterizing properties which are said to inhere in her; (iii) therefore, Tibbles, strictly speaking, is entirely devoid of properties and is thus, implausibly, a bare substratum.

The epistemological worry is often thought to follow immediately from the metaphysical charge of bare particularity. The worry often takes the form of "I know not what" claims echoing the likes of Descartes's "this I know not what of mine" (referring to himself as a mental substance), Locke's characterization of substance as "I know not what," and Reid's (1994: i273) claim that "this obscure something, which is supposed to be the subject or substratum of those qualities." If substances are bare particulars, mere featureless pincushions for properties, then in what sense are they intelligible and capable of being known? In sum, the prospects of formulating real definitions of substances is far too dim given that particular kinds of substances are bare particulars, or something near enough.

As others have aptly pointed out, these charges simply misconstrue the Aristotelian gloss on the relationship between particular substances and their characterizing properties.[72] For one, the earlier move from (ii) to (iii) is a non-sequitur. From the fact that particular substances are numerically distinct from their characterizing properties, it does not follow that they are therefore entirely devoid of properties altogether (nor capable of existing without any properties whatsoever). Numerical distinctness does not, in itself, entail separability. Consider a trope and its bearer by way of analogy. Few trope-theorists would disagree that tropes are numerically distinct from their bearers. Nevertheless, the non-transferability of tropes, on standard accounts, is explained in terms of a trope's being grounded in and thus inseparable from its bearer. Hence, we have numerical distinctness without separability.

A similar relation obtains between a substance of a particular kind and its causal profile. As per KPC, in every possible world in which a substance of a particular kind exists, it is characterized by its respective causal profile; there is no world in which a substance of a certain kind exists and lacks the causal dispositions that characterize things of that kind. On the fundamental ontology I alluded to earlier which countenances tropes as particularized properties, tropes are dependent on and thus non-transferable from their host substances. The substance itself is both the both the bearer and ontological base of its particular dispositional tropes in every world in which it exists. No bare particulars or propertyless substrata need apply.[73]

What, then, are we to make of the epistemological worry regarding our knowledge of the natures of substances? While essences are explanatorily prior to properties in that they serve as their minimal explanatory base (as we will see next), few would deny that we generally come to know the natures of substances by means of how they behave in certain contexts in virtue of their characterizing properties and causal powers. The primary means by which we attain knowledge of a thing's constitutive predicables is through its characterizing causal powers and capacities.

The irreducibility of natures to properties is in no way antithetical to coming to know the former on the basis of the latter; the serious essentialist metaphysic that I am advocating is no *a priori* essentialism, at least when it comes to empirically specifiable entities. This point is nicely underscored by Lowe (2009: 158) concerning the natures of chemical substances:

> It is, of course, perfectly feasible to maintain this while acknowledging that investigation of a chemical specimen's empirically detectable properties *guides* us in classifying it as being an exemplar of this or that chemical kind and hence, say, as being a particular instance of the kind named "gold."
>
> (Lowe 2009a: 158)

Causal powers and dispositions point to the natures of substances. More specifically, since particular causal dispositions, on my view, are non-transferable tropes that modify their bearers, their existence and identity are grounded in their bearers. We might also say that knowledge of the causal profile of a substance constitutes, at the very least, partial knowledge of its nature.[74] For instance my knowledge of the dispositional profile of a particular isotope of gold—its melting point, malleability, ductility, solubility in aqua regia, etc.—constitutes knowledge (albeit partial and defeasible) of its free electron structure, which partly constitutes its nature. This was, in fact, Aquinas's view regarding our knowledge of fundamental substantial natures: "If anybody advances a definition that does not lead him to the properties of a thing, his definition is fanciful, off the subject, merely a debating point" and "the species of a thing is gathered from its proper operation; for the operation manifests the power, which reveals the essence."[75] Such knowledge is, of course, neither exhaustive nor indefeasible.

Not only do the natures of substances necessitate their distinctive causal profiles as per KPC, there is also a rich *explanatory structure* that obtains between the two proper sub-classes included in their modal profile. How, then, might we go about making this explanatory structure more precise? Must the serious essentialist rest content with what Armstrong (1997: 66) has called "mere vague gesture" in distinguishing between that which is constitutive of the nature of a substance and that which characterizes it?

I think not. Recall that I briefly stated earlier that the serious essentialist gloss on the structure of a substance's modal profile (N) is better described as being roughly akin to an ordered *n*-tuple such as N = ⟨$f_1 \ldots f_n$⟩ such that the items in its modal profile stand in certain priority relations to one another, where Fine construed such relations in terms of logical consequence.[76]

In the place of Fine's notion of logical consequence I want to offer a second notion of ordering expressed by the aforementioned scholastic locutions (p. 38) regarding the items in the modal profile of a substance. On the view I am advocating here, there is a privileged subset of items within the modal profile of a substance that are more *explanatorily basic* than others, where the notion of explanation here is understood as a distinctively metaphysical *in virtue of* relation. Metaphysical explanations of this sort—whether they are best understood as species of metaphysical grounding per se or simply backed by metaphysical grounding relations—carve out non-causal, explanatory relations that are asymmetric.[77]

To help unpack this second variety of structure among the items of a substance's modal profile, I recommend something roughly similar to Lewis's (1986: 59–61) notion of a naturalness ordering over properties, albeit one that is extended to *all* predicables and their ontological correlates, both constitutive and characterizing.[78] Further, let us suppose for illustrative purposes here that all predicables—whether constitutive or characterizing—are natural or sparse in that they account for "objective sameness and difference, joints in the world, discriminatory classifications not of our own making."[79]

As we have seen, one can predicate a multiplicity of things to a polar bear, gold, a flower, water, or an electron. While all natural predicables are responsible for the objective and causal joints in nature, some carve much deeper than others. There is, in other words, an inegalitarianism with respect to natural predicables in that some of them are *more natural* than others in that that they are better suited to carve nature at its deepest explanatory joints.[80]

To help elucidate the relationship between the nature of a substance and its characterizing causal profile in terms of a naturalness ordering, let "□ P_S" represent the modal profile of a substance S—that is, the total class of the necessary (natural) predicables of S—and begin by offering the following notion of *explanatory basicness*:

> *Explanatory Basicness*: for any two proper subsets *b* and *c* of □P_S, *b* is explanatorily basic for *c* iff the necessary predicables in *b* explain the necessary predicables in *c*, and not vice versa.

This rather straightforward notion of explanatory basicness is meant to highlight the *asymmetrical* explanatory ordering that governs the necessary predicables (or any features for that matter) included within the modal profile of any particular substance.

The modal profile of plants belonging to the botanical genus *geranium*, for example, include the necessary (characterizing) predicable *being disposed to develop a root system* as well as *being disposed to undergo seed dispersal*; yet the former predicable explains the latter and not vice versa. Geraniums are necessarily disposed to undergo seed dispersal precisely *because* they are disposed to develop a root system. The capacity to develop a root system, then, is explanatorily prior to the power for seed dispersal and thus the former, we might say, is more explanatorily basic for geraniums than the latter. Of course, the aforementioned ordering relation between these two causal powers represents only a small slice of the explanatory structure that obtains between the features that are predicated of a geranium.[81]

On the serious essentialist metaphysic I am developing here, there will be necessary predicables within the modal profile of a substance that are not only more basic than others in the order of explanation, but ones which fail to be explained in terms of any other necessary predicables of that substance.[82] That is, the hierarchy of explanatory ordering for the necessary predicables within a substance's modal profile ultimately terminates in those that are *minimally explanatorily basic* for that substance.

With this concept in hand, we can define the notion of *minimal explanatory basicness* as follows:

Minimal Explanatory Basicness: a proper subset a of $\Box P_S$ is minimally explanatorily basic for $\Box P_S$ iff (i) a is explanatorily basic for every predicable not in a and (ii) there is no proper subset of a, a^*, such that a^* is explanatorily basic for $\Box P_S$.

A naturalness ranking over the modal profile of a particular substance, then, generates a hierarchy of necessary predicables which are ordered by means of their explanatory basicness. The hierarchy of necessary predicables for a substance will ultimately terminate in a minimal explanatory base, a base which is not explained in terms of any other set of predicables within the modal profile of S, and which serves to explain every other set of predicables within S's modal profile.

On the naturalness conception of structure on offer, we can identify the necessary predicables of S's modal profile that carve out the minimal explanatory base for S with its *perfectly natural predicables*:

Perfectly Natural Predicable: F is a perfectly natural predicable of $\Box P_S$ iff F is minimally explanatorily basic for $\Box P_S$.

On my view, the constitutive predicables—those that enter into the real definition of a substance—are perfectly natural in so far as they, more than any other predicables within its modal profile, carve the deepest explanatory joints (and thus are directly definitive of S). The perfectly natural predicables of a substance serve as the minimal explanatory ground as to *why* that substance is characterized the way it is, including its distinctive causal profile. On this score, Harré and Madden (1975: 101–102) highlight the minimal explanatory role of constitutive predicables as follows: "Capacities, just as much as powers, what particulars or substances are liable to undergo as well as what they are able to do, are explained by reference to what the thing is in itself."

Consider some examples. The property of *being malleable* is arguably part of the causal profile of the element of gold. That gold is characterized as such is, on the view offered earlier, explained in terms of the nature or essence of gold, in this case its particular electron configuration (having a free electron structure). The nature of gold as a metal whose atomic constituents have atomic number 79, carves out and unifies a particular range of properties and powers that necessarily accompany substances of that kind. While gold is characterized by its *being malleabe* in every possible world in which it exists, the latter is not a *perfectly* natural predicable of gold and therefore fails to enter into its real definition.

Again, the nature of Ethanol as consisting of a hydroxyl group—a group consisting of an oxygen atom connected by a covalent bond to a hydrogen atom—is what explains its *being miscible with water*, that is, its power to form a homogeneous mixture with water. Moreover, it is in virtue of the nature of a diamond as having a particular crystalline structure that it has the power to exhibit such a high hardness index on the Mohs scale. Having a hydroxyl group and a having a crystalline structure are arguably perfectly natural predicables of Ethanol molecules and diamonds, respectively.

Here we need to consider more closely what sense can be made of the idea that, as Lewis (1986a: 59–61) points out, naturalness admits of degrees. As we saw earlier, one predicable can be more or less natural than another, with perfectly natural predicables serving as the root of the naturalness ordering for various predicables of particular substances.

In Lewisian fashion I want to suggest that we unpack the notion of "comparative" or "relative" naturalness in terms of explanatory "distance" from the perfectly natural predicables.[83] That is, if x is *more natural* than y, then the explanatory chain linking x to the perfectly natural predicables of a substance will be "shorter" than the explanatory chain linking y to those very same predicables.

We can understand the idea of explanatory "distance" between necessary predicables in terms of an *immediate explanatory base* as follows:

Immediate Explanatory Base: F is the immediate explanatory base for G iff (i) F is explanatory basic for G and (ii) there is no F^* such that F is explanatorily basic for F^* and F^* is explanatorily basic for G.[84]

If predicable F is the immediate explanatorily base for predicable G, then there is no intermediary in the order of explanation linking G and F. For

G to be related to F in such a way is an example of an explanatory chain that is maximally "short." If one were to incrementally add explanatory "links" to the chain connecting G to F one would thereby increase the explanatory "distance" between the two predicables.

On this understanding of comparative or relative naturalness, then, non-necessary characterizing predicables (i.e., extraneous accidents) are the least natural of the natural predicables of a substance. The necessary characterizing predicables, however, are more natural than the non-necessary characterizing predicables in that there are fewer explanatory links in the chain connecting them to the perfectly natural predicables (minimal explanatory base). Not all necessary characterizing predicables need have at least one perfectly natural predicable as part of their immediate explanatory base; only those that have the highest degree of naturalness short of being perfectly natural have this status.

Consequently, each necessary characterizing predicable will be linked to the perfectly natural predicables either directly by means of having them as part of their immediate explanatory base, or indirectly by means of an explanatory chain running through the former.[85] As mentioned earlier, a substance's perfectly natural predicables—i.e., constitutive predicables, lay at the root of the explanatory ordering over the necessary predicables within its modal profile. The real definition of a particular substance, then, aims to capture its minimally explanatory basic features or those that are directly definitive of the substance in question which serve to explain all other necessary predicables within its modal profile.

Consider the following examples of comparative naturalness at work. In virtue of its having an asymmetrical (non-uniform) charge distribution (i.e., a high molecular polarity which in turn gives rise to dipole-dipole interactions), a HCl molecule is disposed toward *being acidic* and *boiling at minus 85 degrees celsius*. Plausibly, the molecule's having non-uniform charge distribution is the immediate explanatory base for the aforementioned necessary characterizing predicables that are part of the modal profile of HCl molecules. Even more, however, is the fact that it is precisely because it is part of the essence of HCl that it is a chemical *compound* consisting of at least two atomic parts that it is capable of exhibiting an *aysmmetrical* charge distribution. For HCl, the constitutive predicable *chemical compound* is an immediate explanatory base for the predicable *being asymmetrically charged*.[86]

Again, a mammal's having a certain follicular skin structure is more natural than its having hair. In fact, it would appear that the latter has the former as its immediate explanatory base. As a result, the explanatory chain linking the dispositional property *being disposed to have hair* to the constitutive (perfectly natural) predicables for mammals is "longer" than the chain linking the property *being disposed to have a follicular skin structure* to those very same predicables.[87]

I'll close with an example that is much closer to home for the reader. Human beings, in virtue of *what* they are fundamentally, have the power to lie. Let us assume here for the sake of illustration that the power to lie is a natural predicable. It seems intuitive to say that the power to lie has as its immediate explanatory base the conjunction of the following variety of natural predicables, each of which appear to be *more natural* than the power to lie: the power to form beliefs, the power to communicate (in propositional form), the power to entertain false propositions and intend to report them as true, etc.[88] While we might admit further structure between even these predicables, the point here is that each appear to be more natural than the power to lie; the explanatory chain linking these predicables to the perfectly natural predicables of a human being is shorter than the one linking the power to lie. Arguably, each of the earlier natural predicables that serve as the immediate explanatory base for the power to lie are themselves *less natural* than the power to be rational; it seems plausible that a human being's capacity for rationality is both explanatorily prior to these natural predicables and, in the end, may well be a perfectly natural predicable and thereby partly constitute the nature of a human being.

Consequently, the aforementioned notion of a naturalness ordering over a thing's necessary predicables, together with the distinction between the nature of a substance and its characterizing properties, stand in direct contrast to both ME2a and ME2b of modal essentialism (see the aforementioned). In contrast to Fine's account of the structure among the items of a thing's modal profile in terms of logical consequence, my own conception of such structure in terms of explanatory naturalness is much less restrictive and thus includes certain features of an entity that are closely tied to it, but do not logically follow from its essence (as was stated earlier regarding triangles and having three sides).

Let's take stock of what has turned out to be a rather lengthy chapter. I began by rehearsing several now familiar lines against the sufficiency of a modal-existential account of essence, as stated in ME1. I then set out to unpack my own particular variety of a serious-essentialist ontology, which attempts to ground modality in essence and gives pride of place to a more fine-grained notion of essence in terms of real definition. I then set out to motivate a clean break from modal essentialism in rejecting ME2 and hence the view that essences are unstructured collections of properties. We examined one reason in particular to think that the notion of essence is irreducible to a set or collection of properties: in virtue of *what* do properties and powers systematically cluster in certain particulars to form an integral unity? I argued that a deep and informative explanation of CLUSTER, one that supports the explanatory and predictive aims of the sciences, is best afforded by an ontology of irreducible substantial natures. I then turned to explicate my own medieval Aristotelian inspired account of the twofold structure that governs the necessary predicables of a substance in terms of the *Kind-Power Connection* as well as the notion of an explanatory ordering in terms of Lewisian naturalness.

Notes

1. For some representatives of this line of thinking see Fine (1994a), Klima (2002), Lowe (2008b), Molnar (2003: 37–39), Oderberg (2007), and Ross (1989).
2. Where "E" serves as the existence predicate such that $Ex = df(\exists y)x = y$.
3. Along with Plantinga (1974: 70) and Mackie (2006: 1) cited earlier, the representatives are numerous: Yablo (1987: 297), the essence of a thing is "an assortment of properties in virtue of which it is the entity in question." Chisholm (1989: 43), "the essence of a thing was said to be a property that is essential to the thing and necessarily repugnant to everything else;" Kaplan (1978: 100), "I prefer to think of an essence in this way (as a transworld heir line) rather than in the more familiar way (as a collection of properties) . . . ." Lewis (1968: 120), "the whole of its essence is the intersection of its essential attributes."
4. Although Oderberg (2007, 2011) is a notable exception here as we will see.
5. This is nicely captured in Des Chene (2006).
6. This is adapted from Correia (2008) who attributes the discussion of Socrates and his life to Lowe (1998: 143).
7. Although Nathan Wildman (2013) and Sam Cowling (2013) attempt to salvage the modal account of essence by appealing to the notion of Lewisian naturalness. Skiles (2015) offers a critical response to this move to which I am sympathetic.
8. See Wildman (2016).
9. Also, note that appealing to the notion of trivially necessary properties in order to blunt the force of Fine's counterexamples may not carry over to our second counterexample of the essential asymmetry between Socrates and his life. Whether Socrates's life is construed as an event or a temporally extended trope of some sort, at the very least, it seems that Socrates's life is a non-trivially necessary feature of Socrates as it is more closely tied to *what* he is (a spatiotemporal concrete particular) than the properties *being distinct from the Eiffel Tower* or *being a member of {Socrates}*.
10. This is evidenced by the fact that the view is now widely presupposed rather than argued for in the literature.
11. For historical background see Knuuttila (2011).
12. I should note that Fine (2002) does not say this is the case for all kinds of necessity. Rather, he excludes facts about natural and normative modality as further kinds of modality that are made true by facts about essence. Here I restrict my discussion to metaphysical modality.
13. Other contemporary philosophers who are sympathetic to the idea of real definition (though some more so than others) are B. Ellis (2001), Johnston (2006), Lowe (2012c), Molnar (2003: 38), Oderberg (2011), Rosen (2015), and Ross (1989).
14. Oderberg (2007: 19).
15. For Aristotle's explication of real definition as "a phrase signifying a thing's essence" see *Topics* I.5 101b38, VII.5 154a31 in Aristotle (1984a).
16. See Ross (2008).
17. As noted in Pasnau (2011: 557–564), this distinction between real definition and what I'm calling the particular essence is a long-standing one in the

48 *Serious Essentialism*

history of essentialism, particularly in the work of the scholastics, see especially Suarez (2000).
18. Here I borrow the phrase "particularized-nature" from Lowe (2012d). This, of course, is one particular interpretation of Aristotle's view as stated in *Meta*. Z.6.
19. See Adams (1979), Plantinga (1974), and Rosenkrantz (1993).
20. See Loux (1978).
21. The primary reason being the threat of an infinite regress of essences (essences having essences ad infinitum) as noted by Aristotle in *Meta*. VII.17.
22. See Oderberg (2007) for a different perspective on the relationship between a substance and its essence.
23. I am of the opinion that these ontological commitments in particular provide a robust foundation for much of the machinery underlying the natural sciences such as inductive inferences, laws of nature, causal powers, and causal explanation. For a full-scale defense of these commitments I point the reader to Harré and Madden (1975), Bird (2007), Ellis (2001), and Lowe (1998; 2006).
24. For the empirical adequacy of a robust, Aristotelian essentialism see Devitt (2008), Dumsday (2012), Oderberg (2007), Walsh (2006), and Wilson (1999).
25. See Lowe (2012c).
26. See Oderberg (2011: 87).
27. Morrison (2006: 110) goes on to state, "Socrates steers the conversation by searching for a 'definition.' Socrates asks his conversation partner to give a definition, to 'say what courage is' or 'what justice is.' What Socrates wants is not (what we would call) a dictionary definition, telling how the word is typically used, but (what philosophers have come to call) a 'real definition,' an account displaying the essential nature of, for example, courage or justice."
28. See his *Being and Essence*, 1 in Bobik (1988).
29. Spinoza (1955: 35).
30. Leibniz (1969: 293).
31. Plantinga (1974: 72).
32. Kit Fine (1995: 56).
33. Fine (1994b: 276) also gives the example of Socrates's singleton, where the property of *containing Socrates as a member* would be part of its constitutive essence and the property of containing some member or other being part of its consequential essence.
34. A second reason might be that the use of logical consequence to explicate the structure of a thing's modal profile appears rather unstable in so far as it is questionable whether *being a man or a mountain* characterizes anything at all, let alone Socrates's consequential essence.
35. Cf. Rosen (2010: 122); Cf. Molnar (2003: 38) and Johnston (2006).
36. Fine (1995: 66).
37. For primary sources regarding natures as being modal truth makers as well the ground of a thing's properties and powers in the thought of Thomas Aquinas, see *ST* III, q. 13, a. 1c and *In Meta*. IX, left. 1, n. 1782. For secondary sources regarding late medieval scholastic thought on this matter see Pasnau (2011: Chapter 24); Knuuttila (1993: Chapter 3); and Des Chene (1996: 71).
38. See Oderberg (2007: 160) who therein cites Lowe (2006) as an example of this distinction at work. Also, Heil (2003: 46) explicitly adopts the aforementioned distinction between characterizing and sortal predicates.
39. One of the clearest historical statements of the distinction between properties per se and essence is in Aquinas (1949: a. 11): "A property is like a substantial predicate, inasmuch as it is caused by the essential principles of a species; and consequently a property is demonstrated as belonging to a subject through a

definition that signifies the essence. But it is like an accidental predicate in this sense, that it is neither the essence of a thing, nor a part of the essence, but something outside the essence itself. Whereas it differs from an accidental predicate, because an accidental predicate is not caused by the essential principles of a species, but it accrues to an individual thing as a property accrues to a species, yet sometimes separably, and sometimes inseparably. So, then, the powers of the soul are intermediate between the essence of the soul and an accident, as natural or essential properties, that is, as properties that are a natural consequence of the essence of the soul."

40. I emphasize *fundamental* here in so far as I take there to be other non-fundamental ontological categories.
41. Cf. Heil (2005).
42. Emphasis in original.
43. These examples are taken from Oderberg (2011).
44. See also Armstrong (1997: 67).
45. For more on Boyle's views regarding natural kinds (as well as the general early modern suspicion regarding our ability to identify the objective natural kind structure in the world) see Pasnau (2011) 633–655.
46. This line of reasoning is advanced by Suarez (2000), sections 15.1.14 and 15.10.64 in particular: "The strongest arguments by which substantial form is proven rely on the fact that for the complete constitution of a natural being it is necessary that all the faculties and operations of the same being be rooted in one essential principle (15.10.64)." For contemporary advocates of this line see Des Chene (1996: 71–75), Lowe (2006: 135), Oderberg (2011), and Scaltsas (1994: 78–80) where Oderberg (2011) is by far the most comprehensive and is the line of reasoning that I mirror closely in what follows.
47. Oderberg (2011).
48. This general line is taken by Bird (2007) and Elder (2004: 26).
49. See Oderberg (2011); cf. Schaffer (2003b: 132–133).
50. This line of reasoning is put forward in Ereshefsky (2010b).
51. Which, as many argue, is one that facilitates inductive inferences (i.e., plays a predictive role) and has the ability to support counterfactual reasoning, which appears to be integral to our best explanatory practices. Note that this line of thinking applies equally to both Hume's own view as well as to that of Lewis (1973: 72–77) in so far as both construe laws as mere regularities, i.e. devoid of intrinsic modal content.
52. For a similar critique of an explanation of CLUSTER in such terms see Harré and Madden (1975: 214).
53. The view, of course, is standardly attributed to Dreske (1977), Tooely (1977), and Armstrong (1983). Here I restrict my attention to Armstrong's explication.
54. Armstrong (1978: 62).
55. Thus, Armstrong retains Lewis's doctrine of Independence (no necessary connections between distinct existences) but rejects his notion of Humean Supervenience, that everything supervenenes on the (first-order) mosaic of local property instances.
56. For a contemporary defense of dispositional essentialism see Bird (2007) and Ellis (2001).
57. Bird could contend that by saying that the laws of nature are "epiphenomenal" one means that laws are "nothing over and above" the dispositional properties and their directed manifestations. Without a clear endorsement of the Eleatic principle of "to be is to have causal power," I take an "epiphenomenal" entity to be one that *exists*, but that lacks causal efficacy.

50 *Serious Essentialism*

58. These examples are from Oderberg (2011: 91).
59. This example is from Bird (2012: 100).
60. See Ellis (2001).
61. Who in turn followed Aristotle in *De Anima*, Book II, Ch. IV.
62. Aquinas, SCG 4.14.3508, see Aquinas (1975).
63. Aquinas, SCG IV.14.12/3508, see Aquinas (1975).
64. *ST* 1a.7.3c, see Aquinas (1947)
65. Buridan, *In Phys.* II. 5, f. 33rb, as quoted in Pasnau (2011)
66. Suarez, *Disp. Meta.*. 15. 10.64, see Suarez (2000)
67. *Disp. Meta.*. 15.1.13, see Suarez (2000).
68. Locke (1975): 2.31.13, p. 383.
69. See Freddoso (1986) for a thorough defense of this view.
70. For more on the distinction between the sort of dispositionality operative in power-ascriptions see Anjum and Mumford (2011).
71. In the twentieth century, this objection traces back to Russell (1945: 211) and Mackie (1976: 77) and traces back even further to Descartes and Locke and Hobbes. For Locke in particular, compare Locke (1975: 295ff.) with 443ff. and 587ff.
72. See Broackes (2006), Loux (2006: Chapter 3), Oderberg (2007) and, to some extent, Heil (2012: 284–285).
73. This point is made by Heil (2012: 284–285), Lowe (2006: 27–28) and Moreland (2001: 152).
74. For a novel account of perceptual knowledge of causal dispositions see Mumford and Anjum (2011).
75. Aquinas (1999) I, left 1 and Aquinas (1975) II.94, respectively.
76. Note, however, that there need not be any *single* explanatorily basic feature that serves to explain all the others (as f_1 would suggest).
77. See Kment (2014) for a broadly similar account of the relationship between essence and metaphysical necessity. I recognize the sizable and every-growing literature here on the connection between grounding and metaphysical explanation. While I will have much more to say on grounding in the next chapter, I am inclined to think that the notion of metaphysical explanation employed here is one among the many species of the genus Grounding.
78. See Taylor (1993: 81) for the extension of naturalness to both constitutive and characterizing predicables. Moreover, Lewis (1999b: 65) himself hints at extending naturalness to objects as well as properties.
79. Lewis (1999a: 67).
80. Interestingly enough, there has been empirical research from cognitive psychology offering prima facie support for the aforementioned essentialist explanatory framework. In her 2003 book *The Essential Child*, Susan Gelman records that the classificatory framework of young children exhibits similarities with the earlier view that I am proposing. The inductive reasoning of young children is often governed by category-based inferences which rely on the distinction between explanatory deep features of a thing (which belong to its nature) and those that are more superficial to the thing in question. See also Gelman (2004) and (2009) as well as Keil (1989) for empirical work in this area.
81. See Gorman (2005: 282) for a similar approach to the structure of what I am calling an object's modal profile in terms of metaphysical explanation. My view differs from Gorman's in that I employ the framework of naturalness to make clear the explanatory structure in question.
82. This is, I think, stated nicely in Aquinas (1949), a. 11. See note 65.
83. See Lewis (1999b: 66) for more on the notion of relative or comparative naturalness.

84. I should note that there the immediate explanatory base here, F, can be a plurality of items.
85. Thus, the traditional notions of "propria" (necessary characterizing properties) and "extraneous accidents" can be reformulated in terms of their respective degree of naturalness relative to a thing's nature. Since the former have as their immediate explanatory base the substantial nature, we might call them the "highly natural properties" (for lack of a better phrase), the latter might be explicated as the "lesser natural properties" in so far as they are non-necessary natural properties of a substance.
86. This is not to say that only chemical compounds are characterized as such, just that there is an explanatory relationship between chemical compounds and the property *being asymmetrically charged*. Nor does this mean that *being a chemical compound* is the sole immediate explanatory base for such a property, only that it is, at the very least, one of the immediate explanatory bases for this property.
87. This example is from Oderberg (2011: 103). Moreover, as Bird (1998: 73) notes, it is often the case that providing the immediate explanatory base of a particular predicable of a substance will be relativized to the sort of characteristic behavior of the substance under consideration: "In explaining why benzyl alcohol reacts with phosphorus chloride to form benzyl chloride, we may point out that this is a reaction characteristic of alcohols, while if what needs an explanation is the same substance's volatility and odour, then reference to its being an aromatic compound (a benzene derivative) is called for."
88. This particular example is from Rea (2011).

2 Grounding and Essence

In the previous chapter, I outlined and argued for a version of serious essentialism that glossed the notion of essence in non-modal terms and is captured by real definition. The modal profile of a thing—what it modally necessitates in every world in which it exists—has a rich explanatory structure terminating in what is explanatorily basic to the thing in question, its essence. I now want to turn to the topic of metaphysical grounding or dependence, yet another pillar upon which I will rely in developing the notion of fundamental mereology in the sequel.

The present chapter will proceed as follows. In §2.1 I introduce the notion of metaphysical grounding as a robust form of (non-causal) metaphysical dependence as well as several general background assumptions about grounding that I draw from in the sequel. I explicate a host of axioms and operative assumptions about the formal and structural features of a species of grounding, viz. ontological dependence, that is ubiquitous in the context of mereological metaphysics. I make no claim to originality nor to have argued for my preferred understanding of metaphysical grounding. Given the vast and ever-expanding literature on grounding, such a task is both beyond the scope of a single chapter as well as the scope of my project here. Rather, my principal aim in this chapter is to get before us a specific class of grounding concepts that are sufficient to provide the requisite metaphysical underpinning for answering the question of fundamental mereology, whether wholes or their parts are metaphysically prior. In §2.2 I take a closer look at the diverse family of ontological dependence relations. I employ the serious-essentialist framework developed in the previous chapter to specify a species of grounding that employs a non-modal view of essence and that is well suited to generate relations of metaphysical priority and posteriority.

2.1 Metaphysical Grounding

As a piece of metaphysical machinery, grounding has an impressive historical pedigree. The list of those who have put the concept to use in one way or another reads like a who's-who in the history of Western philosophy:

Plato, Aristotle, Augustine, Aquinas, Scotus, Descartes, Spinoza, Leibniz, Brentano, and Husserl, to name a few. More recently, however, grounding has presented itself as a remarkably useful piece of metaphysical machinery. It has been argued that an appeal to grounding as a form of non-causal, metaphysical dependence improves our understanding of truthmaking (Schaffer 2009a; Lowe 2009b, Inman 2012), physicalism (Schaffer 2009a; Loewer 2001: 39), intrinsicality (Witmer et al. 2005), objective similarity (Sider 2012), perfectly natural properties (Schaffer 2004), the nature of non-causal explanation (Audi 2012; Kim 1994:67), trope inherence (Lowe 2006), and an overall realist approach to metaphysics (Fine 2001; Schaffer 2009a). As a result, grounding has been hailed as a unified and theoretically fruitful notion that undergirds a variety of concepts in metaphysics.

Yet anyone who has spent time with the burgeoning contemporary literature on grounding knows that sharp disagreement abounds, even among close friends of grounding. Here I do not want to enter into the thicket of the debates concerning the nature and structure of grounding. Rather, for my purposes in unpacking the project of fundamental mereology, I will simply assume and will not argue for the particular gloss on metaphysical grounding I offer next. As I will make clear in this section and the next, I am principally concerned with explicating a non-causal, metaphysical priority relation that obtains between composite objects and their proper parts (or vice versa).

Let me begin by unpacking a few large-scale background assumptions about grounding that I will employ throughout the course of the book, and then turn to unpacking the formal and structural features of grounding understood as such.

2.1.1 *On the Intelligibility of Grounding*

To begin, I take the extension of the concept "metaphysical grounding" to be non-empty; I reject the view that all putative cases of metaphysical grounding or priority are either unclear, unintelligible, or in the end cases of some other species of priority such as epistemological, conceptual, or counterfactual.[1] Here one often proceeds on the basis of putative examples of metaphysical grounding. I find intelligible examples of a distinctively metaphysical ordering relation littered throughout contemporary metaphysics, philosophy of science, and philosophy of physics. For many versions of spacetime substantivalism, regions of spacetime are grounded in spacetime as a whole; for certain ontic structural realists, objects are grounded in relational structure; for certain Aristotelians, immanent universals are grounded in their instances; for many trope-theorists, tropes are grounded in their bearers; spatial boundaries are grounded in their hosts; and (non-empty) sets are grounded in their members. All of the above strike me as clear and intelligible cases of a variety of metaphysical dependence and priority, one that is not merely epistemic or conceptual.

2.1.2 On Grounding and Ontological Innocence

Second, I assume that what is grounded does not reduce to its grounds. That is, that which is grounded is a genuine addition to being "over and above" its grounds; grounded entities or facts are neither "ontologically innocent" nor an "ontological free lunch." Positing grounded or derivative entities brings with it genuine ontological commitment.[2]

2.1.3 On Monistic Multivocalism

Third, I incline toward the view that there is a single (basic) grounding relation. This is, of course, entirely consistent with there being many (non-basic) grounding relations each of which bear an important relation to the one basic grounding relation; thus I assume a form of grounding monism.[3] However, I do not think that our semantic use of the term "grounding" is univocal in that it always refers to a single relation on each occasion of use. Rather, as Bradley Rettler (2017) has helpfully pointed out in his defense of what he calls "monistic multivocalism," even if there is a single basic grounding relation (call this relation "Grounding" for short), our use of the term "grounding" is often semantically variant and picks out distinct non-causal dependence relations such as ontological dependence, truthmaking, metaphysical explanation, or reductive analysis (or more besides), depending on the particular context of use. Grounding is a "specification relation" in that it may be either a genus, a determinable, or multiply realizable and thus admit of a variety of "specifics"—i.e., non-causal dependence relations that are either particular species, determinates, or realizers of Grounding.[4]

Understanding our talk of "grounding" as context variable goes some way toward explaining why grounding-theorists differ so widely among themselves about the precise formal and structural features of Grounding. Friends of Grounding disagree about whether it is (i) a relation,[5] (ii) topic-neutral,[6] (iii) a strict partial order,[7] (iv) explanatory,[8] (v) and whether it holds of necessity,[9] just to name a few.[10] Perhaps disagreement abounds because grounding-theorists are latching on to distinct grounding relations that are all species, determinates, or distinct relations that each realize the Grounding role.

There are, on this view, many ways of being Grounded. To illustrate, suppose we think of Grounding as a genus that admits of a variety of distinct species such as ontological dependence, truthmaking, metaphysical explanation, and reductive analysis (perhaps more besides). Since "grounding" talk is multivocal on this view, our use of "grounding" might pick out one of these distinct species of Grounding depending on the particular context ("grounding" might even pick out Grounding itself). Along these lines, Rettler (2017: 12) points out,

The essence of truthmaking is that it's the grounding of a thing's truth in an object. The essence of metaphysical explanation is that it's the grounding of a thing's truth in other, usually more fundamental, truths. The essence of ontological dependence is that it's the grounding of a thing's existence in another thing's existence. The essence of reductive analysis is that it's the grounding of some facts about a thing or kind of thing in some facts about some other (standardly thought to be more fundamental) thing or kind of thing.

In one context, say the question of how a (non-empty) set is grounded in its members, "grounding" might pick out a topic-neutral, strict partial ordering relation (certain forms of ontological dependence). Alternatively, in another context, say the question of how the proposition "Texas summers are hot" relates to its grounds, "grounding" might pick out a relation that is non-reflexive, non-symmetric, and non-transitive (truthmaking). Despite differing with respect to some of their formal and structural features, both relations are species of the genus Grounding. Understanding Grounding as a single genus that admits of distinct species explains the intuitive conceptual link between relations such as ontological dependence, truthmaking, metaphysical explanation, and reductive analysis, each of which are non-causal "in virtue of" relations that carve out distinct facets of the metaphysical structure of the world.

On this view, what unifies each of the earlier grounding relations and makes them all species of the genus Grounding is that each is characterized by something like the following "job description" of Grounding:

> relates the fundamental to the non-fundamental, relates the relatively more fundamental to the relatively less fundamental, lays out the structure of the world, says which things depend on which other things, explains why something exists, and explains why something has a property.
> (Rettler 2017:13–14)

If the putative relation in the specific context is characterized by the aforementioned job description, then it is a genuine grounding relation and thus a species of Grounding.[11]

2.1.4 On Grounding and Supervenience

Fourth, I assume (as is now widely recognized) that supervenience is an ill-suited proxy for metaphysical grounding. One particular example of glossing supervenience as a proxy for grounding is captured by David Lewis (1999a: 29): "A supervenience thesis is, in a broad sense, reductionist. But it is a stripped-down form of reductionism, unencumbered by dubious denials of existence, claims of ontological priority, or claims of translatability."

There are, however, insuperable problems with employing supervenience as a stand-in for grounding. Most fundamentally, there is a lack of isomorphism regarding the formal properties of the two relations. Supervenience is reflexive, transitive, and non-asymmetric, where grounding is commonly thought to be irreflexive, transitive, and asymmetric. More importantly, as Kim (1998) has effectively pointed out, supervenience is mere modal correlation between multiple domains and thus is not a very deep relation at all. By this Kim means that the relation of supervenience is unable to play the role that it is often thought to play in fundamental ontology—namely, to account for the metaphysically fundamental joints of the world. Supervenience is "not a type of dependence relation–it is not a relation that can be placed alongside causal dependence, reductive dependence, mereological dependence, dependence grounded in definability or entailment, and the like" (1998: 14). So much so that Kim argues that views which employ the notion of supervenience toward this end must "look elsewhere for its metaphysical grounding; supervenience itself is not capable of supplying it" (1998: 14).[12]

2.2 The Structure of Grounding

Since my overall aim in this book is to explore the question of fundamental mereology—whether concrete composite objects or their proper parts are metaphysically prior (or more fundamental)—I restrict my talk of "grounding" in what follows to the relation of ontological dependence and its many varieties, the species of Grounding that aims to track (non-causal) metaphysical priority and posteriority relations among entities in particular. In this sense, grounding is minimally the relation that connects fundamental entities to non-fundamental entities. Whether *all* grounding relations are to be glossed in this way and suited to play this characteristic role is a topic for a much wider debate in the literature on grounding.

With this particular species of Grounding as our target, let us turn now to unpacking the formal and structural features of grounding. I take the domain of entities that can serve as the relata of grounding to be maximally general. Grounding, like proper parthood, is *topic neutral*: entities of *any* ontological category can stand in the grounding relation. Thus:

> G1. *Topic Neutrality*: entities of any ontological category can serve as the relata of grounding.

The tenability of G1 stems from the intuitiveness of the following diverse cases of grounding: an individual baseball game is grounded in its constituent sub-events (e.g., innings) out of which it is composed, non-empty sets are grounded in their individual members, the redness trope or mode of an

58 Grounding and Essence

apple is grounded in that very apple, holes in a piece of Swiss cheese are grounded in its particular host, the Aristotelian universal *horseness* is grounded in the existence of individual horses, and the truth of a proposition is grounded in its truthmaker. Thus events, sets, properties, holes, universals, and propositions are all, on my view, potential relata of grounding.

Given my preference for the topic neutrality of grounding, I take the logical form of the relation as best expressed by a two-place predicate such that "$x \triangleright y$" stands for "x is grounded in y:"

$x \triangleright y = x$ is grounded in y

This predicative rendering of grounding claims leaves open, rightly so in my opinion, the possibility that substances, properties, events, states of affairs, and so on may serve as the relata of grounding.

Stated simply, I take grounding to be a type of metaphysical ordering relation that generates a strict partial order over a domain of entities. Thus, grounding is

G2. *Irreflexive*: $\neg(x \triangleright x)$
G3. *Asymmetric*: $(y \triangleright x) \rightarrow \neg(x \triangleright y)$
G4. *Transitive*: $(y \triangleright x \land z \triangleright y) \rightarrow (z \triangleright x)$

It must be underscored that while it is common to think that axioms G2–G4 hold for the species of Grounding exclusively in question, viz. ontological dependence, they are not entirely uncontroversial in so far as there have been proposed counterexamples, particularly to G2 and G3.[13] But as I noted earlier, since we are concerned solely with a grounding relation that plays the characteristic role of generating relations of metaphysical priority and posteriority (as well as relative fundamentality) between entities, the debates as to whether *all* species of Grounding generate a strict partial order is one that we need not settle at this point (more on this next).[14] As I do not claim to offer a full-fledged account here, I will simply work with one particular, albeit very common notion of grounding—indeed Michael Raven (2013) renders it the status of "Orthodoxy"—at work in the contemporary literature.

Grounding can be *total* as well as *partial*. This is an important structural feature of grounding as there are many instances where the relation may be one-many such that a single entity may have a plurality of partial grounds. Particularly clear examples of an entity having a plurality of grounds are found in the case of a non-empty set being partially grounded in each of its individual members, a state of affairs being partially grounded in each of its non-mereological constituents, and certain kinds of mereological wholes being partially grounded in each of their individual proper parts.

A clear statement of total and partial grounding requires the use of plural variables. Let the variables x, y, z stand for singular variables and a and b for singular or plural variables. In this way, quantifying over a domain including *a* and *b* allows us to represent cases of either singular or plural grounding in a precise manner. In addition to the use of variables whose values include both single and multiple grounds, I rely on the primitive two-place predicate "ϵ" of singular inclusion, where "$a\epsilon b$" stands for "*a* is one of the *b*'s."[15] In employing the machinery of singular inclusion, we remain neutral regarding the degree to which the following grounding axioms rely on set-theoretic notions, particularly the relation of set-membership.

With *a* and *b* as our singular or plural variables, together with the aforementioned notion of singular inclusion, we can begin to work our way toward defining the axioms of total and partial grounding. With "E" as the existence predicate, we begin by defining "E*a*" in term of the existence of one or many entities that is (are) identical to *a*:

$$Ea =_{def} (\exists b)(a = b)$$

We can then define total grounding as follows:

G5. *Total Grounding*: $x \triangleright_t a =_{def} Ea \wedge (\forall z)(z \epsilon a \leftrightarrow x \triangleright z)$

In words: *x* is totally grounded in *a* if and only if *a* exists and *x* is grounded in every entity that is one of the *a*'s. To illustrate, consider a rather common analysis of the nature of events in terms of the triple [o, P, t], where "o" stands for some object or objects, "P" a property (whether monadic or polyadic), and "t" a time. On this account of events, the event [o, P, t] exists just in case o has P at t. The total grounds for the event of the *the collision of the Titanic with an iceberg on April 14, 1912*, for example, include the objects of the Titanic and the iceberg, the dyadic relation *colliding with*, and the particular time of April 14, 1912; the event is totally grounded in every item that is among its constituents.

For partial grounding, we begin with the notion of *containment*, where "$a \subset b$" is read as "*a* is contained in *b*" and can be defined in terms of singular inclusion as follows:

Containment: $a \subset b =_{def} (\forall y)(y \epsilon a \rightarrow y \epsilon b)$

That is, *a* is contained in *b* just in case every entity that is one of the *a*'s is one of the *b*'s. We can now define partial grounding in terms of total grounding and containment in the following manner:

G6. *Partial Grounding*: $x \triangleright_p a =_{def} Ea \wedge (\exists b)(x \triangleright_t b \wedge a \subset b)$

In words: *x* is partially grounded in *a* just in case *a* exists, *x* is totally grounded in *b*, and *a* is contained in *b*. On this construal of partial grounding, $x \triangleright_p y$ is entirely consistent with $x \triangleright_p z$, where $y \neq z$. Note that in stating an entities' partial ground one need not appeal to a plurality of entities among its total grounds. This is because a single entity may be partially grounded in another single entity (one-one partial grounding) or a plurality of entities (one-many partial grounding).

To illustrate, take the set {x, y, z} as an example of the various ways a single entity can exhibit both one-one and one-many partial grounding. Now, according to one standard description of sets, {x, y, z} is totally grounded in x, y, and z collectively. However, as the set has y as a member, it is partially (one-one) grounded in y in so far as it is totally grounded in the members collectively and y is contained in that collection. Likewise, {x, y, z} is also partially (one-many) grounded in both x and z in so far as it is totally grounded in the members collectively and x and z are contained in that collection. The point here is simply that there are many ways to be partially grounded.

In addition to being total or partial, I consider grounding to be both an existence entailing relation:

G7. *Existence Entailing*: $\Box(x \triangleright y \rightarrow (Ex \wedge Ey))$

and one that holds of necessity:

G8. *Necessity*: $(x \triangleright y \rightarrow \Box(Ex \rightarrow x \triangleright y))$

G7 states that necessarily, if x is grounded in y then both x and y exist. Regarding G8, if x is grounded in y, then it is necessarily the case that if x exists, then it is grounded in y. G8 tracks the intuition that an entity's being grounded in another entity is a non-contingent feature of that entity.

I am also inclined to endorse the well-foundedness of grounding in that for any non-empty grounding domain D there must be at least one metaphysically basic entity in D.[16] To unpack this idea, call a *minimal element*, e, of a non-empty grounding domain D one such that there is no y in D such that e is grounded in y. The minimal elements for D are those that are ungrounded—i.e., basic. This need not imply that the minimal elements of a domain also serve as grounds, just that they themselves remain ungrounded. With this notion of a minimal element for a domain in hand, we can then state the well-foundedness of grounding as follows:

G9. *Well-Foundedness*: for any non-empty grounding domain D there is, of necessity, at least one minimal element in D.[17]

The basic idea underlying G9 is that there must be at least one ungrounded entity in D. G9 is the metaphysical analogue of the axiom of foundation in set theory that every non-empty set contains a minimal element (as a member). The denial of G9 amounts to the possibility that the exhaustive inventory of reality consists entirely of grounded entities: its just one grounded thing after another such that a exists in virtue of b, b exists in virtue of *c*, *c* in virtue of *d*, and so on ad infinitum. On this view, there is no minimal grounding element and thus no metaphysically basic entity—i.e., there is no substantial being to use the traditional terminology.

Why might one endorse G9 as a constraint on grounding? Many who feel the pull of G9 justify their acceptance of it on the basis of its naturalness or intuitiveness; G9 strikes them as a reasonable thesis that, in the absence of overriding considerations to the contrary, is more plausible than its denial.[18] Some proponents of G9 take its underlying motivation to be that if there were no lower-bound to the grounding domain of a world, then nothing would exist in that world. Leibniz, for instance, in his June 30, 1704 letter to de Volder stated thus: "Where there is no reality that is not borrowed, there will never be any reality, since it must belong ultimately to some subject."[19]

Schaffer (2010b: 62) shares the Leibnizian intuition in that "endless dependence conflicts with the foundationalist requirement that there be basic objects (§1.2). On this option nothing is basic at gunky worlds. There would be no ultimate ground. Being would be infinitely deferred, never achieved." Others simply report their inability to comprehend the denial of G9. On this score, Lowe (1998: 158) candidly states, "All real existence must be 'grounded' or 'well-founded.' Such an 'axiom of foundation' is quite probably beyond conclusive proof and yet I find the vertiginous implications of its denial barely comprehensible." While I myself take the intuition driving G9 to be a strong one, I am aware that many will not share this opinion. I am also of the view that any argument in favor of G9 will, most likely, fail to carry the same intuitive force as the axiom itself. Be that as it may, such a task is not entirely without merit as I think there are ways to gesture toward the well-foundedness of grounding.

One might suggest here that accepting G9 has a certain theoretical utility in that it offers a unified explanatory ground for the existence of each grounded entity in a domain.[20] In a domain deprived of ungrounded entities, the existence of each grounded entity is explained in terms of a distinct (albeit immediate) ground or collection of grounds, which are themselves grounded entities. Accepting the well-foundedness of grounding, on the other hand, allows the ungrounded entity (or class of ungrounded entities) to serve as one and the same explanation for the existence of each grounded entity in that domain. This preserves the theoretical principle that it is better to have a single explanatory ground for each phenomenon (i.e. the existence of each individual grounded entity) than to have a distinct explanatory ground for each phenomenon. Even more, however, positing at least one ungrounded entity in a grounding domain lends an explanation for not only the existence of each grounded entity in that domain, but also for the existence of grounded entities *per se* in that domain. It is one thing for there to be an explanation for the existence of each grounded entity in a domain, quite another for there to be an explanation for why the class of grounded entities exist in that domain *in the first place*. Accepting

G9 affords both theoretical simplicity as well as explanatory power with respect to the existence of grounded entities.

While I noted that the prospects of employing supervenience as a stand-in for grounding are dim, there nonetheless exists an intimate relationship between the two concepts. Kim (1993: 148), after rightly distinguishing the covariation element of supervenience from the alleged dependence ordering it is claimed to secure, nevertheless argues, "But the two components are not entirely independent; for it seems that the following is true: for there to be property dependence there must be property covariation." While supervenience analyses of grounding fail, it is plausible to think that grounding entails supervenience.[21] Again, Kim (1993: 167) suggests, "It [supervenience] is not a 'deep' metaphysical relation; rather, it is a 'surface' relation that reports a pattern of property covariation, suggesting the presence of an interesting dependency relation that might explain it."

Consider the following case of grounding: a trope's being grounded in its bearer. Here the bearer of the trope, the particular object, is the ground and the trope is what is grounded. It is plausible to assume that there can be no difference in the trope—that which is grounded—without there being a difference in the particular object—that which does the grounding. In other words, there is no variation in that which is grounded without there being a variation in the ground. This is just to say that the trope's being grounded in its bearer entails that the trope supervenes on its bearer (but not the converse).

Where "S" denotes the relation of supervenience and "P_x" and "P_y" the class of properties belonging to x and y, respectively:

G10. *Supervenience Entailment*: $\Box(x \triangleright y \rightarrow S(P_x, P_y))$

The core insight behind G10 is that there can be no property-difference in the grounded without a property-difference in the grounds. Here I want to underscore an important insight regarding G10 that will prove essential in my arguments against the metaphysical priority of parts over wholes in the sequel. Regarding the modal consequences of grounding, Schaffer (2009: 364) mentions in passing the prospects for using the failure of supervenience as an indication of the failure of grounding.[22] As per G10, since it is necessarily the case that if x is grounded in y, then the properties of x supervene on the properties of y, a failure of supervence in this sense indicates that x thereby fails to be grounded in y. Consequently, if the supervening domain fails to covary with its subvening base, this is reason enough to conclude that it thereby fails to be grounded in its base.

2.3 Varieties of Metaphysical Grounding

We have been concerned up to this point with getting clear on the formal and structural features of a particular species of Grounding—ontological dependence—as a non-causal dependence relation that generates relations of metaphysical priority and posteriority between concrete entities in particular. However, it is important to point out that this particular species of Grounding is itself a genus that admits of a variety of different species, not all of which are equally suited to play this characteristic role in fundamental ontology. And since our immediate context is that of mereological metaphysics where talk of a composite material object's being "grounded in," "dependent on," "posterior to," or "less fundamental" than its proper parts (or vice versa) is commonplace, it is important to get clear on a particular species of ontological dependence that fits the bill in question.[23]

2.3.1 Existential Grounding

In contemporary mereological metaphysics, grounding claims like "ordinary composite objects are grounded in their proper parts" and "the cosmos grounds each of its proper parts" naturally give expression to the idea that, at the very least, the existence of the one is grounded in the existence of the other(s). Ordinary composite objects exist *in virtue of* the existence and structure of their proper parts; or ordinary composite objects exist *in virtue of* the existence and structure of the cosmos. These grounding claims are explicated in modal terms such that it is metaphysically necessary that composite objects exist only if their proper parts exist (or vice versa).

One common way of formulating this variety of existential grounding is in the following modal terms:[24]

(RG) x is *rigidly existentially grounded* in $y =_{def} \Box(Ex \rightarrow Ey)$

As a rigid form of existential grounding, rigidly grounded (RG) captures the insight that one thing (x) may depend on another *specific* entity (y) for its existence: it is metaphysically impossible for x to exist unless y—*that very entity*—exists. In this way, the proponent of RG takes there to be relations of necessitation in the world such that the mere existence of x necessitates the existence of y.

Examples of RG in contemporary metaphysics are commonplace. On one view of the ontology of events, the existence of, say, *the presidential inauguration of Barack Obama*, necessitates the existence of Barack Obama; it is impossible that the event exist unless Barack Obama exists. As I have already indicated, events, immanent universals, and regions of spacetime on substantivalism, are all plausible candidates of entities that stand in the relation captured by RG to their grounds. In addition, many advocates of a trope ontology take the sort of grounding or dependence relation between a trope and its bearer to be an instance of RG. The existence of the redness of this particular apple is rigidly grounded in that very apple, it cannot exist unless that specific property-bearer exists.

We may, however, distinguish RG from a more generic variety of existential grounding. One might hold that while the existence of one entity may not require the existence of any specific entity or entities in particular, it may nevertheless exist only if some entity or other of a particular type exists. That is, an entity may be existentially grounded in a type of entity that satisfies predicate F (call these Fs), it need not be grounded in any *particular* object that satisfies F. We can formulate this generic variety of existential grounding more precisely as follows:

(GG) x is *generically existentially grounded* in Fs $=_{def} \Box(Ex \rightarrow \exists y Fy)$

There are two ways in which GG is weaker than RG. First, GG is much less restrictive in scope than RG: x exists only if there is some entity or other that satisfies F, yet x does not need any F in particular in order to exist. The immanent universal *electron*, for instance, exists only if there exists at least one thing that falls under the kind *electron*. If there were no such instances, then the kind-universal *electron* would fail to exist. However, the universal is not rigidly grounded in any one electron in particular. And while a living organism may not necessitate the existence of any of its proper part in particular, it arguably necessitates the existence of some some proper parts or other out of which it is composed.

A second sense in which GG is weaker than RG is that RG entails GG, but not the converse. If x is rigidly grounded in y, then the existence of x requires at least the existence of an object that satisfies F, where F in this case might stand for "an entity that is identical to y." In virtue of being rigidly grounded in y (where y satisfies F), x cannot exist unless *something*, that very y, satisfies F. But we must not allow the value of F to be completely unrestricted on pains of rendering generic existential grounding trivial. If F were the predicate "is self-identical," for instance, then x would be generically grounded in every existing entity, on the assumption that every existing entity is identical to itself. In the case of the immanent universal *humanity*, we might say that *humanity* is generically existentially grounded in Fs, where the predicate F is restricted to "is a human being;" it is necessarily the case that *humanity* exists only if at least one particular entity satisfies the predicate "is a human being."

Recall that grounding claims regarding the relationship between composite objects and their proper parts are naturally taken to carve out relations of metaphysical priority and posteriority; wholes are either *prior* to (more fundamental than) or *posterior* to (less fundamental than) their proper parts. It is this very feature of talk of "grounding" in a mereological context that renders our initial modal gloss of grounding in terms of RG and GG inadequate.

Arguably, neither form of existential grounding is suited to carve out relations that underpin a composite object's being more fundamental than or metaphysically prior to its proper parts (or vice versa). First, while relations of priority and posteriority are naturally thought of as strictly asymmetric, existential grounding is *non-symmetric* in so far as there are plausible instances where existential grounding is *symmetric*.[25] Consider the following intelligible examples of mutual or symmetric existential grounding. On one particular brand of trope-bundle theory defended by Peter Simons (1994), objects consist of a two-tiered bundle of tropes. On the one hand, the essential features of an object are determined by a bundle of mutually dependent tropes (what Simons calls the "nucleus"), while the non-essential features are determined by a further bundle of tropes that inhere in the nucleus. Or consider the grounding relations that obtain between Socrates and his life, that extended temporal event that was his biological life. Arguably, the existence of Socrates's life is rigidly existentially grounded in Socrates (necessarily, it exists only if Socrates exists), and Socrates is rigidly existentially grounded in his biological life (necessarily, he exists only if his life exists).

Second, recall that both RG and GG were analyzed purely in modal-existential terms: x is grounded in y if and only if necessarily, x exists only if y exists (where y was taken to be either a particular entity or a generic type of entity). For reasons that largely mirror those raised against modal essentialism in Chapter 1 (§1.1–1.2), an analysis of grounding in terms of modal requirement for existence is much too course-grained to undergird claims to metaphysical priority and posteriority.

One rather prominent shortcoming of RG in this regard is that it comes out vacuous for necessarily existing entities. If there are necessarily existing entities such as numbers, propositions, or God, then according to RG *every* existing thing is grounded in and hence dependent on such entities. The reason being that it follows rather trivially that every existing entity modally necessitates the existence of any necessary being (since it is necessarily the case that in every world in which that thing exists is a world in which the necessary being exists).[26] But this seems to many to be wholly unintuitive, as Peter Simons (1987: 295) puts it, "Pythagoreanism aside, I am not ontologically dependent on the number 23." If every existing thing necessitates the existence of any necessary being (and is thereby grounded in and posterior to it), it follows that the coffee mug on my desk could not have existed without the proposition <aqua regia has the power to dissolve gold>. But surely coffee mugs do not depend for their existence on propositions of *any* sort.

As an extension of the modal essentialist account of essence (see §1.1 of Chapter 1), RG generates a grounding-ordering between entities that appear to be wholly unrelated. Irrespective of whether necessary beings such as God, numbers, and propositions exist, the substantive point here is that merely accepting some objects as existing in every possible world should not result in such an implausible characterization of the dependence ordering in those worlds.

The basic point made earlier can be generalized to form a similar line of reasoning to what was advanced in our discussion of modal essentialism in the previous chapter.[27] Though it is necessarily the case that Socrates necessitates the existence of his singleton (RG: necessarily, if Socrates exists then his singleton exists), surely Socrates is not grounded in, less fundamental than, or posterior to his singleton (Fine 1994b: 271). But this is precisely the grounding description RG delivers concerning the relationship between Socrates and his singleton. Consequently, the very same lines of reasoning put forward against modal essentialism are relevant in showing that a gloss on grounding in terms of RG is too coarse-grained to do the ontological work demanded of it in mereological metaphysics.[28] What is needed, then, is a more fine-grained gloss on grounding that is both (i) non-modal and (ii) asymmetric and thus suitable for generating relations of metaphysical priority and posteriority (and thus relations of relative fundamentality, i.e. "more fundamental than").

Recall from the previous chapter that on serious essentialism, essence is irreducible to necessity (the denial of ME1) and is much more fine-grained than mere modal requirement for existence. Employing our serious essentialist framework here is one way, though certainly not the only way, of moving toward a species of grounding that is suited to track relations of (relative) fundamentality and priority/posteriority.[29]

2.3.1.1 A Precursory Note: Duns Scotus on Essential Order

There is a more fine-grained notion of grounding that has a rich historical precedent in the work of the medieval scholastics, with perhaps the most well-developed account having been advanced by Duns Scotus. Scotus's most nuanced treatment of the notion of dependence is found in his *De Primo Principio*. There, Scotus unpacks the notion of metaphysical posteriority and priority, what he calls "essential order," and explicates two distinct varieties of essential order: the order of eminence and the order of dependence.[30] On the one hand, the order of eminence pertains to the notion of perfection; x is eminently ordered with respect to y if x's perfection exceeds the perfection of y, and is thereby said to be prior to y in the order of eminence. The order of dependence, on the other hand, involves the notion of priority and posteriority with respect to the essence or nature of the two relata involved; "the dependent is said to be posterior whereas that on which it depends is prior."[31]

Scotus maintains that the relata of essential ordering relations are *essences*. In the specific theological context of the union of the two natures of Christ, Scotus explicitly endorses the notion that the relata of essential ordering relations are essences, "As for the case at hand, the personal or hypostatic entity has no essential priority in respect to creatures, for an essential order obtains per se only between essences (in contrast to hypostatic entities), since it is forms (i.e. essences) that are like numbers."[32] Elsewhere, Scotus unpacks the locution "the essence of x" as "that which is included per se in the quidditative concept of x and therefore, is posited in the essential notion of its quiddity, and not as something added."[33] In short, the order is one of essential dependence in so far as the priority or posteriority stems from the natures or essences of the entities in question.

For Scotus, essential ordering relations imply a sort of existential dependence of the posterior on that which is prior, "the prior according to nature and essence can exist without the posterior but the reverse is not true."[34] He continues,

> And this I understand as follows. Even though the prior should produce the posterior necessarily and consequently could not exist without it, it would not be because the prior requires the posterior for its own existence, but it is rather the other way about. For even assuming that posterior did not exist, the existence of the prior would not entail a contradiction. But the converse is not true, for the posterior needs the prior. This need we can call dependence, so that we can say that anything which is essentially posterior [in this way] depends necessarily upon what is prior but not vice versa, even should the posterior at times proceed from it necessarily.
>
> (Ibid.)

In short, Scotus maintains that if x is essentially posterior to y, then x depends on y for its existence. He states that if x is essentially ordered to y, then x's existence "needs" or "requires" y's existence—i.e., it is impossible that x exist without y's existing.

Here it is vital to note that Scotus appears to distinguish between a posterior (grounded entity in our terminology) proceeding from that which is prior (ground) *necessarily* and a posterior proceeding from that which is prior *essentially*. More specifically, just because something posterior could not fail to proceed from that which is prior, one cannot infer that the thing is therefore essentially posterior to it. While something's being essentially prior entails its being necessarily prior, the converse does not hold for Scotus. In this sense, I take Scotus to be a proponent of something in the general vicinity of a more fine-grained, non-modal conception of grounding as defended by Fine (1994b) and Lowe (2005b).

While it is not clear as to which notion of existential dependence Scotus takes essential order to entail (whether RG or GG as stated earlier), it is evident that he is of the opinion that if an entity is essentially ordered to another entity, then the former is existentially dependent on the latter *in some sense or other*. However, for illustrative purposes, I will formulate his notion of essential order in terms of the stronger variety of existential grounding stated in terms of RG.

Scotus's non-modal conception of grounding or dependence in terms of essence can be stated using our sentential operator "$\Box_x$" for "it is part of the essence of x":

(EO): x is *essentially ordered* to y $=_{def} \Box_x(Ex \rightarrow Ey)$.

EO is to be read as follows: x is essentially ordered to y if and only if it is part of the essence of x that it exists only if y exists. Michael Gorman (1993) has pointed out that Scotus endorses several structural principles regarding essential ordering relations, principles that correspond nicely to our initial formulation of grounding in terms of G2–G4. Taking "O_e" to stand for the relation of essential order, Scotus maintains that essential ordering relations are governed by the following axioms:

> *Irreflexive*: "Nothing whatever is essentially ordered to itself:" $\neg(O_e(x, x))$[35]
> *Asymmetric*: "In any essential order a circle is impossible:" $O_e(x, y) \rightarrow \neg(O_e(y, x))$[36]
> *Transitive*: "What is not subsequent to the prior is not subsequent to the posterior:" $(O_e(x, y) \wedge O_e(y, z)) \rightarrow (O_e(x, z))$[37]

Our brief excursus into Scotus's view of grounding reveals an account of grounding that is non-modal (one that entails but is not entailed by modal views) and is governed by the axioms of irreflexivity, asymmetry, and transitivity.[38]

2.3.2 Essential Grounding

Here I recommend that we take a page from the Subtle Doctor in explicating a more fine-grained notion of existential grounding in essentialist or non-modal terms. With the notion of essence as primitive as per serious essentialism, we can formulate the following non-modal species of existential grounding (call it "essential$_E$ grounding"):

(REG) x is *rigidly essentially$_E$ grounded* in y $=_{def} \Box_x(Ex \rightarrow Ey)$

As with EO, REG is read as "it is part of the essence of x that it exists only if y exists." Likewise, we can then go on to define generic essential grounding as follows:

(GEG) x is *generically essentially$_E$ grounded* in Fy $=_{def} \Box_x(Ex \rightarrow \exists y Fy)$

where GEG states that it is part of the essence of x such that x exists only if some F exists.

It is crucial to note that REG and GEG are more fine-grained than RG and GG precisely because they entail (but are not entailed by) their respective modal counterparts, while every case of rigid essential$_E$ grounding is a case of rigid existential grounding, the converse does not hold (mutatis mutandis for generic grounding). More specifically, if it is part of the nature or essence of Socrates's singleton that it exist only if Socrates exists (REG), then it is necessary that if Socrates's singleton exists then

Socrates exists (RG). In general, since the real definition of a singleton involves reference to the existence of its sole member, the existence of the singleton both *essentially* and *existentially* necessitates the existence of its sole member.

It is important to underscore that the aforementioned distinction between a modal and a non-modal gloss on grounding hinges on the irreducibility of essence to modality. On modal essentialism as defined in the previous chapter, REG and GEG are *equivalent* to RG and GG in so far as a thing's essence *just is* what it modally requires for its existence. That is, every instance of $\Box_x(Ex \to \Phi x)$ is equivalent to an instance of $\Box(Ex \to \Phi x)$. The point is commonly overlooked: availing oneself of REG and GEG as distinct and more fine-grained grounding relations presupposes a serious-essentialist metaphysic.

The virtues of explicating grounding along the lines of REG and GEG are many. First, a non-modal gloss on grounding avoids the charge that grounding runs vacuous for necessary beings; while one could infer from the existence of a necessary being that therefore every existing thing is rigidly existentially grounded in it as per RG, this does not hold for REG. One cannot infer from the existence of a necessary being that therefore every existing thing is REG in it; it is no part of the *nature* or *essence* of a boson, for instance, that it exists only if the number 23 exists.

Likewise, in contrast to RG, REG does not entail that the identity and nature of the ground is wholly irrelevant to the existence of that which is grounded. According to RG, since it is necessarily the case that in every world in which Socrates exists his singleton exists, Socrates is rigidly existentially grounded in his singleton; Socrates, the grounded, necessitates the existence of his singleton, the ground. Yet intuitively the existence of a set-theoretic entity seems wholly irrelevant to whether or not Socrates exists. In contrast to RG, REG has no such implication. According to REG, from the fact that it is necessarily the case that in every world in which Socrates exists his singleton exists, it does not follow that Socrates is REG in his singleton; it is no part of the *essence* of Socrates that he exists only if such a set-theoretic entity exists. Again, the relevant grounding ordering intuitively runs *from* Socrates *to* Socrates's singleton, not the other way around. Similarly, from the fact that it is necessarily the case that in every world in which Socrates exists the temporal event that is his life exists, it does not follow that therefore Socrates is REG in his life; arguably the event exists and *is what it is* (and *which* particular event it is) in virtue of Socrates, not the other way around. In so far as REG entails but is not entailed by RG, it rightly models the order of grounding as facts about Socrates are arguably more fundamental than facts about either his singleton or the temporally extended event that is his life.

There is, however, reason to think that even the aforementioned non-modal gloss on grounding in terms of REG and GEG is neither fine-grained enough nor suited to track relations of metaphysical priority and posteriority. First, some have argued that there are plausible cases where *x* is essentially$_E$ grounded in *y*, where nevertheless the *identity* of *x* fails to be grounded in the *identity* of *y*. Lowe (2006: 199–200), for instance, has argued, "Very plausibly, an entity can, for example, depend essentially for its *existence* on one or more other entities, without necessarily depending essentially for its *identity* upon those other entities." Lowe points to an Aristotelian immanent universal, *roundness*, as an example. As an immanent universal, *roundness* is such that it is part of its essence that it exist only if some instance or other exists and is round; thus immanent universals are entities that are generically essentially$_E$ grounded (GEG). However, the real definition of the universal *roundness*—*what* it is fundamentally and *which* entity it is—does not involve reference to any single round object nor the totality of all actually existing round objects. We will examine in more detail this further species of essential grounding next.

Second, some have argued that there are plausible cases of essential$_E$ grounding that are symmetric, and that arguably *all* forms of existential grounding, whether modal or non-modal, are best characterized as *non-symmetric*. For instance, on certain (realist) structuralist mathematical ontologies that explicate numbers as nodes in a structural network, it is part of the essence of each number that it exists in virtue of the other nodes in the network. If so, then structuralist views in the philosophy of mathematics provide plausible examples of symmetric essential$_E$ grounding.[39]

Third, as Fine (1995a: 274) and Koslicki (2013a: 51–60) have argued, all forms of existential grounding, whether modal or non-modal, are too weak in so far as they characterize grounding strictly in terms of what an entity requires for its existence. Perhaps there is more to the nature or essence of a thing than what that thing requires for its existence. As Fine (1995a: 274) points out,

> The present examples [viz. impossible objects and identity properties] highlight a problem that besets any existential account of dependence, whether it be modal or essentialist in form. For, it does not seem right to identify the "being" of an object, its being what it is, with its existence. In one respect, existence is too weak; for there is more to what an object is than its mere existence. In another respect, existence is too strong; for what an object is, its nature, need not include existence as a part.[40]

That is to say, perhaps some species of grounding more thoroughly capture the identity of a thing—what that thing is; not all forms of grounding are species of existential grounding. If so, then the serious essentialist may want to carve out an even more fine-grained notion of essential grounding, strictly in terms of what the thing requires for its *identity* and not merely its existence.

For neo-Aristotelians like Lowe (2005b) and Koslicki (2013a), non-modal varieties of grounding (they prefer "dependence") admit of further classification to include *identity grounding*, cases where the *identity* of x and *which* thing of its kind x is are grounded in the *identity* of y and *which* thing of its kind y is. Mark Johnston (2006: 676) captures this more robust connection between essence and grounding nicely,

> Associated with the ideas of real definition and essence is the idea of the ontological dependence of one item on another; where an item x is ontologically dependent on an item y just when y features at some point in the full account of the essence of x (the real definition of x), but not vice versa.

In the same vein, Fine (2010) notes, "One object may be (*ontologically*) *prior* to another in the sense that it is possible to provide an explanation of the identity of the one object, to explain *what it is*, with the help of the other object."

Following Lowe and Tahko (2015) we can formulate this further species of essential grounding in the following manner (call it "essential$_I$ grounding"):

(IG) x is *essentially$_I$ grounded* in y $=_{def}$ there is a two-place predicate "F" such that it is part of the identity of x that x is *related by F* to y.

IG moves beyond purely existential grounding (whether modal or non-modal) in the sense that it specifies what is required not simply for x's existence per se but for *what x* is and *which* thing of a certain kind x is. The set {Fido, Wilber}, for example, is essentially$_I$ grounded in its members, Fido and Wilber, in that there is a two-place predicate *being a member of* and it is part of the essence of {Fido, Wilber} that Fido and Wilber be a member of it; the identity of the set—*what* the set is and *which* set it is—is totally grounded in its members.

Thus I follow Lowe (2012b) in taking essential$_I$ grounding to be a relation of individuation; if x essentially$_I$ grounds y, then the individuality of y is fixed by the individuality of x, where x serves as the individuator of y. Since sets are totally essentially$_I$ grounded in their members, Fido and Wilber individuate the set {Fido, Wilber}, *which* set {Fido, Wilber} is is fixed solely by Fido and Wilber. Or, consider once again an ontology of events that construes events as a triple [o, P, t], where "o" stands for some object or objects, "P" a property (whether monadic or polyadic), and "t" a time. If [o, P, t] is essentially$_I$ grounded in o, P, and t as its constituents, then the latter ground not only the essence of [o, P, t] generally, an event, but also *which* individual event it is, say the sinking of the Titanic (as opposed to the Battle of Hastings). The identity of the event [o, P, t]—*what* it is and *which* event it is—is fixed by its essential$_I$ grounds, its individual constituents.

By specifying the essential$_I$ grounds for particular instances of kind K, one thereby specifies a (synchronic) principle of individuation for K. The principle of individuation for (non-empty) *sets*, for example, specifies those items that make a set the very set that it is, its members; or, the principle of individuation for *events* specifies the items that make an event the very event that it is, its constituents. Moreover, as Lowe (2012b) points out, relations of essential$_I$ grounding also generate criteria of identity, that is, criteria that determine when two entities of the same kind stand in the identity relation to one another (i.e., identity understood here in the standard logical sense of equality, "="). The fact that (non-empty) sets are totally essentially$_I$ grounded in their individual members, for example, lends the Axiom of Extensionality as the criterion of identity governing sets: if x and y are sets, then x and y are the same set just in case x and y have the same members.

As before, IG entails but is not entailed by the broader species of essential grounding in terms of REG and GEG. If a set {Fido, Wilber} is IG in its individual members Fido and Wilber, then it is rigidly existentially (RG) as well as rigidly essentially$_E$ grounded (REG) in Fido and Wilber as its members. And since a heap of sand is arguably essentially$_I$ grounded in the individual grains of sand it has as proper parts, it is thus rigidly existentially grounded as well as rigidly essentially$_E$ grounded in those proper parts.

A thing may fail to be essentially$_I$ grounded, yet be both generically existentially (GG) and generically essentially$_E$ grounded. Arguably, a living organism is not essentially$_I$ grounded in any of its individual proper parts; *which* entity a living organism is is not determined by *which objects* is proper parts are. A living organism remains the very organism it is despite gaining and losing parts over time. Consequently, an organism fails to be both RG as well as rigidly essentially$_E$ grounded (REG) in its proper parts (and their specific arrangements). Be that as it may, a living organism may well be generically existentially grounded as well as generically essentially$_E$ grounded in its composing parts. It is part of the essence of living organisms that they exist only if they are composed of *some proper parts or other* that are suitably arranged along the lines of what our best empirical theories specify.

As a species of non-modal grounding, IG moves beyond characterizing grounding in purely existential terms (whether modal or non-modal) and arguably provides the requisite asymmetry we are looking for in a grounding relation that tracks relations of metaphysical priority and posteriority. While two entities may be mutually essentially$_E$ grounded in one another, this is arguably not the case for essential$_I$ grounding.

As a strict partial ordering relation (G2–G4), IG is well suited to carve out relations of metaphysical priority and posteriority and support talk of one concrete entity's being more or less fundamental than another.[41] For instance, an event's being metaphysically posterior to or less fundamental than its constituents is understood in terms of the fact that the event is *what* it is and is individuated by its constituents and not vice versa. The same applies to the case of an occupant of spacetime being metaphysically prior to its spatial boundary. Spatial boundaries are what they are in general and are the very boundaries they are in particular in virtue of their hosts and not vice versa. *What* a redness trope is in general, as well as *which* redness trope it is in particular, is grounded in the nature of its bearer and not vice versa. We could multiply examples.

Accordingly, when I speak of "grounding" in the context of mereological metaphysics in the sequel, I mean IG in particular unless otherwise stated. While there are many varieties of ontological dependence as the particular species of Grounding in question (RG, GG, REG, GEG), I think that IG is the only species that is suited to the task at hand going forward. I leave it to the reader who is inclined to take grounding in this context as primitive to make the relevant substitutions in what follows.

Notes

1. See Hofweber (2009) for a representative of a view of this sort.
2. See Audi (2012).
3. Proponents of grounding Monism include Fine (2012) and Schaffer (2016). For a notable defense of Pluralism see Wilson (2014).
4. Bennett (2017) takes a genus-species approach to what she calls "building relations." This view also has precedent in Rodriguez-Pereyra (2015). Rodriguez-Pereyra (2015: 519) notes, "Grounding is the non-causal generic relation of *being F in virtue of* (or, equivalently, the generic relation of *being F non-causally in virtue of*). Thus a relation is a case or species of grounding if it is a specification of the non-causal generic relation of *being F in virtue of*. Therefore, truth-making is a case or species of grounding since it is the non-causal relation of *being true in virtue of*: the proposition <Socrates is white> is true in virtue of the fact that Socrates is white. Similarly, *being right in virtue of*, *being blue in virtue of*, *existing in virtue of*, and many other such relations are also cases or species of grounding."
5. Schaffer (2009a) and Koslicki (2013a) think that it is, while Fine (2012a) and Correia (2010) think that it's a logical operator or connective.
6. For topic-neutrality see Schaffer (2009a) and Cameron (2008); for facts see Rosen (2010) and Audi (2012); for propositions see Fine (2012a).
7. For a helpful overview of this particular aspect of grounding see Raven (2013). For a sampling of those who reject grounding as a strict partial order (in some way or other) see Jenkins (2011), Schaffer (2012), Rodriguez-Pereyra (2015), and Fine (2010).
8. For grounding as a kind of metaphysical explanation see Fine (2012a) and deRosset (2013). Audi (2012) disagrees.
9. For grounding necessitarianism see Trogdon (2013) and Correia (2010). For grounding contingentism see Schnieder (2006), and Skiles (2015).
10. I owe these citations to Rettler (2017). See also Trogdon (2013) for a very helpful survey of the grounding literature up to 2013.
11. As Rettler (2017:14) points out, "And Grounding is the relation that does all of those things essentially. No property other than Grounding realizes grounding in all instances of grounding. A relation is a grounding relation because it satisfies (enough of) the job description in a particular instance. Most properties that play the grounding role do so accidentally; Grounding is the unifier of them because it plays the grounding role essentially."
12. To illustrate, the neo-Humean and the neo-Aristotelian could agree about all of the supervenience facts about a particular domain—e.g., that all modal facts

74 *Grounding and Essence*

supervene on the spatiotemporal distribution of local property instances—yet adamantly disagree about the grounding or fundamental facts regarding that domain (neo-Aristotelians taking local dispositional properties to be the ground of modal truths, while neo-Humeans claiming that our world is fundamentally devoid of intrinsic modal structure).

13. See Fine (1995: 286), Barnes (forthcoming), and Thompson (2016).
14. See Raven (2013) and Rodriguez-Pereyra (2015) for relevant discussion.
15. See Simons (1987: 21).
16. Where a grounding domain D is *non-empty* just in case there are at least two existing entities in D (as per G2 and G7) that stand in the grounding relation with respect to one another (remaining neutral as to which grounds which).
17. There need not be a *single* minimal grounding element in D, however. Here I leave open the possibility of there being a multiplicity of minimal grounding elements in D.
18. See Fine (1991: 267).
19. Quoted in Adams (1994: 335).
20. See Cameron (2008) for instance.
21. Cf. Kim (1993: 167).
22. See also Schaffer and Ismael (2016, §2.2.3).
23. My discussion of the varieties of metaphysical grounding follows closely the work of Lowe and Tahko (2015). See Koslicki (2013a) for an excellent overview of the varieties of ontological dependence in the neo-Aristotelian literature.
24. As per Chapter 1, here I use the sentential operator "E" for the existence predicate and define it in terms of the existential quantifier: $Ex =_{def} (\exists y)(x = y)$
25. See Barnes (forthcoming) and Thompson (2016).
26. As Correia (2005: 47) rightly points out, the source of the worry here is the validity of $\Box B \rightarrow \Box(A \rightarrow B)$.
27. General forms of this problem as applied to grounding or dependence can be found in Simons (1987: 295).
28. It is interesting to note that Fine's (1994b) own critique of RG followed his (1994a) critique of modal essentialism.
29. Or one might, following Schaffer (2009, 2010), take grounding here to be a primitive, strict partial ordering relation that carves out relations of metaphysical priority and posteriority.
30. Here I rely on the Scotus (1949) edition of *De Primo Principio* (DPP) in what follows; see 1.6 in particular.
31. DPP, 1.8.
32. *Quod.* 19, n. 19., see Scotus (1975).
33. *Quest.* 7, q. 1, see Scotus (1997).
34. DPP, 1.8.
35. DPP, 2.2.
36. DPP, 2.4.
37. DPP, 2.6.
38. See Inman (2012) for a more thorough discussion of grounding concepts (esp. ontological dependence and truthmaking) in medieval metaphysics.
39. Barnes (forthcoming). Although see Lowe (2012b) for a critical discussion of alleged cases of symmetrical identity grounding or dependence (see the following) in structuralist ontologies.
40. As quoted in Koslicki (2013a).
41. If one allows for the possibility of self-individuation, then essential$_I$ grounding will be *non-reflexive*.

3 Fundamental Mereology and the Priority of Substance

3.1 The Structure of the Mereological Hierarchy

The contemporary *locus classicus* of the notion that concrete material reality exhibits mereological structure is Paul Oppenheim and Hilary Putnam's 1958 paper "Unity of Science as a Working Hypothesis." Oppenheim and Putnam put forward a reductive account of the hierarchy of levels where each of the following levels is said to correlate with the various branches of the natural sciences:

6. Social groups
5. (Multicellular) living things
4. Cells
3. Molecules
2. Atoms
1. Elementary particles

According to Oppenheim and Putnam, "Any thing of any level except the lowest must possess a decomposition into things belonging to the next lower level" (1958: 9). It is claimed that the entities occupying level $n+1$ or higher are ultimately decomposable into n-level entities in the sense that they are somehow contained or latent in level n and thereby micro-reducible to it. For Oppenheim and Putnam, then, all $n+1$ level entities are micro-reducible to entities occupying the level of fundamental physics.

Though the strong reductive letter of Oppenheim and Putnam's account of the mereological ordering of reality has been largely abandoned (for reasons we will see in the course of this essay), many contemporary philosophers are apt to endorse something similar in spirit. Perhaps the clearest statement of the mereological structure of (concrete) reality that permeates contemporary analytic philosophy is by Kim (1998: 15):[1]

> What has replaced the picture of a dichotomized world is the familiar multilayered model that views the world as stratified into different

"levels," "orders," or "tiers" organized in a hierarchical structure. The bottom level is usually thought to consist of elementary particles, or whatever our best physics is going to tell us are the basic bits of matter out of which all material things are composed. As we go up the ladder, we successively encounter atoms, molecules, cells larger living organisms, and so on. The ordering relation that generates the hierarchical structure is the mereological (part-whole) relation: entities belonging to a given level, except those at the very bottom, have an exhaustive decomposition, without remainder, into entities belonging to the lower levels. Entities at the bottom level have no physically significant parts.

(Kim 1998: 15)

As will become evident shortly, though Kim's statement of the view favors an atomistic understanding of the levels conception of reality, it is nonetheless a widespread assumption among most contemporary analytic philosophers that reality is ordered by the part-whole relation such that mereologically complex wholes are *composed* of objects occupying a lower-order level, with such a succession potentially extending *ad infinitum*. This is, of course, not to say that parthood relations are the only relations that obtain between the various "levels" or "layers" of the mereological hierarchy.

There are two general considerations that are taken to undergird a layered model of reality, both of which involve reality's exhibiting distinct kinds of *structure*. We will look at each in turn.

3.1.1 Mereological Structure

We can do no better than start with the notion that concrete material reality exhibits *mereological (part-whole) structure*. Everyone, *pace* the mereological nihilist, takes the motorcycle to be *composed* of its many mechanical parts, the building to be *composed* of its materials, and a human being to be (partly) *composed* of various organs, organs being *composed* of cells, and so on. While this entire essay can be seen as an attempt to undermine mereological nihilism, here I assume that the nihilist is mistaken and that reality exhibits mereological structure. By my lights, if one were to point out the existence of a molecule and its atoms but failed to take note of the parthood relations that obtain between them, one would have missed a deep structural feature of reality.

In light of this, many advocates of a layered conception of reality express the core notion of the thesis as follows:

Hierarchy: The natural world is divided into a hierarchy of levels generated by the part-whole relation.[2]

As stated, **Hierarchy** is a rather uncontroversial thesis concerning the *existence* of mereological ordering in the natural world and one that only the mereological nihilist is apt to deny; as stated, it is simply the thesis that entities stand in a part-whole relations to one another thereby generating ascending levels of composition and descending levels of decomposition. Electrons are proper parts of atoms; space-time points are proper parts of regions; instantaneous temporal parts are proper parts of extended space-time worms, etc. As a result, **Hierarchy** is generally accepted by all save those with an appetite for the austere in mereology.

To illustrate, consider some entities at a lower lower-order level (l) that compose some composite entities at a higher-order level ($l + 1, l + 2, l + 3$). Roughly, we can understand the notion of a level or layer of the mereological hierarchy being "higher" or "lower" than another in terms of the various formal properties of the proper parthood relation that generate them. Level $l + 2$ is "higher" than $l + 1$ precisely because entities occupying $l + 1$ (which are composed of entities occupying level l) enter into the asymmetrical relation of proper parthood with mereologically complex entities at $l + 2$. Given the asymmetry of proper parthood, the same does not apply to the entities at $l + 2$—i.e., entities occupying level $l + 2$ are not proper parts of entities occupying $l + 1$. If one were to admit the existence of the Universe as per classical extensional mereology, such a mereologically complex entity (the mereological fusion of all concrete objects) would serve as the "highest" level of the mereological hierarchy such that every thing is part of it and it is not a proper part of anything. From the assumption that the mereological hierarchy is governed by the partial ordering relation of proper parthood, we can say that for any level on the mereological hierarchy (where "$\succ$" stands for "higher than"), the following holds:

Irreflexivity: $\neg(l \succ l)$
No level is higher than itself.

Transitivity: $((l + 2 \succ l + 1 \wedge l + 1 \succ l) \rightarrow l + 2 \succ l)$
If level x is higher than level y, and y is higher than z, then x is higher than z.

Asymmetricality: $((l + 2 \succ l + 1 \rightarrow \neg(l + 1 \succ l + 2))$
If level x is higher than level y, then it is not the case that level y is higher than level x.

As we will see shortly, is that there is nothing about **Hierarchy** *in itself* that precludes a series of levels with infinite descent. Nonetheless, I take it that many philosophers will find plausible the thesis that the world admits of mereological structure, for both philosophical and empirical reasons alike.[3]

We come now to the question of whether **Hierarchy** admits of a fundamental level or "ground floor," so to speak. That is, we can inquire as to whether or not the following thesis is true:

> **Fundamentality:** There is a fundamental or basic level of the mereological hierarchy.

It is often the case in discussions concerning the structure of the natural world, the question as to whether there is a "fundamental level of reality" is associated with the question of whether reality exhibits an ultimate *mereological* terminus in particular. In this sense, **Fundamentality** conveys the idea that the hierarchy of composition "bottoms out" in a fundamental level containing entities devoid of proper parts—i.e., mereological simples.[4] On this particular understanding of **Fundamentality**, mereological simples serve as the fundamental "building blocks" from which all else is composed.

Call this the "compositional fundamentality" variant of **Fundamentality**:

> **Compositional Fundamentality:** The entities at the fundamental level are mereologically simple and are the building blocks from which the rest of the mereological hierarchy is composed.

Much of the debate surrounding the levels conception of reality pertains to whether or not the world has a fundamental level in the sense of **Compositional Fundamentality**. For instance, Schaffer (2003) considers the question of whether or not there is a fundamental level to reality as being synonymous with the question of whether mereological Atomism is true. Given that our best science gives no credence to the existence of material simples, claims Schaffer, we should reject the thesis that the mereological hierarchy "bottoms out" in a level whose occupants lack proper parts. In the same vein, Ladyman and Ross (2007: 53–57) consider the question of the truth of **Fundamentality** to be equivalent to the question of whether **Compositional Fundamentality** is true; on their view **Hierarchy** is suspect precisely on the grounds that there is no adequate evidence in favor of mereological simples.

However, many have rightly pointed out that there is nothing inherent in the layered conception of reality as stated in **Hierarchy** that requires **Compositional Fundamentality**; the existence of mereological simples need not be a core tenet of this general view regarding the compositional ordering of reality. As stated, **Hierarchy** is entirely consistent with what David Lewis (1986a) has famously labeled "atomless gunk:" objects each of whose parts have proper parts. As Jaegwon Kim (1998: 123) notes, "The layered model as such of course does not need to posit a bottom level; it is consistent with an infinitely descending series of levels." What's more, as Peter Simons has shown, classical-extensional mereology is entirely consistent with the existence of gunk. As an example of a gunky mereology, Simons (1987: 41) points to "the regular open sets of a Euclidean space, the part-relation being set-inclusion confined to these sets."[5]

All this to say that **Hierarchy** is consistent with a wide range of mereologies in so far as it is neutral as to whether reality is infinite in descent with respect to its part-whole ordering. To put this a bit more precisely, the claim is that **Hierarchy** is consistent with the following mereologies (where "A" stands for atom, "≤" parthood, and "<" proper parthood):

Atomic: $(\forall x)(\exists y)(Ay \wedge y \leq x))$
Gunky: $(\forall x)(\exists y)(y < x)$
Non-Atomic: $(\exists x)(Ax \wedge (\exists x)(\forall y)(y \leq x \rightarrow (\exists z)(z < y)))$

An *atomic* understanding of **Hierarchy** holds that every existent is either itself an atom (A) or is mereologically composed of atoms. A *gunky* interpretation of **Hierarchy**, on the other hand, states that every existent on the hierarchy has at least one proper part. On this reading of the hierarchy, **Compositional Fundamentality** is false in so far as no level "bottoms out" in mereological simples. Lastly, a *non-atomic* reading of **Hierarchy** is such that some of the existents on the hierarchy are atomic and others are gunky. As a result, both the gunky and the non-atomic conceptions of the mereological hierarchy are committed to the view that the domain that is governed by the mereological relations is infinite, it's "turtles all the way down" as the saying goes. The layered model of reality as stated in **Hierarchy**, then, is *neutral* concerning the existence of mereological simples; Atomism need not be built into the view from the start. There is, then, a minimal core to the view that realty admits of mereological structure, which includes the conjunction of **Hierarchy** together with either an atomic, gunky, or non-atomic mereology.

3.1.2 Metaphysical Structure

Let's turn now to the second variety of structure that is often conjoined with **Hierarchy**—namely, *metaphysical structure*. By "metaphysical structure" here I simply mean the (non-causal) structure in reality that is generated by metaphysical grounding relations. As the nature and logical structure of grounding was the subject of Chapter 2, we need not rehearse our previous discussion here. Here I will assume, for reasons outlined in Chapter 2, that grounding relations, understood along the lines of essential$_I$ grounding, carve out relations of metaphysical priority and posteriority among concrete entities in the world.[6]

When we conjoin **Hierarchy** with the notion that reality exhibits grounding structure, we get the thesis that objects at a given mereological level, together with their properties, powers, and behaviors, are either metaphysically prior or posterior to objects at distinct mereological levels.[7] Concrete material reality displays not only mereological structure (as represented by our minimal core of **Hierarchy** together with an atomic, gunky, or non-atomic mereology), but also metaphysical grounding structure which generates relations of priority and posteriority.

And since it is natural, albeit not entirely uncontroversial, to suppose that grounding relations are well-founded as per G9 (see §2.1.4), admitting the existence of this kind of metaphysical structure raises the question of a metaphysically fundamental or minimal ontological base upon which all else depends for its existence and identity on the hierarchy.

Here we must be careful to distinguish between *relative* and *absolute* metaphysical fundamentality. The former states that one entity *grounds* or is *is more fundamental than* some distinct entity, and the latter maintains that one entity (or collection of entities) not only grounds or is more fundamental than some distinct entity or class of entities, but that entity is itself ungrounded. The general idea here is straightforward: something can be *relatively* fundamental without itself being *absolutely* fundamental. For instance, the individual members of the baseball team may ground or be more fundamental than the team as a group, without thereby being absolutely fundamental in the sense of being ungrounded.

The question of whether there is anything that is absolutely fundamental *tout court* has traditionally been a wider metaphysical and theological question than the one at hand. Theists, for example, will maintain that all reality, including the mereological hierarchy of concrete material beings, is grounded in God who alone is absolutely fundamental *full stop*.[8] On this view, all fundamental concrete reality that is not God is relatively fundamental with respect to the class of non-fundamental concreta. By contrast, if the concrete *material* reality exhausts concrete reality per se, then anything that is absolutely fundamental will be located at some level of the hierarchy of composition (assuming that grounding is well-founded, see G9 from Chapter 2, §1.1). Since our aim in this essay is limited to fundamentality as it pertains to the mereological ordering among concrete material beings in particular, I restrict the scope of "absolute fundamentality" to what is on the hierarchy of composition for concrete material objects. The question of fundamental mereology, then, concerns which concrete item/items on the compositional hierarchy is/are absolutely fundamental, leaving open the question of whether those items are also absolutely fundamental *tout court*.

Whether or not those who endorse **Hierarchy** are also committed to the further thesis of **Compositional Fundamentality**, many are inclined to think that there are items on the compositional hierarchy that are more fundamental than all the rest.[9] Such entities are taken to be metaphysically independent in the sense that in addition to ultimately grounding all distinct (concrete) material reality on the compositional hierarchy, they also fail to be grounded in any distinct entity on the hierarchy. The metaphysically fundamental entities (or entity) are commonly thought to be either

(i) "maximally real" or (ii) metaphysically ungrounded and thus prior to non-fundamental entities on the hierarchy.

We can capture this particular variety of **Fundamentality** in terms of grounding and metaphysical structure as follows:

> **Metaphysical Fundamentality:** The (absolutely) metaphysically fundamental entity or entities are (i) "more real" than the non-fundamental (derivative) entities, and/or (ii) metaphysically prior to the non-fundamental (derivative) entities in so far as they ground non-fundamental entities and are themselves ungrounded.

Though common, I wish to dismiss tenet (i) of **Metaphysical Fundamentality** at the outset. Several philosophers, mistakenly I believe, take it that if x is grounded in or dependent on y, then x is somehow "more real" than y. For instance, Markosian (2005: 74) explicates what he calls "ontological fundamentalism" as the thesis that "ours is fundamentally a world of mereological simples, which are in some sense more real than the entities that are composed of them." He goes on to state, "And there is a long tradition in philosophy that involves saying that whenever x depends for its existence on y, then y exists more fully, and is more real, than x."[10]

I must admit that I myself am at a loss as to what these claims are supposed to mean. Thankfully, the commitment to various degrees of existence is no part of the commitment to claims of metaphysical grounding. An entity's being metaphysically grounded in another in no way implies that the former is somehow "less real" than the latter; or at least *I* am unable to see such an implication. Rather, in claims of grounding, dependence, or priority, "existence" is used univocally such that both relata of grounding relations exist *in precisely the same sense*.

With that clarification in mind it should be pointed out that in contrast to **Compositional Fundamentality**, many philosophers who endorse a hierarchical conception of reality are apt to consider **Metaphysical Fundamentality** as a core thesis of such a view, together with **Hierarchy** and the choice of an accompanying atomic, atomless, or non-atomic mereology. I say this precisely because a good many views in metaphysics and the philosophy of mind are explicated (though not always explicitly) in terms of the notion that a metaphysically elite class of entities "fix" or "determine" the properties and behaviors of other entities at a distinct mereological level, where the such relations are understood as asymmetric. In this way, entities occupying the metaphysically fundamental level of the hierarchy of composition form the ultimate ontological base on which the hierarchy rests, everything else being grounded in such entities. An oft repeated slogan: fix the fundamentals, and you thereby fix everything else.

A few important things to note about **Metaphysical Fundamentality** and its relation to **Compositional Fundamentality**. First, while not all hierarchy theorists who endorse **Metaphysical Fundamentality** go on to endorse **Compositional Fundamentality**, the converse is almost always the case. That is, those who adopt **Compositional Fundamentality** take the mereologically fundamental entities to be metaphysically fundamental as well. For those who include simples in their ontology, it is often claimed that such entities are *metaphysically prior to the wholes they compose* and that composite entities are built up out of these fundamental entities. Second, **Metaphysical Fundamentality** is silent as to which ontological category the fundamental entities belong. As far as **Metaphysical Fundamentality** is concerned, the fundamental entities could be substances, events, properties, relations, structures, etc. Finally, **Metaphysical Fundamentality** is neutral as to the size of the fundamental units of being, that is, whether such entities (or entity) are microscopic (as in particles, fields distributed across spacetime, etc.), macroscopic (ordinary material objects), or the entire cosmos.

3.2 Fundamental Mereology

A commitment to **Metaphysical Fundamentality**, together with the thesis that reality has mereological structure (**Hierarchy**), gives rise to what Jonathan Schaffer (2010b) has recently called *the question of fundamental mereology*: what is the (absolute) metaphysical ground of the mereological hierarchy. That is, the question of fundamental mereology inquires as to which objects are the fundamental units of being that serve as the absolute terminus of the grounding ordering of the mereological hierarchy. The question of fundamental mereology has an impressive historical pedigree and provides much of the underlying framework for many of the debates in contemporary metaphysics, philosophy of science, and the philosophy of mind.

3.2.1 Schaffer on Fundamental Mereology

While the concept of fundamental mereology is one with a long-standing historical precedent, the most extensive treatment of the idea in the recent literature is provided by Jonathan Schaffer. To help motivate the notion of metaphysical priority and posteriority as applied to wholes and their parts, Schaffer (2010: 31) begins by asking the reader to consider the question as to which is prior: a circle or its pair of semicircles? He asks, "Are the semicircles dependent abstractions from their whole, or is the circle a derivative construction from its parts?" Schaffer then asks the reader to consider the cosmos as a whole and whether or not it is prior to its parts or vice versa. It is this latter question that he takes to be at the heart of fundamental mereology.[11]

The project of fundamental mereology rests on several assumptions that need to be stated at the outset. First, as was argued for in the previous chapter, fundamental mereology proceeds on the assumption that there is a relation of metaphysical grounding or priority, that reality has distinctively metaphysical joints ordered by relations of priority and posteriority. Second, fundamental mereology assumes that the items generated by part-whole relations are numerically distinct from the items from which they are generated; that is, *composition is not identity*.[12] By this I mean to reject the thesis that the relation a whole bears to its parts *is one and the same as* (or even sufficiently similar to) the relation of numerical identity. Though controversial, I take this assumption to be well-warranted given the distinct modal and historical properties of wholes and their parts as well as the existence (and ipso facto possibility) of strongly emergent properties which I take to be incompatible with composition as identity.[13] According to fundamental mereology, then, there are no "free ontological lunches" when it comes to composite objects; mereological wholes are not "ontologically innocent"; they exist "over and above" their parts.

3.2.1.1 The Tiling Constraint

Schaffer begins his discussion of fundamental mereology by putting forward what he calls a "tiling constraint" on possible answers to the question of fundamental mereology. He argues that the metaphysically fundamental entities (the entities that satisfy what I have labeled **Metaphysical Fundamentality**) ought to collectively cover the cosmos without overlapping. For the fundamental entities, then, *there are no gaps and no overlaps*. To help get clear on the tiling constraint as well as the possible answers to the question of fundamental mereology, let us adopt the following notation:

$x < y = x$ is a proper part of y
$x \triangleright y = x$ is grounded in y
$u =$ the cosmos
$F =$ fundamental (concrete) object

By "the cosmos" (u) here Schaffer is explicit that he means the (actual) concrete sum of which all other concrete entities are proper parts. It is well-known that classical extensional mereology includes as a basic axiom the principle of Unrestricted Composition—informally, whenever there are some things, then there exists a fusion of those things. As such, a commitment to classical mereology guarantees the existence of a unique sum of all (actual) concrete objects, i.e. the cosmos.

As for Schaffer's conception of a fundamental or basic concrete entity, he has in mind something along the general lines of the traditional Aristotelian notion of a substance in terms of a variety of metaphysical independence, which he goes on to define in terms of grounding as follows:

$Fx = Cx \land \neg(\exists y)(Cy \land x \triangleright y)$

That is, an entity is fundamental just in case it is concrete and there is no distinct concrete entity in which it is grounded.

With the earlier notation and the working definition of a fundamental or substantial entity in hand, Schaffer goes on to explicate the following two tenets that jointly constitute the tiling constraint for the fundamental entities (or entity) in one's fundamental mereology (where "σx: (Φx)" denotes the sum of all entities that satisfy the description Φ):

Covering: σx: (Fx) = u
No Fundamental Parthood: $(\forall x)(\forall y)((Fx \wedge Fy \wedge x \neq y) \rightarrow \neg(x < y))$[14]

Regarding **Covering**, Schaffer argues that the fundamental entities must be *complete* in that their collective duplication, together with the relations that obtain between them, suffices to duplicate the entire cosmos. The notion of completeness here is one such that a set of entities S at world w is complete for w if and only if S serves to provide a grounding base for w, without remainder. **Covering**, then, requires the basics to serve as the exhaustive grounding base of w; *all* non-fundamental or derivative entities must be grounded in the fundamentals. It is important to note here that Schaffer's formation of **Covering** *assumes* that there is a mereological sum that is identical to the cosmos—i.e., the maximal mereological fusion of classical mereology. While this assumption is harmless for our purposes at this stage in setting up the question of fundamental mereology, it is important to note that the core notion behind **Covering** can be formulated without this metaphysically loaded assumption.[15]

Covering is a mereological extension of David Lewis's (1986a: 60) notion that the sparse or natural properties ought to "characterize things completely and without redundancy." Following Lewis (1986a: 59–63), we can take x and y to be duplicates just in case there is a one-one correspondence between their parts that preserves perfectly natural properties and relations. On this score, **Covering** is the thesis that there ought to be a one-one correspondence between the sum or fusion of the fundamental entities and the entire cosmos itself. If the sum of the fundamental entities ($σx$: (Fx)) failed to stand in a one-one correspondence to the entire cosmos (u) it would be incomplete in so far as there would be segments of reality that would remain unaccounted for in such an inventory.

As a constraint on possible answers to the question of fundamental mereology, **Covering** is meant to exclude as fundamental entities whose duplication would leave out large portions of reality, say, the total collection of books in all the libraries in the world. It also follows from **Covering** that if there is but a single fundamental entity, that entity is the fusion of all concrete reality—i.e., the cosmos; there is nothing other than the cosmos whose duplication could suffice *on its own* to preserve the natural properties and relations of the totality of concrete reality.

No Fundamental Parthood, on the other hand, is the claim that the fundamental entities fail to stand in part-whole relations to one another. In other words, no fundamental entity has another fundamental entity as a proper part. This is not to say, however, that fundamental substances need be mereologically simple and thus lacking proper parts *altogether*.[16] Rather, **No Fundamental Parthood** is simply the claim that fundamental substances fail to be composed of other fundamental substances (according to Schaffer, the cosmos is *not* mereologically simple in so far as it has non-fundamental or derivative proper parts). Given **No Fundamental Parthood** it follows that if there is more than one fundamental entity on the hierarchy of composition, then the cosmos is not a fundamental entity as the former would be fundamental parts of the cosmos, thereby rendering the cosmos as non-fundamental.

No Fundamental Parthood will strike the reader as being an extremely strong claim regarding the relation between the mereological and the metaphysical ordering of reality. And strong it is! Nonetheless, as we will examine next, **No Fundamental Parthood** is an enduring piece of classical metaphysics concerning the mereological structure of fundamental objects.[17] What's more, it is a thesis that plays an absolutely central role in my overall neo-Aristotelian metaphysic of material objects. In light of the fact that I will examine **No Fundamental Parthood** and Schaffer's arguments in favor of it in much greater detail in what is to come, I simply mention it here as a part of Schaffer's tiling constraint on fundamental mereology.

3.2.1.2 *Monism and Pluralism*

With the aforementioned tiling constraint in place, Schaffer proceeds to offer two exhaustive and mutually exclusive *general* answers to the question of fundamental mereology—*Monism* and *Pluralism*—each differentiated by the direction of grounding that obtains between the cosmos and its many proper parts:

> The Monist holds that the whole is prior to its parts, and thus views the cosmos as fundamental, with metaphysical explanation dangling downward from the One. The pluralist holds that the parts are prior to their whole, and thus tends to consider particles fundamental, with metaphysical explanation snaking upward from the many.
> (Schaffer 2010b: 31–32)

According to Schaffer, the core tenet driving Monism is the idea that *the whole is metaphysically prior to its proper parts*. By the use of the definite article here Schaffer intends to refer to the unique maximal sum of all concrete reality, the cosmos (u). On this view, the cosmos serves as the metaphysical ground of the mereological hierarchy in that it grounds the existence and identity of its many proper parts and is in no way grounded by any distinct concrete entity on the hierarchy of composition. Given the tiling constraint, if the cosmos is the metaphysical ground of the hierarchy, then it is the *sole* fundamental substance on the hierarchy of composition since everything else at a "lower" level of decomposition would be a non-fundamental part of it.

The core tenet of Pluralism, on the other hand, is the thesis that *the parts are metaphysically prior to the whole cosmos*. Hence, the many proper parts of the cosmos are metaphysically prior in that they collectively ground the existence and nature of the cosmos, and a privileged subclass of the parts of cosmos are themselves ungrounded. Pluralism entails the denial of Monism as, per the tiling constraint, the cosmos cannot be fundamental in so far as at least one of its parts is fundamental.

As is well known, Schaffer ingeniously defends a monistic fundamental mereology that takes the cosmos to be the sole metaphysically fundamental entity with its many parts (planets, humans, bicycles, etc.) being derivative on it. Schaffer argues against what he takes to be the main pluralistic rival to Monism: an atomistic variant that takes the *minimal* or mereologically simple parts of the cosmos (what he refers to as "particles") as being absolutely fundamental or metaphysically ultimate.

As a version of Pluralism, Atomism is the view that (i) there are at least two metaphysically fundamental entities, (ii) such entities are proper parts of the cosmos, and that (iii) these entities are the *minimal* or smallest proper parts of the cosmos (subatomic particles, waves, fields, etc.). For the Atomist, then, it is the mereologically simple parts of the cosmos that are metaphysically fundamental and thus metaphysically prior to both intermediate mereological wholes as well as the entire cosmos. In our earlier terminology, Schaffer's Atomism is committed to **Compositional Fundamentality** as well as **Metaphysical Fundamentality**. For the Atomist, the mereologically simple entities are (absolutely) metaphysically fundamental. Though at times Schaffer appears to use the terms "Pluralism" and "Atomism" synonymously, he is clear that the latter should not be built into the definition of the former given the availability of alternative versions of Pluralism (as we will see shortly).

Given that Pluralism encompasses a variety of options in fundamental mereology and thus is not limited to Atomism, Schaffer defines Monism and Pluralism in light of the tiling constraint as follows:

(M) **Monism:** $(\forall x)(x < u \rightarrow x \triangleright u)$
(P) **Pluralism:** $(\exists x)(x < u \wedge u \triangleright x)$[18]

What's crucial for my purpose here is that Schaffer classifies the live options in fundamental mereology (M and P)—including the two core tenets driving Monism and Pluralism—primarily in terms of the cosmos as the maximal sum of classical mereology. More on this later.

To help illustrate the various options in fundamental mereology, it will be helpful to utilize the three-atom model of classical extensional mereology. Consider the following very general slice of the mereological structure of the world as captured by the three-atom model of classical extensional mereology:[19]

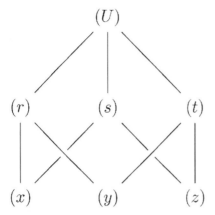

Figure 3.1 Three-Atom Model

At the top of the mereological hierarchy is the Universe (U)—the unique mereological sum of all concrete reality (Schaffer's cosmos)—and our respective atoms occupying the lowest mereological level (x, y, z). Schaffer uses "molecules" to denote the mereologically intermediate entitities (r, s, t) each of which are proper parts of U and have at least two atoms as proper parts.

Now, using the aforementioned three-atom model, Schaffer's more finegrained classification of the options in fundamental mereology are as follows:[20]

Monism: $x, y, z \triangleright r, s, t \triangleright U$[21]
Intermediate: $(x, y, z \triangleright r, s, t) \wedge (U \triangleright r, s, t)$[22]
Atomism: $U \triangleright r, s, t \triangleright x, y, z$

According to Monism, the grounding chain begins with the atoms, extends through the intermediates, and ultimately terminates in the Universe. Intermediate holds that all grounding chains within the mereological hierarchy terminate in the mereological intermediates, whether originating from the atoms or from the Universe. For the Atomist, the grounding chain begins with the Universe, proceeds through the intermediates, and ultimately terminates in the atoms. While Schaffer is unequivocal that the most defensible of the three options are Monism and Atomism (for reasons that will become clear in what follows), he does not exclude Intermediate as a potential option in fundamental mereology.

3.2.2 Where Have All the Fundamental Intermediates Gone?

While Schaffer gives lip service to the notion that Intermediate (or any variant thereof) carves out a position in logical space, he often weds what I'll call Whole-Priority, the view that wholes are prior to their proper parts, and Part-Priority, the view that proper parts are prior to their wholes, to Monism and Pluralism respectively. In doing so, Schaffer gives the impression that the defender of Monism has exclusive rights to Whole-Priority.

To see this, it is important to underscore that Schaffer often alternates between the following variants of Whole-Priority:

(WP_a) Whole-Priority$_a$: The whole is metaphysically prior to its parts.
(WP_b) Whole-Priority$_b$: Wholes *per se* are metaphysically prior to their parts.

Schaffer's use of WP_a is often signified by the use of the definite article, which as we have seen, he takes to refer to the cosmos, the unique sum of classical mereology. And as the above quote makes clear, Schaffer takes Monism to be *equivalent* to WP_a.[23]

However, Schaffer often speaks of Whole-Priority in a much more general way in terms of WP_b. For instance, Schaffer labels the Intermediate position "quasi-monistic" in virtue of ascribing metaphysical priority to intermediate wholes. Using "molecules" as a stand-in for fundamental intermediate composite objects, Schaffer (2010b: 63–64) argues,

> Further, the use of basic molecules is already *quasi-monistic*. Given the tiling constraint (§1.3), no proper parts of any basic molecules can themselves be basic. Hence the use of basic molecules involves treating the whole as prior to its parts, with respect to the basic molecules and their derivative parts. So it is hard to see how the molecular pluralist could have any principled objection to monism.
>
> (2010b: 63–64)

This is a puzzling statement indeed. Surely Schaffer doesn't mean that the Intermediate position is "quasi-monistic" in the sense that it takes "the whole as prior to its parts" (note the use of the definite article) to mean that the *cosmos* is prior to its parts; such a reading would subsume Intermediate into Monism. Rather, what he means here is that Intermediate is "quasi-monistic" in that it ascribes metaphysical fundamentality to molecules as intermediate wholes. At work here are two different interpretations of the phrase "the whole is prior to its parts," one that is equivalent to Monism (WP_a), and another that refers to the much more general mereological thesis that wholes *per se* are metaphysically prior to their proper parts (WP_b). The latter is more inclusive than the former in the sense that it is neutral as to *which* exist and are metaphysically prior to their parts, whether the cosmos or some privileged subset of intermediates (e.g., molecules).

In branding non-monistic views that favor WP$_b$ as "quasi-monistic," Schaffer gives the impression that a commitment to WP$_b$, *on its own*, brings with it a commitment to WP$_a$; any view that embraces Whole-Priority is in danger of collapsing into Monism.[24] Perhaps the clearest example of this is the following quote, where Schaffer again considers the Intermediate position which takes a subclass of intermediate wholes to be fundamental and thus metaphysically prior to their parts (thereby adopting WP$_b$):

> Second, the priority pluralist might (on wanting to maintain basic entities in a gunky scenario, but not wanting to take the whole as basic) take some intermediate level of mereological structure to be basic. But this is hardly thematic for the pluralist, as now she would be treating these intermediate structures monistically, as prior to their parts.
> (2014, §3.2.3)

Where the intermediate position (which endorses WP$_b$ but not WP$_a$) was previously described as "quasi-monistic" in virtue of adopting WP$_b$, here we see that the prefix "quasi" has been dropped to give us the much stronger claim that WP$_b$ *just is* a monistic fundamental mereology. One is left with the impression that to take seriously the ontological priority of wholes per se over their parts is *equivalent* to adopting Monism.

There are further traces of this wedding of Monism to WP$_b$ throughout Schaffer's "Monism: Priority of the Whole." Schaffer often uses the locution "priority of whole to part," which on the surface appears to denote the more general thesis of WP$_b$, to characterize what he takes to be the core notion of the monistic tradition.[25] But the use of such a phrase (given the absence of the definite article that serves to distinguish the two variants of Whole-Priority) tends to gloss over the aforementioned distinction between WP$_a$ and WP$_b$ and serves to reinforce the idea that Monism has exclusive rights to WP$_b$.

But why think that WP$_b$ is "monistic" or even "quasi-monistic" simply in virtue of appropriating the insight that wholes *per se* are prior to their parts? As a general mereological thesis concerning the relationship between wholes *per se* and their parts, WP$_b$ is entirely *neutral* as to *which* mereological wholes one ought to be ontologically committed.[26] Accordingly, it is difficult to see how endorsing WP$_b$ implies a commitment to the existence of the unique sum of classical mereology, the cosmos? The fact that Schaffer says as much reveals that he takes the general mereological insight of the ontological priority of wholes *per se* over their parts (WP$_b$) to be wedded to a monistic fundamental mereology.

But of course the Monist has no right to stake out WP$_b$ as a piece of monistic metaphysics. In doing so, they fail to account for important logical space regarding the options in fundamental mereology. While Schaffer gives lip service to views like Intermediate as a viable option in fundamental mereology at the outset, his tendency to wed WP$_b$ to Monism prohibits all non-monistic views from appropriating the core insight underlying WP$_b$. This of course precludes views like Intermediate (or any that assign metaphysical fundamentality to a subclass of ordinary composite objects) as a live option in fundamental mereology, an option with as much historical precedent as Monism and Atomism.[27]

Monism and WP$_b$ are logically independent views concerning the intersection of mereological and metaphysical structure. This is evidenced by the simple fact that *it is possible that WP$_b$ be true and Monism turn out false*.[28] Consider a world where WP$_b$ is true and composite objects are prior to their parts, and yet the maximal sum of classical mereology does not exist (for a variety of reasons).[29] In such a world, WP$_b$ is true yet Monism is false.

One reason that contributes to Schaffer's wedding of WP$_b$ to Monism is that he begins with the cosmos as his point of reference in characterizing the options in fundamental mereology. According to Schaffer, the following options are exhaustive and exclusive: either the entire cosmos is metaphysically fundamental or its proper parts are fundamental (whether intermediate or minimal). We have seen that, for Schaffer, this is just *equivalent* to whether the one whole or its parts are ontologically prior. But why take as the locus of one's classification the *maximal whole*—the cosmos—instead of the *many intermediate wholes* at a lower level of decomposition? Why privilege Spinoza over Aristotle here? If one takes as one's starting point the unique maximal whole of classical mereology, then *anything* and *everything* at a lower level of decomposition will be a part of that whole. As a result, *any* fundamental mereology that takes there to be metaphysically fundamental entities at a lower level of decomposition than the cosmos will be misclassified as rejecting a fundamental mereology that gives metaphysical pride of place to wholes over their parts.

3.3 Fundamental Mereology Reformulated

It is important to note here that Schaffer is representative of the ubiquitous assumption among contemporary metaphysicians that the tenable options in fundamental mereology exclude views that assign metaphysical fundamentality to *any* ordinary, medium-sized objects; the metaphysically fundamental entities reside exclusively at either the "top" or "bottom" level of the hierarchy of composition. Another way of stating this deeply entrenched assumption is that all chains of metaphysical dependence run *through* intermediate composite objects without ever terminating *in* them. Conspicuously absent from recent discussions in fundamental mereology, then, is an explication and defense of the metaphysical fundamentality of at least some "intermediate" composite objects that correspond to ordinary, medium-sized objects.[30]

Indeed, given the modal status commonly assigned to fundamental mereologies such that whatever view is true is true of necessity, the widespread assumption regarding fundamental intermediates involves the even stronger claim that necessarily, no intermediates are fundamental; or, alternatively, necessarily all intermediates are derivative.[31] In what follows, I'll refer to this ubiquitous assumption as "No Fundamental Intermediates" (let "I" stand for "intermediate (concrete) object"):

No Fundamental Intermediates: □ (∀x)(Ix → ¬(Fx)).

My aim in Chapters 4, 5, and 6 is to argue against the widespread rejection of fundamental, intermediate composite objects as expressed in *No Fundamental Intermediates*.

While I disagree with Schaffer's commitment to *No Fundamental Intermediates*, I am in substantial agreement with much of what he has to say about the overall constraints on fundamental mereology. In fact much of what I will have to say in the sequel is an attempt to build on and supplement his own arguments in favor of Whole-Priority as a *general* thesis in fundamental mereology. For my purposes in this essay, I follow Schaffer in adopting the tiling constraint to govern the potential options in fundamental mereology.

I recognize the controversial nature of proceeding on the basis of such strong preliminary assumptions. For some, **No Fundamental Parthood** will seem excessively restrictive, even demonstrably false. Though I ultimately disagree with this sentiment, my purpose for proceeding with **No Fundamental Parthood** for fundamental substances is threefold.

First, **No Fundamental Parthood** is a constraint on the notion of a substance qua fundamental or independent entity that has a rich historical precedent, boasting adherents from the ancient, medieval, and early modern periods.[32] While these historical considerations are certainly no infallible guide to truth, at the very least, they suggest that **No Fundamental Parthood** is not an unprecedented assumption regarding the intersection of metaphysical grounding and mereology.

Second, in so far as the question of fundamental mereology has recently been reinstated by Schaffer in terms that explicitly make use of the tiling constraint, I think it wise and dialectically advantageous to defend my own position from within the same broad parameters in which the debate has been situated.

Finally, I will argue in the sequel that a particular application of **No Fundamental Parthood** to certain ordinary composite substances yields a unified solution to a host of conundrums that occupy center-stage in the metaphysics of material objects. Thus I consider any theoretical advantages that accrue to my fundamental mereology along these lines to be indirect support for **No Fundamental Parthood** as a tenable constraint regarding the grounding structure of fundamental substances.

Nonetheless, given the widespread tendency to either wed Whole-Priority (WP$_b$) to Monism (as per Schaffer) or to exclude the application of Whole-Priority to ordinary composite objects altogether, it will prove helpful at this point to reorient the locus of classification of views in fundamental mereology so as to not stack the deck against the fundamental mereology I defend in the sequel.

3.3.1 The Direction of Mereological Grounding

If we part company with Schaffer in taking the maximal sum or cosmos as the locus of classification for options in fundamental mereology, how then are we to proceed? To begin, I propose the following alternative formulation of the question of fundamental mereology in terms of what I will call "the direction of mereological grounding" as applied to the hierarchy of composition:

> (DG) **Direction of Mereological Grounding:** Are wholes *per se* metaphysically prior to their parts or vice versa?

The various answers to DG will seek to get clear on whether a composite whole in general or its many parts are prior, that is, whether wholes *per se* ground their parts or vice versa.[33]

Here we do not start with one *particular* whole, the cosmos, and formulate the live options in fundamental mereology in relation to it. Rather we are, at least at this stage, concerned primarily with how mereological and grounding structure intersect in the most general terms—and thus not with how such structure comes together in any one whole in particular.

With DG in hand, consider a rather simple chain consisting of four objects standing in the proper parthood relation: $o_1 < o_2 < o_3 < o_4$. For ease of illustration, suppose we adopt an atomistic reading of the hierarchy of composition and take o_1 to be mereologically simple. As an alternative formulation of the question of fundamental mereology, DG will replace Schaffer's Monism and Pluralism with the following *general* descriptions of the order of grounding in the aforementioned chain.

According to a "Part-Priority" description of the representative slice of mereological structure, the grounding chain begins with o_4 and terminates in o_1 such that o_4 is grounded in o_3, o_3 in o_2, and o_2 in o_1–where the latter serves as the fundamental entity in the grounding chain. On this construal, the composite object o_4–whether it be the cosmos or an intermediate whole–is totally grounded in its proper parts o_1-o_3 as well as partially grounded in each one individually.[34] On a Part-Priority fundamental mereology, according to Kim (1978: 154), "[w]holes are completely *determined*, causally and *ontologically*, by their parts."[35]

On Part-Priority, composite objects per se are derivative (non-fundamental) entities in so far as they are totally grounded in their proper parts. If grounding is transitive (see G4 of Chapter 2) then composite objects on this view will *ultimately* be grounded in either a fundamental base that lacks proper parts or, as per gunky worlds, will proceed infinitely and never reach "ontological bedrock."[36]

Alternatively, on a "Whole-Priority" description, the aforementioned chain begins with o_1 and terminates in o_4. A whole, irrespective of its size, is metaphysically prior to its proper parts and, depending on whether it itself is part of a higher-level composite object, would serve as one of the (absolutely) fundamental units of reality upon which the mereological hierarchy terminates. And on the assumption that a fundamental entity is one that is ungrounded, it follows that no proper part of the composite object is itself a fundamental substance. Again, the *level* of o_4 on the hierarchy of composition–whether it be an intermediate or the maximal whole—is irrelevant for the purposes of classification at this point.

Here it is important to point out the implications of the tiling constraint for Part-Priority and Whole-Priority. On a Part-Priority view, for any composite object you choose on the hierarchy of composition, it will be the first member of a grounding chain that will either terminate in mereologically simple parts or will proceed *ad infinitum* as per a gunky world.[37] Either way, Part-Priority has it that the parts of all composite objects are themselves metaphysically prior and in no way grounded in the wholes of which they are a part.

On this description, the mereological hierarchy consists of nested wholes composed of *separable* parts, each of which are ontologically prior and whose existence and identity are independent of those wholes. A bit more precisely (as per Chapter 2, the sentential operator "$\Box_x$" is to be read as "it is part of the essence of x"):

Separable Part: x is a *separable part* of $y =_{def} x < y \land \neg\Box_x(Ex \rightarrow x < y)$

In words, a proper part is separable from its whole just in case it is not (rigidly) grounded in the whole of which it is a proper part.

Corresponding to the earlier notion of a separable part, a Whole-Priority description of the mereological hierarchy utilizes the notion of an *inseparable part*, a part that is (rigidly) grounded in the whole of which it is a part:

Inseparable Part: x is a *inseparable part* of $y =_{def} x < y \land \Box_x(Ex \rightarrow x < y)$

The distinction between a separable and an inseparable part is a far reaching one in the history of Western philosophy. Having first been introduced to the Western philosophical tradition by Plato, the notion was given its most explicit and detailed formulation by Edmund Husserl in part three of his *Logical Investigations*.[38] If wholes are prior to parts in that they rigidly ground their existence and identity, it follows that no proper part of a composite object is capable of existing independently of that very whole.

3.3.2 *Minimal Fundamental Mereology*

But here it is important to note that Whole-Priority and Part-Priority are exclusive answers to DG only on the additional assumption that there is a single category of whole or object at play in fundamental mereology. It is often assumed by those working in contemporary mereological metaphysics—in part due to the pervasive influence of classical extentional mereology as applied to ordinary objects—that there is a uniform answer at play in whether composite objects per se are prior to their parts or vice versa.

However, if we follow Aristotle, Aquinas, Husserl as well as a handful of contemporary philosophers such as Kit Fine, Mark Johnston, Kathrin Koslicki, E. J. Lowe, J. P. Moreland, David Oderberg, Peter Simons, and even Schaffer himself, and countenance distinct *kinds* of mereological wholes with differing existence and identity conditions, then it is entirely reasonable to maintain that some are governed by Whole-Priority and others by Part-Priority.[39]

I propose we follow this venerable Aristotelian tradition and distinguish between two kinds or categories of composite objects—*substances* and *aggregates*—that are each characterized by distinct dependence or grounding descriptions in relation to their parts.[40]

The idea here is that instead of taking the locus of classification in fundamental mereology to be any one whole or mereological level in particular, we instead situate the question of whether wholes or their parts are prior in terms of *ontological category*. On this view the direction of grounding that obtains between a whole and its proper parts is determined by *what* the object is in terms of its ontological category, whether a substance or an aggregate, irrespective of the size or mereological level occupied by the whole in question. The central question of fundamental mereology (DG) asks, "Are wholes per se prior to their parts or vice versa?" Our venerable tradition answers: "Sometimes wholes are prior, and sometimes parts are prior; it depends on the *ontological category* of the whole in question."

If we reorient the locus of classification in fundamental mereology in terms of ontological category, we arrive at what I'll call "Minimal Fundamental Mereology":

> **Minimal Fundamental Mereology:** *Substances* are metaphysically fundamental and are either mereologically simple or metaphysically prior to their parts; *aggregates* are metaphysically derivative and are metaphysically posterior to either (i) their proper parts or (ii) the composite substances of which they are parts.[41]

All fundamental mereologies are committed to **Minimal Fundamental Mereology** and hence the existence of both fundamental and derivative objects, what I am calling "substances" and "aggregates" respectively. **Minimal Fundamental Mereology** makes no ontological commitments concerning any *particular* composite objects (e.g. the cosmos), and is neutral as to which objects fall under the extension of "substance" and "aggregate."

We then can go on to build upon **Minimal Fundamental Mereology** and specify individual variants of Whole-Priority and Part-Priority in terms of additional ontological and mereological commitments as follows:

> **Priority Monism:** The maximal mereological whole, the cosmos, is a fundamental substance and is metaphysically prior to its proper parts.
> **Priority Macrophysicalism:** Intermediate macrophysical wholes are fundamental substances and are metaphysically prior to their proper parts.
> **Priority Microphysicalism:** The microphysical parts of composite wholes are fundamental substances and are metaphysically prior to their wholes.

In addition to **Minimal Fundamental Mereology**, proponents of Priority Monism go on to affirm the existence and fundamentality of the cosmos as a substance that is prior to each of its parts, all of the latter of which are derivative aggregates in virtue of being parts of the cosmos (i.e., in virtue of satisfying clause (ii)).

Proponents of Priority Macrophysicalism, by contrast, claim that the extension of "substance" is reserved exclusively for the class of intermediate composite objects; all other objects are classified as aggregates and thus derivative in virtue of being posterior to either their substantial parts (clause i), or to the composite substance of which they are a part (clause ii).

Finally, Priority Microphysicalism (PM) opts instead for a plurality of microphysical substances that are prior to each of the composite objects they compose, the latter being derivative aggregates in virtue of being posterior to their microphysical proper parts (i.e., in virtue of satisfying clause (i)). Consequently, what distinguishes the aforementioned fundamental mereologies from one another is the substantive metaphysical question of which wholes exist and belong in the extension of "substance" and "aggregate."

On this taxonomy, it is clear that both Priority Monism and Priority Macrophysicalism are variants of a Whole-Priority fundamental mereology; both views take wholes per se to be prior to their parts and thus composed of only inseparable parts. Where Priority Monism and Priority Macrophysicalism principally differ is not with respect to *whether* wholes are prior to their proper parts but rather *which* wholes exist and are fundamental (and perhaps which formal theory of parts and wholes one adopts more broadly); what cuts the divide between these two views involves wider formal and ontological commitments, in particular, the existence and fundamentality of either the maximal sum of classical mereology or medium-sized, macrophysical objects. The point deserves underscoring: for the proponent of a non-monistic version of Whole-Priority, the disassociation of Priority Monism and Whole-Priority is absolutely vital if they do not want their view to be rejected along with Priority Monism as a fundamental mereology.

To take stock, we have been concerned with shifting the locus of classification in fundamental mereology from the cosmos to mereological wholes *per se* in order to make room for the possibility of fundamental intermediate objects (i.e. those composite objects that occupy a lower level of decomposition than the cosmos but one that is higher than the atoms) that are prior to their proper parts. Toward this aim, we introduced the question of *the DG*, which thereby generated two general positions in fundamental mereology—Whole-Priority and Part-Priority—which were intended to supplant Schaffer's characterization of fundamental mereology in terms of Monism and Pluralism, respectively. We then introduced **Minimal Fundamental Mereology** as a non-uniform answer to DG in which the grounding structure of composite objects is specified in terms of the category, type, or kind of composite object in question. I offered **Minimal Fundamental Mereology** as the minimal core to which all fundamental mereologies are committed, irrespective of additional formal and ontological commitments. We then examined the following species of these two general answers to the direction of grounding: **Priority Monism, Priority Macrophysicalism, and PM.**[42]

3.4 Substantial Priority

The reformulation of the core of fundamental mereology in terms of **Minimal Fundamental Mereology** opens up the possibility of a mixed view concerning the mereological level at which the fundamental substances reside. As stated, Priority Monism, Priority Macrophysicalism, and PM are differentiated not merely in terms of Whole-Priority and Part-Priority and by additional formal and ontological commitments, but also by the *level of the mereological hierarchy at which the fundamental entities exclusively reside*.

What differentiates Priority Microphysicalism and Priority Macrophysicalism, for instance, is that the latter takes the metaphysically fundamental beings to *exclusively* occupy the intermediate level of the hierarchy of composition, the former the atomic level. But this requires, rather implausibly in my opinion, that the fundamental entities must be *either* (exclusively) medium-sized *or* maximally small. On the surface, this seems needlessly restrictive as nothing demands that we take the fundamental entities to exhibit such uniformity regarding their level of occupation on the mereological hierarchy. Unless we are given reason to think otherwise, we should allow for the possibility that the fundamental entities occupy a multiplicity of levels on the mereological hierarchy, as long as this remains consistent with the tiling constraint as per **No Fundamental Parthood.**[43]

The fundamental mereology I aim to defend in this book builds on **Minimal Fundamental Mereology** by affirming the existence of at least some intermediate fundamental substances. I call this view "Substantial Priority:"

> **Substantial Priority**: There are intermediate composite objects in the category of *substance*.

Substantial Priority stands in sharp contrast to the ubiquitous assumption among friends of fundamental mereology enshrined in *No Fundamental Intermediates*, that all intermediate composite objects are metaphysically derivative. According to Substantial Priority, at least some denizens of the class of ordinary material objects are metaphysically fundamental.[44]

While Substantial Priority is minimally committed to the fundamentality of at least some intermediate composite objects, it does not claim that *all* macrophysical objects are fundamental (as does Priority Macrophysicalism); not all such medium-sized composite objects fall within the extension of "substance." As with all fundamental mereologies that affirm **Minimal Fundamental Mereology**, Substantial Priority maintains that not all composite objects are created equal with respect to their metaphysical status; some are derivative and some are fundamental. In contrast to other views, however, Substantial Priority maintains that some *intermediate* composite objects in particular carve nature at its fundamental joints more closely than others. Some intermediates fall under the extension "aggregate," and others under the extension "substance."

Those with traditional neo-Aristotelian sympathies, for example, might think that living organisms are fundamental substances, composite objects that lack fundamental proper parts along the lines of **No Fundamental Parthood**, yet think that ping-pong tables and automobiles are derivative grounded wholes in so far as they are totally or partially grounded in their fundamental atomic parts and the relations between them. Fundamental and derivative intermediate objects are, on this view, distinct categories of object that are governed by distinct grounding relations with respect to their proper parts.

Moreover, Substantial Priority allows for the possibility of a mixed view in which the fundamental substances are scattered across both the intermediate and atomic mereological levels. The only constraint here is that such a mixed view must adhere to the tiling constraint, in particular **No Fundamental Parthood**. It may turn out that, in light of metaphysical and empirical considerations, that the composite objects within the extension of "substance" reside at multiple mereological levels. In allowing for a mixed view, the proponent of Substantial Priority must offer an account as to *how* fundamental substances can reside at multiple mereological levels without standing in part-whole relations to one another. I take up this task in the final chapter when I consider objections to Substantial Priority.

Given the tiling constraint, Substantial Priority entails the falsity of Priority Monism and PM; if even a proper subset of the set of intermediate composites fall under the category of *substance*, then neither the cosmos nor the proper parts that compose intermediate substances are fundamental substances in their own right given the tiling constraint. While Substantial Priority rules out the fundamentality of the cosmos, it is entirely compatible with the existence of the cosmos qua aggregate or derivative composite. In addition, Substantial Priority entails that Priority Microphsyicalism as a *global* fundamental mereology is mistaken; if some intermediates are fundamental substances, then microphysical reality does not exhaustively ground all macrophysical reality.

But how exactly are we to gloss the notion of substance at the heart of **Minimal Fundamental Mereology** and **Substantial Priority**? The question of the criteria for substantiality is well-traveled and I certainly don't intend to say anything new on the matter here. I do, however, want to underscore in particular the importance of unity considerations when it comes to delineating fundamental substances from derivative aggregates.

Borrowing from Gorman (2006), Lowe (2010), and Toner (2010), I propose the following necessary conditions for the concept of a substance in terms of ungroundedness and unity:

> **Substance:** x is a *substance* only if (a) there is no y such that (i) y is concrete, (ii) y is not identical with x, (iii) x is (essentially$_I$) grounded in y and (b) x is unified in the right kind of way.[45]

Clause (a) of **Substance** employs the notion of essential$_I$ grounding as explicated in chapter 2 in order to capture a vital aspect of the metaphysical fundamentality of substances; the real definitions of substances are not derived from the real definition of any distinct concrete entity (or collection of entities). *Which* entity a particular substance is not fixed by any distinct concrete thing. It is the fundamentality of substances per se (whether complex or simple) that is captured by Schaffer's notion of **Covering** as per the tiling constraint. As constituting the metaphysical foundation of the domain of the compositional hierarchy, substances are complete for that domain in that they collectively provide a grounding base for it; all derivative entities on the hierarchy are grounded in the substances.[46] Substances, on this reading, are metaphysically prior to aggregates precisely *because* they serve as their grounds and are themselves ungrounded entities—i.e., their natures are fundamental or primary. In contrast to existential and essential$_E$ grounding, the asymmetry of essential$_I$ grounding is aptly suited to capture the ontological *priority* of substances which has traditionally been at the heart of the notion of substance.

Clause (a) states that there is no distinct concrete entity in which a substance is grounded. This might seem problematic for classical theists who have traditionally ascribed to God alone the status of being absolutely ungrounded in the respective sense (the only *absolutely* fundamental being). The theist, however, can take one of the following routes.

First, theists might affirm clause (a) in an unqualified sense and claim that it holds even for those who think that God creates, conserves, and sustains the existence of every distinct entity whatsoever (or perhaps every distinct concrete entity). While every (concrete) entity that is not identical to God is rigidly essentially$_E$ grounded in God's creative activity, they might argue that this does not imply that every entity is therefore essentially$_I$ grounded in God's creative causal power. While it may be part of the essence of all concrete substances (other than God) that they depend for their moment-by-moment existence on the sustaining power of God, on this view, arguably *what* they are fundamentally as expressed by their real definition and *which* thing of their kind they are need not make reference to the existence and sustaining power of God.[47]

Alternatively, the theist might consider restricting the scope of **Substance** to either (i) *created* substances in general or (ii) concrete entities on the hierarchy of composition in particular (see §1.2 above), and thus add to clause (a) further qualifying conditions (e.g., y is not a creature). On this theistic route, the fundamental substances in purview in **Substance** ought to be characterized in terms of (qualified) absolute fundamentality—i.e., absolutely fundamental with respect to all other created concrete entities on the compositional hierarchy.

While the identity of the composite substance might fail to be (essentially$_I$) grounded in any of its proper parts in particular, its existence may be *generically* grounded in its parts, whether existentially or essentially$_E$ (see Chapter 2, §2). Suppose that the *ps* are the actual parts that compose x at t; if we were to take a snapshot of the mereological structure of x at t we would find all and only the *ps* among the proper parts of x. It is true to say of x that it is generically essentially$_E$ grounded in the *ps*, since it is part of the essence of x that it exists only if *some parts composing it exist at t* exist, and the *ps* are, as a matter of fact, the parts that compose x at t. But it is also true that x is not rigidly existentially or essentially$_E$ grounded in any one p among *ps* nor in the *ps* in particular; it is part of the nature of x that it exist and be composed of an entirely different set of parts at t, say the *qs*.

Accordingly, clause (a) of **Substance** implies that a composite substance fails to be rigidly existentially as well as rigidly essentially$_E$ grounded in anything, including its proper parts. Yet it is widespread among those with neo-Aristotelian sympathies to find a definition of substance as a metaphysically fundamental or independent entity to include an exception clause for its being rigidly grounded in or dependent on its proper parts (if it has any). Fine (1995), for instance, notes "A substance may be taken to be anything that does not depend upon anything else *or, at least, upon anything other than its parts*."[48] In like manner, Simons (1998: 236) states,

> The ontological primacy of substances arises chiefly from their independence, or ability to subsist alone ... An object is independent in the corresponding sense when it depends on nothing apart from itself *and*

perhaps parts of itself, giving a sense to the idea of something depending on nothing "outside itself".[49]

Lastly, Gorman (2006) includes the following exception clause for proper parts in his definition of substance, where x is a substance such that there is no particular y such that "y is not one of x's proper parts and the identity of x depends on the identity of y."

But if complex substances are truly metaphysically fundamental, then the inclusion of the aforementioned exception clauses for the proper parts of substances seems misplaced.[50] As Robb (2009) has aptly pointed out, "[i]f something exists because its parts do, then it's not basic, doesn't exist in its own right. This premise also seems to be self-evident." No object is identical with any of its (proper) parts, and so if an object exists because its individual parts exist, it is parasitic on something else and therefore not a substance. On the assumption that composite objects are numerically distinct from their proper parts, I am inclined to think that any definition of the notion of substance in terms of ontological independence or metaphysical fundamentality ought to say that substances fail to be essentially$_I$ grounded (which entails the failure of both rigid existential and rigid essential$_E$ grounding) in any distinct entity *tout court*, including their proper parts.

At this point, neo-Aristotelians who endorse a version of a hylomorphic ontology of material objects—minimally the view material objects are compounds of matter (*hyle*) and form (*morphe*)—will retort that clause (a) of **Substance** conflicts with the fact that a composite substance is (rigidly) grounded in its form and matter for what it is fundamentally.[51] This is an important point for those who favor a version of hylomorphism who might be attracted to Substantial Priority.

I admit that the heavyweight notion of metaphysical fundamentality expressed in clause (a) of **Substance** does indeed lead away from the view that composite substances are grounded in their form and matter as (concrete) elements of the compound. However, I do think a weaker sense of the fundamentality of composite substances can be preserved for the proponent of hylomorphism who favors Substantial Priority. Following the lead of some neo-Aristotelians, this would involve distinguishing between the relation of *parthood* and the sui-generis relation of *constituency*.[52] As the only elements of the substantial compound that factor into its real definition and determines the identity of the compound, form and matter are constituents and not, strictly speaking, proper parts of the hylomorphic compound. There does indeed seem to be an intuitive (albeit hard to define) difference between the relations that obtain between a living organism and its proper parts (e.g., atoms, cells, organs) and that between an organism and its metaphysical constituents (substantial form and prime matter) that factor into its real definition.

If this route is taken, the proponent of a hylomorphic ontology would need to include an additional item in clause (a) of **Substance** that would allow hylomorphic compounds to be grounded in their (concrete) formal and material constituents.[53] And since Substantial Priority is principally a claim about the existence of fundamental intermediate substances and the grounding relations that obtain between substances and their proper parts in particular (as per **No Fundamental Parthood**), the exclusion clause for formal and material constituents allows one to endorse Substantial Priority and its accompanying theoretical benefits.

This brings us to clause (b) of **Substance.** In contrast to the foregoing neo-Aristotelians who maintain that the fundamentality of substances is compatible with their being rigidly grounded—whether existentially or essentially—in their proper parts (if they exhibit mereological structure at all), Lowe (2012) maintains that composite substances are neither rigidly existentially nor rigidly essentially grounded as such. For Lowe, the identity of composite substances such as living organisms fail to be grounded in *any* distinct thing, including their proper parts. While I am in wholehearted agreement with Lowe that the metaphysical fundamentality of substances is rightly captured by their failing to be grounded in *any* distinct thing whatsoever (including their proper parts), we differ as to whether the fundamentality of substances is exhausted by clause (a) of **Substance** noted earlier.

In contrast to Lowe, I consider the fundamentality of substances to be inextricably tied to not only their being ungrounded as in (a), but also to their exhibiting a high degree of unity as stated in (b) earlier. But how exactly we unpack the unity involved in (b) is a difficult matter that has been at the heart of the debate concerning the definition of substance throughout the history of Western philosophy. The view that I take to be at the heart of Substantial Priority and one that I will be defending in the course of this essay, which has a rich historical precedent and finds a handful of contemporary defender, is that a substance's being "unified in the right kind of way" involves its lacking *separable parts* (see above) and thus adhering to **No Fundamental Parthood**.[54]

We must proceed with caution at this point as the preceding claim is liable to misrepresentation. There are two distinct ways a composite object might lack separable parts: either by (i) lacking proper parts altogether or (ii) having only proper parts that are *inseparable*. The unity clause as understood in terms of lacking separable parts is satisfied by both simple substances (if there are any) in so far as they conform to (i) as well as composite substances in so far as they adhere to (ii).

More specifically, on the view that I am recommending here, substances are not only the terminus of grounding relations, they also place certain grounding constraints on their proper parts (if they have any). The unity that is said to characterize a substantial whole as per clause (b) is precisely one that stems from its serving as the essential ground for each of its proper parts. The proper parts of substances are, to borrow an apt phrase from Verity Harte (2002: 165) employed in the context of Plato's view of wholes, "structure-laden" in that "they get their identity

102   Fundamental Mereology

only in the context of the structure of which they are part." In contrast to Lowe, I am inclined to think that the notion of fundamentality undergirding the concept of substance suggests that substances are not only *complete* but *minimally complete*, where a set S of entities is minimally complete for a domain D iff (i) S is complete for D, and (ii) no proper subset of S is complete for D. Substances—whether simple or complex—fail to have a proper sub-plurality that are themselves basic or fundamental. As a result, both clauses (a) and (b) of **Substance** aim to explicate the defining feature of a substance qua metaphysically fundamental or non-derivative entity.

The earlier conception of a composite substance as one that exhibits a grounding ordering over its proper parts (as per (b)) whereby the parts are "structure-laden" gives us a way to account for the deep difference between fundamental substances and derivative aggregates.[55] Let us distinguish between what I will henceforth call *grounding wholes* and *grounded wholes*, the former corresponding to (composite) substances and the latter to aggregates. Using "O" to signify (actual) concrete objects, we can state this a bit more precisely as follows:

Grounding Whole: x is a *grounding whole* $=_{def}$
$(\exists y)(Oy \land y < x \land (\forall z)(z < x \to \Box_z(z \rhd_t x)))$

Grounded Whole: x is a *grounded whole* $=_{def}$
$(\exists y)(Oy \land y < x \land (\exists z)(z < x \to \Box_x(x \rhd z)))$[56]

In words, x is a *grounding whole* just in case there is at least one individual object that is a proper part of x, and every proper part of x is such that it is (totally) grounded in x. On the other hand, x is a *grounded whole* if and only if there is at least one individual object that is a proper part of x, and there is at least one proper part of x such that x is grounded in it.[57]

It should be emphasized that I take the earlier grounding descriptions to apply to the *individual* or *objectual* proper parts of grounding and grounded wholes—i.e., those parts that belong to the category of *object*, *thing*, or *individual* (I use these interchangeably in what follows). Here I help myself to the fundamental distinction between an entity that is structured in a particular manner—what I refer to as an "individual" or "object"—and that which is structured to make an individual or object—what I refer to as "stuff."[58] More specifically, by "object" here I simply mean an entity that has both determinate identity conditions as well as determinate countability.[59] It is part of the nature of entities belonging to the category *object* that if x and y are both objects, then there must be a fact of the matter as to whether $x = y$. The determinate countability of objects stems from their being intrinsically unified or structured—x's being determinately countable obtains in virtue of its being *one* thing, a singular unit of being in contrast to a plurality. While all substances are objects in so far as they have determine identity conditions and they are intrinsically unified, not all objects are substances (grounded wholes being an example of a non-substantial object). When I henceforth speak of the proper parts of a composite object in the sequel I mean those proper parts that are objects or individuals in the sense specified earlier.

As a grounding whole, a substance not only fails to be grounded in any distinct entity, it is also metaphysically prior to its proper parts in so far as it serves as their total ground. As a result, grounding wholes are governed by Schaffer's **No Fundamental Parthood** constraint on fundamental entities in that they lack substantial or basic proper parts. A grounding whole is unified to the highest degree in virtue of being composed of all and only grounded or dependent parts (i.e. inseparable), parts whose existence and identity are defined in terms of the particular whole of which they are a part.

Grounded wholes are non-substantial composite objects and thus exhibit a much weaker kind of unity in so far as they are composed of separable parts. In reference to the Part-Priority fundamental mereology of many of the early modern philosophers (in the form of what he calls "the actual parts doctrine"), Thomas Holden (2004: 150) draws out the traditional difference between grounding and grounded wholes as follows:

> The actual parts doctrine states that the parts of bodies are each fully-fledged distinct entities. This implies that the whole gross extended body is a composite or compound entity: a structured aggregate of these pre-existing, independently existing parts. Since each actual part is a distinct entity, the whole must be conceptualized as a composite structure, a compound built up from ontologically prior concrete elements . . . A second important corollary is sometimes thought to follow from this first point. Since extended entities constructed from actual parts are aggregates, they fail to meet two traditional criteria for substancehood. First, as aggregates, their existence is a derivative one, depending on the ontologically prior existence of their parts . . . Second, as aggregates, bodies lack the unity typically required for substancehood. Thus those who follow through the actual parts view to this corollary will deny that material bodies are substances in full metaphysical rigor: at best they are collections of substances . . . in Leibniz's phrase "substantiata," "of-substances."
>
> (Holden 2004: 150)

Some will no doubt object that requiring substances to be unified in such a way as to be either mereologically simple or be composed of only inseparable parts as much too restrictive. What arguments might be offered in favor of such a radical view? In the sequel I'll argue that the aforementioned notion of a substance as a fundamental entity lacking separable proper

104 Fundamental Mereology

parts is both scientifically serious as well as philosophically fruitful in its ability to dissolve a host of puzzle in contemporary metaphysics. However, in addition to this line of thinking in the sequel, it might be helpful at this point to consider several historical and contemporary considerations in favor of substances as grounding wholes.

We can do no better than begin with an interpretation of Aristotle's own unity constraint on substantial wholes. As noted by Theodore Scaltsas (1994), one particular interpretation of Aristotle's account of the unified nature of substances is aptly described as "substantial holism." Scaltsas remarks,

> This is Aristotle's way of establishing that a substance is not a cluster of copresent (even interrelated) components, but a single, unified whole. The form unifies the components of a substance, not by relating them (which would leave their distinctness in tact), but by *reidentifying* them, that is, by making them identity-dependent on the whole. It is not *relation* that unites, but the *identity dependence* of the constituents on the whole, in accordance with the principle of form.
>
> (1994: 3)

Aristotle's substantial holism sheds light on his well-known "homonymy principle:" that a severed hand and an eye that cannot see is a "hand" and an "eye" in name only. In his own words, "For they [the parts of a whole] cannot even exist if severed from the whole; for it is not a finger in any and every state that is the finger of a living thing, but a dead finger is a finger only in name."[60] Aristotle's principle reason for endorsing substantial holism stems from his desire to safeguard the unity of fundamental wholes: a substance's having a *plurality* of substantial parts would undermine its being a *single* fundamental entity.

Many of Aristotle's medieval interpreters, most notably Thomas Aquinas, followed suit in thinking that a substance's being composed of a plurality of distinct substances would compromise the intrinsic (*per se*) unity of the substance. The rather lively scholastic debate concerning the unicity or plurality of substantial forms in a substance was one that dominated the medieval metaphysical landscape. Citing one common argument for the unicity of substantial form (what I am calling **No Fundamental Parthood**), Duns Scotus remarks (without endorsing),

> Substance understood as one of the [ten] most general categories, is an *ens per se*. No part of a substance is an *ens per se* when it is part of a substance, because then it would be a particular thing (*hoc aliquid*), and one substance would be a particular thing from many particular things, which does not seem true.[61]

Aquinas, following Aristotle, took considerations of unity to be at the heart of what it means for a substance to be fundamental (or "complete in its species" as he would put it). Generally, Aquinas considered composition as a type of unifying relation such that if the *xs* compose *y* then *y* is unified to a certain degree.[62] As a *single* composite object, a mereological whole can be either "one thing" *simpliciter (per se)* or "one thing" *secundum quid (per accidens)*, what we might think of as roughly either an intrinsically or extrinsically unified concrete object. Along these lines, he states,

> One thing *simpliciter* is produced out of many actually existing things only if there is something uniting and in some way tying them to each other. In this way, then, if Socrates were an animal and were rational in virtue of different forms, then these two, in order to be united simpliciter, would need something to make them one. Therefore, since nothing is available to do this, the result will be that a human being is one thing only as an aggregate, like a heap, which is one thing *secundum quid* and many things *simpliciter*.[63]

Here Aquinas states that since the intrinsic unity of a substance requires the existence of a unifying relation or relations, and since there is no such relation that grounds the fact that *animality* and *rationality* are substantial forms of a *single* substance as opposed to two numerically distinct substances that are related to each other, Socrates is therefore fundamentally a "many" and a "one" only in a secondary or derivative sense.

But as Lowe (2012) has pointed out, the earlier Aristotelian line of reasoning in favor of **No Fundamental Parthood** conflates the *composition* relation with the relation of *identity*.[64] Lowe argues, rightly in my opinion, that the plurality at play in the case at hand is to be attributed not to Socrates but to his proper parts. Though the proper parts of Socrates are many, Socrates himself is a *single* unified whole. If Socrates were *identical* to his proper parts, then he would be a plurality in virtue of being identical to a plurality of proper parts. If composition is not identity, however, then a substances' being composed of a plurality of substantial proper parts does not compromise the intrinsic unity of the substance itself.

While I grant Lowe's point in general, I am inclined to think the earlier Aristotelian line can be salvaged. By my lights, Lowe fails to appreciate the fact that composition is a type of generative or "building" operation, which presumably explains why its application gives rise to a numerically distinct entity.[65] While composite objects are numerically distinct from their many proper parts, they do not merely *contain* such parts as a region of spacetime contains a material object; rather it is natural to think that composite objects are *constructed* or *generated* from their parts.

An entities' being the product of a generative operation is fairly easy to see in the case of the construction of a set, where the set $\{x, y, z\}$ is the result of the application of the *set-builder* operation S on x, y, and z. Intuitively, it is precisely *because* the objects from which $\{x, y, z\}$ is generated remain essentially *as such* after the application of S that we commonly take them to be more fundamental than the set itself; the existence and identity of the item constructed is grounded in the entities from which it is constructed. Similarly, consider the generation of a mereological sum or fusion as on classical mereology, where fusion f with x_1, x_2, x_3 as proper parts is the product of the application of the fusion operation O on x_1, x_2, x_3. As with sets, the entities over which O is applied remain *as such* after F is generated or constructed, which again plausibly explains *why* many are apt to think fusions are grounded in their parts, that the parts of fusions are more metaphysically fundamental even though the axioms of classical mereology *per se* are entirely non-modal.[66]

Consider, then, a substantial whole w and the two proper parts a and b from which it is generated by means of applying the *substantial composition* operation C.[67] Quite simply: w is the result of applying C to a and b. But here is where I think the Aristotelian intuition gets its traction: if substantial composition is generative in that it gives rise to a distinct entity w by means of C, and were a and b to remain essentially unaltered after the generation of w, it is difficult to see how w could fail to be *what it is* in virtue of a and b, and thus derivative on its proper parts.[68] That is, it is natural indeed to think that if that from which a substance is generated (a and b) continues to exist *as such* as part of its compositional base (whether such parts are substantial or non-substantial), that the substance would thereby be *dependent* on these objects for its fundamental identity and hence fail to be a substance in so far as it fails to satisfy clause (a) of **Substance**. This, I submit, is *precisely* what underlies the widespread adherence to the view that parts are ontologically prior to their wholes (Part-Priority).

The Aristotelian intuition states that the substantial whole will remain grounded in the objects from which it is generated unless such objects are essentially altered upon the generation of the substance. On the natural assumption that composition is a generative operation, those with neo-Aristotelian sympathies who are keen to retain a robust account of the fundamentality of substances is faced with the following dilemma: either (i) substances are not robustly fundamental entities in so far as they are grounded in (and thus posterior to) the numerically distinct objects from which they are generated, or (ii) the objects from which a substantial whole is generated are essentially altered upon composition and are now grounded in the whole. The second horn (ii) is consistent with the objects either ceasing to exist full stop upon the generation of a substance, or their coming to have a different nature subsequent to their generating a substance.[69]

On one standard interpretation of Aquinas's mereology, he opts for (ii). In contemporary parlance, his view is that the priority of substances with respect to their parts demands not only their completeness but rather their minimal completeness in that they serve to ground each of their proper parts. This interpretation of Aquinas, as well as the views of his teacher Albert the Great, is offered by Calvin Normore (2006: 740–741) concerning the question of "whether a substance could be composed of items which had a claim to themselves be substances:"

> On these issues Albertus Magnus and his protege Thomas Aquinas had taken a radical stand. They insisted that in a composite substance there were no parts, integral or essential, which were ontologically prior to the substance. A composite substance, an animal, for example, comes to be out of other substances; but only the prime matter of that out of which it comes to be remains in the new substance, and that prime matter has no existence of its own . . . Moreover, while a composite substance always has integral parts—hands, blood vessels, and the like—these parts are themselves ontologically dependent on the substance: a severed hand is only homonymously a hand, and once severed, a hand is no longer a thing of the kind it was—indeed is likely no longer one thing at all.

Consider Aquinas in his own words:

> A substantial form perfects not only the whole, but each part. *For since the whole is made up of its parts*, a form of the whole that does not give existence to the individual parts of the body is a form that is a composition and ordering (the form of a house, for example), and such a form is accidental.[70]

Of course, the earlier considerations do not amount to an argument in favor of the Aristotelian intuition, which is precisely why I persist in calling it an intuition. Other than putting on display the theoretical utility of such a view (which will be the focus of Chapters 5, 6, and 7), I do not know of any straightforward philosophical argument that one might offer in its favor, either. Be that as it may, I think the Aristotelian intuition noted earlier is both intuitively plausible and is (as we will see in Chapter 4) consistent with our empirical theories concerning the actual structure of wholes and their parts across multiple empirical domains.

In addition to the aforementioned considerations involving the generative nature of composition, John Heil (2012) has argued that substances fail to have other substances as proper parts on the grounds that the primary role of substances qua property bearers requires it. Property-possession, for Heil, requires the right sort of metaphysical underpinning: bearers of properties must be *singular* units of being and thus sufficiently *unified*. Since objects that have substances as proper parts are, according to Heil, pluralities or complexes of substances that stand in relations to one another, they are unfit to bear properties according to Heil. With the tradition role of substances as being primary property bearers in hand, **No Fundamental Parthood** follows quite naturally. Since Heil takes complex objects such as tables, turnips, and spires as being ultimately composed of substances (particles), such ordinary macrophysical objects are rendered non-substantial and thereby fail to be property bearers (they are, he claims, "quasi-substances," substances by courtesy, and their properties "quasi-properties").

Turning now to Schaffer's own considerations for favoring **No Fundamental Parthood**, he offers two primary reasons to endorse this traditional Aristotelian insight. The first states that the substances—as fundamental units of being—must be modally unconstrained in their relation to one another. To illustrate, consider two substances x and y, where x is a proper part of y and both of which are characterized by the intrinsic property F. For our purposes here, assume also that x is the only proper part of y that bears F. In virtue of x being a proper part of y, x and y share a common part, in this case x (where x is an improper part of itself and y has x as a proper part). Now suppose it to be the case that x undergoes intrinsic alteration and ceases to be F. It follows, in virtue of their overlap, that y would thereby cease to be F as well. More generally, x and y would be modally constrained such that "it is not possible to vary the intrinsic properties of the common part with respect to the one overlapping thing, without varying the intrinsic properties or composition of the other (ibid.)." Consequently, in so far as substances would be modally constrained were they to exhibit mereological overlap, they cannot stand in part-whole relations to one another.

The second argument hinges on considerations in ontological economy: since one should not multiply fundamental substances beyond necessity, and that since substances which stand in part-whole relations are redundant, it follows that substances fail to stand in part-whole relations to one another. The first premise is uncontroversial in so far as most would grant the truth of its weaker cousin that one ought not multiply entities without necessity; its plausible that such a principle applies all the more to *fundamental* entities. The second premise—that basics related by means of part-whole relations are redundant—relies on the notion that the duplication of the whole entails the duplication of all of its proper parts and thus "adding the parts contributes nothing new to the characterization of reality already provided by the whole."[71] Schaffer gives the example of Socrates having the property of *being snub nosed* intrinsically. Any intrinsic duplicate of Socrates as a whole will (must) have a snub nose as a proper part. In the same manner, any intrinsic duplicate of a substantial whole will suffice to duplicate all of its proper parts and their intrinsic properties and relations. If the duplication of the whole automatically secures the existence and intrinsic properties of its proper parts, then to maintain that the proper parts of substances are substances in their own right would be to multiply substances beyond necessity.

Whether or not the previously mentioned arguments in favor of **No Fundamental Parthood** are ultimately persuasive is not my immediate concern at this point (I myself am not in full agreement with all of them). While I consider **No Fundamental Parthood** to be a reasonable constraint that ought to guide the project of fundamental mereology, the primary aim of this essay is to defend Substantial Priority as a *particular* application of this enduring piece of philosophical wisdom. It is to this task that I now turn.

Notes

1. I henceforth assume that while abstract objects (if there are any) can stand in mereological relations, the mereological hierarchy consists solely of *concrete* entities standing in part-whole relations.
2. For a few proponents see Cameron (2008), Kim (1993, 1998), Markosian (2005), Oppenheim and Putnam (1958), Paseau (2010), Schaffer (2003).
3. See Markosian (2005) and Schaffer (2003: 498).
4. In particular, see Kim (1998), Oppenheim and Putnam (1958), and Schaffer (2003).
5. See also Simons (2004: 373).
6. Of course, one *need* not endorse such a view of the interrelationship between grounding and essence to take up the task of fundamental mereology going forward.
7. Consider Hütteman (2004: 10) on microphysicalism, "Microphysicalism provides a decisive interpretation of the multilayered conception of reality. The properties on the macro-level—i.e., the properties of biological and neurophysiological systems or systems with mental states, are completely determined by microphysical properties. The microphysical laws govern the macro-systems. The causal relations among the macro-systems turn out to derive from those on the micro-level. Microphysicalism thus provides on ontological interpretation of the hierarchical structure of the many layers of reality."
8. See Pearce (forthcoming, 2018) for a theistic account of God's relationship to concrete material reality in terms of grounding.
9. For a sampling of those that gloss a metaphysically fundamental layer of reality in terms of ontological independence see Cameron (2008) and Paseau (2010).
10. See also Murphy (2007) for another example.
11. Kim (1993) hints at the intersection of mereological and metaphysical structure when he states, "One interesting application of the supervenience concept is mereological supervenience, the doctrine that the character of a whole is supervenient on the properties and relationships holding for its parts. This apparently calls for two distinct domains: one domain consisting of wholes and another consisting of their parts. It would be of interest to know how a dependency relation can be formulated across two domains."
12. The contemporary locus classicus here in favor of a strong reading of composition as identity is Donald Baxter (1988).
13. For more on this line see McDaniel (2008).
14. I've changed Schaffer's "**No Parthood**" to "**No Fundamental Parthood**" as I think the latter better captures the view in question. Also, it is worth pointing out that Schaffer initially relies on a much stronger thesis he calls NO OVERLAP: $(\forall x)(\forall y)((Fx \land Fy \land x \neq y) \rightarrow \neg(\exists z)(z < x \land z < y))$, but later weakens this to **No Fundamental Parthood** as explicated earlier.
15. Example: one might simply say that while the basics *collectively* provide a grounding base for w, this does not entail that there is some *one* thing that is the sum of the basics which plays this role. One might say that it is the *Plural Duplication* of all of the basic entities (with their basic relations) that suffices to duplicate the entire cosmos.

16. Thus, Morganti (2009: 276) misconstrues Schaffer's tiling constraint to include the following: "Schaffer's tiling constraint and the view that composition is not identity will not be questioned. First, it is very plausible that basic entities are simple, and so cannot overlap or share parts."
17. See section III titled "Ancient Structure-Based Mereologies" in Koslicki (2008) for a nice overview of the notion in the metaphysics of Plato and Aristotle.
18. Note that on Schaffer's view, even the universe's being *partially* grounded in one of its proper parts renders it non-fundamental or derivative.
19. Although we have already seen that the mereological hierarchy does not require an atomic gloss and is entirely consistent with either a gunky or a non-atomic mereology.
20. At their core, Monism and Atomism are minimally committed to the view that every concrete entity is either grounded in U or in x, y, z respectively. Strictly speaking, the views are neutral as to the dependence ordering that obtains between the non-fundamental or derivative objects—i.e., r, s, t and x, y, z on Monism and U and r, s, t on Atomism. My explication of Monism and Atomism here are what I take to be the most thematic formulations of these positions.
21. Strictly speaking, Schaffer's view is called "Priority Monism" but since I am considering options in fundamental mereology (where the notion of priority and posteriority are already being assumed), I use "Monism" for short.
22. The addition of U to the formulation of **Intermediate** will obviously depend on whether one countenances the universe U of classical extensional mereology qua composite individual. For reservations, see Simons (2003: 249).
23. He states, "Monism is equivalent to the thesis that every proper part of the cosmos depends on the cosmos."
24. Cameron (2010a) expresses something similar when he says, "A sum is ontologically dependent on its parts, if priority pluralism is true—and vice-versa if priority monism is true . . . " Here again we see the wedding of Part-Priority with Pluralism and Whole-Priority with Monism.
25. Schaffer (2010b: 66).
26. I follow Koslicki (2008: 171), "Thus, mereology, on this conception, does not settle matters of ontological commitment; rather, it presupposes them to be resolved elsewhere within metaphysics or outside of philosophy altogether."
27. Think here of the many adherents of the view throughout the span of the Aristotelian tradition in Western philosophy.
28. Here it is important to note that my concern here is not to argue that the cosmos is not a whole in its own right (and thereby undermine Priority Monism). Rather, it is strictly methodological in showing that Schaffer's chosen characterization of fundamental mereology is far from exhaustive.
29. Consider an example of a non-monistic endorsement of Whole-Priority (WP$_b$) in the recent work of Kit Fine (2010). Fine takes there to be what he calls "generative operations"—operations the application of which are identity-explaining—that proceed from whole to part and not vice versa. He remarks, "[I]t seems to me that some basic generative operations are in fact *de*-compositional. Far from serving to account for the identity of the whole in terms of its parts, they serve to account for the parts in terms of the whole."
30. Other representatives of this ubiquitous assumption among contemporary metaphysicians are Ross Cameron (2010a), Louis deRosset (2010), and Jonathan Tallant (2013). deRosset (2010) has stated that a fundamental mereology (what he calls a "priority theory") is best captured by the conjunction of three theses, one of which is "Explanation," which states, "The existence and features of the macroscopic concrete objects alleged by common sense abetted by science can be completely explained solely by reference to the existence

and properties of other things." Instead of simply assuming the untenebilty of fundamental intermediates (as does deRosset), Tallant (2013) and Schaffer provide several arguments against the existence of fundamental intermediate objects. I evaluate Tallant's and Schaffer's objections to fundamental intermediates in Chapter 8.
31. Schaffer (2010b) argues that fundamental mereologies are theses about "the laws of metaphysics"—i.e., laws that govern what depends on what, concerning the dependence ordering of the part-whole structure of reality.
32. For a sampling of the relevant histories here see Harte (2002), Koslicki (2008), and Scaltsas (1994) for ancient; Pasnau (2011: Chapters 25–26) for medieval; and Holden (2004) for early modern.
33. Recall from Chapter 2 that I am working with a notion of metaphysical grounding that I take to be suited to carve out relations of priority and posteriority— i.e., essential$_1$ grounding. Hereafter "grounding" for short.
34. Although o_2 and o_3 are complex objects as well and hence grounded in o_1.
35. Emphasis in original.
36. This feature of Part-Priority will, as we will see, serve to generate a disjunctive dilemma such that either the Part-Priority theorists rejects the well-foundedness of grounding (or supervenience) or the possibility of gunky worlds, neither of which seem plausible, therefore Part-Priority is suspect.
37. As we will see, for gunky worlds it follows on Part-Priority that grounding is non-well-founded.
38. For Plato, see Harte (2002) where she refers to the inseparability feature what I am calling inseparable parts as their being "structure-laden."
39. Consider the following representatives of this line of thinking: Lowe (2009: 94) states, "What I do think is that mereological sums and things like cats have different principles of composition, just as they have different criteria of identity, and that the principle of composition for mereological sums is simply that some things, the xs, have a mereological sum, y, just so long as the xs (all of them) exist. Hence, I maintain, if one or more of the xs ceases to exist, so does y. Things like cats have a much more complicated and interesting principle of composition." Further, Simons (1987: 324), "That the distinction between sums and non-sums—which we may call *complexes*—is an ontological one may be seen by comparing their existence conditions. For sums these are minimal: the sum exists just when all the constituent parts exist . . . By contrast, a complex constituted of the same parts as the sum only exists if a further constitutive condition is fulfilled." Lastly, Johnston (2006) states, "Each genuine kind of complex item will have associated with it a characteristic principle of unity; for arguably, it is sameness in principle of unity and kinds of parts than in turn qualifies the members of a given kind to be included in the complex whole that is the kind."
40. See Fine (1994c) and (2010: 585); Johnston (2006: 678), Lowe (2012), and Schaffer (2010: 47) in particular. Schaffer (2010: 47) remarks, "I think common sense distinguishes *mere aggregates* from *integrated wholes* . . . Common sense probably does endorse the priority of the parts in cases of mere aggregation, such as with the heap. Yet common sense probably endorses the priority of the whole in cases of integrated wholes, such as with the syllable."
41. **Minimal Fundamental Mereology**, as a broad classificatory schema, is meant to mirror what Simons (1987:31) calls "Minimal Extensional Mereology" in so far as it does not guarantee the existence of arbitrary sums (including the maximal sum) and thus "anything we can take as being too strong an assumption" (Simons 1987:31).

42. I take these to represent the most widely held fundamental mereologies in the Western tradition as well as the contemporary literature. I make no claim as to whether or not they exhaust the options.
43. Of course, if the cosmos is fundamental, then nothing else on the hierarchy is fundamental and, *ipso facto*, no fundamental occupies a level of decomposition lower than the cosmos. Thus, when I allow for the fundamentals to occupy a multiplicity of mereological levels as consistent with **No Fundamental Parthood**, my aim is to allow for some intermediate fundamental entity (a molecule, for example) that does not enter into the composition of a fundamental whole at a higher-level (whether or not there are such entities).
44. Substantial Priority bears a family resemblance to what Koons and Pickavance (2015:144–145) call "Compositional Pluralism", the view that "there exists at least one emergent [an object that is not a mere heap of its parts] and autonomous thing [a dependent fragment of some larger fundamental entity]." While Substantial Priority and Compositional Pluralism have much in common, there are important differences. Compositional Pluralism allows for (i) mutual grounding or determination between substance and their parts, and (ii) substances to have other substances as proper parts, i.e. denial of **No Fundamental Parthood**.
45. I assume here that substances are concrete in so far as I take them to be (at the very least) capable of persisting (although they need not in fact persist as with the possibility of substances that exist only for an instant and thus have zero temporal extant) and are the locus of fundamental causal powers. Both of these conditions, as I see it, exclude abstract objects from playing the role of substances, although I won't argue for this thesis here.
46. The traditional statement of this is found in Aristotle's *Categories* 2b6-7 (see 1984: 5): "So if the primary substances did not exist it would be impossible for any of the other things to exist."
47. Gorman (2006: 7) argues that this was Aquinas's view regarding the dependence of creatures on God. See Aquinas *ST* 1, q.44, a.1, ad. 1.
48. Emphasis mine.
49. Emphasis mine.
50. This is underscored by Toner (2010). See Koslicki (2013b) for discussion of the exclusion of proper parts from the definition of substance.
51. Koslicki (2013b). Also, Koons (2014) offers a partisan overview of what he calls "fainthearted" and "stalwart" versions of hylomorphism in the recent literature. Evnine (2016: 10) refers to these as "principle-based" and "powers-based" varieties of hylomorphism, respectively.
52. See Brown (2005), Oderberg (2008), and Rea (2011) for examples of this route. Along these lines, Oderberg (2008: 65–66) states, "Now substantial form is intrinsic since it is a constituent solely of the substance. It is a constituent because it is a real part or element of it, though not on the same level as a substance's natural parts such as the branch of a tree or the leg of a dog. Rather, substantial form is a radical or fundamental part of the substance in the sense of constituting it as the kind of substance it is."
53. An alternative route here would be to follow Koslicki (2013b) and drop clause (a) entirely and thus abandon the requirement that substances be metaphysically fundamental in the noted sense.
54. See Christopher Brown (2005), J.P. Moreland (2009), Schaffer (2010b), and Patrick Toner (2010).
55. My "substance" and "aggregate" here track Schaffer's (2010b: 347) "organic unity" and "mere heap." This, in fact, is the precise way that Aquinas (1947) distinguishes between substances and non-substances: "A substantial form

perfects not only the whole, but each part. For since the whole is made up of its parts, a form of the whole that does not give existence to the individual parts of the body is a form that is a composition and ordering (the form of a house, for example), and such a form is accidental. The soul, on the other hand, is a substantial form, and so it must be the form and actuality not only of the whole, but of each part" (*ST*, 1a.76.8c).

56. Where "▷" can denote either total or partial grounding depending on whether the grounding base for *x* is one or many.
57. While the grounding base for grounded wholes will more often than not be a multiplicity of items, this formulation allows for the possibility of a grounded whole being (totally) grounded in just a single proper part.
58. The question as to whether fundamental ontology can be accounted for using a thing, stuff, or a mixed ontology of both things and stuff is a matter of considerable debate in the literature.
59. See Lowe (1998) and (2006) in particular.
60. *Metaphysics* 1035b23–25, see his (1984b).
61. *In Praed.* 15.1 as cited in Pasnau (2011: 607–608).
62. See *ST* III, q. 90, a. 3, ad. 3 in particular.
63. Aquinas (1984: 11c.)
64. See also Harte (2002) for this same objection albeit applied to the general mereological insight among the ancients, what Harte calls "the pluralizing parts principle," that an object is just as many as its parts; objects are pluralized in virtue of their many parts.
65. See Fine (2010: 582), Paul (2012a), as well as Bennett (2011).
66. The assumption that fusions or mereological sums are grounded in their proper parts is widespread indeed, although there are some exceptions. For a more detailed discussion of the interplay between classical mereology and modality see Uzquiano (2014).
67. Here I presuppose for illustration that there are multiple composition operations each giving rise to distinct kinds of mereological wholes (although these operations need not be fundamental or basic). Or, at the very least, a distinction between the generative operations that govern substances and those that govern fusions or sums.
68. In Paul Humphrey's (1997) terminology, substantial composition is a type of "fusion operation" such that the entities over which it operates "no longer have an independent existence within the fusion" and "have been 'used up' in forming the fused property instance" (where he takes property-instances in particular to be the entities governed by the fusional operation). Interestingly enough, Humphreys acknowledges the shortcoming of his chosen label for such an operation, "[s]ince this paper was first drafted in 1991 I have realized that the term 'fusion' has a standard use in the mereological literature that is almost opposite to its use here."
69. See Koons (2014) for a very insightful discussion of the various ways in which items are changed when they enter into the composition of a fundamental substance.
70. *ST* 1.76.8c, emphasis mine.
71. Schaffer (2010b: 41).

4 Against Part-Priority

My aim in this chapter is to examine the predominant fundamental mereology on offer in the contemporary literature, Part-Priority, as expressed in its most popular guise, Priority Microphysicalism (PM). I begin by unpacking a few of the core tenets of PM in particular and then consider some of the lines of reasoning that have been advanced in its favor. I then set my sights on Part-Priority in general arguing that it is ill-suited to account for the metaphysical possibility of gunky worlds, worlds devoid of mereological simples. I then turn to considerations regarding the failure of whole-part supervenience within the domain of physics, chemistry, and biology with respect to both microphysical and macrophysical wholes, thereby taking aim at both Part-Priority and PM.[1]

4.1 Priority Microphysicalism

Arguably, the predominant fundamental mereology at work in contemporary metaphysics is PM:

> **(PM) Priority Microphysicalism:** The microphysical parts of composite wholes are fundamental substances and are metaphysically prior to their wholes.[2]

As an ontological interpretation of the mereological hierarchy, PM holds (broadly) that all macrophysical reality is metaphysically grounded in microphysics.[3] While there is an intimate relationship between Part-Priority and PM, the latter does not entail the former. As we will see shortly, PM need not be committed to Part-Priority as a *global* fundamental mereology. Before we turn to examine the merits of Part-Priority and PM in detail, we need to get clear on the latter as it permeates many of the contemporary debates in metaphysics, philosophy of science, and philosophy of mind.

While PM is often formulated as a supervenience thesis, it is often the case that it is intended to denote a much stronger thesis than is captured by the mere covariance between properties or classes thereof. It is often pronounced that supervening properties are "determined" or "fixed" by their subveneing base.[4] As Jaegwon Kim (1998: 11) rightly notes,

> [I]t is customary to associate supervenience with the idea of dependence or determination: if the mental supervenes on the physical, the mental is dependent on the physical, or the physical determines the mental, roughly in the sense that the mental nature of a thing is entirely fixed by its physical nature . . . In fact common expressions like "supervenience base" and "base property" all but explicitly suggest asymmetric dependence.
>
> (1998:11)

According to PM, microphysical entities serve as the ultimate ontological base—the terminus of the grounding sequence—that grounds the mereological structure we see in reality.

One need not look far to note the prevalence of PM in contemporary philosophy. Terrence Horgan (1982: 29) puts it well when he states,

> Many contemporary philosophers believe there is something ontologically fundamental about physics, particularly microphysics. They believe that all the facts about our world are somehow fully determined by the microphysical facts concerning the subatomic "building blocks" of the world.
>
> (Horgan 1982: 29)

In like manner, Brian Ellis (2001: 64) remarks,

> The accepted paradigm of ontological dependence is to be found in the theory of micro-reduction. Methane molecules, for example, are said to depend ontologically on their constituent hydrogen and carbon atoms. They are said to be ontologically dependent because the methane molecules could not in fact exist if these atoms did not exist. Conversely, however, the atoms could exist, even though the molecules did not exist.
>
> (Ellis 2001: 64)

One often finds PM formulated in broad terms as the view that the properties, behaviors, laws, and/or facts about macro-entities are grounded in the properties, behaviors, laws, and/or facts of micro-entities. In addition to Horgan's earlier formulation of PM in terms of facts, Theodore Sider (2003: 2) defines PM in terms of properties (both monadic and polyadic) as "the attractive principle that the properties of wholes, in the actual world anyway, are determined by the properties of and relations between their atomic parts (where 'atom' means 'atom of physics', not 'partless simple')."

What's more, Andreas Hütteman and David Papineau (2005: 2) include microphysical laws in their characterization of PM as the view that "macroscopic physical entities are asymmetrically determined by their microscopic physical parts and the microphysical laws that apply to those parts." After discussing the nature of mereological supervenience—that the properties of wholes are fixed by the properties of their parts—Kim (1998: 18) goes on to note the natural progression to PM, "A general claim of macro-micro supervenience then becomes the Democritean atomistic doctrine that the world is the way it is because the microworld is the way it is."

In what is perhaps the most exhaustive critique of PM on offer, Hütteman (2004) considers three theses that he takes to be jointly constitutive of PM, all of which encompass the many divergent explications of PM in the literature:

> (MD) *Micro-Determination:* "The behavior or the properties of compound systems are determined by the behavior or the properties of their constituents and the relations among them but not vice versa."
>
> (2004: 7)
>
> (MG) *Micro-Government:* "The laws of the micro-level govern the systems on the macro-levels."
>
> (2004: 7)
>
> (MC) *Micro-Causation:* "All causation takes place in virtue of the causation on the level of the (ultimate parts)–or the micro-level. Macro-causation is entirely derivative and piggybacks on the causation of the micro-constituents."
>
> (2004: 7–8)

According to Hütteman (2004: 7), the core doctrine that binds the aforementioned three "micro-theses" together is "the affirmation of an *ontological priority of the micro-level.*" In fact, he explicitly ties his threefold formulation of PM to the question of what I am calling fundamental mereology: "The theses of micro-determination, micro-government and micro-causation concern the question of whether there is an ontological priority of the level the fundamental parts vis-à-vis the level of the compounds."[5] Hütteman is clear that PM "provides a decisive interpretation of the multilayered conception of reality," in particular, "an ontological interpretation of the hierarchical structure of the many layers of reality."[6]

In a similar fashion, Nancy Murphy (2007: 21–22) rightly notes that the ontological priority of the parts over the whole is the explanatory ground as to *why* the of aforementioned micro-theses were obtained. Speaking of a view she calls "atomistic reductionism," Murphy states,

> Causation on this view is "bottom-up"; that is, the parts of an entity are located one rung *downward* in the hierarchy of complexity, and it is the parts that determine the characteristics of the whole, not the other way around. So *ultimate* causal explanations are thought to be based on laws pertaining to the lowest levels of the hierarchy. The crucial *metaphysical* assumption embodied in this view is the ontological priority of the atoms over that which they compose. This is metaphysical atomism-reductionism.
>
> (2007: 21)

From here on I will follow Hütteman and Murphy in thinking that the core unifying feature of PM to be the metaphysical thesis of the metaphysical priority of the microphysical level of being, with the aforementioned micro-theses being consequences thereof.

Let us begin, then, by getting clear on the precise tenets of PM, beginning with the mereological structure of the basic entities that are said to occupy the smallest level of the hierarchy of composition. There are several options available to the advocate of PM on this score. Let us consider just a few of what I take to be the most interesting variants of PM.

First, the advocate of PM may adopt an *atomistic* (i.e., mereologically simple) interpretation of the basic microphysical entities and thus take either simple subatomic particles (quarks, leptons, bosons, etc.), spacetime points, or extended mereological simples (perhaps strings) as metaphysically fundamental.[7] The idea here is that the metaphysically fundamental base is populated by entities that are mereologically fundamental, i.e. lacking proper parts, which serve to exhaustively ground the existence, properties, and behaviors of macro-entities. A concise statement of a particle variant of PM is given by Louis deRosset (2010: 4) from whom I borrow the label "Priority Microphysicalism," though deRosset is clear that he in no way takes PM to entail such an interpretation:

> Priority Microphysicalism holds that the fundamental concrete individuals are very small. On this view, the existence and features of tables, raindrops, tectonic plates, and galaxies are ultimately explicable solely by reference to the existence and features of particles, including which particles are arranged table-wise, tectonic-plate-wise, etc.
>
> (deRosset 2010:4)

One might, on the other hand, reject the premise that microphysical being need be mereologically fundamental, thereby adopting an *atomless* interpretation of the ultimate ontological base of the hierarchy. After all, there is no scientific constraint on the content of our best physics being atomistic in this sense (cf. Schaffer 2003). A further option here is to maintain that microphysical being is ontologically basic in its serving as an *atomless* supervenience base for all of non-microphysical reality.[8] According to Schaffer (2003), an atomless supervenience base of this kind could take one of two forms. The supervenience base could either bottom out in an *ultimate* ontological base (well-founded) or it might simply be a point in the mereological hierarchy that follows, which there is an infinite descent of *symmetric* supervenience relations. On the latter, the infinite descent here would be, in Schaffer's terms, "boring" in that microphysical wholes below such a threshold would supervene on their parts and vice versa.

The precise nature of the atomless supervenience base, which would serve to metaphysically ground the existence of macro-phenomena will, no doubt, be tied to the content of our best fundamental physics.[9] By way of illustration, one particular option (though not the only option of course) is to adopt a wave-theoretic view of the (well-founded) supervenience base that takes the mereological hierarchy to terminate in "wavefunction-stuff" as per the Ghirardi-Rimini-Weber interpretation of quantum mechanics. On this view, one might think that various aspects of the universal wavefunction that serve to metaphysically ground the existence of some composite object at a some higher level in the hierarchy. To say that wavefunction stuff as per the Ghirardi-Rimini-Weber theory is metaphysically basic would be to say, for example, that the existence and nature of a particular chair is ultimately metaphysically grounded in a "chair-like" distribution of "wavefunction stuff" or "chair-like" behavior of the universal wavefunction in a certain locality.[10]

In addition to the question of the specific mereological structure of the metaphysically basic entities at the micro-level, PM comes in varying degrees of strength depending on the kind of relations that are thought to hold between entities at the minimal grounding base. Perhaps the strongest form of PM in the literature is defended (however tentatively) by David Lewis and is known as *Humean Supervenience*: that all facts are metaphysically determined by the intrinsic properties of point-sized parts, together with the spatiotemporal relationships between these parts.[11] Lewis (1986b: ix) famously states this doctrine as follows:

> All there is to the world is a vast mosaic of local matters of particular fact, just one little thing and then another . . . We have geometry: a system of external relations of spatiotemporal distances between points. Maybe points of space-time itself, maybe point-sized bits of matter or aether or fields, maybe both. And at those points we have local qualities: perfectly natural intrinsic properties which need nothing bigger than a point at which to be instantiated. For short: we have an arrangement of qualities. And that is all. There is no difference without difference in the arrangement of qualities. All else supervenes on that.
> (Lewis 1986b: ix)

The rigidity of Lewis's particular version of PM is evident in that spatiotemporal relations are the *only* fundamental relations allowed to hold between the point-sized entities of the ultimate supervenience base.[12] Though Lewis withholds judgment about the type of micro-entity taken as fundamental (particles, points, fields, etc.), the picture is a rather austere one indeed: a mosaic of microphysical point-parts related solely by spatiotemporal relations (for example, *being-one-meter-away-from*). The spatiotemporally related point-parts of the mosaic, together with the intrinsic qualities instantiated (locally) at such points, serves to constitute the Humean Supervenience base upon which all else depends.

Lewis is clear in his characterization of the notion of supervenience as the denial of independent variation: if x supervenes on y, there can be no difference in x without a difference in y. He states,

> To say that so-and-so supervenes on such-and-such is to say that there can be no difference in respect of so-and-so without difference in respect of such-and-such. Beauty of statues supervenes on their shape, size and colour, for instance, if no two statues, in the same or different worlds, ever differ in beauty without also differing in shape or size or size or colour.
>
> (1999a: 29)

Elsewhere, Lewis (1986b: 15) is unequivocal that the supervenience relation has modal import saying "Supervenience means that there *could* be no difference of the one sort without difference of the other sort. Clearly, this "could" indicates modality. Without the modality we have nothing of interest." On this score, it is *impossible* for a macrophysical whole to instantiate a supervenient property without first instantiating the corresponding subvenient property at the Humean base.

Though Lewis expresses some reserve about there being any privileged metaphysically deep notion of priority (Lewis 1999a: 29), the notion of supervenience operative in Humean Supervenience is strikingly similar to the modal explication of grounding we examined in Chapter 2: x is (rigidly) existentially grounded in y just in case necessarily, if x exists, then y exists ($\Box(Ex \rightarrow Ey)$). Not only is it impossible for a macrophysical whole to exhibit supervenient features without first instantiating the respective subvenient features, the latter are also *sufficient* for the instantiation of the former (which suggests that the latter metaphysically *fix* or *determine* the former).

As an example of the relationship between macrophysical objects and their features (properties, behaviors) and the ultimate Humean Supervenience base, Lewis offers the metaphor of a dot-matrix (1986a: 14) and a grid of pixels (1999b: 294). He asks us to consider a grid of a million tiny pixels each of which are capable of instantiating some property or other (light/dark in his example). Together, the pixels form a picture which itself instantiates various global intrinsic properties such that there is "a supervenience of the large upon the small and many" (1999b: 294). While the picture exists, claims Lewis, it along with its global intrinsic features *reduces* to the particular arrangement of the individual pixels and their intrinsic properties. Such a reduction obtains precisely because

> the picture supervenes on the pixels: there could be no difference in the picture and its properties without some difference in the arrangement of light and dark pixels . . . In such a case, say I, supervenience is reduction.
> (Ibid.)

According to Humean Supervenience, the picture and its global properties are nothing "over and above" the local intrinsic qualities of the individual pixels and their arrangements in that they "could go unmentioned in an inventory of what there is without thereby rendering that inventory incomplete."[13]

Now, on the surface, the claim that the picture is "nothing over and above" the pixels and the arrangements thereof is puzzling in that it seems to suggest that the picture does not exist *in any sense*. The aforementioned statement that concluded the previous paragraph reinforces this reading; one can provide an exhaustive inventory of *existing* entities per se without mention of supervenient entities. On the other hand, Lewis is unequivocal when he states, "Yes, the picture really does exist. Yes, it really does have those gestalt properties" (ibid.).

One particular suggestion here is that what Lewis is aiming for is the thesis that while supervenient entities exist, they do not carve nature at the joints in the sense of constituting the sparse structure of being.[14] For Lewis, sparse or natural properties, in contrast to abundant properties, "carve nature at the joints" in that they are responsible for grounding (i) qualitative similarities, (ii) causal powers, and (iii) the minimal ontological base for properties. Regarding the role of sparse properties as providing the minimal ontological base for the class of properties, Lewis (1986a: 60) elaborates as follows: "There are only just enough of them to characterize things completely and without redundancy." This, together with Lewis's admission that an adequate account of reality ought to accommodate both the sparse *and* abundant properties or objects, leads one to think that it is the duplication of the subvening entities at the Humean base that suffices to provide a complete inventory of the sparse structure of being in particular (not the inventory of being *tout court*). While supervenient entities exist, they do not carve nature at its sparse joints.

Moreover, Lewis elsewhere offers a more precise characterization of the relationship between supervenience and reduction that further bolsters the earlier reading of the status of supervening entities:

> A supervenience thesis is, in a broad sense, reductionist. But it is a stripped-down form of reductionism, unencumbered by dubious denials

of existence, claims of ontological priority, or claims of translatability. One might wish to say that in some sense the beauty of statues is nothing over and above the shape and size and colour that beholders appreciate, but without denying that there is such a thing as beauty, without claiming that beauty exists only in some less-than-fundamental way, and without undertaking to paraphrase ascriptions of beauty in terms of shape, etc. A supervenience thesis seems to capture what the cautious reductionist wishes to say.

(1999b: 29)

Lewis is clear that the sort of supervenience he employs in Humean Supervenience does not deny the existence of supervening entities (i.e., beauty in the earlier example) and thus serves more as a "cautious reductionism."

The application of Lewis's particular brand of fundamental mereology to macrophysical objects and their microphysical constituents is straightforward. We have seen from Lewis's illustration of the grid of pixels that entities at the macrophysical level asymmetrically supervene on their microphysical point-sized constituents, with the former reducing to the latter in the sense of being no addition to the *fundamental* or *sparse* inventory of reality. While Lewis countenances macrophysical objects as being composed of point-sized parts occupying the Humean base, the existence and nature of these "higher-level" wholes depend entirely on the distribution and arrangement of the point-parts of the mosaic.

Consequently, it is a very small step indeed to the thesis that the composite objects that have point-sized objects as parts are not metaphysically basic, i.e. are not fundamental substances. This stems from Lewis's contention (as hinted at earlier) that in order to provide a complete or exhaustive sparse inventory of reality one need only duplicate the metaphysically basic or fundamental entities. And, if one need not include that which supervenes on the Humean base in order to arrive at such an inventory, it follows that all ordinary composite objects (as well as everything that supervenes on the mosaic) are not metaphysically basic.

Given the widespread influence the earlier picture (as well as Lewis in general) has had on the present metaphysical landscape, the aforementioned consequence of Humean Supervenience (and PM in general) concerning ordinary macrophysical objects is no trivial matter. In fact, as we will see in more detail in the sequel, the primacy of the microphysical is a deeply entrenched background assumption in contemporary metaphysics.

4.2 Why Priority Microphysicalism?

But what exactly is the lure of ascribing metaphysical primacy to the microphysical parts of composite objects? Why endorse the particular fundamental mereology advocated by Lewis, or something similar? Here I will briefly consider three lines in favor of Part-Priority and PM: (i) physicalism demands it, (ii) the unrivaled success of micro-explanation in the natural sciences is evidence for PM, and (iii) common sense takes parts to be metaphysically prior to wholes.

4.2.1 *Physicalism Demands It!*

Let us begin with the contention that physicalism regarding the mental demands an unwavering commitment to the metaphysical priority of parts over their wholes, particularly those occupying the level of microphysics. While I am in no way sympathetic to physicalism about the mental, it is important to show that the rejection of Part-Priority is consistent with such a widespread view in the metaphysics of mind. Compare the following two claims that often accompany versions of physicalism:

> (P) All facts are identical to, or at least are metaphysically grounded in, physical facts.
>
> (P*) All facts are identical to, or at least are metaphysically grounded in, microphysical facts.

The question before us is whether P entails P*, that is, whether physicalism per se entails the truth of PM. Now, certainly some self-proclaimed physicalists affirm such an entailment. For instance, Philip Pettit (1993: 220–1) remarks, "The fundamentalism that the physicalist defends gives total hegemony, as we might say, to the microphysical order: it introduces the dictatorship of the proletariat." Pettit builds P* into the doctrine of physicalism without reserve.

But our concern here is whether the card-carrying physicalist *must* endorse P* on pains of giving up the label of physicalism. Here a great deal hinges on the precise meaning of "physical" at work in P. If "physical" facts are taken to denote facts corresponding to the domain of microphysics, then P trivially entails P*. But why understand "physical" in this sense? It certainly looks as if P and P* are independent theses, one being a claim about how things go *within* the physical (i.e. non-mental) domain (P*) and the other about how the allegedly non-physical (mental) domain relates to the physical domain (P). P is a claim about the metaphysical primacy of certain *kinds* of facts (all facts supervene on facts whose contents are expressed by our best empirical theories), P* is a claim about the metaphysical primacy of facts involving the smallest *parts* of the physical domain.

As stated, P* is a substantive metaphysical claim regarding the intersection of mereological and grounding structure within the physical domain: the fundamental entities (along with the fundamental facts involving such entities) correspond exclusively to the lowest mereological level, the domain of microphysics. But on first pass, it would appear that physicalism *per se* need not take a stand on such a heavyweight metaphysical position regarding which physical level hosts the metaphysically basic or fundamental entities. As Papineau (2008) points out, the physicalist is under no obligation *qua physicalist* to think that a fact's being characterized as "physical" is determined entirely by whether or not that fact is identical to or supervenes on a *microphysical* fact. As long as every putative non-physical entity is identical to or metaphysically supervenient on a physical entity or process, this is enough to secure a commitment to physicalism. Or so it seems to me at least.[15]

An example may help clearly distinguish between P and P*. Consider sensorimotor theories of phenomenal consciousness which argue that qualitative conscious experiences consist of patterns of interaction involving the environment and the experiencing subject. On this view, qualia *just are* patterned ways organisms go about engaging in externally directed activities in relation to their environment, and thus can be given an exhaustive *physical* (i.e. non-mental) description in terms of the characteristic physical capacities of the organism in question. However, the range of capacities that enable the organism to engage in such activities—such as bodily movement, speech and rational thought perhaps—may very well be higher-level physical capacities which belong to the organism as a whole and thus fail to be instantiated by any of its microphysical parts (P*). Nonetheless, sensorimotor theories of consciousness are rightly classified as providing a physicalist account of phenomenal consciousness in so far as they construe all facts (including facts concerning phenomenal consciousness) as being *identical* to facts about the physical domain.

Perhaps one might respond that considerations regarding the causal closure of the physical domain might help tip the scales in favor of the claim that P entails P*. Again, a great deal hinges on the precise meaning of the slogan in question. If by the "causal closure of the physical domain" one means that every physical event (which has a cause) has a sufficient microphysical cause then this clearly begs the question against any view that endorses P yet takes there to be higher-level (non-mental) properties and causal powers that are irreducible to fundamental physics—e.g., emergentism.[16] The alleged conflict between the denial of Part-Priority and PM and physicalism per se stems from conflating what goes on within a particular domain (the macrophysical supervening on the microphysical) with the relationship between that domain and other allegedly distinct domains (physical vs. mental). Thus the rejection of P*, I submit, in no way threatens the truth of P. There is no incompatibility between the thesis that everything that exists is physical (insert your favorite account of *being physical* here, such as being spatiotemporally located or extended) or, at the very least, supervenes on the physical with the claim that macrophysical wholes do not exhaustively depend on the properties of their proper parts (and their basic relations). By all appearances, the truth of physicalism seems entirely independent of the truth of microphysicalism.

Even more, Papineau (2008: 144–147) makes the more general point that the question of physicalism per se (P) is entirely *neutral* with respect to the dependence ordering between empirically specifiable wholes and their proper parts. Even if wholes failed to exhaustively depend on their proper parts in virtue of instantiating ontologically emergent properties or dispositions, this would (by itself) in no way undermine the *physicality* of the wholes nor the physicality of their emergent properties. While a commitment to P certainly does exclude the ontological emergence of irreducibly mental (i.e., non-physical) substances or properties, it does not exclude the emergence of physical substances or properties *per se*.

4.2.2 The Unrivaled Success of Microphysical Explanation

The second line in favor of Part-Priority and PM is from the empirical success of micro-explanations regarding the properties and causal activity of macrophysical wholes. This is stated succinctly by Sider (2003: 140):

> Why accept supervenience on the small? Because of the unrivaled success of the physics of the small. Physics and related disciplines have been so successful at explaining macroscopic phenomena that it would take a very powerful argument indeed to undermine our faith in this principle.[17]

Sider's point seems to be that the sheer explanatory power of microphysics in explaining the properties and causal powers of macrophysical wholes provides evidence in favor of PM, at least in the absence of any overriding considerations to the contrary. Note the generality of Sider's claim that *all* macroscopic wholes and their accompanying phenomena appear to be explainable in terms of their microphysical constituents. This is a sweeping claim indeed. Even if we grant Sider that the bottom-up explanatory story applies to a great many macrophysical composite objects, it is not at all obvious that *all* macrophysical composites are characterized as such.

But what exactly warrants the general inference from the success of microphysical *explanation* to the stronger thesis of the *metaphysical priority* of the microphysical? While metaphysical priority is arguably a genuine (non-causal) explanatory relation, not all explanatory relations are metaphysical priority relations. Suppose we assume what Kim (1988) has called "explanatory realism," the view that explanations track objective dependence relations in the world. But note that not just *any* dependence relation will support the move from *explanation* to metaphysical *priority*. What the Priority Microphysicalist needs is a relation that is both (i) *non-causal* and (ii) *asymmetric*, in so far as metaphysical priority is both non-causal and asymmetric (see §2.1.4.).

Arguably, neither (i) nor (ii) can be "read off" of the explanatory relations that obtain between the microphysical and macrophysical noted by Sider earlier. From the fact that *some* dependence relation must obtain between the two domains in order to ground successful micro-explanations of macrophysical phenomena, it does not immediately follow that this relation must be an asymmetrical, non-causal grounding relation.

The objector to PM may even grant that many of the processes and mechanisms at work at the macrophysical level *causally depend* (both synchronically and diachronically) on processes and mechanisms operative at the microphysical level of reality. But to infer from this the stronger claim that therefore microphysical reality *asymmetrically* and *non-causally* grounds macrophysical reality is much too quick.

For instance, not all accounts of causation involve determination or necessitation. One notable example of this would be the view defended by Stephen Mumford and Rani Lill Anjum (2011) called *causal dispositionalism*: the view that causes do not determine or necessitate their effects but merely dispose toward them; the presence of interfering factors may prevent a cause from bringing about its effect. Thus even if macrophysical composites are disposed to bring about a certain range of effects *in virtue of* the causal activity of their microphysical parts, this in no way implies that the former are metaphysically grounded in or determined by the latter.

Moreover, the claim that causation, and ipso facto causal explanation, is asymmetric is not entirely uncontroversial. Again, causal dispositionalism admits cases of causal production that are reciprocal or symmetric; causation, on this view, is best characterized as a *non-symmetric* rather than an asymmetric relation. Consequently, the denial of PM is consistent with the claim that the properties and causal mechanisms at the level of microphysics *causally* explain many of the properties and causal mechanisms at the level of macrophysics. This is precisely because mere causal dependence between two domains does not, by itself, secure the stronger thesis that one domain is metaphysically grounded in the other.[18]

More importantly, to secure the asymmetry needed to ground the inference from the success of micro-explanation to the thesis of micro-grounding, Sider needs not only the minimal claim regarding the *ubiquity* of microphysical explanation—that microphysical laws govern the features and dynamics of *all* macro-phenomena—but also the *supremacy* or *hegemony* of microphysical explanation—the distribution of microphysical laws and properties is sufficient to fix or determine the *total* behavior of each macro-system. But this is just to assume micro-determination (MD) above and hence the truth of PM.

The distinction between the ubiquity of microphysics and the hegemony of microphysics is underscored by Carl Hoefer (2003: 1408) when he says,

> A fundamentalist thinks that the phenomena studied in chemistry, biology, meteorology, etc., all are composed of the doings of atoms,

molecules, photons, fields, and so on; and that these constituents are perfectly governed by the fundamental laws. But she need not believe *any* sort of thesis of the reducibility of biology, chemistry, or meteorology to physics!

While PM may perhaps entail the ubiquity of microphysical explanation, the converse does not hold; one may grant that the behavior of higher-level composite objects are *governed* by microphysical laws without endorsing the stronger thesis that such behavior is wholly *grounded* in or *determined* by such laws.

Even if we grant Sider's sweeping claim about the success of microphysical explanation, it is not at all clear how to offer a non-question begging way to secure the asymmetry required to support the inference from successful microphysical explanations of macrophysical phenomena to the truth of PM. This is *not*, however, to say that PM is false as a result; perhaps some or even all composite objects are grounded in their microphysical constituents as per PM. Rather, it is to point out that the widespread success of microphysical explanation in the natural sciences fails, on its own, to provide *positive evidence* in favor of PM. The defender of PM must supplement the argument from the success of microphysical explanations with further arguments in support of their position.

4.2.3 Mereological Mooreanism

Perhaps one such argument available to the defender of Part-Priority is that common sense dictates that parts are metaphysically prior to their composite wholes. It is a Moorean fact, it is argued, that at any given time a composite object is "built up" out of *separable* proper parts, parts whose existence and nature are independent of the whole in question. The atoms in a molecule, for instance, are separable parts of the molecule and thus capable of existing *as such* without being a proper part of that very molecule. Here the analogy of a whole, like a building, as being constructed out of prior independent materials illustrates this insight well.

The intuition can also be stated diachronically as follows: it seems natural to think that one is capable of tracing out the compositional history of one and the same carbon atom throughout its spatiotemporal career, the atom being a proper part of a host of distinct composite objects at different times. We have, then, the following claim attributed to common sense regarding the relationship between wholes and their proper parts:

(PS) *Part-Separability*: One and the same object, O, can exist both as a proper part of a composite object, O_1, at t as well as a proper part of a numerically distinct composite object, O_2, at t_1.

128 *Against Part-Priority*

If a fundamental mereology entails the denial of PS as a dictate of common sense about material objects and the parthood relations in which they stand, then so much the worse for that theory. It is argued that Part-Priority can claim the mantle of common sense in so far as it's the only fundamental mereology consistent with the truth of PS.

But note that the force of the argument from common sense hinges not only on PS being a dictate of common sense but also the general methodological principle known as *particularism* or *Mooreanism* with respect to the domain of material objects and their proper parts. Let's call this view "mereological Mooreanism." As a general guiding methodological principle, particularism is the view that our commonsense judgments about cases in the target domain of philosophical inquiry (ethics, epistemic justification, composition, etc.) are largely correct and carry (defeasible) epistemic weight—that is, they are epistemic difference-makers; when conflict arises between general principles and intuitive judgments, the latter may epistemically defeat the former.[19] Since PS is a deliverance of common sense regarding material objects, and such deliverances carry epistemic authority in the absence of overriding defeaters as per mereological Mooreanism, we have reason to endorse Part-Priority.

As I am strongly inclined to accept mereological Mooreanism as well as particularism as applied to other domains of philosophical inquiry, the earlier argument from common sense carries a great deal of weight in my opinion. But those who are inclined to eschew particularism in general and mereological Mooreanism in particular (which is becoming an increasing lot as of late) will likely part company at the second step of the argument from common sense.[20] In doing so, they reject the view that the deliverances of common sense regarding material objects and their parts constitute epistemic difference-makers.

Note, however, that the defender of Substantial Priority is well positioned to embrace PS with respect to the proper parts of a limited subclass of composite objects—namely, what I referred to in the previous chapter as "aggregates" or "grounded wholes." If so, then there is no straightforward path to Part-Priority as a *wholesale* fundamental mereology from PS as a dictate of common sense. Substantial Priority is not only compatible with PS, it is build into the view from the very start in its drawing a distinction between different kinds of composite objects that are governed by different grounding descriptions.[21]

The proponent of the argument from common sense in favor of Part-Priority has a straightforward rejoinder. Simply replace PS with the following thesis:

(PS*) *Part-Separability**: One and the same object, O, can exist both as a proper part of a composite substance (grounding whole), O_1, at t as well as a proper part of a numerically distinct composite substance, O_2, at t_1.

PS* amounts to the claim that numerically one and the same proper part of a substance can retain its identity upon composing distinct substances at different times. Here the defender of Part-Priority can simply restate the argument from common sense in terms of PS*.

It is true that the defender of Substantial Priority cannot accept PS* in so far as they maintain that the proper parts of composite substances (grounding wholes) are grounded entities and therefore *inseparable* parts of their substantial wholes. But here we come to what I take to be the crux of the matter regarding the argument from common sense. The argument gets its traction by assuming that both PS and PS* are, in fact, deliverances of common sense regarding the relationship between parts and their wholes.

Consider PS* in particular. Strictly speaking, PS* is the claim, allegedly warranted on the basis of common sense alone, that numerically one and the same material object can be a proper part of distinct composite substances at different times. But why think a claim like PS* is capable of being justified solely on the basis of common sense? Why think that PS* inherits its positive epistemic status solely by way of intuitive judgments about the persistence of material objects?

Here I must confess that I have my doubts as to whether common sense *alone* can pull this particular kind of philosophical weight. To motivate Part-Priority on the basis of common sense alone assumes that our folk judgments about material objects and the nature of diachronic persistence are discerning enough to adjudicate between cases of numerical and qualitative identity, at least enough to single-handedly support a full-blown metaphysical thesis such as Part-Priority.[22] But why think that our stock of commonsense beliefs include beliefs such as "the carbon atom that was once a proper part of a substance S at t is *numerically identical* to the carbon atom that is now a proper part of a distinct substance S* at t_1?" How, we might ask, can pre-theoretical reflection on the world's structure adjudicate between the earlier belief and the following: "the carbon atom that was once a proper part of a substance S at t is *qualitatively identical* to the carbon atom that is now a proper part of a distinct substance S* at t_1?"

Frankly, I do not see how it could. For one, it seems that our folk or commonsense beliefs about numerical identity (both synchronic and diachronic) would be exactly the same whether or not the carbon atom at t_1 was numerically or qualitatively identical to the carbon atom at t. Whether two exactly resembling sticks of chalk resting on the blackboard—one on Monday the other on Friday—are numerically or qualitatively identical to one another is a question that cannot, even in principle, be decided on the grounds of common sense alone. Or so it seems to me. If such a question could be decided in such a manner, then views in the metaphysics of persistence that eschew strict numerical identity through time, e.g. stage theory and mereological essentialism, would be non-starters in so far as they would be blatantly incompatible with the straightforward deliverances of common sense. But of course stage theory and mereological essentialism are live metaphysical options on the table, and in no way immediately ruled out by common sense alone. These views need to be substantively engaged, and not simply dismissed on the grounds that they are in tension with the deliverances of common sense.

As a result, while it may be plausible to include among our stock of commonsense beliefs those involving qualitative sameness or exact resemblance (the Monday-chalk and the Friday-chalk are *exactly* alike), I am inclined to think that common sense is simply too coarse-grained to adjudicate between such claims and those of numerical sameness (the Monday chalk is *one and the same* as the Friday chalk). At the very least, we need to be given a reason to think that commonsense intuitions are fine-grained enough to track these differences. Without such a reason, the argument from common sense carries little weight as a stand-alone argument in favor of a Part-Priority fundamental mereology.

4.3 The Argument from the Possibility of Gunk

Having explicated Part-Priority and PM as well as a sampling of considerations in favor of such views, let us turn now to examine the merits of each fundamental mereology. The first argument I want to offer against Part-Priority in particular stems from the metaphysical possibility of gunky worlds.[23] Gunky worlds are worlds devoid of mereological simples. For each mereologically complex whole in a gunky world there are infinitely many proper parts, each with infinitely many proper parts, and so on. The question before us here is whether or not such worlds are *metaphysically* possible (just "possible" henceforth) given a Part-Priority fundamental mereology.

Let me attempt to motivate the prima facie tension between the possibility of gunky worlds and Part-Priority. First, as per Part-Priority, if every complex whole is a grounded whole, then each whole is grounded in its proper parts. In gunky worlds where Part-Priority holds, we have a grounding chain of infinite descent which tracks infinite mereological descent. If decomposition of proper parts continues ad infinitum in gunky worlds, and if wholes are grounded in their proper parts, then it follows that there are no metaphysically basic (ungrounded) entities in gunky worlds. But surely it is not possible for *every* existing entity to borrow its existence from another; there must be a metaphysical foundation from which the derivatives *ultimately* derive their existence. If not, it is difficult to see how anything exists in the first place. As a result, Part-Priority seems ill-equipped to handle the mere possibility of gunky worlds.

The *the argument from the possibility of gunk* against Part-Priority can be stated as a reductio as follows:

1. Necessarily, composite objects are rigidly grounded in their proper parts.[24] (assume Part-Priority for reductio)
2. Gunky worlds are possible.
3. If gunky worlds are possible, then it is possible that there are no fundamental entities in such worlds.
4. It is not possible that there are no fundamental entities in such worlds (the necessity of well-foundedness of grounding).
5. Therefore, it is false that necessarily, composite objects are grounded in their proper parts.

The rationale for premise 1 stems from the necessity of grounding as per G8 (see §2.1.4.), that grounding is a non-contingent relation between that which is grounded and its grounds, in this case, a mereological whole and its proper parts.[25] More specifically, premise 1 is the application of the necessity of grounding to Part-Priority in that if mereological wholes are grounded in their proper parts in the actual world, then (by G8) it follows that in every world in which composite objects exist they are grounded as such.[26]

I take the key premises in the argument from the possibility of gunk to be 2 and 4. Let us begin with premise 2. The mere possibility of gunky worlds is a rather minimal claim, one that may not turn many heads in the ontology room. As many have pointed out, gunk meets several of our best criteria for possibility such as conceivability (or, minimally, the lack of an inconceivability argument against it) and coherence.[27] What's more, in so far as the axioms of standard mereology reflect possible mereological structures, then the availability of gunky mereologies as noted in Chapter 3 suggests the possibility of worlds with infinite mereological descent. Lastly, the actuality of gunk has, as Schaffer (2010b: 61) notes, been taken seriously as an empirical hypothesis.[28] Consequently, the mere possibility of gunk seems plausible, at least in the absence of considerations to the contrary.

There are, however, those that *have* offered considerations to the contrary, that is, considerations against the possibility of gunky worlds. While I take such a thesis to be plausible in its own right (albeit one that lacks any knockdown arguments in its favor), a defense of premise 2 will inevitably involve rebutting potential defeaters to the possibility of gunky worlds.

Most notably, Hudson (2001: 84–90) has advanced an argument against the possibility of gunk that turns on the fact that the most defensible answers to The Simple Question (i.e., what are the necessary and jointly sufficient conditions for an object to be a material simple?) entail the impossibility of gunk. The two accounts of material simplicity Hudson considers are (i) x is a material simple iff x is *point-sized* (Pointy View for short) and (ii) x is a material simple iff x occupies a *maximally continuous* region of space (MaxCon for short).[29] The general structure of Hudson's argument proceeds as follows: (i) either the Pointy View or MaxCon is true, (ii) if MaxCon is true then gunk is impossible, (iii) if the Pointy View is true then gunk is impossible, (iv) hence, gunk is impossible.

Let me begin by highlighting the fact that Hudson *assumes* the disjunction that either the Pointy View or MaxCon is the correct answer to the Simple Question. It is far from obvious, however, that these options have exclusive rights as the only defensible answers to the Simple Question. For one, McDaniel (2007a) highlights six different answers to the Simple Question, only two of which are the Pointy View and MaxCon (both of which he classifies as "spatial accounts," the others being "fundamentality accounts" and "indivisibility accounts"). McDaniel himself argues indirectly for a seventh view–what he calls *The Brutal View*–that there is no non-mereological criterion for being a material simple by showing that each of the other options face serious difficulties. Now, my aim here is not to delve into the various answers to the Simple Question and argue that one is more plausible than another. Rather, it is the more minimal claim that the earlier argument against the possibility of gunk will only carry weight with those who are already convinced of the superiority of the Pointy View and MaxCon as answers to the Simple Question. But this is no lightweight assumption given the presence of alternative, defensible answers as well as the presence of positive reasons to reject both the Pointy View and MaxCon.[30] Consequently, we have reason to be suspicious of the exclusivity of (i).

Moving on from (i), let us consider Hudson's reasons for thinking that the Pointy View entails the impossibility of gunk as per (iii).[31] Hudson argues that the following jointly entail the impossibility of gunk:

H1. The Doctrine of Arbitrary Undetached Parts (DAUP).
H2. Necessarily, no hunk of gunk exactly occupies a point-sized region of space.
H3. Necessarily, any hunk of gunk exactly occupies some region or other.
H4. Necessarily, any region has at least one point-sized sub-region.
H5. Necessarily, any point-sized region is exactly occupiable.

Roughly, DAUP is the thesis that necessarily, for every material object o and its occupying region R, and for any occupiable sub-region of R, r^*, there is a material object o^* that occupies r^* and is a proper part of o. Premise H2, that (necessarily) no hunk of gunk exactly occupies a point-sized region, immediately follows from the Pointy View of material simples. While a hunk of gunk fails to exactly occupy a point-sized region of space, it nevertheless is highly plausible to think that it, being *material*, must occupy some region of space or other, hence H3. But for any region of space R you choose, there must be at least one point-sized subregion of R, r^*, such that r^* is exactly occupiable. From this, together with DAUP, it follows that there must be a material object that occupies r^*, which is to say that r^* must be occupied by a material simple. Hence, gunk is impossible on the Pointy View of simples.

The argument is subtle, yet powerful. I take the driving premise to be the truth of DAUP (H1), although one might also consider taking issue with

H4. What reasons does Hudson offer in favor of DAUP? The only factor cited by Hudson is that the defender of gunk ought to be inclined to accept H1 on the grounds that gunk is itself motivated by DAUP.[32] Whether or not gunk has been historically motivated by an appeal to DAUP or something similar I do not know.[33] But whether or not gunky worlds are possible certainly *need* not rely on the tenability of DAUP. A world every object of which has proper parts, yet one where the proper parts of objects fail to be isomorphic with the mereological structure of their occupiable sub-regions is entirely conceivable.[34] Thus, there is no conceptual constraint on the proponent of gunk to side with DAUP in order to motivate the possibility of gunk. Apart from its motivating role, we are simply given no other reason as to why the proponent of the possibility of gunk ought to look favorably on DAUP.

We need not rehearse the standard arguments against DAUP here as they will be familiar enough to many.[35] I instead want to gesture toward an independent (though often neglected) reason to hedge one's confidence in DAUP: the possibility of extended simples.[36] Whether one endorses DAUP will, as is common in metaphysics, partly depend on one's wider sympathies regarding the conceivability and possibility of other metaphysical theses. The possibility of extended simples—spatiotemporally extended hunks of matter lacking proper parts—offers a counterexample to DAUP (a thesis that is necessarily true if true at all) in that *no* sub-region of the hunk's occupying region hosts a material object that is a proper part of that hunk. For those who look favorably on the possibility (and actuality) of extended simples, the path from (a) necessarily, there is at least one exactly occupiable point-sized sub-region (r^*) of the region (R) occupied by o (premise H4) to (b) necessarily, there is an object that occupies r^* and is a *proper part* of o, is suspect (o could exactly occupy an extended region of space without having proper parts that correspond to point-sized sub-regions within its boundaries).[37] As a result, the truth of DAUP will need to be weighed by other considerations involving possible mereological structures, such as extended simples. But Hudson has offered no principled reason to prefer DAUP over the possibility of extended simples other than the fact that gunk would be unmotivated if DAUP were denied, a reason we have already shown to be without merit. In sum, at the very least, I take the possibility of gunk to be undefeated by Hudson's arguments earlier.

Let us proceed, then, to premise 4 of the argument from the possibility of gunk: that it is not possible that there are no fundamental entities in gunky worlds. The premise is simply a negative formulation of the well-foundedness of grounding discussed in Chapter 2 under the label G9 (§2.1.4.). G9 claims that non-empty grounding domains devoid of at least one basic entity are metaphysically impossible (positively, for any non-empty grounding domain, it is necessary that at least one basic entity exists in that domain). Schaffer illustrates the insight behind the well-foundedness of grounding by appealing to the analogue of foundationalism with respect to epistemic justification. If one's noetic structure were devoid of justified *basic* beliefs (beliefs which do not derive their epistemic justification from other beliefs), then it is difficult to see how any *non-basic* beliefs would be epistemically justified. Alternatively, if there were no *non-inferentially* justified beliefs, then there would be no *inferentially* justified beliefs.

Interestingly enough, Leibniz's commitment to a Part-Priority fundamental mereology seems to have directly influenced his further claim that there *must* be mereological simples (and hence the impossibility of gunky worlds):

> *I believe that where there are only beings by aggregation, there will not even be real beings.* For every being by aggregation presupposes beings endowed with true unity, because it has its reality only from that of its components, so that it will have none at all if each being of which it is composed is again a being by aggregation; or else yet another foundation of its reality must be sought, which cannot ever be found in this way if one must always go on seeking.[38]

On this view, since composite objects exist and are grounded in their proper parts (Part-Priority), there *must* be a terminus to descending mereological structure (simples), or else there would be no composite objects.

Schaffer (2010b: 62) shares the Leibnizian intuition in that "endless dependence conflicts with the foundationalist requirement that there be basic objects (1.2). On this option nothing is basic at gunky worlds. There would be no ultimate ground. Being would be infinitely deferred, never achieved." Others simply report their inability to comprehend the denial of G9 (and hence premise 4). On this score, Lowe (1998: 158) candidly states, "All real existence must be 'grounded' or 'well-founded'. Such an 'axiom of foundation' is quite probably beyond conclusive proof and yet I find the vertiginous implications of its denial barely comprehensible." While I myself take the intuition driving premise 4 (and G9) to be a strong one, I am aware that many will not share this opinion. I am also of the view that any argument in favor of premise 4 will, most likely, fail to carry the same intuitive force as the premise itself. Be that as it may, such a task is not entirely without merit as I think there are ways to gesture toward the well-foundedness of grounding as per G9.

One may, following Ross Cameron (2008), argue that accepting G9 has a certain theoretical utility in that it offers a unified explanatory ground for the existence of each grounded entity in a domain. In a domain deprived of ungrounded entities, the existence of each grounded entity is explained in terms of a distinct (albeit immediate) ground or collection of grounds, which are themselves grounded entities. Accepting the well-foundedness of grounding (and hence premise 4), on the other hand, allows the ungrounded entity (or class of ungrounded entities) to serve as one and the same explanation for the existence of each grounded entity in that domain. This preserves the theoretical principle that it is better to have a single explanatory ground for each phenomena (the phenomena here is the existence of each individual grounded entity) than to have a distinct explanatory ground for each phenomena. Even more, however, positing at least one ungrounded entity in a grounding domain lends an explanation for not only the existence of each grounded entity in that domain, but also for the existence of grounded entities *per se* in that domain. It is one thing for there to be an explanation for the existence of each grounded entity in a domain, quite another for there to be an explanation for why the class of grounded entities exist in that domain *in the first place*. Accepting premise 4 affords both theoretical simplicity as well as explanatory power with respect to the existence of grounded entities.

Interestingly enough, Schaffer (2010: 62–65) has argued that the possibility of gunk poses a problem not only for what I am calling Part-Priority (which, for our purposes here, includes PM), but for *any* non-monistic fundamental mereology, including Substantial Priority. In Schaffer's terminology, any pluralistic fundamental mereology (i.e., one that posits metaphysically basic sub-world entities) is unable to accommodate the possibility of gunk without doing an injustice to our intuitions regarding the well-foundedness of grounding. I disagree. But I will hold off on interacting with Schaffer's objection until chapter 8 where I engage objections to Substantial Priority.

4.4 The Failure of Whole-Part Supervenience

I turn now to a second variety of argument aimed at Part-Priority, particularly PM, the latter being the predominant fundamental mereology in the literature. The general type of argument I advance in what follows hinges on the idea that Part-Priority and PM rule out, a priori, the thesis that composite objects per se as well as macrophysical wholes (respectively) instantiate ontologically emergent properties, including perfectly natural properties. In this section I want to argue that the properties and behavior of at least some composite objects taken from total science are genuinely emergent in the sense that they fail to supervene on the properties and behavior of their proper parts and their basic arrangements. If so, then such wholes fail to be grounded in their proper parts and thereby serve to undermine both Part-Priority and PM.

4.4.1 Against Part-Priority

Recall from our previous discussion that a Part-Priority fundamental mereology is a *global* thesis regarding the intersection of mereological and grounding structure: *all* composite objects are grounded wholes that are composed of separable proper parts and thus are freely recombinable with one another. On a well-founded Part-Priority mereology, some of the proper parts of composite wholes are basic or substantial in their own right, and thereby (ultimately) explain the existence and nature of the wholes of which they are a part. Part-Priority, as stated by Kim (1978: 154), maintains, "Wholes are completely *determined*, causally and *ontologically*, by their parts."[39]

With this in mind, consider the following argument against Part-Priority, what I call *the argument from the failure of whole-part supervenience*:

1. If a whole exhibits emergent properties, then it fails to be grounded in its proper parts.
2. Some wholes exhibit emergent properties.
3. Therefore, some wholes fail to be grounded in their proper parts.[40]

The argument from the failure of whole-part supervenience is aimed at undermining the *global* nature of Part-Priority: that *all* complex wholes are grounded wholes (see §3.4). While it is plausible that *some* intermediate wholes may be grounded as such (aggregates or artifacts), there are grounds for thinking that not *all* composite objects fit this grounding description.

Before I turn to the premises themselves let me say a bit about the notion of emergence at play in the argument. By "emergence" here I have in mind *ontological emergence* (as opposed to epistemic or structural emergence), properties of systems or wholes that include causal properties not reducible to any of the intrinsic causal properties of the parts or to any of the fundamental relations between them. More precisely, we can say that for some property F and some complex whole x, F is an ontologically emergent property of x iff (i) x instantiates F, (ii) F is a perfectly natural property, and (iii) x's instantiating F does not supervene on the intrinsic properties of, and spatiotemporal relations among, x's proper parts. As Michael Silberstein and John McGeever (1999: 182) point out, "[o]ntological emergence entails the failure of mereological supervenenience" and Schaffer (2009) "the intended notion of an emergent property is one for which mereological supervenience fails."

Elaborating on (ii) I, like many, presuppose a naturalness ordering over properties, with the *perfectly natural properties* being those elite natural properties that (i) ground objective similarities between things and (ii) carve out the non-redundant causal powers in the world.[41] While natural properties per se carve out the distinctively causal structure of the world, some carve the causal structure of the world *more precisely* than others. For instance, the power to tell a lie is, arguably, redundant in that it can be explained or reduced in terms of the *more natural* (although not necessarily perfectly natural) properties involved: the power to take a doxastic attitude toward a proposition (i.e. form beliefs), the power to speak, the power to entertain false propositions and to intend to report them as true, etc. As such, the power to tell a lie is not a perfectly natural property in so far as it can be reduced to more basic causal powers.[42]

With the notion of a perfectly natural property in hand, we can elucidate tenet (ii) by following Lewis (1999a: 27) in taking two complex objects to be *duplicates* if and only if there is a one-one correspondence between their parts that preserves perfectly natural properties (and perfectly natural relations). In like manner, let us say the *xs* are *plural duplicates* of the *ys* if and only if the *xs* and the *ys* can be put in one-one correspondence that preserves perfectly natural properties and relations.

Recall that on a Part-Priority fundamental mereology "[w]holes are completely *determined*, causally and *ontologically*, by their parts."[43] The qualitative and causal profiles of mereological wholes, then, supervene entirely on the profiles of their proper parts, together with their fundamental arrangements. In other words, Part-Priority adheres to the following *Plural Duplication Principle* (PDP) for mereological wholes and their parts:

(PDP) *Plural Duplication Principle*: For any *xs*, *w*, and *z*, if the *xs* compose *w*, then *z* is a duplicate of *w* if and only if there are some *ys* that are plural duplicates of the *xs*, and the *ys* compose *z*.[44]

As a thesis about composite objects, PDP claims that *duplicating the perfectly natural properties of the parts and their basic arrangements suffices to duplicate the perfectly natural properties (and relations) of the whole.* The argument from the failure of whole-part supervenience sets out to establish the falsity of PDP as a universal principle governing composite objects; there are perfectly natural properties of certain composite objects that fail to supervene on the properties and powers of their proper parts, together with their basic arrangements; for a subclass of intermediate wholes, duplicating the parts and their basic arrangements does not preserve the properties and causal dispositions of the whole.

With the aforementioned groundwork in place, let us turn to the argument itself. At its core, premise 1 is warranted on the basis of the more general thesis concerning the nature of grounding expressed by G10, the thesis that grounding entails supervenience (see §2.1.4). As was noted previously, while much of the recent literature on grounding has been quick to acknowledge the failure of analyzing grounding in terms of supervenience, there is an equal consensus that the two concepts are indeed intimately related. In fact, Kim (1993: 148), after rightly distinguishing the covariation element of supervenience from the alleged dependence ordering it is claimed to secure, argues, "But the two components are not entirely independent; for it seems that the following is true: for there to be property dependence there must be property covariation." While supervenience does not entail grounding, it is plausible to think that the converse does in fact hold.[45] Again, Kim (1993: 167) suggests that supervenience, "is not a 'deep' metaphysical relation; rather, it is a 'surface' relation that reports a pattern of property covariation, suggesting the presence of an interesting dependency relation that might explain it."

Consider the following case of grounding: a event's being grounded in its constituents. Here the constituents of the event of the presidential inauguration of Barack Obama (which include, at the very least, Barack Obama and the time at which the inauguration took place) ground the existence of the event itself. The thesis on the table here is that there can be no difference in the event—that which is grounded–without a difference in the constituents—that which does the grounding. In other words, there can be no variation in that which is grounded without a variation in the ground. This is just to say that the event's being grounded in its constituents entails that the event supervenes on its constituents (but not the converse).

Given the modal consequences of grounding, the failure of grounding follows quite naturally from the failure of supervenience. If the supervening entity fails to covary with its subvening base, this is reason enough to conclude that it thereby fails to be grounded in its base.

4.4.1.1 Quantum Entanglement

What then of 2, the claim that some composite wholes instantiate emergent properties? Perhaps one of the most plausible instances of the failure of PDP (and thus ontological emergence) is *quantum entanglement*. One of the hallmarks of classical physics is the *separability* of physical systems: that the state of a compound physical system S consisting of n point particles is determined by the local magnitudes of its constituent particles which occupy distinct spacetime points.[46] Thus, the pure (i.e. unmixed) state of a classical system at any given time consists entirely of the pure states of its subsystems. Facts about S involving classical physical quantities such as mass, momentum, or kinetic energy supervene on local facts regarding the corresponding quantities of their constituent subsystems. We can capture the separability of classical physical systems by the following principle:

> *Separability Principle*: The states of any spatiotemporally separated subsystems $S_1, S_2, \ldots, S_n$ of a compound system S are individually well-defined and the states of the compound system are wholly and completely determined by them and their physical interactions including their spatiotemporal relations.
>
> (Karakostas 2007)[47]

Consequently, for any compound physical system in a classical universe, its constituent subsystems are separable, individual parts that exhaustively determine the states of the systems in which they are embedded.

As many have pointed out, quantum mechanical systems exhibit a behavior that is radically at odds with the *Separability Principle*. To illustrate this, suppose we have two non-identical particles, call them a and b, where a and b each occupy distinct regions of space and jointly compose a compound system S. The individual spin states of a and b are associated with a two-dimensional vector (Hilbert) space H_a and H_b (in the z-direction) as follows (where "$|\uparrow\rangle_n$" is to be read as "particle n is in spin-up state"):

H_a: $|z\uparrow\rangle_a |z\downarrow\rangle_a$
H_b: $|z\uparrow\rangle_b |z\downarrow\rangle_b$.

We can represent the four-dimensional vector space for the entire system S, call it H_S, as the tensor product ($\otimes$) of H_a and H_b, where $H_S = H_a \otimes H_b$:

H_S:

i. $|z\uparrow\rangle_a \otimes |z\downarrow\rangle_b$
ii. $|z\downarrow\rangle_a \otimes |z\uparrow\rangle_b$.

States i and ii of H_S represent a few of the possible vector states of the compound system S, composed of a and b. States i and ii are easily expressed as the tensor product of the pair of vectors as per H_a and H_b and hence are exhaustively explained in terms of the spin states of S's component parts.

In addition to i and ii, however, S includes further spin states that are no mere product of the spin states of its components. Perhaps the best example of such a state is the *singlet state*, a *superposition* of a pair of particles with anti-correlated spin states, in this case $|z\uparrow\rangle_a|z\downarrow\rangle_b$ and $|z\downarrow\rangle_a|z\uparrow\rangle_b$:[48]

iii. $\frac{1}{\sqrt{2}}|z\uparrow\rangle_a|z\downarrow\rangle_b - \frac{1}{\sqrt{2}}|z\downarrow\rangle_a|z\uparrow\rangle_b$.

As per Born's rule, for each individual particle in the singlet state, a and b, there is a 50% chance that a will be $|z\uparrow\rangle$ and b will be $|z\downarrow\rangle$ and a 50% chance that a will measure $|z\downarrow\rangle$ and b $|z\uparrow\rangle$.[49] Here, however, we must note that things are quite different with respect to the entire system of which both a and b are components. The total spin for systems in the singlet state is zero. It is a fact about S alone that each of its component particles are disposed to yield opposite results if both spins are measured in the same direction (z-direction). The spin probability distribution of the system— that there is a zero chance of *both* a and b being measured at $|z\uparrow\rangle$ (or $|z\downarrow\rangle$ alternatively)—is an *irreducible, holistic* feature of S that is not capable of being derived from the facts concerning the expectation values of the spin of the individual particles themselves. The singlet state of S is a pure (un-mixed) state that can be attributed to neither a nor b individually, it is a genuine addition to being, it is ontologically emergent.

Consequently, S is an *entangled quantum system* given that its total vector state fails to be the tensor product of the vector states of its sub-components *a* and *b*: $H_S \neq H_a \otimes H_b$.[50] While the proper parts of a non-entangled whole *w* may be plural duplicates of the proper parts of an entangled whole *w**, it is evident that *w* and *w** are not duplicates *per se*. This is precisely because there are perfectly natural properties instantiated by entangled wholes, such as *having spin state zero* in the case of a system composed of two spin-1/2 particles in the singlet state, that fail to be instantiated by non-entangled wholes. As a result, an exhaustive inventory of the world's perfectly natural properties that omitted features of entangled quantum wholes would be radically incomplete. The *holism* at work in quantum entanglement is such that the total system has features or states (singlet) that are irreducible to the features or states of its component particles. As Karakostas (2009: 10) puts it, "the entangled state W represents global properties for the whole system S that are neither *dependent* upon nor *determined* by any properties of its parts." The holism of entangled quantum systems, then, suggests the failure of whole-part supervenience.

Reflecting on quantum entanglement and its significance for mereological metaphysics, Maudlin (1998: 55) concludes,

> The physical state of a complex whole cannot always be reduced to those of its parts, or to those of its parts together with their spatiotemporal relations, even when the parts inhabit distinct regions of space. Modern science, and modern physics in particular, can hardly be accused of holding reductionism as a central premise, given that the result of the most intensive scientific investigations in history is a theory that contains an ineliminable holism.

In similar fashion, Heil (2012: 47) concurs,

> Suppose quantum systems, systems of "entangled" particles, are genuinely "holistic," suppose their characteristics really do outstrip characteristics of their ingredients . . . [t]he "parts" of such systems would have the status of modes: the wholes of which they are parts would not depend on the parts, the parts would depend on the wholes.

In short: quantum entanglement undermines the *Separability Principle* of classical physics, together with the metaphysical thesis of PDP upon which it rests.

Here the proponent of Part-Priority might retort that entangled wholes can be accounted for without dispensing with PDP and hence the metaphysical priority of parts over their wholes. To preserve Part-Priority, one might introduce primitive (external) *entanglement* or *correlation relations* in addition to those spatiotemporal relations that obtain between the components of an entangled system. The vector state of the entire quantum whole, on this view, would be a *structural property*, one that is nothing more than the vector states of its sub-components *together with the spatiotemporal and fundamental entanglement relations that obtain between them*. Ontological emergence at the quantum level, on this view, would undermine Part-Priority only if it were shown that entangled systems failed to supervene on the intrinsic properties of their proper parts, together with any fundamental relations among such parts (not just spatiotemporal relations).[51] With fundamental entanglement relations in hand, no irreducible quantum states of the whole need apply.

I take this to be a compelling rejoinder on behalf of Part-Priority in response to the failure of PDP with respect to quantum wholes. There are, however, a few concerns with this line of reasoning. First, amounts to denying an otherwise straightforward and natural reading of the results of Bell's Theorem, most notably the fact that the entangled state is a *global property* and thus appears to be encoded in the entire entangled system. We need, then, plausible grounds for introducing sui generis entanglement relations between individual particles, ones that are independently motivated apart from a desire to safeguard PDP and thus a Part-Priority fundamental mereology.

Second, such a maneuver comes at a high price for those who prefer a staunch neo-Humean gloss on Part-Priority. Including brute entanglement relations as part of the microphysical supervenience base is tantamount to the denial of Humean Supervenience as traditionally stated. A world that is replete with basic entanglement relations is one that flies directly in the face of the thesis that reality is made up of intrinsically unconnected, independently existing concrete particulars.

Lastly, Kris McDaniel (2008: 132) has argued that this move requires that a perfectly natural property (spin zero) necessarily covaries with a perfectly natural relation (entanglement relation). But this seems to deny what many take to be at the heart of the very concept of perfect naturalness: that perfectly natural properties and relations are modally free with respect to one another.[52]

4.4.2 Against Priority Microphysicalism

While quantum entanglement offers compelling grounds for the falsity of PDP per se, the resilient defender of a particular variant of Part-Priority has a response close at hand. As stated, the conclusion of the argument from the failure of whole-part supervenience noted earlier is entirely compatible with PM; even if PDP fails as a *global* thesis regarding the mereological ordering of the world, we need not rid PDP entirely in so far as we may put it to use in a more restricted capacity. Even if duplicating the parts and their basic arrangements does not suffice to duplicate *all* mereological wholes, this is plausibly true for all macrophysical or "higher-level" wholes such as molecules and living organisms. In other words, the failure of whole-part supervenience obtains solely at the quantum

142 *Against Part-Priority*

level. PM may be true even if Part-Priority as a global fundamental mereology is false.[53]

This rejoinder on behalf of the Priority Microphysicalist surfaces the following dilemma at this stage in the argument: either every macrophysical object is grounded in its microphysical parts or it is not. If every macrophysical object is grounded in its microphysical parts, then the failure of PDP is a pervasive feature of the world given the ubiquity of quantum entanglement. If, however, not every macrophysical object is grounded in its microphysical parts—if PDP fails for at least some macrophysical wholes—then Priority Microphysicalism is false.[54] Either way, PDP fails.

The above argument, however, can be easily adapted to cover Priority Microphysicalism as well.[55] If whole-part supervenience fails for some macrophysical wholes in virtue of their possessing emergent properties, this is evidence for the falsity of PM. We can then revise premise 2 of the earlier argument to the following:

2*. Some macrophysical wholes exhibit emergent properties.

The revised conclusion of *the argument from the failure of whole-part supervenience* being:

3*. Therefore, some macrophysical wholes fail to be grounded in their proper parts.

As was noted in §1 of this chapter, one important tenet of PM is that the occupants of the microphysical level are the exclusive bearers of the perfectly natural properties. Recall that the defender of an atomistic gloss on PM—the view that the mereologically simple microphysical parts of wholes are basic and are ontologically prior to their wholes—is committed to the following thesis concerning the various levels from which the non-redundant or fundamental causal powers of the world are to be drawn:

(MC) *Micro-Causation*: All macro-causation takes place in virtue of the causation on the level of the (ultimate parts) or the micro-level. Macro-causation is entirely derivative and piggybacks on the causation of the micro-constituents.

(Hütteman 2004)[56]

On MC the facts concerning the *non-redundant* causal joints of reality are calibrated exclusively by (ideal) fundamental physics. Hence, all macro-causation, on this view, is redundant in that it can be exhaustively explained in terms of the causal powers of microphysical entities. While the causal powers of molecules and biological organisms may be *relatively* natural with respect to the perfectly natural properties instantiated at the level of fundamental physics, such properties need not be invoked in our inventory of scientifically *irreducible* facts about the world.[57]

4.4.2.1 *Chemical Structure*

But might the irreducible holism distinctive of entangled systems extend beyond the quantum realm to molecules and biological organisms? I take this to be a question best answered by a metaphysically informed examination of the status of reductionism in chemistry and biology. My own inclination is the same as Papineau's (2008: 146):

> Non-local entanglement is ubiquitous in the real world. I illustrated it above by considering a system of two separated electrons. But it will also be present in systems comprising basic physical persisting objects, like atoms and molecules. The joint state of the local components of such composite systems will characteristically contain information additional to that implied by the local properties of the components ... There are facts about persisting objects like atoms and molecules that transcend the intrinsic physical properties of their spatial parts plus the spatial and causal relations between them.

What Papineau is suggesting is that PDP may well be falsified not only by quantum wholes, but by atomic and molecular wholes as well; there are facts involving the instantiation of perfectly natural properties by composite objects that are not reducible to facts about the perfectly natural properties (and relations) of their proper parts.

Let us begin at the intersection of physics and chemistry: *quantum chemistry*. At the heart of quantum chemistry is the appropriation of quantum mechanics to explain chemical bonding and structure. Following Robin Hendry (2010; forthcoming), for any isolated atom or molecule, there is a resultant Hamiltonian, a quantum mechanical description of the energetic properties of the entire system. The resultant Hamiltonian for an atom or molecule is determined by enumerating the various nuclei and electrons in the system, together with their interacting forces, the most prominent determinant of molecular structure and bonding being the electrostatic (Coulomb) force between charged particles.

As Hendry points out, it is very often the case that molecular structure is *holistic* in that it fails to be adequately captured in terms of resultant (Coulombic) Hamiltonians alone.[58] In other words, the mere enumeration of electrons and nuclei together with electrostatic forces does not yield the distinctive properties and causal dispositions that characterize chemical structures. Hendry (2010: 186) notes:

> Molecular structures cannot be recovered from the Coulomb Schrödinger equations, but not because of any mathematical intractability.

144 *Against Part-Priority*

The problem is that they are not there to begin with. The Coulomb Schrödinger equations describe mere assemblages of electrons and nuclei rather than molecules, which are structured entities.

Commenting on the calculation of the total energy state of complex molecules (by solving the molecular wave function by means of the Born-Oppenheimer approximation), Robert Bishop (2005: 714) makes precisely the same point:

> The Born-Oppenheimer approach amounts to a *change in topology*—i.e., a change in the mathematical elements modeling physical phenomena—as well as a *change in ontology*, including fundamental physical elements absent in the quantum description; in the case of molecular chemistry, the new ontological elements are structures absent from quantum mechanics . . . Now the molecular structure challenge to reduction can be put very succinctly: Neither the topology nor the ontology appropriate to molecular structure can be derived from or found in quantum mechanics alone . . . Hence, an empirically and explanatorily important structure in molecular chemistry looks to be missing from quantum mechanics.[59]

The ontological underpinnings that account for the existence of holistic molecular structure (including novel powers and dispositions,), according to Hendry and Bishop, simply cannot be accounted for in terms of quantum states alone.

One particular example cited by Hendry of the holism exhibited by certain chemical structures is Hydrogen Chloride. As a complex polyatomic molecule, the resultant Coulomb Hamiltonian for HCl can be determined by (i) specifying the electrostatic force predicted by Coulomb's law (ii) enumerating the charges, masses, and values (etc.) for both chlorine (partial negative charge) and hydrogen (partial positive charge), (iii) listing the polar covalent bond that obtains between chlorine and hydrogen, which therein gives rise to a dipole moment, and finally (iv) using the results of steps (i)-(iii) to list the kinetic and potential energy operators and adding them.[60] The resultant Hamiltonian for HCl, on this method, gives rise to a charge distribution that is spherically *symmetrical*. But, as Hendry points out, the charge distribution for HCl cannot be spherically symmetrical in so far as its acidic behavior and distinctive boiling point obtain in virtue of its being an *asymmetrically* charged molecule. The chemical whole HCl, which includes its distinctive causal powers and capacities, cannot be reduced to the features and relations between its component atoms, it is ontologically emergent.

In the case of HCl qua molecular whole, duplicating the parts and their basic arrangements does not suffice to duplicate the whole in that HCl instantiates certain natural properties that fail to supervene on the

Against Part-Priority 145

natural properties of chlorine or hydrogen taken individually or as a pair. Hendry (2010: 187) draws the following conclusion,

> If molecules are ontologically reducible to their physical bases, then they ought to have no causal powers beyond those that are conferred by those physical bases . . . if the acidic behavior of the hydrogen chloride molecule is conferred by its asymmetry, and the asymmetry is not conferred by the molecule's physical basis according to physical laws, then surely there is a prima facie argument that ontological reduction fails.

Since there arguably are causal powers possessed by HCl beyond those conferred by its fundamental physical parts, one can infer that PDP fails with respect to such wholes.

4.4.2.2 *Biological Structure*

Biological explanation is replete with talk of novelty, organization, and structure. Consider the following passage from a standard biology textbook:

> Identifying biological organization at its many levels is fundamental to the study of life . . . With each step upward in the hierarchy of biological order, novel properties emerge that were not present at the simpler levels of organization . . . A molecule such as a protein has attributes not exhibited by any of its component atoms, and a cell is certainly much more than a bag of molecules. If the intricate organization of the human brain is disrupted by a head injury, that organ will cease to function properly, even though all its parts may still be present. And an organism is a living whole greater than the sum of its parts . . . [W]e cannot fully explain a higher level of order by breaking it down into parts. A dissected animal no longer functions; a cell reduced to its chemical ingredients is not longer a cell. Disrupting a living system interferes with the meaningful explanation of its processes.[61]

Following the lead of Manfred Laubichler and Günter Wagner (2001), molecular biology centers on the investigation of the mechanisms that ground the fundamental processes of life, such as DNA replication, protein synthesis, regulation of gene expression, cross-membrane transport, metabolic pathways, and intracellular communication. By their lights, the developmental mechanisms that ground the earlier processes are features of *structured* cellular *wholes*. Explanations in developmental molecular biology are irreducibly *holistic* in that they make reference to either the cell qua biological whole or the dynamical properties of developing systems; an appeal to component molecular properties (and their interactions) to explain the mechanisms that guide the unfolding of cellular growth and spatial differentiation are incomplete. All of the earlier developmental mechanisms take place within, and are enabled and constrained by, cellular wholes themselves. Lenny Moss (2003:95) argues along similar lines that "cellular context as a whole is basic to the nature and continuity of living beings and is irreducible to any of its constituent parts." As a result, duplicating the molecular parts and their basic arrangements does not suffice to duplicate the cellular whole with its accompanying perfectly natural properties (developmental mechanisms). Arguably, PDP fails with respect to cellular wholes.

John Dupré (2010) cites the phenomena of protein folding as an example of the emergent causal dispositions of cells at work. One particularly thorny problem in developmental molecular biology is accounting for the "transition from an amino acid sequence to the baroquely complex structure that results as this sequence folds into a three-dimensional shape." Dupré notes that while the precise topology of the protein structure is essential to its proper functioning, such structure is "strongly undetermined by the chemical properties of the links between successive amino acids." What is required "over and above" the chemical properties of the component sequence are further "chaperone" proteins to help aid in correct unfolding. Dupré argues that it is the structural context of the cellular whole (in its supplying the requisite chaperone proteins) that causally disposes the parts of the genome to produce an appropriately folded protein. Hütteman and Love (2011: 540) concur in stating, "Scientists now recognize that the causal powers requisite for folding are not all contained within the parts of the linear polypeptide." Dupré himself concludes, "The cell, I think we must say, with all its intricate structure and diverse contents, is what causes these contents to behave in these life-sustaining ways."

All of the earlier examples from physics, chemistry, and biology suggest that PDP fails with respect to certain microphysical *and* macrophysical wholes, thereby calling into question both Part-Priority as well as PM.

4.4.3 *Whole-Priority and Empirical Adequacy*

I want to conclude this chapter by exploring the prospects of moving from the failure of a Part-Priority grounding description for certain composite objects to the stronger thesis that there are empirical considerations that are consistent with (and are highly suggestive of) Whole-Priority grounding structure in nature (and hence instances of grounding wholes). That is, the existence of grounding wholes is not inconsistent with what we know to be the case from our best empirical knowledge of the world.

In certain cases of ontological emergence, we have not only the *whole's* failure to supervene on its proper parts, but the causal properties as well as the very *parts* themselves appear to be inseparably tied to or constrained by their respective wholes. A word of caution at this point. While I think the empirical considerations that follow show that the metaphysical priority of wholes over parts is not in tension with well-entrenched empirical theory in each respective domain, they do not constitute demonstrative evidence in favor such a view. While fundamental metaphysics ought to be guided and constrained by our best empirical theories (see the Introduction), I am not attempting to straightforwardly "read off" a Whole-Priority fundamental mereology from empirical data (given that empirical data is often metaphysically underdetermined). In my estimation, empirical theory is insufficient, on its own, to dictate fundamental metaphysics. At minimum, then, the empirical considerations from quantum mechanics, chemistry, and biology to follow can be said to show that Whole-Priority is empirically adequate and not in tension with our best empirical theories; Whole-Priority is scientifically serious. At best, these considerations are *suggestive* of the metaphysical priority of wholes over their parts and the existence of grounding wholes in nature.[62]

4.4.3.1 Whole-Priority in Quantum Mechanics

Consider quantum entangled wholes once more. The spin states of the particles that now compose an entangled whole in the singlet state can no longer be defined apart from the whole of which they are a part. As parts of a genuinely non-separable system, neither particle instantiates a *pure* (unmixed) spin state, a state that can be individuated apart from the other particles in the entangled whole. The components of entangled systems, then, are "structure-laden" in that the spin state of each individual particle can be specified only by reference to the entangled whole. Karakostas (2009:12, 17–18) summarizes this nicely:

> In considering any entangled compound system, the nature and properties of component parts may only be determined from their "role"—the forming pattern of the inseparable web of relations—within the whole ... In a truly non-separable physical system, as in an entangled quantum system, the part does acquire a different identification within the whole from what it does outside the whole, in its own "isolated," separate state.

And,

> for the non-separable character of the behavior of an entangled quantum system precludes in a novel way the possibility of describing its component subsystems as well-defined individuals, each with its own pure state or pre-determined physical properties. Upon any case of quantum entanglement, it is not permissible to consider the parts of a quantum whole as self-autonomous, intrinsically defined individual entities.
>
> (Ibid., p. 14)

The fact remains that many philosophers interpret the holistic implications of quantum entangled wholes to suggest that such wholes fit the description of what we have been calling grounding wholes (§3.4). Heil (2012: 47) is worth reiterating on this score:

> Suppose quantum systems, systems of "entangled" particles, are genuinely "holistic," suppose their characteristics really do outstrip characteristics of their ingredients . . . [t]he "parts" of such systems would have the status of modes: the wholes of which they are parts would not depend on the parts, the parts would depend on the wholes.
> (Heil 2012: 47)

According to Heil, the grounding structure that obtains between an entangled whole and its proper parts is precisely that of Whole-Priority.[63] So much so that he emphasizes that fundamental particles "are abstractions, the nature and identity of which is dependent on systems to which they belong" (ibid., 48).

In a similar manner, Josh Parsons (unpublished) makes the explicit connection between the holism embodied in entanglement and fundamental mereology:

> This proposal is really nothing more than the application of a fairly traditional metaphysical idea–the idea that the fundamental ontology of the world consists of substances–where that means things that exist independently of each other. The elements of a non-separable quantum system don't seem to exist independently. Therefore, they are not substances, and if you buy into an ontology of substances, then they are not part of the fundamental ontology of the world.

Moreover, cosmologist George Ellis (2001: 270) writes,

> Most quantum states are entangled states. This means that instead of thinking of bottom-up action by invariant constituents, one must consider cooperative effects between the constituent components that *modify their very nature* . . . In principle the particles have *no separate existence*. It can be suggested that our worldview should take this seriously, if indeed we take quantum theory seriously.[64]

Lastly, philosophers of physics Fredrick Kronz and Justin Tiehen (2002: 346) refer to entangled quantum wholes as exhibiting what they call "dynamic emergence" which they characterize in the following manner:

> Emergent wholes have contemporaneous parts, but these parts cannot be characterized independently from their respective wholes . . . it does not make sense to talk about reducing an emergent whole to its

parts, since the parts are in some sense constructs of our characterization of the whole . . . Emergent wholes are produced by an essential ongoing interaction of its parts, and *when that interaction ensues the independent particles become dependent*. But, if some of those parts are identical particles, then *they cannot be identified with those that existed prior to the interaction*, as a result of Pauli's exclusion principle. That is to say, *the independent parts cease to exist and the dependent parts come into existence*.[65]

Not only does quantum entanglement provide a counterexample to PDP as we have seen, it also suggests a more radical dependence ordering between entangled wholes and their proper parts such that even the very parts themselves are inseparable from the entangled whole.

4.4.3.2 Whole-Priority in Chemistry

Lest anyone think that the Whole-Priority grounding structure that is thought to characterize entangled wholes is a phenomenon unique to the domain of quantum mechanics, consider the following charge by philosopher of chemistry Joseph Earley (2003: 89):

> Most philosophers have yet to recognize that, when components enter into chemical combination, *those components do not, in general, maintain the same identity that they would have had absent that combination* . . . Interactions of such insights with the philosophical study of wholes and parts (mereology) is in its initial stages. It would be useful to develop a mereology adequate to deal with chemical systems, in order to facilitate future progress in dealing with other and more complex problems.[66]

And,

> An adequate theory of wholes and parts (mereology) must take into account that when individuals enter combinations of interesting sorts they no longer are the very same individuals that existed prior to the composition. It appears that no such formal theory now *actually* exists.

Earley appeals to the dissolving of sodium chloride (NaCl) in water to form a saline solution. When the saline solution is produced, Earley argues:

> [B]oth the constituents of the salt and also the solvent water are significantly changed. Parts are modified by their composition into a whole. This situation is excluded, by definition, from standard mereology. Mereology needs to be extended, to apply to cases where the assumption that wholes do not influence parts is not applicable.

150 *Against Part-Priority*

Earley is no lone voice in the philosophy of chemistry regarding the robust constraints on the parts of chemical compounds. There has been recent efforts by the likes of philosopher of science Rom Harré and chemist Jean-Pierre Llored (2010, 2011) to develop a formal mereological framework that mirrors the real unity and structure that characterize chemical compounds. Harré and Llored (2011) point to one of the most influential theories of chemical bonding of the twentieth century—molecular orbital approximation—as an example of the need for an alternative mereological framework that takes seriously the integral unity of chemical wholes as suggested by Earley.[67]

Classical accounts of molecular bonding centered on a molecule being a collection of atoms, each sustained by their individual combining power. This understanding of the molecule eventually gave rise to the shared electron theory of chemical bonding in which the positively charged nuclei of the atoms attract the shared negatively charged electrons. According to molecular orbital theory as advanced by the Nobel prize-winning chemist Robert Mulliken (1932, 1981), the bonding between the individual atoms is understood as a combination of their electronic wave functions (atomic orbitals). The total electronic wave function for the entire molecule (molecular orbital) is then calculated as the weighted sum of its constituent atomic orbitals. According to Mulliken, the electrons are "delocalized" in the sense that they are not assigned to individual bonds between atoms, rather, they are treated in relation to the nuclei of the entire molecular whole itself.

Mulliken offered the example of the molecule helium hydride (HeH) where "the atom of helium He disappears during the synthesis of the molecule HeH" such that "even ion-cores lose their thing-like status."[68] For Mulliken, then, a molecule is a composite whole in which the atoms "lose their singularity."[69] Reflecting on the implications of molecular orbital theory for mereology, Harré and Llored (2011: 73) remark:

> Using the expression "diatomic molecule" for such a thing as a molecule of HCl or H2 suggests that the mereological analysis of these complex entities should lead us to say that the parts of such molecules are hydrogen and chlorine *atoms*. However, Mulliken's solution to the problem of how atoms are bound into molecules involves electron orbits that are not centered on the nuclei of the constituent atoms. Instead the one-electron wave function approximation for an electron becomes molecule centered, the paired nuclei serving as the reference for the model interpretation of the new orbital as a linear function of the wave equations for each electron considered with respect to each of the apparently constituent nuclei. If the criterion of identity for an atom or the ionic residue of such an atom, is the composition of the electron shells then these criteria could not be satisfied by the components of a complex molecule. The relevant nuclei form a doublet which, speaking in the accent of Mulliken, are a unit without parts, using the molecular orbital theory of electrons

as the criterion for an individual part. A molecule does not have atoms or ions or even the nuclei of ions as its parts.

Again, noting the implications for mereology,

> We could express this insight in a mereological principle: Constituent atoms of molecules are not parts of those molecules when we look at the total entity in the light of molecular orbitals. Unlike chair parts which preserve their material properties whether in the chair or on the bench. Nor are they parts in the sense that buckets of water are parts of the ocean . . . looked at from the point of view of their constituent parts they are potentialities, not the things that are thereby afforded.
> (74)

Consequently, it is not unreasonable to think that chemical combination is such that the elements that are combined are substantially altered such that "when individuals enter combinations of interesting sorts they no longer are the very same individuals that existed prior to the composition."[70] That is to say, established empirical theory about chemical bonding (molecular orbital theory) is consistent with understanding chemical wholes along the lines of grounding wholes as per Substantial Priority.

4.4.3.3 Whole-Priority in Biology

Turning again to the domain of biology, not only do certain biological organisms instantiate emergent properties, there is also good reason to think that the proper parts of organisms are inseparably related to the organisms of which they are a part. In fact, philosopher of biology Evelyn Fox Keller (2010: 22) cites "the dependence of the identity of parts, and the interactions among them, on higher-order effects" as one of the defining features of biological explanation. Citing the example of a cell and its constituent genome, Keller goes on to claim that the global properties of biological wholes can not only causally influence but also fix the very identity of the parts of such wholes: "the very definition of what (if anything) a gene is depends on the properties of the cell in which the DNA is embedded."[71]

The recent advent of systems biology illustrates a biological holism with respect to the proper parts of living organisms. Biological organisms are *autopoietic systems*: self-organizing and self-regulating systems that perform the necessary operations to maintain their own identity. According to philosopher of biology Alicia Juarrero (2000: 31), autopoietic systems are "dissipative structures" that exhibit constraints on the powers and identities of their proper parts:

> By delimiting the parts' initial repertoire of behavior, the structured whole in which the elements are suddenly embedded also redefines

them. They are now something they were not before, nodes in a network, components of a system. As such, they are unable to access states that might have been available to them as independent entities.

Some philosophers of biology explicitly endorse what I am calling Whole-Priority with respect to biological organisms. Again, theoretical biologist Manfrid Laubichler and evolutionary biologist Günter Wagner (2000: 23) represent this view nicely:

> In many cases, and in particular in the most problematic ones, the theories we are concerned with refer to sub-organismal objects, such as genes, or cellular and organismal characters (traits). The relationship of these objects to the individual organism can be of one of two kinds: (i) the organism can be thought of as a composite entity "made up" of its traits and characters, or (ii) the traits can be thought of as (conceptual) abstractions of the organism. These two scenarios differ as to which object—part or whole—is ontologically prior. In the first case the characters or parts are ontologically prior to the higher level object or the organism . . . In the second case the higher level unit is ontologically prior. In this instance the sub-organismal objects (characters) are defined as conceptual abstractions of a higher level integrated whole and thus ontologically secondary. Here we argue that most biological objects at the sub-organismal scale are of the second kind. *In other words, we assume the ontological primacy of organisms and derive the objects relevant to the theory, i. e. the biological characters, by means of a conceptual decomposition of the organism.*[72]

The kind of structure that defines living organisms not only threatens to undermine PDP, but also provides plausible grounds for thinking that Whole-Priority is consistent with well-established theories in biology.

We have examined what is perhaps the predominant fundamental mereology on offer in the recent literature, Part-Priority, in its most prevalent form, PM. I argued that Part-Priority in particular is faced with the challenge of accounting for the metaphysical possibility of gunk as well as the fact that both Part-Priority and PM are ill suited to account for instances of whole-part supervenience failure in the domain of quantum mechanics, chemistry, and systems biology.

Kim (1999: 28) has argued that a whole's exhibiting constraints and causal influence on its proper parts borders on the incoherent: "But how is it possible for the whole to causally affect its constituent parts on which its very existence and nature depend?" I think Kim is right on point in this regard. But far from substantiating the alleged incoherence of a whole exhibiting causal influence on its parts, the earlier insights, I think, serve to stand Kim's conclusion on its head: it is precisely *because* some wholes exhibit such influence that they thereby fail to be grounded in their proper parts. We also noted that the failure of a Part-Priority grounding description for certain wholes is suggestive of (but does not entail) a stronger dependence ordering between a whole and its parts, namely, one that conforms to the notion of a grounding whole as per Substantial Priority. I turn now to a more direct attempt to motivate my preferred fundamental mereology, Substantial Priority, by showing that if offers a unified solution to a host of conundrums in the metaphysics of material objects.

Notes

1. As we will see in what follows, I do not take the falsity of Part-Priority *per se* to entail the falsity of PM; the latter could be true even if the former were false. Hence the need to offer independent arguments against PM in addition to those aimed at Part-Priority.
2. I borrow the term "Priority Microphysicalism" from deRosset (2010).
3. For a recent defense of PM that is sensitive to the question of fundamental mereology, see Heil (2012).
4. For a thorough treatment of supervenience as a stronger determination relation, see Heil (1998).
5. See Hütteman (2004: 122).
6. Ibid. 10.
7. Regarding the option of taking the atomic entities to be extended instead of point-sized, consider the following remarks by physicist Brian Greene: "What are strings made of? There are two possible answers to this question. First, strings are truly fundamental—they are 'atoms,' uncuttable constituents . . . As the absolute smallest constituents of anything and everything, they represent the end of the line . . . in the numerous layers of substructure in the microscopic world. From this perspective, even though strings have spatial extent, the question of their composition is without any content. Were strings to be made of something smaller they would not be fundamental. Instead, whatever strings were composed of would immediately displace them and lay claim to being an even more basic constituent of the universe . . . [A] string is simply a string—as there is nothing more fundamental, it can't be described as being composed of any other substance." (1999: 141–142). Consequently, on this option, the advocate of PM may accept the mereological fundamentality of micro-entities while, at the same, time reject the thesis that such entities are point-sized—i.e., unextended. Some have argued that there are good physical considerations to go this route in so far as entities that occupy a point of space at any given time would exhibit an infinite energy-density. The defender of extended simples argues just this, see Simons (2004: 373).
8. This option is noted by Schaffer (2003: 509–512).
9. Again, the options here for an atomless supervenience are many. A few other suggestions would be where quantum theory is best construed as pertaining to various kinds of stuff (Lavine 1991) or perhaps even to quantized excitations of a field as suggested by Redhead (1988) and Ginsberg (1984).
10. cf. Lewis (2006).
11. Here I restrict myself to Lewis's own preferred gloss on PM. There are, however, various non-Humean views that, with Lewis, locate the metaphysically basic entities at the microphysical level yet, contra Lewis, are much more liberal concerning the range of fundamental external relations that

154 *Against Part-Priority*

     relate the occupants of the microphysical level. See Hawley (2001), Oppy (2000: 77), and Zimmerman (1997). On such views, the riches of the world (including facts about the laws of nature as well as the unity of perduring or exduring particulars) cannot be adequately accounted for along the austere lines of Humean Supervenience as stated by Lewis.

12. See Lewis (1999c: 226).
13. Recall Armstrong (1997: 12): "[W]hatever supervenes or, as we can also say, is entailed or necessitated, . . . is not something ontologically additional to the subvenient, or necessitating, entity or entities. What supervenes is no addition to being."
14. See Schaffer (2004). Also, Lewis explicitly states that there is a certain naturalness ranking for objects as well as properties: "Among all the countless things and classes that there are, most are miscellaneous, gerrymandered, ill-demarcated. Only an elite minority are carved at the joints, so that their boundaries are established by objective sameness and difference in nature. Only these elite things and classes are eligible to serve as referents." (1999d: 65).
15. Papineau actually argues for the stronger claim that the physicalist *ought not* follow suit precisely in virtue of the existence of higher-level physical properties that are not reducible to properties occupying the level of fundamental physics.
16. This is underscored nicely by Corry (2012).
17. Note that Sider intends a much stronger thesis here than simply that the macroscopic covaries with the microscopic. Rather, he has in mind a determination thesis: the properties of macroscopic wholes are *determined* by properties and relations between their microphysical parts (140).
18. See Hütteman (2004) for a full-scale critique of PM and the the argument from the unrivaled success of microphysical explanation.
19. Where by "common sense" I simply mean propositions that are believed pre-theoretically with respect to the domain in question.
20. See Ladyman and Ross (2007, esp. Chapter 1) and Sider (2013) for an example of the outright rejection of what I am calling mereological Mooreanism.
21. Note Schaffer (2010b: 47): "I think common sense distinguishes mere aggregates from integrated wholes . . . Common sense probably does endorse the priority of the parts in cases of mere aggregation, such as with the heap. Yet common sense probably endorses the priority of the whole in cases of integrated wholes, such as with the syllable."
22. As was noted earlier, Substantial Priority endorses PS with respect to grounded wholes. But, and this is key, it does not do so *on the basis of* common sense alone as is argued here. Although see the previous note where Schaffer appeals to common sense to establish the truth of PS for what he calls "aggregates."
23. The argument is advanced by Schaffer (2010b) and hinted at in Cameron (2008).
24. I grant that Lewis himself would be weary of this first premise in so far as he was inclined to endorse the contingency of Humean Supervenience. Even so, it is difficult to see what substantive *metaphysical* content is to be given to the claim that wholes are metaphysically determined by their parts without taking grounding to be a non-contingent affair as per G8.
25. Recall that G8 states: $(x \triangleright y \rightarrow \Box(Ex \rightarrow x \triangleright y))$.
26. Independent support for this insight here would be the non-contingency of composition conditions for objects. If one takes an composite object's composition conditions to be a part of the nature or the ontological category to which that object belongs (substance or aggregate, for instance), and in so far as the content of ontological categories remains fixed across possible worlds including such categories, then so will the composition conditions.

Against Part-Priority   155

27. See Schaffer (2003) and McDaniel (2006) in particular.
28. For example, see Dehmelt (1989), Georgi (1989: 456), Greene (1999: 141–42).
29. Where a region of space is maximally continuous iff (i) it is filled with matter, (ii) it is a continuous region, and (iii) it is not a proper sub-region of some continuous matter-filled region.
30. For instance, it has been argued that there may very well be empirical considerations that count against the Pointy View in that entities with zero-dimensional spatial extent would have infinite density, which thereby causes difficulties for the Dirac equation, "A version of the nonrelativistic Schrödinger equation taking special relativity theory into account . . . and is needed to discuss the quantum mechanical states of heavy atoms and the fine structural features of atomic spectra generally" (Martin, 2010). Both Simons (2004: 373) and Lowe (2006: 139) argue along these lines. In particular, Simons notes, "However, such point-particles are physically impossible because they would have to have infinite density, being a finite mass in zero volume. Leaving this minor embarrassment aside as a product of idealization may be acceptable for physicists, but a metaphysician has to take it literally and seriously. Therefore there can be no point-particles." For further reference on the physics underlying the objection, see Daintith (2000: 141). In addition, McDaniel (2003) argues that both the Pointy View and MaxCon are incompatible with the metaphysical possibility of co-located material objects. For friends of constitutionalism, this is evidence enough against the Pointy View and MaxCon.
31. Given that Hudson needs *both* (ii) and (iii) for the argument to go through, I take it that blocking one such entailment suffices to block the conclusion.
32. See Hudson (2001: 89).
33. For a nice historical treatment of gunk and indivisibility, see Zimmerman (1996).
34. Or, at the very least, there is no reason to think that such a world is inconceivable.
35. For a classic objection to DAUP, see van Inwagen (2001: 75–95).
36. This is the route taken by McDaniel (2006) as well.
37. For a nice treatment of the various reasons offered in defense of the possibility of extended simples are possible, see Gilmore (2014).
38. Ibid., p. 336.
39. Kim tends to use the label "mereological supervenience" for what I am calling Priority Microphysicalism. To me, this is rather imprecise in so far as "mereological supervenience" is vague concerning whole-part and part-whole superveneince and the label is silent as to the level of reality that is taken to host the metaphysically basic entities (micro-level).
40. A similar argument is found in Schaffer (2014).
41. Consider Bird (2007: 13), "The fundamental natural properties are those with non-redundant causal powers."
42. The example is from Rea (2012).
43. Kim (1978).
44. McDaniel (2008:129).
45. Cf. Kim (1993: 167). Also, see Karakostas (2009: 6): "if the whole state of a compound system is completely determined by the separate states of its subsystems, then the whole state necessarily supervenes on the separate states."
46. Here I restrict my focus to a particle-theoretic interpretation of classical mechanics. One could easily restate this in field-theoretic terms such that the values of fundamental parameters of a field are well defined at every point of the underlying manifold. See Karakostas (2009) for more along these lines.
47. See also Howard (1989: 226).

156 *Against Part-Priority*

48. I am indebted to Tim Maudlin (2007: 54–61) in what follows.
49. Born's rule (named after the physicist Max Born) is used to determine the expectation value for each spin configuration of a given system. Following Maudlin (1998), "Given the state S, one can calculate expectation values for all of the Hermitean operators in the spin space of each single particle. The calculation is quite simple: for any given direction, there is a 50% chance that the spin will be found up and a 50% chance that it will be found down."
50. In addition to the singlet state as an example of an entangled system, Maudlin (2003: 483) notes that "the failure of the quantum state of the whole to supervene on the quantum states of the parts is most strikingly illustrated by the so-called m = 0 Triplet state." He formulates the m = 0 Triplet state in terms of x-directional spin as follows: $\frac{1}{\sqrt{2}}|x\uparrow\rangle_a|x\uparrow\rangle_b - \frac{1}{\sqrt{2}}|x\downarrow\rangle_a|x\downarrow\rangle_b$. He argues that the mixed state ascribed to each individual particle in the m = 0 Triplet state is identical to the mixed state of each particle in the singlet state (50% chance to each outcome). The difference, argues Maudlin, between the singlet state and the m = 0 Triplet state can only be captured by a "*global measurement* made on both particles, and not by any possible *local* measurement made on one particle" (483). Maudlin again concludes, "The quantum state of a whole therefore does not supervene on the states of its parts, exhibiting a form of holism" (ibid.). In our terminology, the comparison of the singlet and the m = 0 Triplet state reveals that the duplication of the parts does not suffice to duplicate the whole, PDP fails.
51. Note that in claiming that the entangled system as a whole supervenes on its component parts together with the fundamental, non-spatiotemporal entanglement relation requires a weaker version of Humean Supervenience.
52. More precisely, the free recombinability of perfectly natural properties can be stated as follows: If (i) x has F and y has G, (ii) x and y are contingently existing objects, and (iii) F and G are perfectly natural properties, then there is a possible world in which both x and y exist, but in which x has F and y does not have G. See McDaniel (2007b: 247).
53. See Melnyk (2003) for a proposal along these lines.
54. See Silberstein and McGeever (1999: 200).
55. All of the arguments against PM from here on out are likewise arguments against Part-Priority as well.
56. For representatives of MC see Lewis (1999:66) and Sider (2008:4). Lewis remarks, "Indeed physics discovers which things and classes are the most elite of all; but others are elite also, though to a lesser degree. The less elite are so because they are connected to the most elite by chains of definability. Long chains, by the time we reach the moderately elite classes of cats and pencils and puddles; but the chains required to reach the utterly ineligible would be far longer still."
57. Hawthorne (2006: viii) uses the apt term "micro-naturalism" to capture what I am (following Hütteman) calling "micro-causation."
58. This is *not* to say that resultant Hamiltonians fail to accurately describe molecular structure in *any* sense.
59. Interestingly enough, Bishop explicitly identifies what I am calling Part-Priority as the root of the reduction of chemical structure to quantum mechanics stating: "*mereological dependence*, where properties of wholes depend in some way on properties of their parts, looks to indicate that quantum physics supplies the 'parts' for the 'wholes'–molecules–of chemistry. In other words, quantum physics provides the base from which the properties of chemical molecules arise."
60. Hendry (2006: 182).

61. Campbell (1996: 2–4).
62. I recognize that the representative considerations that follow are highly selective and will constitute philosophical "cherry-picking" in the minds of some. I plead guilty, although I emphasize that I'm not asking the reader to take the quotations that follow as positive warrant in favor of Whole-Priority, just that the view is scientifically serious.
63. I hesitate to follow Heil here in characterizing the parts of entangled wholes (particles) as *modes* precisely because I take there to be a distinction between the parthood relation and the characterization relation (although, to be fair, he does put the word "part" in quotation marks). Heil's labeling the entangled particles as modes of the whole, in my opinion, trades on the inference that because the parts of entangled wholes stand in the very same relation to their ground as do modes and their bearers—viz. ontological dependence—that therefore the parts of such systems *just are* modes. But the fact that x and y both stand in R to their individual grounds does not entail that x and y belong to the same ontological category (so if R is the relation of ontological dependence, x could be a number standing in R to a structure as per mathematical structuralism, or y could be a set standing in R to its members collectively). In my opinion, the identification of dependent or grounded parts with modes stems from the overall neglect of the concept of an inseparable part in contemporary metaphysics.
64. Emphasis mine.
65. Emphasis mine.
66. My emphasis.
67. It is important to note that Harré and Llored (2011) explicitly make reference to Earley in that they see their project to be an extension of his. Their remarks echo Earley's: "And that is why again, the topological chemical quantum turn is of the utmost importance for philosophical enquiries such as this. That is why, too, philosophers need to go back to laboratories of research to grasp what scientists are really doing with their new models and apparatus." (2011: 75).
68. Harré and Llored (2011: 70).
69. Ibid.
70. Earley (2005: 85).
71. Cf. Dupré (2010: 41).
72. Emphasis mine.

5 Substantial Priority
Cats, Statues, and Lumps

My aim in this chapter and the next is to argue against the widespread consensus in the literature that no intermediate composite objects, let alone ordinary medium-sized objects like people, trees, and tigers, are fundamental. Recall that a universal assumption shared by Priority Microphysicalists and Priority Monists alike is that the tenable options in fundamental mereology exclude views that assign metaphysical fundamentality to ordinary, medium-sized objects; the metaphysically fundamental entities reside exclusively at either the "top" or "bottom" level of the hierarchy of composition (if there is a bottom). All chains of metaphysical grounding run *through* intermediate composite objects without ever terminating *in* them. Consequently, no mereologically intermediate objects, such as persons and other living organisms, are metaphysically fundamental.

My aim in this chapter is to argue against this widespread assumption in the literature. In §3.3 I referred to this ubiquitous assumption as "No Fundamental Intermediates" and formulated it as follows (where "I" refers to intermediate):

No Fundamental Intermediates: $\Box(\forall x)(Ix \to \neg(Fx))$.

No Fundamental Intermediates is a deeply entrenched assumption in contemporary metaphysics. Even Daniel Korman (2015a), the stalwart defender of conservatism regarding ordinary material objects, remarks "Even those who think that ordinary objects exist will likely find it natural to suppose that no ordinary composites are fundamental: all ordinary composites are ultimately going to be grounded in their simple microscopic parts."

In this chapter, I defend Substantial Priority—and thus the tenability of at least some fundamental intermediate composite objects—by highlighting its theoretical utility in providing a unified solution to a variety of puzzles in material objects.

5.1 A Unified Solution to Puzzles in Material Objects

The burden of the present chapter is to put on display some of the virtues of Substantial Priority. The view, say I and others before me, is worthy of consideration in so far as it offers a unified solution to a host of conundrums in contemporary metaphysics.[1] Substantial Priority is not only scientifically serious (see §4.4) but also preserves many of our cherished intuitions about the denizens of spacetime. By Substantial Priority offering a *unified* solution to the puzzles that follow, I mean the very same metaphysical machinery afforded by Substantial Priority underlies the denial of at least one premise in all of the conundrums to follow.

As those well-traveled in the literature in this area will acknowledge, *every* solution to the following puzzles must learn to live with some counterintuitive consequence or other. And I freely admit Substantial Priority is no exception on this score. I take it as a general methodological principle that we ought to favor a solution to the puzzles that has, on balance, the most important advantages and the least serious drawbacks (see the Introduction). As what one perceives to be "the most important advantages" will inevitably be person-relative to some extent (as well as what counts as a "serious drawback"), I leave it to the reader to decide for themselves the merits of Substantial Priority alongside the likes of mereological essentialism, dominant kinds, constitutionalism, mereological nihilism, stage theory, perdurantism, and alternative neo-Aristotelian solutions. I offer the view here only as a viable option alongside these other models in so far as it aims to offer a unifying solution to puzzles in mereological metaphysics.

To begin, I follow the consensus in taking the following to be prephilosophical beliefs about material objects that are worth preserving:

Existence: There are composite material objects.
Survival: Composite objects survive the loss or replacement of some of their proper parts.
No Coincidence: Two composite material objects cannot exist in the same place at the same time.
Change: Composite material objects persist through time and change.
Identity: Necessarily, identity is a transitive relation.

While I'm of the opinion that we ought to try to accommodate all of the above intuitions in our theorizing about material objects, I do think that some are more deeply entrenched than others. I understand **Identity**, for instance, to be more firmly established as a datum worth preserving than **No Coincidence**, even though I take the denial of the latter to only slightly less counterintuitive than the former. With the aforementioned commonsense intuitions in place, let's turn to the puzzles.

5.1.1 Tib and Tibbles

Tibbles the cat is a mereologically complex object. Among the many proper parts of Tibbles-at-t is her tail, call it "Tail." Now, take all of Tibbles minus Tail, call this "Tib," and suppose that Tibbles undergoes an unfortunate accident at t_1 whereby she loses her tail and thus ceases to have Tail as a part. At t_1, then, Tibbles is a tailless cat. With this much in hand, we can generate the following puzzle:

> T1. **Existence:** Tibbles and Tib exist.
> T2. **Proper Parthood:** Tib-at-t ≠ Tibbles-at-t
> T3. **Change:** Tib-at-t = Tib-at-t_1
> T4. **No Coincidence:** Tib-at-t_1 = Tibbles-at-t_1
> T5. **Survival:** Tibbles-at-t_1 = Tibbles-at-t

As is familiar, the puzzle turns on the fact that T1 together with T3-T5 jointly entail the denial of T2 via the transitivity of identity (**Identity**). Premise T2, however, is true by Leibniz's Law in virtue of Tib and Tibbles having distinct properties (topological, modal, and historical properties). Something must give. There are, of course, a host of solutions on offer to the aforementioned conundrum, each of which have rather counterintuitive consequences in denying one of the earlier well-entrenched intuitions.

One of the most prominent solutions is to deny **No Coincidence** and argue that while Tib and Tibbles occupy one and the same region at t_1, they are numerically distinct, albeit spatiotemporally coincident material objects.[2] Another option would be to deny **Identity** and relativize the identity relation to times, sortals, or possible worlds.[3] Yet another would be to reject **Survival** and argue that upon losing Tail, Tibbles thereby ceases to exist, and thus endorse mereological essentialism.[4] Perhaps, some have argued, upon the loss of Tail there is only a single object where we initially thought there were two, albeit one that now belongs to two distinct kinds at t_1. Since Tibbles's dominant kind (i.e., cat) is associated with Tibbles and not Tib, we ought to identify the surviving object with Tibbles and conclude that Tib has ceased to exist at t_1, thereby denying **Change**.[5]

Moreover, some have found solace in an ontology of temporal parts as a means to reject **No Coincidence**: while Tibbles and Tib are distinct four-dimensional spacetime worms with different temporal parts, they nevertheless are partially spatiotemporally coincident at t_1 in virtue of sharing a common temporal part (more on this in what follows).[6] Or, lastly, one might simply deny **Existence** for at least one of the composite objects upon which the paradox is predicated, whether Tibbles or Tib or both.[7]

The problems with the foregoing solutions to the puzzle of Tib and Tibbles are well rehearsed. Here I want to highlight how the machinery of Substantial Priority affords a solution to the puzzle. As is natural to suppose for living organisms, let's say that Tibbles is a composite substance. As a substance qua grounding whole, Tibbles fails to have proper parts that are themselves substances. Again, this is precisely because the existence and identity of the proper parts of composite substances are grounded in their particular substantial wholes (see §3.4). As per T2, since Tib is a proper part of a substance (Tibbles) at t, it follows that Tib is an inseparable part of Tibbles-at-t, and therefore not a fundamental substance at t. The paradox of Tibbles the Cat gets its bite by assuming that the proper parts of Tibbles are substantial or fundamental in precisely the same sense as Tibbles, that cats and their proper parts are of the same ontological category. From T4, together with the plausible assumption that one's status as a substance or non-substance is among its essential (i.e. non-contingent) features, we can infer the denial of T3 (**Change**). If Tib-at-t is essentially grounded in Tibbles-at-t and thus not a substance at t, then it is impossible for Tib-at-t to be identical to Tib-at-t_1, since the latter *just is* Tibbles on the assumption of **No Coincidence**. As a result, Substantial Priority offers principled, non ad-hoc grounds to reject **Change** as it applies to the proper parts of fundamental substances in general, in this case Tib in particular.

What's more, the earlier solution to the paradox of Tibbles the Cat helps with one notable objection to the standard rejection of **Change** as found in the dominant kinds account of Burke (1994a and 1994b) and Rea (2000). For instance, Theodore Sider (2001: 163) contends that the "good old-fashioned implausibility" of a denial of **Change** in this context stems from the following: "We are asked to believe that an artist can destroy a lump of clay by shaping it into a statue, and that a torso can be destroyed by detaching something external to it!" Note the last comment in particular, the one about the torso (Tib) being *externally* related to Tail. If this was the correct description of the relationship between the many proper parts of a living organism such that they were *externally* related with respect to one another, then it is difficult indeed to explain Tib's ceasing to exist upon the detachment of Tail.

But on Substantial Priority, this description of the mereological structure of substances is precisely what we do not have. As grounding wholes, substances are composed only of inseparable parts; each individual part is grounded in the whole of which it is a part. Moreover, the parts of a substance are together many-one grounded in one and the same substantial whole (see §3.4). As Schaffer (2010a) points out, parts that are collectively grounded in a common whole are *internally* related to one another in some sense. Even on Lewis's (1986a: 62) weaker notion of internal relatedness where an internal relation is one that supervenes on the intrinsic natures of its relata, the parts of substantial wholes are related to one another in virtue of their natures, causal properties, and common ground. While Schaffer has a much stronger notion of internality in mind in his argument for Monism, he offers several candidates for internal relatedness among the parts of a substantially unified whole (for Schaffer: the One whole), one of which is the relation of causal connectedness given a neo-Aristotelian view on natures and the causal powers they necessarily confer (see my *Kind-Power Connection* in Chapter 1, §2.4). On this powers-based ontology, since the parts collectively are what they are in virtue of the whole, it belongs to the essence of the causal powers of the parts of a fundamental substance that they be jointly causally connected in the functioning of the whole.[8] The parts of a substance will be causally connected in virtue of each of their intrinsic causal powers being directed toward the functioning of one and the same the whole. If one is sympathetic to a such a powers-based ontology, which many neo-Aristotelians are, then, contra Sider, Tib is internally related to Tail and every other proper part of Tibbles on Substantial Priority.

Consequently, in rejecting T3 (and thereby **Change** with respect to Tib) Substantial Priority offers a principled grounding story as to *why* Tib ceases to exist upon the loss of Tail. In so far as the removal of Tail amounts to the shrinking of Tibbles from t to t_1, Tib at t thereby ceases to exist precisely because it is impossible for an entity that is derivative and essentially grounded (Tib-at-t) to be identical to an entity that is fundamental and essentially ungrounded (Tibbles). Assuming **No Coincidence** (C2), the detachment of Tail at t_1 brings about Tib's demise at t_1 precisely because of the unique grounding structure of that characterizes fundamental substances and their proper parts.

5.1.2 *Goliath and Lumpl*

Let us move on to what is perhaps the most well-known puzzle in material objects, which turns on the relationship between a statue, "Goliath," and the lump of bronze from which it is made, "Lumpl." The problem was reintroduced onto the contemporary scene by Alan Gibbard (1975) and trades on the tension between several of our commonsense intuitions noted earlier. The puzzle consists in the fact that the following plausible theses regarding Goliath and Lumpl are mutually inconsistent:

- C1. **Existence:** Goliath and Lumpl exist.
- C2. **No Coincidence:** If Goliath and Lumpl both exist, then Goliath = Lumpl.
- C3. Goliath has different properties from Lumpl.
- C4. If Goliath has different properties from Lumpl, then Goliath ≠ Lumpl.

The problem, of course, is that C1-C4 cannot all be true. Common sense commends the existence of statues and lumps of bronze, hence C1. C2 is plausible in so far as both Goliath and Lumpl would appear to occupy the very same place and share a great many (if not all) of their proper parts (at least at some level of decomposition). But surely the following principle holds: for any occupied place p, there is exactly one material object that exactly occupies p. On the other hand, Goliath and Lumpl have very different properties, most notably modal properties that ground distinct persistence conditions. Lumpl is able to survive being melted by the artist, not so with Goliath. The melting of Goliath would seem to result in the complete destruction of Goliath. It follows, by Leibniz's Law, that Goliath is not identical to Lumpl (C4).

Following Fine (2003) and others, we can distinguish two broad categories of responses to the earlier puzzle: monism and pluralism. Monist solutions hold fast to **No Coincidence** and claim that Goliath and Lumpl are numerically identical, while pluralist solutions deny this and reject **No Coincidence**. In what follows my aim is not to provide an exhaustive lay of the land regarding monist and pluralist solutions to puzzles in material constitution. Rather, it is to unpack a few of the most prominent solutions so as to properly situate Substantial Priority within the contemporary landscape.

To begin, a straightforward denial of C1 dissolves the problem at hand: there simply *are* no statues and no lumps of bronze to generate the puzzle.[9] Hence, van Inwagen (1990: 111): "If there are no artifacts, then there are no philosophical problems about artifacts." Again, for many, a denial of **Existence** for such objects is the cure that kills the metaphysical patient.

5.1.2.1 *Some Pluralist Solutions*

Let's turn to examine a few of the most prominent pluralistic solutions to the puzzle that deny **No Coincidence** (C2). As with the previous puzzle, one might argue that the puzzle concerning Goliath and Lumpl warrants a commitment to a four-dimensional ontology, whether of a perdurantist or stage-theoretic variety. As a large number of philosophers endorse four-dimensionalism on the basis of its providing a solution to the puzzle of Goliath and Lump (as well as many other puzzles outlined in this chapter), let me briefly unpack perdurantism here (and stage theory next) and quickly outline why some are inclined to reject the view as a viable solution to the puzzles.

The most common four-dimensionalist solution to the puzzle of Goliath and Lumpl is *perdurantism*. For the perdurantist, material objects are temporally as well as spatially extended particulars. Just as you are located in space by having distinct parts at different regions—i.e., spatial parts—you are also located in time by having distinct parts at different times—i.e., temporal parts. On this view, your entire spatiotemporal career consists of the mereological fusion of all of your spatial and temporal parts throughout the duration of your existence. For any given subinterval of your spatiotemporal career, you exist at that subinterval by having a temporal part that exactly overlaps that subinterval. You, however, are only *partially* located at that interval in virtue of one of your parts existing at that interval.

Perdurantism lends a rather straightforward denial of **No Coincidence** (C2). Goliath and Lumpl are numerically distinct material objects with distinct spatiotemporal careers, albeit ones that share one and the same temporal part during the period of coincidence.[10] The spatiotemporal coincidence between Goliath and Lumpl is no more problematic than the momentary spatiotemporal overlap of two distinct roads, only part of each road is picked out during the time of overlap.

One of the many costs of both perdurantism (and stage theory), according to some, is the denial of the following natural and commonplace truth: the "you" that began reading this sentence and the "you" that will finish reading this sentence pick out one and the same thing in its entirety. Persistence plausibly involves one and same object existing wholly and completely at distinct times.[11] On perdurantism, while distinct temporal parts of the candle bear intrinsic properties at different times—straight-at-t_1 and bent-at-t_2—it is not the case that strictly *one and the same* thing loses a property and gains another at a later time. But the belief that persistence involves the strict and complete diachronic continuity is one that is firmly entrenched for many. Perdurantism seems to substitute the successive *replacement* of temporal parts for the notion of genuine change or alteration over time.

Perhaps the most widespread pluralist response (often called the "standard" solution) is to reject C2 (**No Coincidence**) and endorse *constitutionalism*: while Goliath and Lumpl are non-identical complex objects in virtue of having different properties (C3 and C4), the latter nonetheless *constitutes* the former. Albeit weaker than identity, constitution is an intimate relation that serves to facilitate mutual property sharing between that which constitutes and that which is constituted. The constitution relation, according to one of the view's foremost proponents, is "the metaphysical glue of the natural world."[12] Lumps of bronze constitute statues, portions of steel constitute battle-axes, bodies constitute human persons, and chunks of wood constitute chairs. This line sacrifices **No Coincidence** in order to hold fast to **Existence** for statues and lumps of bronze.

Arguably the most common objection leveled against constitutionalism is what is known as the grounding (or indiscernibility) problem (Olson 2001; Zimmerman 1995). Recall that on constitutionalism, Goliath and Lumpl are atom-for-atom qualitative duplicates, they share precisely the same physical profile (same size, shape, structure, weight, texture, and made of the same bits of matter); as such, each object is empirically indistinguishable and share the precisely the same non-modal profile. Yet, on constitutionalism, Goliath and Lumpl each have radically different modal profiles, including different persistence and identity conditions. But if these objects share precisely the same physical and non-modal profiles, then what accounts for such radical modal differences between them, say, in Lumpl's ability to persist despite being flattened? Herein lies the grounding problem for constitutionalism.[13]

5.1.2.2 Some Monist Solutions

One rather prominent monistic solution to the puzzle is a distinct version of four-dimensionalism known as *stage theory* or *exdurantism*. On *stage theory*, in contrast to perdurantism, ordinary material objects are identical to a single stage that is wholly present at each moment it exists; it turns out, however, that each stage is instantaneous and maximally short-lived.[14] Thus, ordinary material objects such as persons, books, playing cards, and molecules *just are* instantaneous stages.

If so, how then do we account for numerical sameness or identity across time on stage theory? Here the stage theorist takes a page from Lewis (1986a: 9–10) in construing identity across time as being analogous to identity across possible worlds. Individuals, for Lewis, are world-bound—i.e., they exist in only one world. Analogously, individuals exist at only one instant for the stage theorist. An instantaneous stage at t_1 "persists" not by existing at a later time t_4 but, rather, by a numerically distinct instantaneous stage at t_4 standing in the temporal counterpart relation to it.

Stage theory affords a distinct four-dimensional solution to the puzzle of Goliath and Lumpl—namely, the denial of C4. On this view, Goliath is *identical* to Lumpl, there is only one instantaneous stage, call it S, that occupies the region in question. How can this be given the fact that Goliath and Lumpl have different properties (C3), for instance? Answer: one and the same stage can be considered under different temporal counterpart relations. For one, where t^* represents the future time at which S will be flattened, it is currently true that S will not exist at t^* in so far as it fails to stand in the *statue counterpart relation* to a subsequent instantaneous stage that exists at t^* and satisfies the predicate "is a statue." Likewise, it is currently true that S will exist at t^* in so far as it stands in the *lump of bronze counterpart relation* to a subsequent instantaneous stage that exists at t^* and satisfies the predicate "lump of bronze." Considered under the *statue counterpart relation*, S will not survive flattening at t^* by the indecisive artist; under the *lump of bronze counterpart relation*, however, S will survive such flattening. Consequently, the stage theorist pins the differences in temporal properties between Goliath and Lumpl on differences in the temporal counterpart relations S bears to numerically distinct stages (note the similarities to modal counterpart relations in accounting for *de re* modal ascriptions).[15]

One common criticism of stage theory is that it shares perdurantism's rejection of a natural and intuitive understanding of persistence as one and the same object existing wholly and completely at distinct times. On stage theory, since ordinary material objects just are instantaneous stages, we thereby lose the ability to speak of diachronic sameness in terms of strict numerical identity. Here we have an account of "persistence" that precludes one and the same thing existing at distinct times; it's just one numerically distinct instantaneous stage after another.

The plausibility of the stage theorist's solution to the puzzle of Goliath and Lumpl rests on the analysis of *de re* temporal ascriptions in terms of temporal counterpart relations. Its being true that "S will exist at t^*," they argue, *just is* S's being related to some numerically distinct statue counterpart that exists at t^*. For those who already harbor a deep-seated suspicion as to whether modal counterpart theory is well suited to capture *de re* modal ascriptions will, most likely, have the very same reservations about its temporal application in the case noted earlier. For philosophers in this camp, myself included, the reductive base of the *de re* temporal ascription "S will exist at t^*" must somehow be intrinsically linked to S. But how does a numerically distinct temporal counterpart satisfying the predicate "statue" at a later time have *anything* to do with whether or not S *itself* will exist at t^*? The analysans appears to be wholly irrelevant to the existence and identity of S.[16] It is for these reasons and others scattered throughout the literature that I set aside stage theory as a solution to the puzzle at hand.

Of course, the earlier remarks concerning four-dimensionalist solutions to Goliath and Lumpl are in no way novel criticisms, and are ones to which both perdurantists and stage-theorists have lodged detailed responses. In the end, however, I am inclined to think that these rejoinders serve to further underscore the deeply revisionary nature of persistence on a four-dimensional metaphysic. As others have so aptly put it, metaphysics ultimately proceeds not from the head, but from the gut.[17]

A second prominent monist solution to Goliath and Lump is found in the dominant kinds account Burke (1994a and 1994b) and Rea (2000) as mentioned in the context of the previous puzzle. This route holds fast to **Existence** as well as **No Coincidence** and proceeds to identify Lumpl with Goliath; there is only a single material object in the region in question. What then of the fact that Goliath and Lumpl appear to have very different modal and persistence conditions (C3)?

Here Rea (2000) argues for two distinct ways in which an object can satisfy a kind. An object satisfies a kind (e.g. *statue*, *lump*) in a *classificatory way* just in case that kind gives the best answer to the question "What is it?" By contrast, an object satisfies a kind in a *nominal way* just in case "the object exemplifies the distinctive qualitative features of those things that satisfy the sortal in the classificatory way" (172). And it is an object's classificatory kind or sortal that determines its modal properties, including its persistence conditions. Thus on this account it is entirely possible for numerically one and the same object to satisfy distinct kinds, as long as it does so in distinct ways.

Applying this machinery to the puzzle at hand, we can see that the dominant kinds account takes aim at C3 in particular. Consider the kinds *statue* and *lump of bronze*. Rea, loosely following Burke (1994a and 1994b), argues that in the case of Goliath and Lumpl there is a single material object, *o*, that satisfies both *statue* and *lump of bronze*. Yet *o* satisfies the kind *statue* in the classificatory way in so far as it offers the best answer to the question "What is o, fundamentally?" As *statue* best expresses what o is *fundamentally* (i.e., o satisfies *statue* in the classificatory way) o inherits the essential properties, including the persistence conditions, that belong to members of the kind *statue* instead of *lump of bronze*; this is precisely what it means to say that *statue* is o's dominant kind. Even if the real definition of o does not involve reference to the kind *lump of bronze*, o nevertheless satisfies the kind nominally in that it exemplifies the qualitative features of objects that satisfy the kind *lump of bronze* in a classificatory way. C3 is false in so far as o has only a single set of essential properties and persistence conditions—namely, those belonging to the kind *statue*.

There have been several important objections leveled at the dominant kinds account, only two of which I will briefly mention here. First, it has been argued that the dominant kinds account suffers from a "Which one?" question, the question of which kind constitutes an object's dominant kind in any given case. In the case noted earlier, we simply stipulated that the object was a statue in the classificatory sense, that *statue* was the best answer to the classificatory question "What is it, fundamentally?" But the very question is one that tracks the more general metaphysical question of what constitutes the essence of a thing in terms of its deepest explanatory joints (in contrast to its necessary properties), as well as the epistemological question of how we come to grasp the real definitions of things (in whole or in part).[18] What general criteria ought to be employed to determine a thing's real definition (or even whether there are any such criteria) is a question for any proponent of essentialism, not simply the dominant kinds route.

The second objection, which was briefly mentioned in the previous section on Tibbles and Tib, is that the dominant kinds account is committed to what many consider to be some rather strange consequences regarding **Change**. Recall Sider's (2001) words earlier, "We are asked to believe that an artist can destroy a lump of clay by shaping it into a statue, and that a torso can be destroyed by detaching something external to it!" How can such minute changes result in something's coming in to existence in the one case, and something's ceasing to exist on the other?

5.1.2.3 Some Recent Neo-Aristotelian Solutions

In recent years, several novel neo-Aristotelian solutions to the problem of material constitution have emerged on the contemporary scene. Some of these solutions fall squarely within the monist camp and others within the pluralist camp (and for some it's not entirely clear where they fall). In what follows I will briefly consider the monist view of Thomas Sattig (2015), and the pluralist views of Kathrine Koslicki (2008) and Jeffrey Brower (2014), all of which appeal to distinct versions of neo-Aristotelian hylomorphism to ground different solutions to Goliath and Lumpl.

In his 2015 book *The Double Lives of Objects*, Thomas Sattig has argued for *perspectival hylomorphism*: the conjunction of a metaphysical thesis he calls "quasi-hylomorphism" with a semantic thesis he refers to as "perspectivalism." Sattig's carefully argued and nuanced proposal aims to carve a middle-path between a classical-extensional/Lewisian account and a version of hylomorphism.[19]

As a metaphysical thesis, *quasi-hylomorphism* maintains that ordinary material objects like statues and people (what I'll call "om-objects") are composed of a (maximal) material object along the lines of classical mereology (what I'll call "m-objects") and a conjunctive fact, what Sattig calls a "K-path."

Let's start with the classical-extensional aspect of Sattig's quasi-hylomorphism. According to Sattig, the m-object that (together with a K-path) composes Goliath at t is a mereological sum or fusion along the lines of full-scale classical extensional mereology (governed by the axioms of Unrestricted Composition and Uniqueness). As such, an m-object is an unstructred sum whose identity and existence are fixed entirely by the existence and identity of each of its proper parts (and thus cannot survive the loss of parts); Sattig is clear that the parts of an m-object are metaphysically prior to the whole (2015: 2).

In addition to an m-object, om-objects like Goliath are also composed of a K-path, a conjunctive fact consisting of facts about the qualitative features of the distinct m-objects that compose (along with the K-path) Goliath at distinct times (although K-paths can have more than one m-object as a subject at the same time). Roughly, we might think of Goliath's K-path (or that of a statue more generally) as a cross-temporal qualitative profile marking out the range of properties that realize *statuehood*. So suppose Goliath is composed of distinct m-objects o_1, o_2, and o_3 at successive times t_1, t_2, t_3. Goliath's K-path consists of the fact that o_1 is P at t_1, o_2 is F at t_2, o_3 is S at t_3, etc (where P, F, and S are all qualitative profiles of each respective m-object at each time). Quasi-hylomorphism is "de-formed" from a more traditional Aristotelian perspective, not in the sense of being what it ought not be or without a notion of form entirely, but in the sense of lacking a place for the robust role of form as the ground of an object's deep unity and structure (2015:28).

Turn now to the semantic thesis of Sattig's proposal: *perspectivalism*. According to Sattig we employ two modes of predication when we talk about ordinary material objects like Goliath, both of which are context-sensitive depending on which perspective on the object is in view. When one adopts the "sortal-sensitive perspective" on Goliath one focuses on Goliath's K-path (or form). When one takes this perspective on Goliath, one employs a formal mode of predication. By contrast, when one takes a "sortal-abstract perspective" on Goliath one selects for discourse those generalized spatiotemporal features of Goliath's m-object (its "matter"), features that the m-object shares with all m-objects (e.g., occupying some region of spacetime, being extended, having mass, not being in the same place at the same time as a distinct material object). In so doing, one employs the material mode of predication when speaking about Goliath. Descriptions stemming from each perspective on Goliath are made true by each respective component of Goliath, whether his K-path (formal) or the m-object (material).

Sattig puts perspectival hylomorphism to work by solving puzzles in material objects. Relevant to our discussion here is the solution afforded by such a view to puzzles in material constitution like Goliath and Lump. As perspectival hylomorphism is a version of Monism, it affirms **No Coincidence** and maintains that Goliath and Lumpl are strictly identical. What, then, of the seeming incompatible modal properties attributed to Goliath and Lumpl (C3)? Sattig argues that the tension that arises here disappears once we consider the fact that ordinary objects lead "double lives."

As we've seen, when we speak about Goliath (or Lumpl) we can adopt either the sortal-sensitive or the sortal-abstract perspective. It is only because we can adopt these two divergent perspectives on Goliath—hence the "double lives" of such objects—that we can hold C1-C4 together without tension. Since C3 and C4 are *formal* predications and C2 a *material* predication, there is no inconsistency in holding that Goliath is distinct yet exactly coincides with Lumpl (formal predications about K-path), yet at the same time hold that distinct material objects cannot coincide (material predication about m-objects). Since these descriptions employ different modes of predication regarding Goliath, they are not incompatible with one another and the puzzle disappears.

While I do not have the space to offer a full-scale critique of perspectival hylomorphism, let me raise a few worries about Sattig's proposal. First, in true Lewisian fashion, perspectival hylomorphism delivers a massively plenitudinous ontology (Sattig 2015: 24). There are truly more ordinary material objects in Sattig's ontology than meets the eye.

Take the K-path, i, for a human organism. Recall that K-paths are cross-temporal qualitative profiles that can have distinct subjects (m-objects) at the same time, t. So i can have m-objects a, b, and c as subjects at t, which gives rise to the following numerically distinct compound human organisms at t: O(a, i), O(b, i), O(c, i); thus there three distinct human organisms at t that are subjects of i. A plenitudinous ontology gets even stranger still. As a cross-temporal qualitative profile, i has what we might call an *occupation profile*: a function from i to sets of non-empty regions of spacetime for i. On a truly plenitudinous ontology, for *any* subset, s, of an organism's occupation profile, there is at least one object that exactly occupies s. So, take the subset of the occupation profile of i that includes the human organisms O(a, i), O(m, i), and O(z, i). On plenitude (which entails Unrestricted Composition), there is a diachronic human organism that has each of the aforementioned synchronic human organisms as proper parts—i.e., O[O(a, i), O(m, i), O(z, i)]. Thus, a plenitudinous ontology delivers both synchronic and diachronic overabundance. While I do not think that a plenitudinous ontology per se is in tension with a neo-Aristotelian metaphysic of material objects (see

Inman 2014), nevertheless many neo-Aristotelians will balk at such a massively inflated ontology of the ordinary world.

Second, on perspectival hylomorphism, ordinary objects like living organisms are understood in *extensional* terms, that is, as compounds that share the same extensional identity conditions as the m-objects qua classical-mereological sums that compose them (Sattig 2015: 23). Two compounds, say living organisms, are identical just in case all of their components are identical (O(a, i_1) = O(b, i_2) iff $a = b$ and $i_1 = i_2$). As such, all ordinary composite objects are such that duplicating the perfectly natural properties of the parts and their basic arrangements suffices to duplicate the perfectly natural properties (and relations) of the compound.[20] Composite material objects on this view are arguably neither fundamental nor the bearer of non-redundant causal properties. If so, the view faces a version of the Overdetermination Argument (see Chapter 6) for *all* ordinary material objects, including organisms. Moreover, as I will argue in Chapter 7, such an understanding of ordinary material objects is in deep tension with views in the metaphysics of mind and free will that assign fundamental causal and qualitative properties to human persons. Those with neo-Aristotelian sympathies who ascribe metaphysical priority to at least some composite objects will find Sattig's penchant for a Part-Priority fundamental mereology problematic.[21]

Third, Sattig's view also runs roughshod over a plausible principle regarding human persons and their mental lives, what Andrew Bailey (2014) has called the "Priority Principle":

> *Priority Principle:* We human persons possess all our mental properties in the primary and non-derivative sense.

I take it that the principal motivating factor behind the *Priority Principle* is that human persons are the ultimate source of their mental lives. I do not inherit or borrow my mental life from any thing that is not strictly me.

Sattig's quasi-hylomorphism, as with many other versions of hylomorphism, violates the *Priority Principle*. On the assumption that human persons are glossed in terms of this hylomorphic framework, it is (strictly speaking) the m-object and not the om-object, the human person—that is, the subject of the qualitative profile at a time. That is, the primary bearer of the properties that carve out a person's K-path is not the person itself but one of its numerically distinct proper parts, the m-object (Sattig 2015: 26). Thus, human persons think and are the bearers of mental properties in a derivative and not a primary sense. But when I stub my toe and find myself in a qualitative state of pain, *I* possess the mental property of *being in pain*, but not in virtue of any distinct thing's being in pain, in this case one of my proper parts. This is simply to say that it is intuitive to think (non-derivatively!) that I do not inherit my mental life from anything that is not strictly me.

Fourth, Korman (2015b) has raised what he calls "the problem of inaudible readings" for perspectival hylomorphism. Sattig's perspectivalism requires that statements like the following have both a true and a false reading depending on which mode of predication is employed (suppose statue Goliath has lost its head):

S: Goliath once had a head.

If S is a formal predication from the sortal-sensitive perspective, then S is true in so far as Goliath's K-path includes the fact that one of Goliath's m-objects at a previous time had a head. However, if S is a material predication from the sortal-abstract perspective, then S is false since the m-object that now composes Goliath-sans-head is numerically distinct from the m-object that composed Goliath-cum-head; the m-object in the relevant domain of discourse never had a head to begin with.

Korman argues that many, myself included, are hard-pressed to hear *any* reading of S where S comes out false; S seems true and *only* true. More generally, the worry is that the truth or falsity of predications like S involving ordinary objects seem context invariant, not context-sensitive as per perspectivalism. Korman takes our inability to hear a false reading of predications like S as reason to think that we do not adopt divergent perspectives and modes of predication in our discourse about ordinary material objects.

Lastly, while perspectival hylomorphism aims for broad explanatory power and scope regarding puzzles in material objects (including the Problem of the Many), it does not have the same explanatory scope as Substantial Priority (e.g., it does not purport to offer a solution to the Overdetermination Argument).

Let's turn briefly to the neo-Aristotelian solution to Goliath and Lumpl (and related puzzles) outlined by Katherin Koslicki in her 2008 book *The Structure of Objects*. Koslicki's is a pluralist solution which provides a straightforward mereological analysis of the constitution relation. On her view, "[s]ome objects, $m_1, \ldots, m_n$, constitute an object, O, just in case $m_1, \ldots, m_n$ are O's material components" (2008: 185). If constitution is a species of composition, then Goliath and Lumpl share all of the same material components (since Lumpl constitutes Goliath), yet Lumpl turns out to be a proper part of Goliath. Despite sharing all of their material parts in common, Goliath and Lumpl are nevertheless numerically distinct in virtue of having different modal properties. What, then, grounds the crucial modal differences between Goliath and Lumpl? Koslicki's ingenious response to the grounding problem is that "the 'remainder' of the statue is made up of those of its formal or structural components which distinguish it from the clay." In other words, the two material objects are distinct in virtue of Goliath having as a proper part a non-material formal component. And it is this non-material formal component that grounds the modal differences between Goliath and Lumpl.

Koslicki's neo-Aristotelian proposal is plausible on many levels. Indeed, her view that Lumpl is a proper part of Goliath is in line with one of the pluralist solutions afforded by Substantial Priority outlined next (§5.2.6). However, Koslicki's neo-Aristotelian proposal lacks explanatory scope in that it arguably cannot be put to work to help solve other puzzles in material-object metaphysics.

Lastly, following on earlier work (with Michael Rea) explicating a neo-Aristotelian solution to material constitution, Jeffrey Brower, in his *Aquinas's Ontology of the Material World*, offers a interpretation of Aquinas's metaphysics of material objects in terms of what Brower calls "Thomistic Substratum Theory" (TST). Let's unpack the tenets of TST that are relevant to a solution to the puzzle of Goliath and Lumpl.

At the heart of TST is a version of Aristotelian hylomorphism that maintains that material objects are form-matter complexes of either a first or second-order variety (where first and second order complexes are distinguished in terms of what plays the functional role of form and matter for each). Material substances (e.g., Socrates) are first-order complexes of substrata (non-individual stuff) and substantial forms (*humanity*). Accidental unities (e.g., seated-Socrates), on the other hand, are second-order complexes of substrata (material substances, e.g., Socrates) and accidental forms (e.g., *seatedness*).

According to Brower's interpretation of Aquinas, the relationship between first-order and a second-order material complexes (e.g., Socrates and seated-Socrates) is numerical sameness without identity, which Brower unpacks as follows:

> (NSWI) *Numerical Sameness without Identity:* For any complexes x and y, where $x \neq y$, and any time t, x is numerically the same material object as y at t if and only if x and y share all their matter in common at t.

While Socrates and seated-Socrates are non-identical coincident hylomorphic compounds, they are *one and the same* material object in so far as they exhaustively share their matter in common at the relevant time.

As Brower makes clear, an advantage of TST is that if affords a pluralist solution to the earlier puzzle of coincidence in its rejection of C2 (**No Coincidence**), while at the same time affirming the existence of statues and lumps of bronze (C1).[22] However, in contrast to constitutionalism, TST holds that Goliath and Lumpl, while numerically distinct hylomorphic compounds, are to be counted as *one and the same* material object along the lines of NSWI. Since we count material objects by their matter, and since Goliath and Lumpl share all their matter at the time in question, then they are one and the same material object, even though they are strictly distinct hylomorphic compounds.[23]

In spite of the many advantages of Brower's carefully articulated view, let me highlight several costs of TST.

Consider first some general costs of TST. First, as with Sattig's neo-Aristotelian proposal earlier, Brower's view runs roughshod over the *Priority Principle*, which strikes many as a deeply plausible view about human persons and their mental lives. Since an ordinary material substance (first-order compound) like Socrates has the mental properties he does *in virtue of* being a proper part of a numerically distinct second-order complex that itself bears the mental properties *simpliciter*, Socrates does not bear any of his mental properties *simpliciter* or in a non-derivative fashion. Socrates inherits his rich, qualitative mental life—his thoughts of the good life or his hopes and aspirations for life after death—from something that is not (strictly) Socrates (although it is one and the same material object as Socrates). But, again, this seems deeply implausible on its surface.[24]

Indeed the underlying structural worry here would seem to easily generalize to all intrinsic properties of ordinary material substances (and not simply mental properties). For any first-order hylomorphic compound C1, and intrinsic property F, "C is F at t" is true iff C is a proper part of some distinct second-order compound C2 at t and C2 is itself F at *t* (has F non-derivatively at *t*). C2 on this picture is the sole primary property-bearer of F at *t*. But this threatens to render *all* of C1's properties as extrinsic or relational (depending on how one explicates the notion of intrinsicality).[25] Even worse, if Socrates has all of his intrinsic properties *in virtue of* some distinct compound, it is hard to see how Socrates could be the bearer of *non-redundant* causal properties. At the very least it seems odd to say that Socrates, a substance and thus a basic or independent being in the Aristotelian scheme of things, inherits the entirety of his causal and qualitative profile from some distinct entity.

In addition, TST does not aim to offer a unified solution to a variety of puzzles in material objects. While it aims to solve the puzzle of Goliath and Lumpl, it does not appear to be sufficiently generalizable to cover the Overdetermination Argument or the Argument from Vagueness (against restricted composition). TST lacks the explanatory scope that Substantial Priority offers to a host of puzzles in material objects.

The plausibility of TST as a solution to Goliath and Lumpl (and puzzles similar in spirit) depends almost entirely on its reliance on the machinery of NSWI. But many, perhaps most, consider a relation of numerical sameness without strict identity to cut against widespread and well-entrenched intuitions about sameness and counting. Yet we should acknowledge that in the span of Western philosophy these intuitions about identity and sameness were not always as firmly entrenched as they are today.[26] And while others who put a form of NSWI to use seem wholly unmoved by the counterintuitiveness of two strictly non-identical objects being counted as numerically one and the same object, Brower recognizes the high cost of this move. And for some, even in light of the theoretical advantages the view affords, the price tag is simply too steep.[27]

5.1.2.4 Substantial Priority

Let us turn now to Substantial Priority and how it bears on the puzzles of Goliath and Lumpl. Substantial Priority affords either a Monist or a pluralist solution to Goliath and Lumpl. Let's start with the pluralist solution afforded by Substantial Priority that is found in the work of Christopher Brown (2005).

Substantial Priority affords a pluralist solution to Goliath and Lumpl in its rejecting **No Coincidence**, for reasons resembling those offered on behalf of constitutionalism as well as those intrinsic to the view itself. This brand of Substantial Priority and constitutionalism agree in that statues and lumps of bronze are non-identical in virtue of their exemplifying different modal properties and having distinct persistence conditions. It is precisely *because* Goliath and Lumpl are different kinds of composite objects that they exhibit distinct modal properties and persistence conditions.

Christopher Brown (2005) defends a Thomistic solution to Goliath and Lumpl (and other puzzles in material objects) that employs much of the same machinery as Substantial Priority, although there are differences in how the views are unpacked and defended. While Brown's Thomistic solution is not explicitly unpacked in terms Substantial Priority (grounding, grounded wholes, grounding wholes), he argues that the difference in category between Goliath and Lumpl is one that tracks not only a difference between the kinds *bronze* and *statue* but also a deep difference in the ontological categories of *substance* and *non-substance*. Moreover, Brown follows Aquinas in affirming the Aristotelian maxim that substances lack other substances as proper parts (**No Fundamental Parthood**). On Brown's interpretation of Aquinas's view, Goliath is an non-substantial artifact (what Aquinas calls an "accidental unity") and thus, in our terminology, a grounded whole (aggregate). Lumpl, on the other hand, is a substance, and hence a grounding whole. On Substantial Priority, the primary reason why C2 is false is that no grounded whole is (or can be) identical to a grounding whole.

If Goliath and Lumpl are non-identical as per the denial of C2, what exactly is the relationship between statues and their matter according to this pluralist version of Substantial Priority? Must we resort to a *sui generis* constitution relation? Here I think Substantial Priority offers a more defensible denial of **No Coincidence** than standard versions of constitutionalism in that it lends a straightforward *mereological* account of the relationship between Goliath and Lumpl.

Note first that on Substantial Priority, while Goliath and Lump may be plausibly said to occupy one and the same region, they do not share all and only the same proper parts (i.e. they do not *exactly* mereologically coincide with one another); indeed they *cannot* given the different grounding structure that characterizes grounded and grounding wholes in general.[28] As per the nature of grounded wholes, Goliath must have at least one substantial proper part at a level of decomposition that is included among its total grounds. By contrast, in virtue of being a substance, Lumpl is essentially such that it lacks substantial proper parts altogether. While both Goliath and Lumpl exhibit a significantly high degree of mereological overlap, Substantial Priority offers a principled reason for thinking that they do not share *all* of their proper parts in common.

On the pluralist version of Substantial Priority I am unpacking here, one such proper part of Goliath that Lumpl lacks would be Lumpl itself (although Lumpl has itself as an improper part).[29] Lumpl, on this pluralist solution, is best construed as a substantial proper part of Goliath, albeit a very large one indeed. As a bronze statue, the nature of Goliath is defined (grounded in) by the bronze out of which it is made as well as the particular property (form, structure, etc.) that makes it a statue of a (giant) human person instead of, say, a statue of a turnip.[30]

This brand of Substantial Priority, then, rejects **No Coincidence** and maintains the non-identity of Goliath and Lumpl (and artifacts and their matter in general) without introducing a *sui generis* constitution relation to explain the relationship between the two spatially co-located material objects. I take this to be a mark in its favor in so far as it offers a more ideologically parsimonious rejection of **No Coincidence** (C2) than constitutionalism in positing less primitive structure in the world.[31] If one opts for a mereological analysis of constitution, then the advantage of parsimony on behalf of Substantial Priority here would be its positing less world-structure *per se*, and not necessarily less *primitive* world-structure.

But what about the fact that Goliath and Lumpl occupy one and the same spatial region? Is not the admittance of spatial co-location between distinct material objects itself a mark against Substantial Priority?

One might argue that what is objectionable in countenancing distinct coinciding material objects is not the coincidence of such objects *per se*, but the coincidence of *fundamental* material objects in one and the same region. Here we might follow Schaffer (2009a: 361) in endorsing a revised gloss on Ockham's Razor in terms of substances: "Ockham's Razor should only be understood to concern substances: do not multiply basic entities without necessity." As Lumpl is the sole fundamental substance within the boundary of the region occupied by the two distinct objects, no substances are multiplied in the case at hand (let alone without necessity). While Substantial Priority in this case rejects **No Coincidence** regarding Goliath and Lumpl, it affirms what we might call **No Fundamental Coincidence**; since regions of space are unrelentingly monogamous when it comes to hosting *fundamental* material objects, the defender of Substantial Priority is innocent of ontological excess where it matters most. Substantial Priority, in sum, provides a solution to the puzzle of Goliath and Lumpl which preserves **Existence**, **Survival**, **Identity**, and **Change** for ordinary material objects, and upholds **No Fundamental Coincidence** in the place of **No Coincidence**.

One additional virtue of the aforementioned pluralist solution to Goliath and Lumpl afforded by Substantial Priority is that it lends a straightforward solution to the thorny grounding problem for distinct coinciding material objects (see §2.3).[32] Informally, if Goliath and Lumpl are atom-for-atom physical duplicates, what could possibly ground such radical differences concerning their modal and persistence conditions?

The grounding problem can be stated succinctly as follows:[33]

> G1. If Goliath and Lumpl differ modally, then there must be some difference between them that is poised to explain their modal differences.
> G2. There is no difference between Goliath and Lumpl that is poised to explain their modal differences.
> G3. So, Goliath and Lumpl do not differ modally.

But, of course, the apparent modal differences between Goliath and Lumpl are the primary grounds by which pluralists reject **No Coincidence** (C2).

As Daniel Korman (2015a: 213–216) points out, following the work of Noël Saenz (2015), linking the modal differences between Goliath and Lump with grounding differences with respect to their mereological structure can provide the requisite underpinning for the denial of G2. If Goliath and Lumpl differ with respect to the grounding relations they stand in to their proper parts and their structural arrangements, then this arguably suffices to explain their modal differences.

So how might Substantial Priority help here? Suppose Goliath is a grounded whole, a composite that is totally grounded in its proper parts (and their relations). It is part of the essence of Goliath qua aggregate that it is totally grounded in its proper parts and the relations between them. That is, *which* objects the parts of Goliath are fixes *which* object Goliath is. Consequently, it is *impossible* for Goliath to survive flattening since Goliath *is what it is* in virtue of its proper parts and the structural arrangements between them.

Likewise, suppose Lumpl is a grounding whole, an ungrounded composite that also grounds each of its proper parts; it is part of the essence of Lumpl qua substance that it fails to be grounded in any distinct (concrete) entity and that totally grounds each of its proper parts. Alternatively, *which* objects the parts of Lumpl are does not fix *which* object Lumpl is. Consequently, it is *possible* for Lumpl to survive flattening since it is *not* the case that Lumpl *is what it is* in virtue of its individual proper parts and their specific structural arrangements.[34]

Korman (2015a: 213) presses the further objection (he calls it "the revenge objection") to the earlier grounding solution to the grounding problem: what grounds the differences in grounding relations between each whole and their respective parts and arrangements? But notice the revenge objection doesn't arise for those who tie grounding in this mereological context to the nature or essence of a thing and thus what is explanatory basic to it (see §2.3). Since Goliath and Lumpl are characterized by radically different grounding descriptions, and if the grounding descriptions are inextricably tied to the explanatory basic essences of Goliath and Lumpl (§1.2.4), then the further question of what grounds the differences in the essences of Goliath and Lumpl fails to arise. As a result, Substantial Priority has the resources to help the pluralist with the grounding problem.

Let's now turn to the monist solution afforded by Substantial Priority as found in the work of Patrick Toner (2007). Over the course of several articles, Toner has argued for the broad explanatory power of a view of substance in which (composite) substances lack separable parts and thus adhere to **No Fundamental Parthood** (although Toner does not make explicit use of this framework), and are what I refer to as grounding wholes. In fact, a great many of the solutions afforded by Substantial Priority in this chapter find their genesis in Toner's work. Toner distinguishes substances from aggregates in that the latter but not the former are composed of other substances. It is part of the nature of each category of object, whether substance or aggregate, that they either adhere or fail to adhere to **No Fundamental Parthood**.[35]

This monist version of Substantial Priority rejects C3 while preserving **No Coincidence** in so far as Goliath is numerically identical to Lumpl. How, then, does one explain the apparent modal differences in question—i.e., Lumpl's being able to survive flattening and Goliath not (C3)? Following Rea (§2.4), Toner appropriates the distinction between classificatory and nominal kind-membership. As we've already seen earlier, one and the same material object can belong to distinct kinds, albeit in different ways. An object satisfies a kind in the classificatory way in so far as that kind or sortal best carves out the object's fundamental nature or identity; as Rea (2000: 172) puts it, "That sortal gives the metaphysically best answer to the 'What is it?' question for that object." An object has only the essential and modal features that flow from its fundamental nature—i.e., its classificatory kind. An object satisfies a kind in the nominal way, on the other hand, in so far as it has the qualitative features that belong to objects that satisfy that kind in the classificatory sense.

Suppose that the kind *statue* best captures the essence of Goliath. Goliath, then, has all the essential and modal features of a statue; as such, *statue* is Goliath's dominant kind. Suppose further that artifacts like statues are aggregates—i.e., grounded wholes, and thus metaphysically posterior to and grounded in their individual proper parts and structural arrangements. However, on this view, Goliath is also a member of the kind *lump of bronze* in a nominal sense in virtue of having the same qualitative features of objects that are lumps of bronze in a classificatory sense.

On Substantial Priority, if lumps of bronze are composite substances, they are grounding wholes and thus metaphysically prior to each of their proper parts. Since Goliath has the essential and modal features of a statue and not that of a lump of bronze, the assumption that there are two non-identical material objects, Goliath and Lumpl, each with distinct essential and modal features is mistaken. The one material object in the region is both a statue and a lump of bronze, although it is a statue (aggregate/grounded whole) in the classificatory sense and a lump of bronze (substance/grounding whole) in the nominal sense. As aggregates, statues are not able to survive such radical changes to its parts and their relations; as substances, lumps of bronze are able to survive such changes. On Substantial Priority, the differences in modal features and persistence conditions between Goliath and Lumpl are tied to deeper categorial differences involving distinct grounding structure that obtains between the objects and their proper parts.

There is one notable shortcoming for both the pluralist and the Monist solutions to Goliath and Lumpl afforded by Substantial Priority. Both solutions only apply to cases where the material objects in question belong to different kinds, one a substance and other an aggregate. Since they fail to cover cases of same-kind coincidence, they do not aim to be sufficiently general solutions to the problem of material constitution.[36] While I take this to limit the explanatory scope of Substantial Priority, I do not think it renders it any less powerful in explaining many of the more prominent puzzles in the literature. Moreover, we ought not overstate the explanatory scope of Substantial Priority's rivals either, since it is widely acknowledged that extant responses to the puzzle of material constitution "differ with respect to their scope of application . . . most published responses are disunified, using disparate keys to unlock different paradoxes."[37]

Notes

1. Note especially the excellent work of Brown (2005) and Toner (2008) in demonstrating the fecundity of an application of a classical conception of substance to contemporary metaphysics.
2. See Baker (2007), Johnston (1992, 2006: §8), Lowe (1983), Wiggins (1968), for a few representatives of this line.
3. See Myro (1997), Geach (1967), Gibbard (1975), respectively.
4. See Chisholm (1976: Chapter 3).
5. See Burke (1994a and 1994b) and Rea (2000).
6. See Sider (2001: ch. 5).
7. On this line, see Cameron (2010b), Dorr (2005), Hawthorne and Cortens (1995), and van Inwagen (1981).
8. In fact, Schaffer infers the metaphysical priority of the cosmos on the basis of the internal relatedness (causal connectedness) of all of its many parts. Here I am using similar machinery in a more restricted fashion to infer the internal relatedness (causal connectedness) of the many parts of Tibbles (including Tib and Tail) on the grounds that Tibbles is metaphysically prior to its many parts.
9. For representatives of this line of thinking see Heller (1990), van Inwagen (1990: 124–127), Hoffman and Rosenkrantz (1997), Merricks (2001), and Olson (2007).

10. As is well-known, the puzzle can be easily adapted to spell problems for the temporal parts theorist. Suppose Goliath and Lumpl both come into existence and cease to exist at the very same time such that they have one and the same spatiotemporal career (i.e. they exactly overlap with respect to their spatial and temporal parts). The temporal parts theorist is forced to identify Goliath and Lumpl.
11. For those who press this line see McTaggart (1927), Mellor (1998, §8.4), Oderberg (2004), and Simons (1987).
12. Baker (2002: 593).
13. For a more thorough critique of constitutionalism (regarding human persons in particular) see Inman (2018).
14. For representatives, see Hawley (2001) and Sider (2001).
15. I take Sider (2001: 200) as representative of a stage-theoretic solution to Goliath and Lumpl.
16. This is forcibly pressed by Merricks (2003).
17. Heil (2012: 9).
18. See Rea (2000: §5) for an alternative account of dominance that tries to solve the "Which one?" problem.
19. According to Koon's taxonomy (2014), perspectival hylomorphism would be classified as a "fainthearted" version of hylomorphism.
20. We called this the *Plural Duplication Principle* in 4.4.1.
21. Sattig's view also runs in to the Thinking Parts Argument (see Chapter 7).
22. The view has many other virtues as well, one of which is a novel solution to the problem of temporary intrinsics. See Inman (2014) for further benefits of a plenitudinous hylomorphic ontology that is broadly similar in spirit.
23. *Hylomorphic compound* and *material object* are different sortals, the former being governed by strict identity and the latter numerical sameness.
24. This worry for Brower's view is pointed out specifically by Bailey (2014).
25. For example, one might argue that there may be relational intrinsic properties—e.g., *having a proper part that is F*. If so, the argument could be restated as Socrates's lacking non-relational intrinsic properties. It is important to note that this objection to Brower's (2010) novel "constituent solution" to the problem of temporary intrinsics stems from his view's being "structurally identical" (2010: 891) to Lewis's perdurantism (replacing Lewis's temporal parts with second-order complexes as the primary bearer of intrinsics). Brower (2010: 889) himself recognizes that Lewis's view cuts against our "ordinary intuitions" about Socrates being the bearer of intrinsic properties nonderivatively.
26. Brower (2004) demonstrates the historical precedent of a version of NSWI in Peter Abelard, and Rea (1998) in Aristotle.
27. Baker (2007), for instance, seems undeterred by the incredulous stares.
28. Of course, assuming the *non*-identity of Goliath and Lumpl, they cannot share all and only their parts, proper *and* improper. To mereologically overlap with respect to their improper parts would be to identify Goliath and Lumpl. Hence the restriction to proper parts.
29. Following the terminology of Wasserman (2002), Goliath and Lumpl *weakly materially coincide* with one another in that while every part of Lumpl is a part of Goliath, not every part of Goliath is a part of Lumpl. Wasserman raises an important objection to the notion of weak material coincidence. Suppose Goliath and Lumpl weakly materially coincide in the aforementioned sense. Call the part of Goliath that is not a part of Lumpl, Righty. Now take the part of Lumpl that coincides with Righty, call it S-Righty. He asks, what is the relationship between Righty and S-Righty? They cannot be identical, he argues, in so far as we are

assuming that Righty is not a part of Lumpl (and hence something that is not a part of Lumpl cannot be identical with a part of Lumpl). Righty and S-Righty are therefore non-identical. Here we have the problem of Goliath and Lumpl all over again, only on a much smaller scale (what accounts for the difference in modal properties between Righty and S-Righty? Answer: there is a part of Righty that is not had by S-Righty. One can continue this line until one reaches the smallest atomic parts of Goliath and Lumpl). In the end, Wasserman argues, the weak material coincidence view will be committed to saying that Goliath and Lumpl are entirely spatially coincident yet fail to share *any* parts at all, a view he takes to be absurd. My proposal here, I think, simply sidesteps Wasserman's worry. For one, given that we are assuming the *non-identity* of Goliath and Lumpl (as do all views that posit coincidence), weak material coincidence only applies to the *proper* parts of Goliath and Lumpl on pains of identifying the two objects. Second, on my view, the proper part of Goliath that is not a proper part of Lumpl *just is* Lumpl *itself*. Goliath has Lumpl as a proper part but Lumpl does not have itself as a *proper* part, although it does have itself as an *improper* part. That is, for me, Righty *just is* Lumpl in its entirety. Hence (if Righty = Lumpl) the only part of Lumpl that *exactly* spatially coincides with Righty is its improper part— i.e., Lumpl itself. There is, then, no *proper* part of Lumpl that exactly spatially coincides with Lumpl. To say that Goliath and Lumpl weakly materially coincide requires only that Righty not be a *proper* part of Lumpl. Righty, however, is free to be an improper part of Lumpl and hence identical to it, which is precisely what this pluralist solution says.

30. This pluralist solution afforded by Substantial Priority is structurally similar to the one put forward in Fine (1982: 100–101). By Fine's lights, Goliath is what he calls a "qua-object," a distinct whole that is the result of a *basis*, in this case Lumpl, being structured by a *gloss*, in this case a Goliath-type spatial arrangement. Fine's qua-objects are a species of what I am calling grounded wholes. Fine takes qua-objects to be governed by the following axioms: *Existence*: the qua-object x-qua-φ exists at a given time iff x exists and has φ at the given time; *Identity:* (i) two qua-objects are the same only if their bases and glosses are the same, and (ii) a qua-object is distinct from its basis; *Inheritance:* at any time at which a qua-object exists, it has those normal properties possessed by its basis.

31. The ideological parsimony here depends, of course, on how the constitutionalist understands the constitution relation. Some, like Markosian (2004) take it as primitive, others, such as Koslicki (2008) and Zimmerman (2002), analyze the notion in mereological terms, and others still, Baker (2007: 32), in non-mereological terms.

32. See Olson (2001) for a helpful statement of the grounding or indiscernibility problem.

33. This has been adapted from Korman (2015a: 212).

34. This is, of course, consistent with saying that Lumpl is generically existentially grounded in some proper parts or other.

35. It should be noted that in some places Toner (2006: 556) speaks of aggregates like chairs as *pluralities* such that "the chair is identical with the atoms standing in an arranged chair-wise relation," and not unified objects that are strictly composed of parts. Other places (2008: 291), however, he treats aggregates as single, unified objects that are strictly (one-many) composed of proper parts.

36. Thanks to an anonymous reviewer for pointing out the restricted application of Substantial Priority to cases of different-kind coincidence.

37. Sattig (2015: 79–80).

6 Substantial Priority
Vagueness, the Many, and Overdetermination

6.1 Vagueness and Composition

The question concerning the conditions under which composition occurs (if ever) has dominated the contemporary mereological landscape. Roughly, three general answers have reigned supreme in the literature as to when composition occurs: *never* (nihilism), *sometimes* (moderatism), and *always* (universalism). By all appearances, liberalism with respect to composition has won the day. Mereological universalism, more precisely, is the view that for *any* non-overlapping *xs*, there is a *y* such that *y* is composed of the *xs*. On this view, *any* two non-overlapping objects, no matter how gerrymandered or causally disconnected in spacetime, compose a distinct object with those two objects as proper parts. Thus the coin resting on my desk, together with one of Hillary Clinton's gray hairs, compose an object—coin-hair—that is a genuine constituent of reality. Reality truly is, on this view, much more than meets the eye. How could such a radically counterintuitive view win the favor of so many contemporary metaphysicians?

Perhaps the strongest argument in favor of universalism is *the Argument from Vagueness*, first advanced by Lewis (1986a: 212–213) and later developed in more detail by Sider (2001). Strictly speaking, the Argument from Vagueness takes aim at the notion of moderatism in general and is thereby consistent with both nihilism and universalism, although the majority of its adherents wield the argument in defense of the latter. The Argument from Vagueness crucially hinges on the denial of both borderline cases of composition as well as sharp cutoffs on the spectrum of composition.

The *Argument from Vagueness* can be stated more clearly as follows:

> V1. If composition sometimes does and sometimes does not occur, then there is a sorites series for composition—i.e., a pair of cases connected by a continuous series such that in one, composition does not occur, but in the other, composition does occur.
>
> V2. Every sorites series for composition contains either borderline cases of composition or a sharp cutoff with respect to composition.

V3. There are no borderline cases of composition.
V4. There are no sharp cutoffs with respect to composition.
V5. Therefore, composition either always occurs or never occurs.[1]

Take V1 first. If composition is restricted in any sense then we have a pair of cases φ and ψ that are connected by a continuous series such that in φ (for instance) composition does not occur, where in ψ composition does occur. The thrust of V2 is simply the claim that any such continuous composition series involves the transition from non-composition (φ) to composition (ψ), which therein involves cases where it is either determinate or indeterminate as to whether or not composition occurs on the spectrum. But borderline (indeterminate) cases of composition seems to render it vague as to whether certain objects compose a further object (V3) and hence vague as to how many objects exist *per se*. But it is equally implausible to think there are a pair of immediately adjacent cases on the continuous series, say α and β, such that in α composition occurs and in β it doesn't; that such minuscule differences on the continuous series accounts for such radical compositional differences seems to be without explanation (V4). Consequently, to maintain that composition sometimes does and sometimes does not occur is an unstable position. So argues the universalist.

The premises that have generated the most discussion are V3 and V4. Sider's main argument for the truth of V3 rests on the non-vagueness of claims concerning numerical sentences of the form "there are n concrete objects" (for some finite value of n). If there were borderline cases of composition–cases where it is indeterminate whether the xs compose y–then "there are n concrete objects" would lack a determinate truth-value. But in so far as such expressions can be formulated in terms of a purely logical vocabulary (utilizing the existential and universal quantifiers, logical connectives, and the identity relation), they are devoid of vague terms.[2] Hence, there can be no borderline cases of composition.

But as others have been keen to point out, Sider's defense of V3 earlier turns on the fact that whether or not statements of the form "there are n concrete objects" have a determinate truth value depends on the size and extent of the relevant domain of existential quantification and hence one's views regarding *which objects exist in the first place*. That is, the truth-value of the numerical statement hinges on the question of *how many things exist*, which is the very question at hand between the universalist and the defender of moderatism.

More to the point, however, are the various denials of V4 on offer in the literature as well as the prospect of Substantial Priority lending a novel solution to the Argument from Vagueness. A denial of V4 amounts to identifying a *non-arbitrary* cutoff with respect to composition, a sort of non-arbitrary compositional "difference-maker" when it comes to α and β on the continuous series described earlier. The sharp cutoff in question serves as the first instance on the continuous series where composition occurs. But what might account for such a sharp cutoff on the spectrum of composition? What (non-arbitrary) metaphysical feature of composites (α) marks them off from non-composites (β)?

Trenton Merricks (2005) has argued, persuasively in my opinion, that the emergence of irreducible features of composites can serve as a non-vague compositional difference-maker and hence a relevant sharp cutoff on the continuous series. He illustrates this by the following story of "whistling composites:"

> Moreover, pretend the following story is true. Necessarily, simples are silent but composite objects emit a loud whistling noise. (That's right, they whistle.) Their whistling, according to this story, is not reduced to the collective activity of their parts. For example, it is not reduced to the spatial interrelations among the composite's parts, as it would be if the wind's blowing through the composite caused the whistling. Instead, whistling is a necessary result of composition itself. The whistling of composites, according to this story, is in some sense "emergent." And, finally, let us add that it cannot possibly be vague whether the whistling occurs.
>
> (2005: 628)

If we were to move along the continuous series spanning from α to β, it is clear when β obtains—just listen! Note the similarity here between the emergence of "whistling" and our discussion of the failure of PDP (see §4.4.1) for certain mereological wholes in Chapter 4. In essence, Merricks is suggesting that PDP fails with respect to whistling composites, wholes that instantiate properties that are irreducible to the properties of their proper parts together with their basic arrangements. Since it is presumably a non-vague matter as to when such properties are instantiated, their instantiation provides a sharp cutoff as to when composition occurs.

As a more substantive stand-in for "whistling," Merricks proposes the emergence of non-redundant causal powers to provide the metaphysical underpinning for the non-arbitrary cutoff on the continuous series. He states,

> In particular, a composite object causes an effect E non-redundantly only if E is not caused by that object's parts working in concert. Thus a composite object's exercising non-redundant causal power—an object's causing something non-redundantly—cannot be reduced to what its parts cause working in concert. In this way, an object's exercising non-redundant causal power is irreducible to its parts (and their features and interrelations, etc.). I think that each and every composite object has non-redundant causal powers. So I think that composites have irreducible features.
>
> (2005: 631–632)

Merricks goes on to state that, by his lights, the most likely candidate objects that exhibit the aforementioned non-redundant causal powers are objects with a rich and qualitative conscious life (including sentient higher-order animals such as dogs and dolphins). Since *being conscious* for Merricks, is a non-vague matter (there are no borderline cases of consciousness), its presence on the compositional series constitutes the sharp cutoff that undermines V4.[3] It follows from this, however, that the only *composite* objects that exist are those that possess mental properties.[4] Accordingly, Merricks's denial of V4 leaves him in the untoward position of rejecting **Existence** for large classes of composite objects such as artifacts, non-conscious living organisms (cells, bacteria, plants, etc.) and non-living substances (gold, H_2O, DNA, electrons, etc.), many of which play an integral role in some of our best empirical theories about the natural world.

Here I think Substantial Priority offers several theoretical advantages over Merrick's own response to the Argument from Vagueness. To see this, note first that Substantial Priority can offer a structurally similar denial of V4 in terms of the emergence of non-redundant causal powers. In Chapter 4 we highlighted several empirical cases from physics, chemistry, and systems biology which seemed to assign perfectly natural properties to composite objects (both micro and macro), which suggested the failure of PDP for such objects. With Merricks, then, Substantial Priority is well positioned to affirm that the instantiation of perfectly natural properties (non-redundant causal powers) can serve as the requisite sharp cutoff on the continuous series of composition (at least for certain kinds of wholes), therein blocking the Argument from Vagueness.

But here an important difference arises between the two views. Where Merricks endorses the failure of PDP solely for *conscious* composite wholes, the defender of Substantial Priority, as we have seen, makes no such restriction. The examples previously offered in favor of the failure of PDP for certain composites (see §4.4.1 to 4.4.3) were those involving both *non-living* composite wholes (quantum entangled wholes and chemical compounds such as HCl, NaCl, and HeH) as well as *non-conscious* biological organisms (cells). As it stands, Substantial Priority is well suited to affirm *both* a non-arbitrary cutoff for composition via the failure of PDP as well as **Existence** for large classes of composite objects commended by the sciences and common sense. Of course, the difference between Merricks's view and the one I am commending here is one of mere degree and not kind. As such, Merricks is entirely within his rights to appropriate the failure of PDP for non-conscious composites as well (though, as we will see in the sequel, his view that non-conscious composites are causal overdeterminers will prohibit him from taking this route). As it stands, however, in so far as Substantial Priority is better situated in accounting for non-arbitratary cutoffs for composition with respect to a much broader class of composite objects, I take that to be a mark in its favor.

The attentive reader will note that the earlier rejection of V4 on behalf of the defender of Substantial Priority holds only for composite wholes for which PDP fails and thus objects that fit the description of a grounding whole. In so far as the earlier story is incapable of being generalized to grounded wholes, the defender of Substantial Priority is left without a sharp cutoff for the composition of grounded wholes. Although my aim in this chapter is focused solely on the theoretical advantages of *Substantial Priority* (and hence grounding wholes in particular) as applied to conundrums in material objects, let me say a few words in response to this charge, which will bring us to the second consideration in favor of Substantial Priority over Merricks's own denial of V4.

Recall the relevant grounding descriptions that characterize grounding wholes (substances) and grounded wholes (aggregates): the former ground the existence and identity of their proper parts and vice versa for the latter. Presumably, grounding is a non-vague notion. Whether the existence and identity of x being grounded in the existence and identity of y is a vague matter hinges, I suspect, on whether existence and identity are themselves vague notions.[5] But here, with a host of others, I must confess that I find the notions of vague existence and vague identity to be strange indeed. By my lights, the only forms of vagueness are either epistemic or semantic, either the result of gaps in our knowledge or semantic indecision. While this bit of autobiographical detail is certainly no argument against the exclusion of a variety of metaphysical vagueness, and many philosophers to whom I greatly admire think otherwise, I must leave my denial of vague existence and identity at the level of autobiography at this stage.

To be safe: *if* grounding is non-vague and thus it is determinate whether x is grounded in y, then the proponent of Substantial Priority has available to them yet another non-arbitrary cutoff on the compositional series, one that applies to the composition of both grounding and grounded wholes alike.[6] Take the composition of a grounding whole first. If one were to move along the continuous series (say from α to β) connecting cases of the non-composition with cases of the composition of a grounding whole, the sharp cutoff as to when certain parts compose a such whole would be sharp indeed: when the existence and identity of the parts become grounded in a common whole. The parts being jointly grounded as such is a necessary result of the composition of a grounding whole.[7]

The case is analogous for the composition of a grounded whole, simply reverse the direction of grounding from whole-to-parts to parts-to-whole. The non-arbitrary cutoff for when parts on the continuous series compose a grounded whole is when the existence and identity of the parts collectively serve as the total ground of a common whole (the whole being partially grounded in each individual part). The existence and identity of the parts serving to collectively ground the existence and identity of the whole is a necessary result of the composition of a grounded whole. This further story, which is part and parcel of a Substantial Priority fundamental mereology (and hence not an ad hoc response to the Argument from Vagueness), allows one to admit sharp compositional cutoffs for both kinds of mereological wholes, thereby rejecting V4 of the Argument from Vagueness while preserving **Existence** in its broadest application.[8]

6.2 The Problem of the Many

First ushered onto the contemporary scene by Peter Unger (1980), the Problem of the Many has proven to be an intractable puzzle that has led many philosophers to endorse some radically counterintuitive views about the nature of material objects.[9]

Consider Socrates, a living human organism sitting in an armchair at time t. Socrates is composed of a large number of material parts at t, call the sum total of these parts "SOC." At t, SOC composes Socrates, a living human organism. Now consider those bits of matter consisting of all the bits in SOC at t save for a single molecule, m, call these bits "SOC-minus." SOC-minus consists of all the same material elements as SOC, minus m.

If SOC composes a human organism at t, and the difference between SOC-minus and SOC hinges on a single molecule (m), then surely it is plausible to suppose that SOC-minus likewise composes a human organism at t. That is, it seems exceedingly plausible to sign-on to the following biconditional: SOC composes a human organism if and only if SOC-minus composes a human organism. It seems objectionably arbitrary to say that one composes a person and the other not. On the assumption that SOC composes Socrates at t, let us call the human organism composed of SOC-minus at t "Socrates-minus." Both Socrates and Socrates-minus are equally good human organism-candidates in the armchair at t. Thus where we originally thought there was just one human organism in the armchair at t, there are a great many more than meets the eye.

We can state one version of The Problem of the Many succinctly as follows:[10]

> M1. *Equal Candidate:* SOC composes a human organism at t iff SOC-minus composes a human organism at t.
>
> M2. If *Equal Candidate*, then it is not the case that there is exactly one living human organism in the chair at t.
>
> M3. There is at most one human organism in the chair at t.

M1-M3 are mutually inconsistent as the conjunction of M1 and M2 entails the denial of M3.

Solutions to the puzzle abound, some more revisionary than others. Hud Hudson (2001) highlights nine different solutions (excluding his own) ranging from the elimination of Socrates altogether, to identifying Socrates with an immaterial substance, to employing the machinery of fuzzy sets, to altering classical identity in some way, to distinguishing between the one person and its many person-constituters, or simply biting the wildly counterintuitive bullet and admitting a plenitude of human organisms in Socrates's chair. Here my aim is only to offer a brief survey of a few notable solutions on offer, with an eye toward showing how Substantial Priority offers a novel solution to this vexing problem.

To begin, one rather obvious solution here would be to deny the existence of composite objects like Socrates-minus; forbid arbitrary undetached parts like Socrates-minus from the class of existents and the problem disappears. The solution, however, is not so easily disposed of. If one rejects Socrates-minus, one is in effect saying that the bits of matter in SOC-minus do not have what it takes to compose a human organism. But remember, the difference between SOC-minus and SOC hinges on a mere molecule, m. If SOC composes a human organism, then surely SOC-minus would as well. How could one single lonely molecule make the difference in whether a human organism exists or not?

Perhaps another straightforward reaction would be to simply bite the bullet of the many and, contrary to our commonsense intuitions, countenance a multiplicity of persons occupying Socrates's chair at the time in question. Where we originally thought there was only one person in Socrates's chair, there are an innumerable number of non-identical persons each with their own respective conscious lives. **No Coincidence**, in effect, is false. After all, this line reasons, we have little reason to put too much epistemic weight on our commonsense intuitions; it is, then, no surprise that such intuitions fail to track the Many. For obvious reasons, there are very few, if any, who endorse such a no-holds-bared inclusion of the Many.

One rather revisionary way of including the Many candidates while, at the same time, claiming that there is "one" person in the chair—namely, Socrates, is to reevaluate our standard thinking about the identity relation in some form or other. Some have argued that the culprit for the generation of the Many in Socrates's chair is a commitment to classical identity; discharge **Identity** and the Many are evicted. There are multiple forms this route may take; here I focus on a medieval and contemporary variant of this style of response to the problem.

Peter Abelard (1079–1142), the pre-eminent philosopher-theologian of the twelfth century, had a ready solution at hand for the Many person-candidates in Socrates's chair, one that stems from his wider views regarding the concept of identity in general. Abelard famously distinguished between *sameness in essentia* and *numerical sameness*.[11] A and B are the same in *essentia* if and only if they have exactly the same proper (integral) parts; distinct in essentia if they do not. If A and B are the same in essentia, then they are numerically the same entity. For Abelard, while being numerically distinct entails being distinct in essentia, the converse does not hold. That is, A's being distinct from B in essentia does not entail that A and B are numerically distinct. Such a relation may hold between A and B if they exhibit a high degree of mereological overlap. While A and B differ in some respect in their proper parts, they nevertheless share a great many proper parts and thus are numerically the same entity. Consequently, Abelard countenances a relation of numerical sameness without what we would call classical or absolute identity. Thus each of the many overlapping human-candidates in the Problem of the Many, though different in essentia in virtue of their failure to exactly mereologically overlap, are nonetheless numerically one and the same human organism.

Abelard's solution to the Problem of the Many shares many similarities with David Lewis's (1999e) response to the puzzle. While Lewis sees no problem in admitting the Many candidates, he maintains that there is a natural sense in which there is but one person in Socrates's chair at the moment. We often, Lewis claims, count by relations other than strict absolute identity. Suppose we take numerical sameness and distinctness to be a spectrum consisting of absolute identity on the one end and absolute distinctness (or what Lewis calls "disjointness") on the other. Occupying the middle of the spectrum will be cases where two things are not entirely identical, nor entirely distinct in so far as they exhibit a high degree of mereological overlap. Thus, we ought to think of overlap as a species of identity, what we might call "partial identity." Any two of our equally plausible human candidates will almost completely overlap, differing in only a few skin cells or other for example. While the human-candidates fall short of complete identity, they fare nicely when it comes to being partially identical to one another in virtue of overlapping to a significant degree; as Lewis puts it, Socrates and Socrates-minus are "almost-identical."

Another response to the problem is to identify Socrates with an immaterial object, his soul for instance.[12] The defender of this line of reasoning takes the generation of the Many human-candidates to apply to any material object whatsoever. For *any* material occupant of spacetime you choose, the Many can be generated by arbitrarily selecting a material simple just beyond the spatial boundary of that object in precisely the same manner as noted earlier. Solution: human persons fail to be composed of any material occupants of spacetime. They are, instead, immaterial souls causally related to a particular human animal. Persons are immune to the generation of the Many precisely because they are immaterial, or so the argument goes.

The last solution I survey here trades on a distinction between persons and person-constituters, between Socrates and those Socrates-constituting collections of simples or portions of matter. Given that these two sorts of entities have different identity and persistence conditions, it would be a category mistake to identify persons with the portions of matter that constitute them (the statue and the lump of bronze, for instance). While there are a multiplicity of Socrates-constituting aggregates of simples in the region at which Socrates is located, Socrates is the sole human animal that each of them constitutes.[13]

Enter Substantial Priority. Suppose now that Socrates, like every living organism, is a fundamental substance understood along the lines of a grounding whole. As such, no distinct concrete thing grounds Socrates, and Socrates is the total ground for each of his proper parts. That is, *which* objects the proper parts of Socrates are involve exclusive reference to Socrates as their ground. Since Socrates lacks fundamental substances as parts at t as per **No Fundamental Parthood**, SOC-minus does not compose a rival substance at t (Socrates-minus).

The proponent of such a fundamental mereology pushes back on the underlying assumption that generates the multiplicity of rival candidates occupying Socrates's chair at t: that substances like Socrates can have other distinct substances like Socrates-minus as proper parts. If the bits of matter in SOC compose a fundamental substance at t, Socrates, then those bits are what they are in virtue of the substance of which they are a part. By extension, since the bits of matter in SOC-minus are parts of the bits that compose Socrates at t (SOC), they are likewise grounded in Socrates and thereby derivative. SOC-minus, then, is not an equally good candidate to compose a human organism at t precisely because the identities of each of its elements are already totally and exclusively dependent on a distinct fundamental substance at t, Socrates. Substantial Priority offers principled, non-ad hoc grounds for rejecting M1.

The denial of M1 afforded by Substantial Priority is similar in structure to an appeal to the notion of a *maximal property* to ground a similar move. A property F is maximal just in case (roughly) the proper parts of an object that is F are not themselves Fs. Those who employ the notion of maximality in this (or related) context would argue that *being a human organism* is a maximal property. Thus:

Maximality: For any x, if x is a human organism, then there is no y such that x is a proper part of y and y is a human organism.

If *being a human organism* is maximal in the sense prescribed by *Maximality*, then no proper part of a human organism will itself be a human organism. Since Socrates-minus is a proper part of Socrates, Socrates-minus is not a human organism on *Maximality*. This route has an ancient pedigree and has found able defenders in various contexts in contemporary metaphysics.[14] An appeal to maximality here promises to offer non-arbitrary grounds for rejecting *Equal Candidate*.

An appeal to *Maximality* as a stand-alone solution to the Problem of the Many has been subjected to some important objections. Let's consider a few of these objections and see how Substantial Priority helps reinforce the maximality solution where it is the weakest as a stand-alone response to the problem.

First, I'm inclined to think that one of the primary shortcomings of the maximality solution is that it seems contrived and unmotivated as a stand-alone response to the problem. Why, we might ask, does *Maximality* hold in this particular case? What is it about being a human organism *per se* that prohibits the proper parts of objects that bear this property from sharing in this elite status? Doesn't an appeal to *Maximality* here seem *too* convenient as grounds for rejecting *Equal Candidate*? Moreover, in what way does an appeal to *Maximality* above offer a *principled* or *non-arbitrary* reason for rejecting M1? For any problematic instance involving equally good F-candidates (where we intuitively think there is only a single F), are there principled grounds for affirming that F is a maximal property and thus the proper parts of Fs are not themselves F? On its own—i.e., in the absence of broader considerations in fundamental ontology—an appeal to maximality doesn't appear to give us any principled grounds to reject *Equal Candidate*; call a stand-alone solution that employs maximality considerations an "unprincipled maximality solution."

By contrast, Substantial Priority aims to offer a principled maximality solution to the Problem of the Many in that it provides a metaphysical underpinning that can motivate a non-arbitrary appeal to *Maximality* in the case at hand. The specific application of *Maximality* to human organisms obtains precisely because the following truths of fundamental mereology obtain: that living organisms are fundamental composite substances, and fundamental substances fail to stand in part-whole relations to other fundamental substances (**No Fundamental Parthood**). According to Substantial Priority, *being a substance* is maximal in that any object that belongs to the category of *substance* fails to be built up out of distinct fundamental substances as per **No Fundamental Parthood**. The maximality of *substantiality* falls out of the view that fundamental substances are not only complete but minimally complete; no proper sub-plurality of a substance is fundamental.[15] It is an enduring piece classical Aristotelian metaphysics that substances are the ultimate roots of being upon which all other beings are grounded. Substantial Priority offers the maximality move non-arbitrary grounds for appealing to maximality for *any* plausible substance-candidate. Consequently, if Substantial Priority proves independently plausible as a fundamental mereology, then appealing to it in the context of the Problem of the Many is not only principled but well-motivated.

A second objection leveled against an appeal to *Maximality* in this context is that it is unable to ground a sufficiently general solution to the Problem of the Many.[16] There seem to be plausible versions of the problem where the relevant property in question, F (e.g. *being a tile*), is not maximal (tiles arguably can have other tiles as proper parts) and thus the maximality move is left without grounds for excluding equally good F-candidates. An appeal to maximal properties, then, doesn't sufficiently generalize to all plausible cases of the Problem of the Many.

Here I think this charge hits its mark against Substantial Priority. As a principled maximality solution to the Problem of the Many, Substantial

Priority is restricted in its scope of application to composite objects that are plausible candidates for the status of fundamental substance. The same appeal to the machinery of grounding wholes and **No Fundamental Parthood** cannot be made when it comes to aggregates or grounded wholes such as heaps of sand or clouds. But I take it as gain that the solution afforded here delivers principled grounds to winnow away the Many in the types of cases many consider to be most problematic and counterintuitive, living organisms and human persons in particular (see Chapter 7 for more on the application of Substantial Priority to the metaphysics of human persons).

Lastly, perhaps the most serious objection to unprincipled maximality solutions is that they fail to address reinforced versions of the problem that incorporate mereological vagueness or indeterminacy. If it is sometimes indeterminate as to whether an object is a proper part of a composite, then the maximality solution is undercut from the start.[17] Here again, the solution afforded by Substantial Priority can help reinforce the maximality solution and sidestep the noted objection.

To illustrate, consider *m* once again, the single molecule included among the parts of Socrates at *t*. Suppose we now stipulate that it is indeterminate as to whether *m* is a proper part of Socrates at *t*; it is not the case that *m* is definitely a part, nor is it definitely not a part of Socrates at *t*. Now let "SOC-plus" refer to the bits of matter that compose Socrates at *t* that *definitely* has *m* as a part. SOC-plus and our original SOC-minus (all the bits of matter in SOC save *m* that compose Socrates-minus at *t*) appear to be equally good candidates to compose a human organism; neither strikes us as being better suited for the task.

If so, as Korman (2015a: 219–220) has argued, we can now replace M1 with something like the following premise that is immune to maximality considerations:

> M1*: *Equal Candidate**: SOC-plus composes a human organism at *t* iff SOC-minus composes a human organism at *t*.

An unprincipled maximality solution will no longer able to wield *Maximality* here in order to winnow away the *Equal Candidate* in M1*. The reason: if there is no determinate fact of the matter as to whether SOC-minus is a proper part of SOC-plus, then *Maximality* is without grounds for ruling out SOC-minus as equally suited to compose a human organism (Socrates-Minus). We then replace M2 with the following:

> M2*: If *Equal Candidate**, then it is not the case that there is exactly one living human organism in the armchair at *t*.

and the argument now hinges on the mutual incompatibility of M1*, M2* and M3. And since M2* is arguably just as plausible as our original M2, the argument has just a much bite as the original version.

How might the resources of Substantial Priority help reinforce the maximality response to this fortified version of the problem? Recall our previous discussion of Substantial Priority and the Vagueness Argument in §6.1.7. If grounding is non-vague—if there is always a fact of the matter as to whether x is grounded in y (or vice versa)—then it is never indeterminate whether some object is a proper part of a fundamental substance. If fundamental substances metaphysically ground each of their proper parts, and grounding is determinate, then substances do not have imprecise mereological boundaries. This falls right out of the grounding description of fundamental substances as grounding wholes and thus is not an ad hoc stipulation in response to indeterminate versions of the Problem of the Many. While this might serve as a *reductio* of the view to some ("*Of course* the mereological boundaries of organisms are indeterminate. So much the worse for Substantial Priority!"), Substantial Priority naturally shores up an appeal to maximality as a solution to one of the most problematic versions of the Problem of the Many.

While we may not be able to determine *which* parts in the vicinity of Socrates's boundaries are his parts, there is a fact of the matter as to which objects compose him at t (perhaps those whose causal dispositions are directed toward the manifestation of the dispositions of the whole) on the assumption that grounding facts are non-vague (see §6.1.8).[18]

To sum up, viewing Socrates (and living organisms more generally) as a grounding whole provides a principled, non-arbitrary reason to deny that any subset of Socrates's proper parts compose a fundamental substance, a reason that is independently motivated given the considerations offered in the preceding sections.

6.3 Causal Overdetermination

Considerations from causal overdetermination constitute a family of arguments aimed at the denial of **Existence** for either the entire class or a particular subset of the class of composite objects. We commonly take ordinary composite wholes to be causally efficacious in that their activity constitutes the causal fabric of the world. Electrons spin, radium atoms decay, cells undergo protein synthesis, aqua regia dissolves gold, biological systems self-regulate, humans engage in the scientific enterprise, etc. Yet at the same time, many take such wholes to be causally relevant *in virtue* of the causal powers of their parts together and their structural arrangements. In this sense, the *primary* actors on the world's stage are the (ultimate) parts of composite wholes and not the wholes themselves: wholes do things in virtue of their proper parts arranged thus and so.

If so, does this not render complex wholes causally redundant and thus epiphenomenal for any given causal event to which they contribute? If the causal activity of composite objects are rendered explanatorily redundant by the activity of their proper parts, to include them in the exhaustive inventory of reality would be superfluous, a violation of Occam's razor par excellence. Hence, parsimony suggests the elimination of mereological wholes as additional items of the world's furniture over and above their proper parts and the arrangements thereof.

I will work with the following formulation of the Argument from Causal Overdetermination against the existence of ordinary composite objects (where "x" stands for any composite object, "E" for an event, and "atom" as a placeholder for whatever it is our best physics tells us is at the fundamental microphysical level, whether atomic or atomless):[19]

> O1. Every E either is, or is not, caused by atoms arranged x-wise.
> O2. If E is caused by atoms arranged x-wise, then it isn't caused by an x.
> O3. If E isn't caused by atoms arranged x-wise, then it isn't caused by an x.
> O4. If no events are caused by x's, then there are no x's.
> O5. Hence, there are no x's.

The conjunction of O1 through O3 entail that no events are the result of the causal activity of x's which, together with O4, serve to call into question the existence of ordinary composite objects. For some philosophers, few (if any) composites survive the argument. Merricks (2001), for instance, contends that the argument winnows away *all* non-conscious composite objects as "overdeterminers," we are left only with higher-order sentient organisms.[20] In like manner, van Inwagen (1990: 122) remarks:

> All the activities apparently carried out by shelves and stars and other artifacts and natural bodies can be understood as disguised cooperative activities [of simples properly arranged]. And, therefore, we are not forced to grant existence to any artifacts or natural bodies.

In Merricks and van Inwagen we have, once again, the denial of **Existence** for a large class of mereological wholes commended by science and common sense.

I take the most contentious premises in the argument to be O2, O3, and O4. Let's start with O4. The premise derives its warrant from a modified form of Alexander's Dictum (Eleatic Principle) which states "to be a composite material object is to have causal powers."[21] If x's do not cause anything *tout court* (and if we have no other reason for including them in an exhaustive inventory of reality) then we ought to hedge ontological commitment to x's. As many philosophers are sympathetic to Eleatic Principle in its full-strength (i.e. to be *per se* is to have causal powers), very few are inclined to object to this rather weak modified version in terms of composite material objects.

Turn now to O2. At its core, O2 hinges on the denial of causal overdetermination with respect to x and its composing atoms. Say an event E is *causally overdetermined* by objects o_1 and o_2 iff (i) o_1 causes E, (ii) o_2 causes E, (iii) o_1 is not causally relevant to o_2's causing E, (iv) o_2 is not causally relevant to o_1's causing E, and (v) $o_1 \neq o_2$.[22] There are a host of ways for o_1 and o_2 to be *causally relevant* to each other's bringing about E. One such way would be where o_1 and o_2 serve as two individual members of the total cause of E (along with o_3, o_4, o_5, etc.) such that the objects in the class jointly suffice to bring about E. Yet another would be where o_1 causes o_2 to cause E or o_1's being caused by o_2 to cause E. With this notion of causal overdetermination in hand, the argument for O2 proceeds as follows: if E is caused by atoms arranged x-wise then E is caused by x only if E is causally overdetermined by x and the atoms arranged x-wise; but no event is causally overdetermined by an x and atoms arranged x-wise; therefore, O2.[23]

But what exactly is problematic with saying E is causally overdetermined by x and the atoms arranged x-wise? The widespread rejection of causal overdetermination, it seems, stems from its being an overt violation of Ockham's Razor, a theoretical principle that has held sway in the history of metaphysics. If there is no explanatory need to posit some entity x, then one (rationally) ought not posit x. Thus, considerations from ontological and ideological parsimony drive the widespread rejection of E's being causally overdetermined by x and the atoms arranged x-wise. Since both x and the atoms arranged x-wise are causally irrelevant to one another's causing E, and the behavior of x can be explained entirely in terms of the behavior of the atoms arranged x-wise, then positing the existence of x in addition to the atoms would be to multiply entities beyond necessity.

Here the defender of composite objects might reject O2 and argue that not all causal overdetermination is created equal. That is, we must distinguish between *objectionable* and *unobjectionable* overdetermination. One might argue that the sort of overdetermination at play between x and the atoms arranged x-wise is of the unobjectionable variety in that the two causal agents in question in the production of E are *not entirely independent from one another*. An example of two independent causal agents would be two police snipers causing the death of one and the same suspect at the exact same time, each individual shot being sufficient to cause the death of the suspect in question. Here the death of the suspect would be objectionably overdetermined in that there are two, independently related causes of the death, each being sufficient to bring about the event in question.

But, it is argued, the relationship between a whole and its proper parts is crucially dissimilar to the relationship between the two police snipers in the earlier example. The intimacy of the composition relation that obtains between a whole and its proper parts is such that the former (albeit numerically distinct) is not entirely independent of the latter. There are, it is claimed, plausible lines of inheritance that run between a whole and its parts and vice versa. Mereological wholes, for instance, appear to inherit their spatial location from their proper parts. Moreover, it is plausible to think that when certain proper parts of a whole undergo alteration, the whole undergoes alteration.[24] As a result, the intimacy (albeit non-identity) of the composition relation renders the instance of overdetermination in the argument unobjectionable. Thomasson (2006), for instance, argues along these lines:

> But this independence seems to be lacking between the causal claims of the baseball and the atoms arranged baseballwise. So it is not at all obvious that, in cases in which independence does not hold between objects A and B, A and B either provide double the amount of causation or are causal rivals.

With Thomasson, one could argue that given that composite objects and their proper parts fail to be entirely independent from one another, there is nothing problematic about saying that E is overdetermined by x and the atoms arranged x-wise and thereby endorse the denial of O2.

Yet another way to draw the line between objectionable and unobjectionable overdetermination would be in terms of metaphysical *fundamentality* or *basicness*. Schaffer (2007: 189) has argued that the overdetermination between x and the x-wise arrangements of atoms would be rendered objectionable only if both causal agents in the production of E were metaphysically basic or fundamental. For Schaffer, it is the multiplication of basics (and their causal activity) without necessity that gets to the heart of Ockham's Razor. He argues, "Redundancy is tolerable provided the redundant entities are properly grounded in what is basic. What is intolerable is redundancy in what is basic." If Schaffer's "mitigated redundancy" qualifies as overdetermination of the unobjectionable variety, then this route affords yet another way to reject O2 of the argument in question. For Schaffer, given his adherence to the view that the cosmos is the sole fundamental entity and thus neither x (where x is taken as any sub-world entity whatsoever) nor the atoms arranged x-wise are basic, there is no objectionable overdetermination and thus no need to eliminate the existence of ordinary composite objects.

A much neglected rejection of O2 stems from the endorsement of *causal pluralism*: the view that there are multiple kinds of causes and causal relations.[25] If so, then the causal activity of the atoms arranged x-wise and the causal activity of x do not compete for *one and the same causal role in the production of E*. A view of causation that accords nicely with causal pluralism is one that consists in the (mutual) manifestation of causal powers.[26] Suppose E stands for the event of Hydrogen Chloride's dissolving methanol. On this view, E's obtaining is the result of the joint manifestation of the molecule's power of acidity as well as the causal powers belonging to its constituents atoms, perhaps chlorine's being negatively charged and hydrogen's being positively charged (which therein gives rise to a polar covalent bond). *The* cause of E—that which is sufficient to bring about E—will involve reference to the manifestation of the causal powers of Hydrogen Chloride qua whole as well as the powers belonging to hydrogen and chloride. Our selection of a *single* causal factor in the production of E is more of an expression of our pragmatic interests than one that cuts metaphysical ice, or so it is argued.

In essence, this route denies that if E is caused by atoms arranged x-wise (hydrogen and chlorine standing in a polar covalent bond to one another) then E is caused by x (Hydrogen Chloride molecule) *only if* E is causally overdetermined; the reason being that *all* causal production is the result of the joint activity of the manifestation of powers. Since, as we earlier above, an event E is overdetermined only if both causal agents are causally *irrelevant* to each other's causing E, and since all instances of causal production involve the joint manifestation of powers, it follows that *no* event is causally overdetermined in the objectionable sense.

O3 has been challenged on the grounds that some events that are caused by composite objects (x's) are not caused by their composing atoms. One notable rejection of O3 argues that some composite objects exhibit non-redundant casual power in virtue of instantiating emergent causal properties (perfectly natural properties) that are not attributable to their proper parts nor the relations between them.[27]

As with the paradox of Tibbles the Cat, Lumpl and Goliath, the Problem of the Many and the Argument from Vagueness, Substantial Priority affords a solution to the Argument from Causal Overdetermination for composite substances in particular. Suppose we take x to stand for composite substances along the lines of Substantial Priority, composite objects that ground each of their proper parts. Perhaps the most direct way of blocking the aforementioned argument from the perspective of Substantial Priority is to underscore the fact that the view entails a denial of O3 in its rejection of the thesis that *all* mereological wholes are such that they adhere to PDP that to duplicate the perfectly natural properties of the parts and their basic arrangements suffices to duplicate the perfectly natural properties of the whole. As we have seen, according to Substantial Priority, there are mereological wholes for which PDP fails in that they instantiate perfectly natural properties and thus bring about non-redundant causal effects in the world.

According to O3, if E fails to be caused by the proper parts of a whole, then that whole is causally irrelevant to the production of E. This, of course, assumes that the perfectly natural properties (non-redundant causal powers) are instantiated *exclusively* by the proper parts of a mereological whole, something the friend of Substantial Priority denies.

But the resources of Substantial Priority afford a much deeper reason to reject O3 than the fact that some mereological wholes exhibit non-redundant causal powers. The reason is unique to Substantial Priority and stems from the distinctive grounding structure of substances. To see this, recall our previous discussion of the Argument from Vagueness, in particular, the continuous composition series which connects cases of the non-composition to cases of the composition of substances—i.e., grounding wholes. Upon the composition of a grounding whole, we noted that the parts are grounded in a common substantial whole. When this occurs, the relevant grounding description of a substance is such that *there is no individual dependence base at a level of decomposition in which the newly generated substance is grounded*.[28] For the proponents of Substantial Priority, this is precisely what it means to be metaphysically fundamental! The various levels of decomposition for substances contain only grounded entities—i.e., inseparable parts; there are no metaphysically basic entities that make up a substance's compositional base (**No Fundamental Parthood**).

That is, Substantial Priority construes composite substances as not only instantiating ontologically emergent *properties*, but also as ontologically emergent *wholes* in their own right. Following Kronz and Tiehen (2002: 346), substantial wholes exhibit "dynamic emergence" with respect to the existence and identity of their proper parts. Recall Kronz and Tiehen's characterization of a whole (a quantum entangled whole in particular) being dynamically emergent with respect to its proper parts:

> Emergent wholes have contemporaneous parts, but these parts cannot be characterized independently from their respective wholes . . . it does not make sense to talk about reducing an emergent whole to its parts, since the parts are in some sense constructs of our characterization of the whole . . . Emergent wholes are produced by an essential ongoing interaction of its parts, and *when that interaction ensues the independent particles become dependent*. But, if some of those parts are identical particles, then *they cannot be identified with those that existed prior to the interaction*, as a result of Pauli's exclusion principle. That is to say, *the independent parts cease to exist and the dependent parts come into existence*.[29]

On this proposal, grounding wholes are wholes that exhibit dynamic emergence in the earlier sense and thus are metaphysically prior to their proper parts. As such, they do not compete with their proper parts in being the cause of E in so far as none of their parts are metaphysically fundamental entities, entities with non-redundant causal powers with which they rival in bringing about E (although they do exhibit causal powers per se). That is to say, for any region of space hosting a fundamental substance, the sole bearer of perfectly natural properties in that region is the composite substance itself (although this is entirely consistent with saying that the parts of substances may instantiate natural properties *per se*; see Chapter 9).[30]

Consider once again the example of an entangled quantum whole. Recall that upon the composition of an entangled whole, "it is not permissible to consider the parts of a quantum whole as self-autonomous, intrinsically defined individual entities."[31] The causal activity of the particle-parts of an entangled whole do not threaten to render the activity of the entangled whole redundant precisely because their nature and existence now depend on the unified entangled whole. Once they compose an entangled whole, neither particle instantiates a pure spin state, that is, a state that can be individuated apart from the entangled whole. Since entangled wholes serve to ground the intrinsic properties of their particle-parts, including their causal powers and capacities, they can no more be eliminated in favor of such parts and their collective activity any more than the members of a set can be eliminated in favor of the set itself.

The main point here is that Substantial Priority takes aim at the hegemony of the underlying fundamental mereology that serves to generate the Argument from Causal Overdetermination in the first place. Merricks (2001: 60) refers to the rejection of a whole's exhibiting metaphysical constraints on its proper parts as "part of the 'scientific attitude' and 'bottom-up' metaphysics, according to which the final and complete causal stories will involve only the entities over which physics quantifies." We have already examined empirical reasons from quantum mechanics, chemistry, and systems biology which suggest that a "bottom-up" metaphysic (what I am calling Part-Priority and Priority Microphysicalism) is inadequate to capture the structure of certain mereological wholes. In addition, we have encountered empirical cases where certain composite objects plausibly (though not conclusively) conform to a grounding whole description in virtue of fixing the existence and identity of their proper parts (§4.3). Hence, to equate the rejection of a bottom-up metaphysics with the rejection of the "scientific attitude" is much too strong.

We have seen that Substantial Priority rejects a bottom-up metaphysic for substantial wholes in two distinct ways, thus lending a twofold denial of O3 in the Argument from Causal Overdetermination. First, O3 is false for fundamental substances in virtue of their instantiating perfectly natural properties. More importantly, however, is the fact that Substantial Priority construes composite substances *themselves*—the bearers of the perfectly natural properties—as being metaphysically prior to their proper parts such that they serve to ground the existence and identity of their proper parts. As such, the causal activity of the proper parts of a fundamental substance do not threaten to render the causal activity of the fundamental substance redundant (and thus susceptible to elimination) precisely because the identity and existence of such parts *depend* on the substantial whole in question.

As mereological wholes which lack bearers of non-redundant causal powers as proper parts, fundamental substances in no way compete or rival their parts for the causal production of E. While we need not deny that a bottom-up fundamental mereology applies to *some* mereological wholes (perhaps artifacts such as baseballs and billard tables, as well as aggregates such as heaps of sand), endorsing Substantial Priority for ordinary substances (and hence rejecting Part-Priority for such wholes) offers a solution to the Argument from Causal Overdetermination that preserves **Existence** for a host of scientifically serious composite objects. And this in addition to the solutions afforded to the puzzles in the previous sections.

Substantial Priority, we have seen, lends a unified solution to a host of conundrums in material objects: Tib and Tibbles, Goliath and Lumpl, The Problem of the Many, The Argument from Vagueness, and The Argument from Casual Overdetermination. It's virtues, I have argued, are many. First, Substantial Priority is *unifying* in that it provides a single overarching solution to many of the most worrisome of puzzles concerning material objects in the literature. Second, the view has broad *explanatory power*; it explains both a wide range and variety of puzzles about material objects. Third, Substantial Priority is (comparatively) *plausible* in that it does not require a radical revision to our most cherished ordinary beliefs about ordinary composite substances themselves (even if one thinks it calls into question commonsense intuitions about the *proper parts* of ordinary composite substances). Fourth, Substantial Priority is also *simple* in that its explanatory work is achieved by the application of just a few metaphysical resources—namely, **No Fundamental Parthood** for fundamental substances and the grounding structure of composite objects (both grounding and grounded wholes). Lastly, as was noted in Chapter 4, the view is well-entrenched in so far as it plausibly accords with facts about the structure of composite objects in the natural sciences.

Notes

1. Adapted from Sider (2001: 120–125).
2. For instance, where $n=2$, the expression "there are n concrete objects" can be formulated as follows: $(\exists x)(\exists y)(Cx \wedge Cy \wedge x \neq y \wedge (\forall z)(Cz \rightarrow (x = z \vee y = z)))$.
3. This route is also taken by Hawthorne (2006: 106–109).
4. Although, to be fair, Merricks is clear that he remains agnostic about non-conscious composites exhibiting non-redundant causal powers.
5. One could, however, leave open the possibility of vague identity and existence for things (or pluralities) like clouds or heaps of sand. However, in so far as all grounding chains include at least one substance as part of its well-founded ground (see G9 in §2.1.4), the non-vagueness of grounding would hinge directly on the non-vagueness of the identity and existence of basic substances.
6. See Pasnau (2012: 490) for a discussion of how an Aristotelian account of the unity of material substances has resources for avoiding the threat of vagueness.
7. Though I do not think the obtaining of such structure is sufficient for composition to occur.
8. That is, assuming that every mereological whole is either a grounding or grounded whole. Artifacts, on this view, would count as grounded wholes in so far as the case can be made in favor of the fact that their causal profiles can be accounted for entirely in terms of the causal profiles of their proper parts and their basic arrangements.

9. See Hud Hudson (2001) for what I take to be the definitive treatment of the Problem of the Many in the literature.
10. I borrow this concise formulation of the problem from Korman (2011).
11. For more on Abelard's account of identity and sameness see King (2004).
12. See Unger (2006) for a defense of this view.
13. See Mark Johnston (1992) and E. J. Lowe (1982, 1995).
14. See Arlig (2015, §4.1) and Normore (2006) for a brief discussion of medieval solutions to the problem, many of which make some form of appeal to a principle like maximality.
15. Schaffer (2009: 377).
16. Sutton (2014) and Korman (2015a: 218–219).
17. Korman (2015a) cites Lewis (1999: 166–167) as an example of one who formulates the problem to include vagueness.
18. Regarding medieval solutions to the Problem of the Many, Robert Pasnau notes (2012: 490), "Later medieval authors have such a solution ready to hand. For any given region of material stuff, there will be a non-vague fact about whether the bodies in that region are informed by a given substantial form, and whether they continue to be so informed over time. To be sure, we will not be in a position to know the truth about such fine-grained details, and so facts about the unity and identity of substances will look vague to us. The vagueness, however, is purely epistemic; the world is determinate."
19. Here I follow Korman's (2011) formulation of the argument as well as the clarificatory points that follow.
20. See Dorr (2005) for a full-scale rejection of composite objects on similar grounds.
21. See Merricks (2001: 81). Note the qualification to exclude alleged abstracta like numbers, sets, and propositions.
22. Korman (2011).
23. I set aside a rather obvious, though not uncontroversial, way to deny O2: that *x just is* the atoms arranged *x*-wise.
24. Of course, this route would need to be a bit more precise as to how to unpack the notion of "independence" (whether counterfactual, causal, metaphysical independence, etc.).
25. It is a further question as to the precise formulation of causal pluralism. Some present the view as claiming multiple kinds of causes and causal relations, each of which are defined in terms of a single fundamental relation, while others take the view to mirror debates in compositional pluralism and thus claim that the view is committed to there being multiple *fundamental* causal relations. For purposes of illustration here I adopt the first reading.
26. See Anjum and Mumford (2011) for a recent full-length defense of this view. This is obviously not an analysis of causation as the notion of "causal power" invokes the notion of causality.
27. See Elder (2007) and Lowe (2005a).
28. This is, in fact, is precisely what Humphreys (1997) takes his concept of *fusion emergence* to entail with respect to avoiding causal overdetermination, albeit applied to the emergence of property-instances instead of mereological wholes.
29. Emphasis mine.
30. There are several accounts of the precise role the parts of fundamental substances play in the action of the whole. Koons (2014) offers his own novel neo-Aristotelian account he labels "parts as sustaining instruments": even if the non-redundant powers of the whole are not grounded in the parts, the whole acts *through* the powers of the parts as teleologically subordinate instruments.
31. Karakostas (2009: 14).

7 Getting Personal
Substantial Priority and Personal Ontology

In the previous two chapters I argued for the theoretical utility of Substantial Priority on the grounds that it offers a unified solution to a host of puzzles in the metaphysics of material objects. The view commends itself as a neo-Aristotelian mereology worth taking seriously. In this chapter, I offer two additional arguments in favor of Substantial Priority—what I call *the terminus argument* and *the tracking argument*. If all grounding chains run *through* and never terminate *in* intermediate composite objects like you and me, then what follows for the metaphysics of free will and human persons? Here I will attempt to explore the interrelationship between issues in fundamental mereology and the metaphysics of mind and free will.

7.1 The Terminus Argument

The first argument in favor of fundamental intermediates rides on the back of a recent objection to fundamental mereology from the metaphysical possibility of non-well-founded mereological structures. Far from undermining the project of fundamental mereology *per se*, I argue that only a fundamental mereology equipped with at least one fundamental intermediate can allow for a terminus of grounding chains in possible worlds with no bottom or top mereological levels. Call this *the terminus argument*.[1]

In a recent article, Jonathan Tallant (2013) has offered an argument he claims undermines both Monism and Pluralism (by "Pluralism" Tallant means Atomism in particular) and thus spells the end of the project of fundamental mereology. Call a world *w* gunky iff every object in *w* has proper parts. And call a world *w** junky iff every object in *w** *is* a proper part. Lastly, call a world *w*** hunky iff *w*** is both gunky and junky—i.e., a world such that every object in that world both *has* proper parts and *is* itself a proper part of a higher-level whole. On the assumptions that all fundamental mereologies are committed to there being some level that is (absolutely) metaphysically fundamental ("SLF") and that such views are necessarily true if true at all ("MOD"), the general argument against Monism and *Pluralism* runs as follows:

H1. A hunky world is metaphysically possible.
H2. If a hunky world is metaphysically possible, then Monism and Pluralism are false (given SLF and MOD).
H3. Monism and Pluralism are false (given SLF and MOD).[2]

In short: the *prima facie* possibility of a world with both infinite downward and upward mereological complexity undermines Pluralism and Monism in so far as such a world is ordered by non-well-founded dependence chains and thus lacks a fundamental level, a metaphysical terminus. Contrary to fundamental mereology, then, it is possible that no concrete entity in hunky worlds—whether the cosmos or its many proper parts—is metaphysically fundamental. If hunky worlds are possible and Monism and Pluralism are exhaustive answers to the question of fundamental mereology, then fundamental mereology is in trouble.

While there are replies available to Atomists and Monists, each carry significant costs in my estimation. Whether one takes conceivability or modal intuitions or seemings as a guide to metaphysical possibility, it is quite plausible to think that each lend, at the very least, *prima facie* evidence for the possibility of worlds lacking both a top and a bottom mereological level. Moreover, arguing for the impossibility of gunky and junky worlds is a tall-order, and often relies on heavyweight commitments that many take to be less plausible than the modal intuitions that ground views to the contrary.[3] The considerations in favor of the *prima facie* possibility of gunky worlds—namely, their conceivability (or, minimally, the lack of an inconceivability argument against them), logical consistency, and their having a formal analogue in extensional mereologies, seem to equally apply to junky worlds and, by extension, hunky worlds.[4] And many philosophers are prepared to grant the possibility of gunky worlds, some even going so far as to argue that there are good empirical grounds for thinking that our world is, in fact, gunky.[5] A sharp asymmetry between the modal status of gunk and junk will strike many as untenable.

Here I want to argue that far from undermining the project of fundamental mereology *per se*, the argument helps establish the tenability of one such view in particular—namely, a fundamental mereology that countenances at least one fundamental intermediate. As there is no top mereological level in our hunky world w^{**}, the cosmos does not exist in w^{**} and therefore cannot serve as the metaphysical terminus of the part-whole ordering in that world. Likewise, as there is no bottom mereological level in w^{**}, the atoms do not exist in w^{**} and thus are unable to ground the part-whole ordering in w^{**}. *Every* entity on the mereological hierarchy in w^{**} is both composite and intermediate. And since a core tenet of fundamental mereology is that there must, of necessity, be a fundamental ground or terminus to reality (SLF) or else "[t]here would be no ultimate ground. Being would be infinitely deferred, never achieved" (Schaffer 2010: 62), it follows that the fundamental entity or collection of entities in w^{**} is/are intermediate.

If *all* composite objects in w^{**} were themselves dependent on a higher-level whole, there would be no terminus to the upward dependence chain in w^{**} and thus no metaphysically fundamental level. Similarly, if *all* composite objects in w^{**} were dependent on their proper parts, there would be no terminus to the downward dependence chain and thus no metaphysically fundamental level in w^{**}.[6] But on the view I am recommending here, w^{**} includes at least one fundamental intermediate, s, where every proper part of s both *is* a derivative intermediate and *has* derivative intermediates as proper parts (composite objects each of which are intermediate and dependent on s), and where s is itself a proper part of an infinite upward series of derivative intermediates (composite objects each of which are intermediate and dependent on s). Substantial Priority seems uniquely suited among fundamental mereologies to support the metaphysical necessity of the well-foundedness of grounding. While the metaphysical possibility of hunky worlds threatens both Monism and Atomism, Substantial Priority remains unscathed.

As a result, it is precisely because w^{**} consists of both derivative intermediates and at least one fundamental intermediate that its failing to have a top or bottom mereological level in no way precludes its having a fundamental level. Only a fundamental mereology which posits at least one fundamental intermediate remains unscathed in light of the objection from the metaphysical possibility of hunky worlds. As a result, the terminus argument offers grounds in favor of Substantial Priority over its rivals.

But consider a worry for Substantial Priority here as it pertains to its alleged modal status. Given MOD, if Substantial Priority is true then it is true of necessity. If Substantial Priority is a proposition of metaphysics, it's truth ought to remain fixed from world to world. That is,

> *SP-Necessity*: If at least one intermediate substance is fundamental at the actual world, then every possible world w is such that at least one intermediate is fundamental at w.

But *SP-Necessity* doesn't seem to be true given possible worlds that lack intermediate mereological joints altogether.[7] For example, consider a possible world w' with only three concrete material objects: atoms a and b which together compose c. Or consider a nihilistic world w'', devoid of parthood relations, with two lonely atoms a and b. In w' and w'' there are only the atoms and the cosmos, no intermediates; *ipso facto* there is no intermediate to serve as the metaphysical ground of the part-whole ordering in such worlds as per Substantial Priority. Consequently, *SP-Necessity* rules out w' and w'' as genuinely possible worlds. Since these worlds are clearly metaphysically possible, *SP-Necessity* is false and Substantial Priority is not true (given MOD).

There is an ever-growing body of literature on the modal status of metaphysical views in general and mereological metaphysics in particular. One often finds in this literature instances of the following type of reasoning. Some argue *from* the metaphysical possibility of gunk to the (necessary) falsity of nihilism and Part-Priority, and others *from* the (necessary) truth of nihilism and Part-Priority *to* the metaphysical impossibility of gunk. Sider (2013) represents this latter move:

> The argument from the possibility of gunk faces a challenge. Consider this argument for the opposite conclusion: "nihilism is possibly true; nihilism is a proposition of metaphysics and hence is noncontingent; so nihilism is necessarily true; so nihilism is true."

Stalwart nihilists and Monists alike can argue from the necessary truth of their view (nihilism or Monism) to the impossibility of certain mereological strucutures, whether gunk or junk.

In the same way, the stalwart proponent of Substantial Priority can respond to the earlier worry by holding fast to *SP-Necessity* and arguing that w' and w'' are not genuinely possible worlds. In general, I find this general move unpromising. Rather what we need is to assign a modal status to Substantial Priority that is strong enough to back the terminus argument against Monism and Atomism, but not so strong as to require every possible world to include intermediate mereological joints. Here is one attempt that restricts the truth of Substantial Priority to worlds with intermediate mereological joints as follows:

> *SP-Necessity (Restricted)*: If at least one intermediate substance is fundamental at the actual world, then every possible world w with intermediate mereological joints is such that at least one intermediate is fundamental at w.

This restricted modal status for Substantial Priority provides the requisite backing for the terminus argument against Monism and Atomism. On the one hand, Substantial Priority (on *SP-Necessity (Restricted)*) remains uniquely situated to uphold the notion that metaphysical structure is necessarily well-founded (SLF); every possible world includes at least one fundamental being. As we have seen, only Substantial Priority can maintain a metaphysical terminus in hunky worlds, worlds that lack a mereological terminus.

On the other hand, if we assign a modal status to Substantial Priority along the lines of *SP-Necessity (Restricted)* we can allow for a fundamental level even in possible worlds that are devoid of intermediate mereological structure (or even devoid of mereological structure at all). It nevertheless remains that in every possible world with intermediate mereological joints, including gunky and junky worlds, there is at least one fundamental intermediate. Substantial Priority can affirm that c, the cosmos, is fundamental at w' and a and b, the atoms, are fundamental at w'' precisely because these are worlds lacking intermediate joints; all while maintaining that it is metaphysically necessary that there be at least one fundamental intermediate in worlds with intermediate mereological structure.

7.2 The Tracking Argument

The second argument in favor of fundamental intermediates, what I'll call *the tracking argument*, turns on the relationship between the fundamental properties and the bearers of the fundamental properties. As we have previously noted, it is now commonplace to employ a naturalness ordering over the domain of properties; natural properties are to be distinguished from those properties that merely serve as the semantic values for meaningful predicates in that they (among other things) ground objective similarities and carve out the causal structure of the world. Moreover, naturalness is thought to admit of degrees, with the *perfectly natural* or *fundamental* properties being those elite natural properties that (i) ground objective similarities, (ii) carve out the non-redundant causal joints, and (iii) serve as the minimal ontological base for all other properties.[8]

While natural properties *per se* carve out the distinctively causal structure of the world, some natural properties carve out this structure in a non-redundant fashion.[9] Since my aim in what follows is limited to the distinctive causal role played by perfectly natural properties, I restrict my focus to those perfectly natural properties the possession of which carve out the fundamental or non-redundant causal structure in the world.

With the aforementioned machinery in place, we can state the tracking argument simply as follows:

T1. *Tracking*: Necessarily, the fundamental causal properties exclusively track the fundamental bearers of properties.
T2. At least some ordinary, intermediate composites are the bearers of fundamental causal properties.
T3. Therefore, at least some ordinary, intermediate composites are fundamental bearers of properties.

Premise T1, what I've called *Tracking*, is endorsed by many Monists and Atomists alike. Many friends of a naturalness ordering over properties are of the opinion that the most natural causal properties and the bearers of those properties march in step: the fundamental objects exclusively bear the elite or fundamental causal properties.

Lewis (1986b: x), for instance, maintains that the natural properties that carve the deepest causal joints are exclusively microphysical.[10] In a similar manner, Schaffer (2013: 71) assumes something akin to *Tracking* in so far as he argues *from* the fundamentality of the properties and laws of the cosmos *to* the fundamentality of the cosmos.[11] Schaffer (2014) even goes so far to say that what I am calling *Tracking* amounts to a "plausible connection between *being a fundamental object* and *bearing fundamental properties* . . . It would be a cost to sever this connection." Regardless of whether one has a penchant for the fundamentality of microphysics or the cosmos, the point remains that it is natural (though certainly not uncontroversial) to think that the bearers of the fundamental properties that carve the non-redundant causal structure of the world are themselves metaphysically elite.[12] John Heil (2012:28) states (and endorses) what I am calling *Tracking* succinctly as follows: "fundamental properties require, as bearers, fundamental substances."

The key premise to defend is T2, the thesis that at least some intermediate composite objects are the bearers of fundamental causal properties. T2 amounts to the following claim about at least some intermediate wholes: duplicating the natural properties and relations of either the (atomic) parts or the (cosmic) whole of which it is a part fails to duplicate the natural properties and relations of the intermediate whole. In this way, the natural properties of at least some intermediate wholes are genuinely non-redundant.

Premise T2 will, no doubt, carry little force with die-hard proponents of Monism and Atomism; "Surely," the Atomist will retort, "the causal properties of intermediate composites are not perfectly natural or fundamental; how *could* they be given that such properties and their bearers are entirely grounded in the domain of microphysics?" It is a commitment to Atomism that drives the acceptance of what John Hawthorne (2006: viii) has called "micro-naturalism", the view that "the 'maximally' or 'perfectly' natural properties correspond to the primitive predicates of an ideal microphysics," and consequently a rejection of T2. If either micro-naturalism or what I'll call "cosmic-naturalism" is true—the view that the perfectly natural properties exclusively reside at the global, cosmic level—then all the non-redundant, causal structure in the world is confined to either the bottom or the top mereological level.[13]

But if the fundamental properties are those that carve out the non-redundant, causal structure in the world, then the denial of T2 carries with it a high price-tag indeed. My own attempt to motivate T2 will focus on intermediate composite objects that are closer to home, so to speak, and are what I take to be paradigmatic examples of bearers of fundamental causal properties: human persons.[14] Perhaps the most that can be offered here to an audience of "neutral agnostics" with respect to T2 is to underscore the costly nature of its denial. It is to this that I now turn.

Consider first the non-redundant *causal* structure in the world. Is there any reason to think that intermediate composite objects—human persons in particular—help carve out this particular variety of structure in the world? One reason to think so turns on the notion that persons are free with respect to at least some of their actions. It is widely thought that the Consequence Argument is *the* staple argument in defense of incompatibilism, the view that free will and determinism are incompatible. For our purposes here, we can define "determinism" as the view that for any propositions, p_1 and p_2, and times t_1 and t_2, such that p_1 and p_2 each accurately describe the state of the world at t_1 and t_2 respectively, the conjunction of p_1 with the laws of nature entails p_2. That is, there is only one possible future given the past and the laws of nature. An informal statement of the Consequence Argument by its foremost contemporary defender runs as follows:

> If determinism is true, then our acts are the consequences of the laws of nature and events in the remote past. But it is not up to us what went on before we were born, and neither is it up to us what the laws of nature are. Therefore, the consequences of these things (including our present acts) are not up to us.
> (van Inwagen (1983: 56))

If determinism is true, and neither the past nor the laws of nature are up to humans, then humans have no choice about what actions they perform. Something must give.

Some incompatibilists, most notably so-called hard-determinists, accept the conclusion that humans have no choice about what actions they perform and thus that none of their actions are free. Incompatibilists of the "libertarian" variety, on the other hand, deny the truth of determinism in order to safeguard the reality of free will. Philosophical friend and foe of incompatibilism alike have disputed both the validity and the soundness of the Consequence Argument, making the extant literature quite complex to say the least. While I myself think the argument is sound and will proceed on the basis of this assumption, I will not argue the case here. Accordingly, the considerations that follow in favor of T2 will appeal only to incompatibilists who accept the reasoning outlined in the Consequence Argument. While the size of my audience of neutral agnostics concerning T2 may dwindle as a result, the argument is no less interesting or forceful in my estimation.

Perhaps less familiar is an argument offered by Trenton Merricks (2001) and more recently Jason Turner (2009) that precisely parallels the Consequence Argument and, according to its proponents, is just as much of a threat to free will as is determinism.[15] Roughly, the argument hinges on the same core insight of the Consequence Argument—that the fixity of certain conditions (together with a suitable closure principle) rules out any actions being up to an agent—yet appeals not to the fixity of the past and laws of nature but to the activity or qualitative character of the agent's microphysical parts and the relations that obtain between them. And since the activity or qualitative character of microphysical reality is not up to agents, it follows that the consequences of the activity or qualitative character of their microphysical parts and their relations—including their present actions—are not up to agents either. And since free will requires that at least some actions be up to human agents, free will seems to be undermined, this time by what Merricks calls "the bottom-up metaphysics." For friends of the Consequence Argument, the threat to free will from the "the bottom-up metaphysics" is very real indeed.[16]

To put this close cousin of the Consequence Argument to work in supporting T2 of the tracking argument, we'll need to get clear on what exactly an agent's "having a choice" or something's being "up to an agent" amounts to. For my purposes here, I follow Turner (2009), who in turn follows Finch and Warfield (1998), in understanding "its being up to an agent A whether p" and "A has the choice about whether p" as "A could have acted to ensure the falsity of p". My having a choice or its being up to me whether *the match ignites at 2:00 p.m.*, for instance, amounts to my having the ability to ensure that *the match ignites at 2:00 p.m.* is false or fails to obtain; if I lack such an ability, then neither do I have a choice nor is it up to me whether *the match ignites at 2:00 p.m.*

To be of use to us in demonstrating the high-cost of the denial of T2, however, the argument needs to be generalized to include the threat from "the bottom-up metaphysics" (Atomism) to free will as well as from what we might call "the Top-down metaphysics," where I use the capital "T" in reference to the topmost mereological level in which everything else is grounded (the cosmos) according to Monism:

C1. The following is not up to human agents: every action human agents perform is grounded in or dependent on either the activity or qualitative character of the cosmos, or the activity or qualitative character of their microphysical parts and the relations between them.
C2. The activity or qualitative character of the cosmos, and the activity or qualitative character of the microphysical parts and the relations between them is not up to human agents.
C3. Therefore, it is not up to human agents what actions they perform.[17]

C1 follows from both micro-naturalism and cosmic-naturalism, which in turn are part and parcel of Atomism and Monism respectively. If the non-redundant causal properties are exclusively instantiated by either the cosmos or by the entities of microphysics, then all other properties and activities depend on the natural properties and activity of either the cosmos or the entities of microphysics. And presumably human agents could not have acted in such a way as to ensure the falsity of Atomism or Monism.

Schaffer (2014: §3.2.5) illustrates the truth of cosmic-naturalism nicely in his description of *his own* activity as a "subcosmic" agent—i.e., an agent that is a proper part of the cosmos: "I am sitting in virtue of the cosmos being as it is;" more generally, he notes "For if a given subcosmic object a has property F, the Monist will say that a is F in virtue of the fact that the cosmos is such and so, where the cosmos is not part of a."[18] Not only is determinism incompatible with any actions being up to human agents, so is a commitment to both micro-naturalism and cosmic-naturalism, and with them Atomism and Monism respectively.

We have reached the following decision point for incompatibilists who accept the reasoning outlined in the Consequence Argument: either (a) reject C1 and thereby *both* micro-naturalism and cosmic-naturalism and with them Atomism and Monism, (b) deny C2 and affirm that the activity and qualitative character of either the cosmos or their microphysical parts and the relations between them is up to human agents, or (c) affirm the argument's soundness and conclude that it is not up to human agents what actions they perform.[19]

Option (c), I take it, is in deep tension with our first-person phenomenological experience of ourselves as human agents with a choice about what actions we perform. We sometimes act freely. For those whose belief in the reality of agency and free will commands their attention, option (c) is a non-starter.

This leaves us with options (a) and (b). Proponents of Atomism and Monism who are incompatibilists and who think agents sometimes act freely, will side with (b) and finger C2 as the culprit: human agents *do* have a choice about either the activity or qualitative character of the cosmos or their microphysical parts and the relations between them. The denial of C2 amounts to the claim that human agents can act in such a way as to ensure the falsity of facts or propositions about the activity and qualitative character of either the cosmos or their microphysical parts and relations between them.

But note here that there are a variety of ways to ensure the falsity of some proposition. There are a host of what we might call "sub-facts" that help make it the case that *the match ignites at 2:00 p.m.*, for example, such as the presence of oxygen in the relevant region of space-time, the particular time at which the match was struck (e.g., the match's being struck at 2:00 p.m. instead of 1:59 p.m.), facts about the properties of the match and the surface on which it is struck (e.g., that the match and surface are dry), and facts about the laws of nature (e.g., that the laws are such that matches struck in those particular circumstances tend to ignite).

As a result, agents may act to ensure the falsity of some proposition p in one of two ways, either *directly* by ensuring the falsity of p itself, or *indirectly* by ensuring the falsity of at least one of the various sub-facts that help make it the case that p.[20] It is plausible to think that it is necessary that in order for it to be "up to me" or "to have a choice about" whether *the match ignites at 2:00 p.m.* I need to have the the ability to ensure the falsity of this proposition, either (i) *directly* by ensuring the falsity of *the match ignites at 2:00 p.m.* itself—i.e., without ensuring the falsity of any of the sub-facts that help make it the case, or (ii) *indirectly* in virtue of ensuring the falsity of at least one of the earlier sub-facts that help make it the case that *the match ignites at 2:00 p.m.*—i.e., ensuring that it is false that *the match is dry, the match is struck at 2:00 p.m.*, etc.

Now consider the following proposition concerning the activity of a small subset of my microphysical parts: *the electrons in the nerves of my toes are in motion*. The proponent of Atomism might argue that while there are a host of sub-facts that help make it the case that *the electrons in the nerves of my toes are in motion*, one salient sub-fact along these lines is the macrophysical fact *that my toes are wiggling*; the electrons in my toes are the way they are and behave the way they do partly in virtue of the fact *that my toes are wiggling*. And it is arguably the case that the fact *that my toes are wiggling* is up to me in so far as I have the ability to directly ensure its falsity—namely, by my refraining from wiggling my toes. Easy enough. If so, then there is no problem with my being able to act in such a way as to ensure the falsity of propositions or facts concerning the activity or character of my microphysical parts and the relations between them, albeit in an indirect sense in virtue of having a choice about various macrophysical sub-facts that make them true. Contra C2, then, human agents *do* have a choice about the activity and character of their microphysical parts and relations between them. So argues the Atomist.[21]

But it is not at all clear whether on Atomism and Monism agents can act in such a way as to ensure the falsity of propositions or facts about the activity or qualitative character of the cosmos or their microphysical parts, even in the indirect sense. On Atomism and Monism, and with them micro-naturalism and cosmic-naturalism, every object and property that is not at the cosmic or the microphysical level is totally grounded in or dependent on the items (and relations) belonging to one of these two domains. This includes both agents themselves as intermediate composite objects as well as the properties that enable them to bring about toe-wiggling sorts of actions. If metaphysical grounding is an asymmetric relation, then the way the top and bottom mereological levels are determines the way the intermediates are and behave the way they do *and not vice versa*; fixing the natural properties and relations of either the cosmos or the domain of microphysics suffices to fix the natural properties and relations of all intermediates in between.

In the example noted earlier, it is questionable given the assumption of Atomism whether the macrophysical fact *that my toes are wiggling* can be among the sub-facts that *make it the case* that the proposition *the electrons in the nerves of my toes are in motion* is true. Likewise, on the assumption of Monism where "I am sitting in virtue of the cosmos being as it is" and not vice versa, it cannot be the case that the proposition *the cosmos is in such-and-such a state* obtains in virtue of the macrophysical fact *I am sitting*.

On this picture, the prospects look rather dim for *any* sort of in-virtue-of or explanatory relations proceeding from intermediate-to-cosmos or intermediate-to-microphysics. As Kim (1999: 28) once asked, "But how is it possible for the whole to causally affect its constituent parts on which its very existence and nature depend?" And if, as deRosset (2010) notes regarding intermediate composite objects, the "existence and features of the macroscopic concrete objects alleged by common sense and abetted by science can be completely explained solely by reference to the existence and properties of other things", then the activity or qualitative character of intermediates is the way it is in virtue of either the cosmos or the domain of microphysics, and not the other way around. A denial of C2 here is against the spirit if not the letter of Atomism and Monism.[22]

It will come as no surprise to the reader that my sympathies lie with option (a) and thus the rejection of C1: in the same way that determinism ought to be rejected in order to make room for free will, "the bottom-up" and "the Top-down metaphysics" ought to be rejected for the very same reason. If every action intermediate agents perform obtains in virtue of either the causal activity or the qualitative character of the cosmos or their microphysical parts and not vice versa, then none of the actions of agents are up to them. If the actions of persons as agents in no way carve reality at its non-redundant causal joints, then it is difficult to see what room there is for free will in such a scenario.

If option (c) is a pill too difficult to swallow for incompatibilists who are friends of the Consequence Argument, then they do well to reject C1 and with it Atomism and Monism. But this is just to say that libertarians about free will who accept the reasoning outlined in the Consequence Argument have grounds for accepting premise T2 of the tracking argument, that at least some intermediate composites are the bearers of fundamental properties, most notably intermediate agents like ourselves who bear non-redundant causal powers.

A second consideration in favor of T2 of the tracking argument concerns the causal and qualitative structure carved out by the phenomenal, conscious properties of human persons. As is well-known, arguments abound in the metaphysics of mind in support of the irreducibility of the mental to the physical. Thought experiments involving inverted qualia, the possibility of zombie worlds, and Mary the neurophysiologist coming to learn genuinely new non-physical facts, all converge on the view that phenomenal mental states are irreducible to physical states. The arguments, of course, are very controversial, and I will not rehearse them here as they are now standard. Nevertheless, a not-so-insignificant number of philosophers have been inclined to accept these arguments and that conscious, qualitative mental properties are fundamental causal properties (and thus not epiphenomenal).

Yet relatively few of these philosophers have made explicit the connection between the fundamentality of phenomenal conscious properties with their being perfectly natural in the Lewisian sense. If phenomenal mental properties are indeed perfectly natural and thus fundamental in their own right, then those who are independently committed to the fundamentality of the mental in the metaphysics of mind will have yet another reason to endorse T2 of the tracking argument, that at least some intermediate composites are the bearers of fundamental properties.

Dean Zimmerman (2010) and Kris McDaniel (2007) are two philosophers who endorse the fundamentality of phenomenal, conscious properties and who explicitly gloss these properties in the ideology of perfect naturalness. Zimmerman (2010: 125) is unequivocal that

> the conclusion supported by appeal to zombies and their ilk is, then, a thesis about which properties are the most natural ones—which ones "carve nature at the joints", being responsible for the most fundamental kinds of objective resemblance among things

and that phenomenal properties are "as natural as the most natural properties that would be mentioned in a 'final physics' description of just the non-sentient material objects and systems."

In like manner, Kris McDaniel (2007: 248–249) has argued for both the existence of phenomenal mental properties, as well as their being perfectly natural or fundamental in their own right. In fact, in arguing against an answer to The Simple Question—i.e., x is a material simple iff_____, that plugs in "x instantiates a perfectly natural property" on the right hand side of the biconditional, McDaniel argues that there is at least one intermediate composite object—namely *himself*—that instantiates perfectly natural properties such as *being in pain* or *having a blue sensation*:

> I am a mereologically complex material object who instantiates perfectly natural properties. I hold that certain mental properties, such as having a blue sensation or being in pain, are perfectly natural properties, or, at the very least, supervene on perfectly natural properties had by complex objects.

For those who come to T2 of the tracking argument with antecedent grounds for thinking that persons are the bearers of perfectly natural phenomenal properties have yet another reason to sign-on to the view that at least some intermediate objects—namely *themselves*—are the bearers of fundamental or perfectly natural properties.

Consequently, if all of the fundamental causal or perfectly natural properties are instantiated at either the cosmic or the microphysical level, then there is a genuine threat to both free will and the existence of non-redundant, phenomenal mental properties. On both Atomism and Monism, the causal and qualitative structure carved out by intermediate objects *per se* is wholly redundant, grounded in, and explained by the activity and character of either the cosmos or their microphysical parts and relations between them.

Of course libertarianism about free will and the existence of fundamental, phenomenal properties are not uncontroversial philosophical positions, to say the least. And the arguments mentioned earlier in favor of T2 of the tracking argument will have only as much pull as the philosophical and pre-philosophical considerations that might lead one to adopt these controversial positions in the first place. At the very least this shows that the question of fundamental mereology is not at all separate from wider issues in the metaphysics of mind and free will. Nor should we pretend that it is. For the not-so-insignificant number of philosophers who side with the earlier views in the metaphysics of mind and free will, the cost of denying T2 will simply be too high of a price to pay. For philosophers in one of these two camps, the tracking argument offers grounds for thinking that at least some ordinary, intermediate composites are fundamental property-bearers in their own right.

In sum, then, *the tracking argument* and *the terminus argument* lend support to the view that at least some intermediates are fundamental, and thus call into question the widespread consensus enshrined in *No Fundamental Intermediates*.

7.3 Substantial Priority and the Metaphysics of Human Persons

It is fitting that we bring our defense of Substantial Priority to an end on a more personal note. In what follows I'd like to consider the bearing Substantial Priority has on a few selective issues in personal ontology. In his book *What Are We? A Study in Personal Ontology*, Eric Olson makes the point that questions about the nature of human persons are, at some level of analysis, inextricably bound up with matters concerning composition and mereology (even if one thinks that persons are simple).[23] Here I'll assume that this assessment is largely correct. I what follows I want to explore how Substantial Priority is uniquely positioned to carve out important dialectical space concerning debates in the metaphysics of mind and human persons.

7.3.1 On Mereology and Personal Ontology

Many contemporary philosophers are of the opinion that consciousness is a highly unified affair; it belongs to the very nature of conscious activity that it cannot be a joint or cooperative production. As such, thinking or consciousness requires that the subject of such states be deeply unified. Intuitively, neither pluralities, collections, nor simples-arranged in a particular manner offer the requisite metaphysical underpinning for conscious mental activity. Mental properties are what Rob Koons and Timothy Pickavance (2017: 487) call "essentially unitary properties," which they define as follows:

> *Essentially Unitary Property*: A property is *essentially unitary* if and only if it is a fundamental property that could by its very nature be possessed only by a single entity, not collectively possessed by a plurality of entities.

For some, the fact that organisms exhibit essentially unitary properties is the sole grounds by which they survive elimination. Since only living organisms exhibit the kinds of properties and can perform the kinds of actions that cannot be accounted for in terms of the joint or cooperative activity of atoms arranged in certain ways, living organisms are the only unified composite objects that exist.[24]

The intuition that conscious thought requires deep metaphysical unity is ubiquitous in the philosophy of mind. As David Barnett (2008) has insightfully pointed out, it is not uncommon to find cases or thought experiments in the metaphysics of mind that hinge directly on the deep unity and mereological structure of the bearers of consciousness. Consider the following cases or counterexamples cited by Barnett (2008, 2010):[25]

> **Person-Pair:** Since a pair of people is a composite, it is absurd to think that a pair of people can itself be conscious. (Barnett, 2008, 2010)
> **Swarm of Bees:** A swarm of bees cannot itself be conscious. (Putnam, 1967)
> **Tiny People in the Head:** A plurality of tiny people in the head jointly realizing the same functional properties of a brain could not itself be conscious. (Block, 1978)
> **Chinese Nation:** A plurality of people jointly realizing the same functional properties of a brain could not itself be conscious. (Block, 1978)
> **Chinese Room:** A system consisting of a monolingual English-speaker, a written set of instructions or rules, and pieces of paper could not itself understand Chinese. (Searle, 1980)
> **Explanatory Gap:** It is hard to see how there could be an explanation of how consciousness arises from the mere interactions of a collection of bits of matter. (Huxley, 1866; Hasker, 2010; Kant, 1965; Leibniz, 1951)

What undergirds the deep plausibility of each of these cases is the intuition that consciousness is essentially unitary whose subject is a single, unified property-bearer.

But what *kind* of unity in particular must bearers of essentially unitary properties possess? Assuming unity is a degreed notion, we might ask *how* unified must such objects be? At this point, one might think that all that is needed is that the bearer of such properties be a single, composite object; no further unity constraints are required in order to be conscious or engage in mental activity.[26] Yet Barnett himself has argued that the intuition underlying each of the cases noted earlier is best explained by the notion that the bearer of consciousness—you and me to be precise—must be *maximally unified*, indeed a single object that is devoid of proper parts entirely. For Barnett, as the bearers of essentially unitary mental properties, human persons must be mereologically simple.

The claim that human persons are mereologically simple substances is, of course, one that has a rich historical precedent in the Western philosophical tradition. The claim is, however, subject to ambiguity as it often is interpreted to mean different things by different proponents of the view. Let us refer to this datum of personal ontology as follows:

CLAIM: Human persons are mereologically simple substances.

CLAIM admits of both a strong and a weak reading in the mouth of its proponents, both past and present. On the strong reading of CLAIM, persons lack proper parts entirely and have no mereological structure whatsoever; they are not strictly composed of anything. This is the more straightforward sense of "mereologically simple" and is how Barnett understands CLAIM.

Yet CLAIM can also be taken in a weaker sense as the view that persons lack not proper parts *per se* but *substantial* proper parts, parts that are themselves full-fledged substances in their own right. Persons need not lack proper parts entirely as on the strong reading. A weak reading of CLAIM amounts to our now familiar tiling constraint in fundamental mereology applied to human persons, **No Fundamental Parthood**. Roderick Chisholm (1991), for example, argued, "I think; therefore I am not a compound." Chisholm (1991: 168) explains,

> According to the thesis of "the simplicity of the soul," we are substances but not compounds of substances; we are, therefore, monads. We are not like pieces of furniture, for such things are composed of other substances—as this chair is composed of back, seat and legs.

By Chisholm's lights, since persons essentially lack substances as proper parts, and compounds essentially have substances as proper parts, persons are not compounds. But of course such a view need not entail that persons lack proper parts altogether. Others have followed suit in reading CLAIM in the weak sense. Thus J. P. Moreland (2009:106) notes "it is directly evident to me that an object composed of separable parts lacks the sort of simple unity necessary for a conscious, thinking being." Likewise, Jonathan Lowe (1996: 39) has argued for the view that "if the self is a substance, it must indeed be a simple substance, entirely lacking substantial parts." While Lowe (1998: 199) takes human persons to lack substantial parts, he grants that they may have spatial parts (and spatial extension) understood as "objects which cannot be individuated or identified without reference to the [object] of which they are parts."

Let's set aside the strong reading of CLAIM and focus on the weak sense in which human persons fail to have substances as proper parts along the lines of **No Fundamental Parthood**. Do essentially unitary properties require the bearers of such properties to adhere to **No Fundamental Parthood**?

Arguably so. To see why, we need to take closer look at the nature of essentially unitary properties. The key notion here is that essentially unitary properties are *fundamental* in the sense that they enable their bearers to carry out activities that cannot be carried out by the cooperative activity of their proper parts; they confer on their bearers the power to bring about genuinely non-redundant effects in the world. As van Inwagen (1990: 118) points out, "Now, surely planning for tomorrow or feeling pain cannot be activities that a lot of simples can perform collectively." If these were activities that could be performed by the activities of some proper sub-plurality of the person as thinker, then they would not be essentially unitary (and van Inwagen and Merricks would have no principled grounds to keep organisms in their fundamental ontology).[27]

But to claim that essentially unitary properties, in this case consciousness and thought, are fundamental or non-redundant is just to say that PDP (§4.4.1) fails for the bearers of such properties and their parts. Recall that two objects are *duplicates* iff there is a one-one correspondence between their parts that preserves perfectly natural properties (and relations). PDP says that for any xs, w, and z, if the xs compose w, then z is a duplicate of w iff there are some ys that are plural duplicates of the xs, and the ys compose z. Thus, duplicating the perfectly natural properties of the parts and their basic arrangements suffices to duplicate the perfectly natural properties (and relations) of the whole. But duplicating the perfectly natural properties of the parts of human persons and their basic arrangements does not suffice to duplicate the perfectly natural properties of the whole, in this case conscious mental properties. There is, then, an important failure of property covariation between human persons and their proper parts and their arrangements. Consequently, if consciousness is an essentially unitary property of human persons and thus genuinely non-redundant, then PDP fails for human persons.

Given the modal consequences of grounding, where the failure of grounding follows from the failure of supervenience (see G10 in §2.1.1), we can infer that human persons as the bearers of essentially unitary properties fail to be grounded in their proper parts and basic arrangements. As a result, human persons at the very least fail to be grounded wholes (aggregates).

We can go further. Suppose one takes the insights undergirding the tracking argument to be sound (§7.2). In particular, suppose one signs on to *Tracking* (T1), the view that the fundamental causal properties exclusively track the fundamental bearers of properties (substances). If so, then one will have reason to think that human persons not only fail to be grounded wholes but are grounding wholes or fundamental substances in their own right. If all the fundamental or non-redundant properties are instantiated at either the microphysical or the cosmic level as per micro-naturalism and cosmic-naturalism (respectively), then there are no non-redundant properties at the level of ordinary, medium-sized objects, including human persons. On a "bottom-up" (Atomism) or a "Top-down" (Priority Monism) metaphysic, the causal and qualitative profile of human persons as ordinary objects is the way it is *in virtue of* either the very small or the very large, and not the other way around. Thus, if human persons as ordinary, medium-sized composites possess non-redundant mental properties, they must be fundamental in their own right. To restate Heil (2012: 28), "Fundamental properties require, as bearers, fundamental substances."

Interestingly enough, while Barnett himself sides with the view that mereological simplicity full stop best explains the intuition underlying the earlier cases in philosophy of mind, he takes seriously the prospects of an explanation that appeals to the connection between consciousness and fundamentality. That is, perhaps only fundamental beings can be conscious, and a pair of persons is not fundamental. Barnett (2008: 320) explains,

> We might have the core intuition because our naïve conception of a conscious being demands that conscious beings are *fundamental beings* (and a pair of people is not a fundamental being, for it owes its existence to two other beings). Granted that composites cannot be fundamental beings, this hypothesis does not rival *Simplicity*. For it may be that, by making the composite aspect of an object salient, we make salient the fact that the object is not a fundamental being. While I am sympathetic to the idea that our simplicity intuitions might be explained in terms of a more basic fundamental-being intuition, I cannot explore it here.

If there are fundamental composites as per Substantial Priority, then perhaps the underlying intuition in the earlier cases can be adequately explained by the fact that composite conscious beings must be metaphysically fundamental, they must not be grounded in anything else. Since on Substantial Priority being composite per se does not render a human person derivative or non-fundamental (contra Barnett), the view affords an explanation of why a pair of people cannot be conscious in terms of fundamentality, one that is worth taking seriously alongside Barnett's explanation in terms of strict mereological simplicity.

We have seen, then, that Substantial Priority offers a metaphysical framework in which to situate certain natural views about the requisite unity and mereological structure of human persons as conscious beings. I want to consider one final point about how Substantial Priority bears on a common argument in the ontology of human persons that is thought to cut against materialism and hylomorphism.

Both the strong and the weak readings of CLAIM—i.e. that human persons are strictly mereologically simple (strong reading) or lack substantial proper parts (weak reading)—have been employed in standard unity arguments against materialism, often in favor of a form of substance dualism that identifies persons with immaterial substances. Consider the following auxiliary premises that are commonly conjoined to CLAIM and

Leibniz's Law to yield the non-identity of persons with their bodies (or any material object for that matter):

- "The brain and nervous system, and the entire body, is nothing more than a collection of physical parts organized in a certain way" (Hasker, 2010: 182).
- "Any physical body is essentially a complex entity (any physical body has separable parts)" (Goetz, 2001).
- "Every composite substance is an aggregate of several substances, and the action of a composite . . . is an aggregate of several actions or accidents, distributed among the plurality of substances" (Kant, 1965, 335).
- "It must be confessed, moreover, that perception, and that which depends on it, are inexplicable by mechanical causes, that is by figures and motions . . . This must be sought for, therefore, in the simple substance and not in the composite or in the machine" (Leibniz, 1951:536).
- "I recognize and conceive very clearly that I am a thing which is absolutely unitary and entire . . . But just the contrary is the case with corporeal or extended objects, for I cannot imagine any, however small they might be, which my mind does not very easily divine into several parts" (Descartes, 2008).
- "Granted that we are not simply physical particles, this argument [that what best explains why pairs of persons cannot be conscious is that conscious beings must be simple] goes against materialism" (Barnett, 2010: 172).
- "There is something that is metaphysically unique about persons: we have a nature wholly unlike anything that is known to be true of things that are known to be compound physical things . . . . the doctrine of the simplicity of the soul is . . . very much a live option" (Chisholm, 1991: 167).

The core unifying assumption underlying these remarks is that all composite material objects (or at least human bodies) are aggregates (grounded wholes) and thereby composed of distinct substances—i.e., separable parts. If persons are not composed of separable parts, and all material objects are composed of separable parts, it follows (by Leibniz's Law) that persons are not identical to material objects. If the underlying mereological assumption is correct, then even the weak reading of CLAIM on which persons only lack substantial parts is inconsistent with materialism, indeed any ontology of the human person that fails to identify persons with simple, immaterial substances. That is, material substances are simply not the right *kinds* of substances to provide the requisite underlying unity for conscious, mental activity. Moreover, this extends to all versions of Aristotelian hylomorphism that consider human persons to be rational animals and thus certain kinds of material substances (albeit not wholly material substances in so far as persons have immaterial rational souls as parts or constituents). If the mereological assumption is true, then the decision is clear: either hold fast to materialism or hylomorphism and reject the deeply plausible unity-intuitions regarding conscious thought, or uphold the unity-intuitions and reject materialism or hylomorphism.

It should be clear by now how Substantial Priority carves out important dialectical space at this juncture. For those who are sympathetic to imposing strong unity constraints on persons as the bearers of consciousness (as per a weak reading of CLAIM), while maintaining that persons are material substances in some sense or other, Substantial Priority fits the bill nicely. On Substantial Priority, the fact that conscious human persons lack substantial proper parts and are not composed of more fundamental parts has no straightforward anti-materialistic or anti-hylomorphic consequences; on Substantial Priority, there is no straight line from lacking substantial parts to being purely immaterial.

I should note that if by "materialism" one means the view that human persons are wholly material, I am in no way sympathetic with materialism as a metaphysic of human persons. Rather, my own preferred view is more in line with a hylomorphic ontology of the human person; human persons are material substances that have an immaterial soul as a proper part or constituent (and thus no living human body is purely material). Accordingly, I have a vested interest in opening up dialectical possibilities for hylomorphism in particular. My overall aim in this section has been to underscore how Substantial Priority as a neo-Aristotelian fundamental mereology bears on one aspect of personal ontology, in particular how it opens up dialectical space for materialist and hylomorphic views of the human person.

7.3.2 Substantial Priority and the Thinking Parts Argument

Again, let "materialism" be the view that human persons are objects that are wholly material. On materialism, you are a material object, whether a human organism, a brain, a nervous system, or perhaps some other exotic material candidate. One rather popular variety of materialism on the market is animalism, the view that human persons are identical to biological organisms that are members of the primate species *Homo Sapiens*.[28]

Consider the following well-known argument against materialism in general, the Thinking Parts Argument. In its broadest application, the Thinking Parts Argument aims to show that among the proper parts of human persons as thinking, conscious beings there is at least one distinct object that is equally suited to think the person's thoughts.[29] Yet the claim that there are multiple, distinct beings who think my thoughts flies in the face of the very natural claim that my mental life belongs exclusively to me.

222 *Getting Personal*

Consider the following informal statement of the Thinking Parts Argument against materialism in general (TPA) as stated (but not endorsed) by Bailey (2014):

> There is exactly one being thinking my thoughts. Materialism cannot accommodate this truth. For if materialism is true, then I am a material object (e.g., a brain, a nervous system, or an organism). Whichever of these things I am, it seems that there is something very much like me but slightly smaller. Suppose I am an organism. Then there is something very much like that organism, overlapping me on all parts but one atom, say; let's call it MiniMe. Is MiniMe a thinking thing? It seems that it is; surely one atom can't make the difference between something's being a thinking thing and not. But what thoughts would MiniMe be thinking but just the ones I am? So if materialism is true, then there isn't, after all, exactly one being thinking my thoughts. So much the worse for materialism.

The argument is generalizable to all forms materialism and is a species of the Problem of the Many within the domain of personal ontology in particular. To unpack the argument in more detail, let's taylor the argument to animalism in particular.

Assuming that I am a human animal as per animalism, we can state TPA as an argument against animalism more formally as follows:

1. **No Rival Thinker:** For any x and y, if x is conscious and thinks my thoughts and y is conscious and thinks my thoughts, then $x = y$ (premise).
2. **Activity:** For any object x, if x has an object y as a proper or improper part, where the nature and activity of y is sufficient for conscious thought and y is appropriately integrated with the other proper parts of x, then x is conscious[30] (premise).
3. **Thinking Part:** I have a proper part the nature and activity of which is sufficient for conscious thought, my brain, and is appropriately integrated with my other parts (premise).
4. I have a proper part, my brain, that is conscious (2–3).
5. **Like-Minded:** If my brain is conscious, then it thinks the same thoughts as me (premise).
6. **Overcrowding:** There are at least two distinct conscious beings that think my thoughts.

Premises 1–6 are mutually inconsistent as the conjunction of 2–6 entails the denial of 1, **No Rival Thinker**. If 2–6 are true, then there are at least two distinct conscious beings that think my thoughts: myself and my brain. Animalists are pushed, given **No Rival Thinker**, to identify the human person with the part that thinks, the brain. The argument spells bad news for animalism. Herein lies the Thinking Parts Argument.

Premise 1, **No Rival Thinker**, is the deeply intuitive notion that I am the unique bearer of my mental profile; nothing that is not strictly me thinks my thoughts. Premise 2, **Activity**, serves to generate at least one rival thinking-candidate to the human animal. If the nature and activity of x is sufficient for thinking, then x is a thinker. Consequently, premise 2 states that whether an object *is* or *has* an object as a proper part whose nature and activity suffices for consciousness, then that object is conscious. For the animalist, **Activity** is grounded in the fact that the nature and activity of a properly functioning and appropriately integrated human brain seems *sufficient* for conscious activity; just as the nature and primary aim of the heart is to pump blood, so too the nature and job description of the brain is to think.

Premise 3, **Thinking Part**, is the straightforward claim that human persons do, in fact, have at least one proper part the activity of which suffices for conscious thought, the brain. But note that human brains are not the only candidate thinkers of my thoughts among my proper parts. Take my head, for instance. Arguably, my head has my brain as one of its proper parts. If we assume with the animalist that the activity of my brain is sufficient for conscious thought, and my brain is appropriately integrated with the other parts of my head (3), it follows by **Activity** that my head is also conscious. And what might my head be thinking about? Well, it's hard to tell for sure. But it would be rather strange to say that my head is occupied with completely different thoughts other than my own; after all, for the materialist, it is in virtue of the very same part and its activity, the brain, that my head and I are both thinkers. We have, then, two other equally plausible candidates that are conscious and that think my thoughts: my brain and my head.

The problem looms even larger, unfortunately. So far we have fixed on the reasonably well-defined proper parts of human persons such as brains and heads as the plausible thinker-candidates that share my mental life. But there are many more besides. Take the proper part of me that consists of all of me minus my right arm, call this object "Ross-minus". Since Ross-minus has a proper part the nature and activity of which suffices for conscious thought, a brain, Ross-minus is also conscious. As with the Problem of the Many discussed in the previous chapter, we can repeat this very same line of reasoning to generate a overabundance of conscious thinkers among my proper parts that think my thoughts. This, of course, violates **No Rival Thinker** in the extreme.

The animalist can regroup here and argue that while objects like my head and my brain are, in fact, thinkers in addition to me, only the entire animal thinks in a non-derivative sense; brains and heads think, but only derivatively, in virtue of the fact that the animal thinks non-derivatively. But here things seem to be the exact opposite of what is described. If anything, the animalist ought to say that I am a thinking, conscious being *in virtue* of my brain and not vice versa. It seems rather odd for an animalist to say that my brain is conscious in virtue of my being conscious. Rather, it is the presence of a brain that explains why I am the kind of object that is capable of conscious thought, not the other way around.

Premise 5, **Like-Minded**, trades on the intuitive idea that what my brain thinks, I think; likewise for my head and Ross-minus. After all, it is in virtue of the very same object and its activity that my brain, my head, and Ross-minus and I are all conscious thinkers. If the mental life of these candidate objects radically diverged from my own (while sharing one and the same brain), what could possibly explain such divergence?

I'll examine only two general routes in responding to TPA on behalf of the animalist (other than denying **No Rival Thinker**). Both routes take aim at **Thinking Part** and attempt to rule out the rival thinking candidates that give rise to **Overcrowding**. The first route points to some principled reason as to why objects like heads, brains, and Ross-minus are disqualified from being thinkers in their own right. The second route outright denies the existence of the rival thinking candidates altogether; eliminate the problematic parts of human persons such as brains, heads, and Ross-minus and the worry disappears. I'll take a brief look at both of these routes with an eye toward how Substantial Priority can help reinforce animalism as a metaphysics of the human person (although Substantial Priority in no way entails animalism).

The first solution available to the animalist is to reject 3, **Thinking Part**, and aim to offer a principled reason as to *why* the proper parts of human persons are ill-suited to be rival thinkers. We have already discussed a similar strategy in our discussion of the Problem of the Many in Chapter 6 (§6.2). If the property of *being conscious* is a *maximal property*, then we have grounds for ruling out brains, heads, and Ross-minus as candidate thinkers. Recall that a property F is maximal just in case no proper parts of an F are themselves Fs. To say that the property of being conscious is maximal, then, is make the following claim:

> **C-Maximality:** For any x, if x is conscious, then there is no y such that x is a proper part of y and y is conscious.

If **C-Maximality** is true, then no proper part of a conscious being will itself be conscious.[31] And since persons are indeed conscious beings, **C-Maximality** offers a straightforward reason to think that the brain is not conscious and thus does not think my thoughts.

Since we have already examined an appeal to maximality as a stand-alone solution to the Problem of the Many, my remarks here will be limited. Recall that I mentioned that a *stand-alone* appeal to maximality was (i) unmotivated and unprincipled, (ii) ungeneralizable to all cases of the puzzle at hand, and (iii) failed to account for fortified versions of puzzles that incorporate mereological vagueness or indeterminacy. In my estimation, only the last charge, (iii), rings true of an appeal to maximality as a solution to the Thinking Parts Argument. Since the scope of the Thinking Parts Argument is restricted to human persons and the property of *consciousness* in particular, the need for both a generalizable solution to other cases as well as non-arbitrary grounds to determine *which* properties are maximal is not pressing. Moreover, I think the intuition that *consciousness* is maximal is very strong indeed, and thus the appeal here seems properly motivated.

However, as with the Problem of the Many, the Thinking Parts Argument can be fortified by introducing an element of mereological vagueness or indeterminacy. And here a bare appeal to maximality, what I previously called an "unprincipled maximality solution", loses some of its force as a solution to the Thinking Parts Argument. In brief, if it can be vague as to whether objects are proper parts of other objects, then it can be vague whether the equal candidates here, brains, heads, and Ross-minus in particular, are proper parts of the human person. If so, then **C-Maximality** is unavailable as a way to pair down the rival thinking candidates in order to preserve **No Rival Thinker**.

As with the Problem of the Many, Substantial Priority can help reinforce the maximality solution to the Thinking Parts Argument. If persons are fundamental substances, then they are grounding wholes and each of their proper parts are grounded in the substance as a whole. If Substantial Priority is true and grounding is determinate and non-vague, then it cannot be indeterminate as to whether the rival thinking candidates in question (brain, head, Ross-minus) are proper parts of the person.[32] The close connection between grounding, parthood, and the fundamentality of substances on Substantial Priority offers animalists who favor **C-Maximality** a helping hand.

Turning to the second animalist solution to the Thinking Parts Argument, many prominent animalists such as Merricks, Olson, and van Inwagen have sought refuge in the outright denial of the existence of the rival thinking candidates such as brains, heads, Ross-minus and the like. **Thinking Part** is false; persons fail to have as a proper part an object the activity of which is sufficient for conscious thought precisely because *they have no composite objects as parts whatsoever*. To be clear: while there are no composite objects that satisfy the predicates "brain," "head," and "Ross-Minus," there certainly are particles arranged "brain-wise" (or perhaps "cerebrally"), "head-wise," and perhaps even "Ross-minus-wise." This route—what Olson (2007) calls the way of *sparse ontology*—takes the very radical line in denying **Existence** regarding a large class of composite material objects commended by common sense. In spite of our rather strong intuitions to the contrary, there are no such objects as brains or heads that are composed of parts.

To be fair, the way of sparse ontology derives its primary motivation from considerations outside the Thinking Parts Argument, such as the denial of DAUP as well as its offering a unified solution to a host of the puzzles in material objects we've considered in previous chapters. If there are no such composite objects as statues, brains, heads, Ross-minus, and Tib then puzzles generated by such objects dissipate.[33]

Yet the elimination of ordinary objects like heads and brains is a very significant cost to standard versions of animalism. By contrast, Substantial Priority can preserve **No Rival Thinker** without altogether eliminating ordinary objects like heads, brains, and the more exotic Ross-minus. For those inclined toward animalism, there is a better way forward than the way of sparse ontology.

As was discussed earlier in §7.3.1, many are of the opinion that thinking or conscious mental activity is a highly unified affair. Whatever one's view of the precise nature of substance, it seems intuitive to think that being a substance involves a very high degree of unity. It is natural, then, for one to endorse the following connection between the unitary nature of consciousness and thinking, on the one hand, and the unitary nature of the subjects of these activities, on the other:

> *SUB-Thinker*: Necessarily, for all x, if x is a conscious, thinking being, then x is a substance.

Why then, on the conjunction of Substantial Priority and *SUB-Thinker*, are parts like heads, brains, and Ross-minus not equally plausible candidates to think my thoughts? It is because my head, my brain, and Ross-minus are not fundamental substances in their own right; as derivative on the organism of which they are a part, they are not the right *sorts* of things to think. In general, we can reject **Thinking Part** for human organisms on the grounds that the nature of their proper parts as derivative and grounded wholes is not sufficient for conscious thought. Consequently, the animalist need not deny **Thinking Part** by eliminating the rival thinking candidates in order to preserve **No Rival Thinker**. Substantial Priority, together with *SUB-Thinker*, does the trick. Brains, heads, and arbitrary undetached parts exist, they just are not substances. As Olson notes, "There is something at least a little bit peculiar about undetached brains and heads—not to mention upper halves and left-hand complements . . . Aristotle denied their existence, or at least denied that they were substances." If, with Aristotle, we bar *all* of the proper parts of human organisms—brains, heads, and Ross-minus included—from the elite class of *substance*, they in no way rival human organisms in thinking their thoughts.[34]

Lastly, Substantial Priority, when conjoined with *SUB-Thinker*, offers the stand-alone maximality response the needed grounds to infer that the brain itself cannot think, and *ipso facto* cannot think the human animal's thoughts. As Olson (2007:82) has argued, an appeal to maximality *on its own* does not necessarily give one reason to think that the animal, and not the brain, is the thinker. Olson (2007: 82) remarks "In any case, the maximality of thought would not explain why our brains cannot think. It implies that if a whole human being can think then its brain cannot. But it also implies that if the brain can think, the human being cannot. And by itself it provides no support for one starting point over the other." Human organisms are paradigmatic examples of substances. On Substantial Priority, human organisms can think precisely because they are substances. As derivative parts of a substantial living organism, heads, brains, and Ross-minus cannot think precisely because they are not the right *kinds* of things to engage in the activity of thinking, they are not fundamental substances in their own right. The reasoning is as follows: I think; only substances can think; thus, I am a substance. My brain is a proper part of me; thus, my brain is not a substance; thus my brain does not (cannot) think. Consequently, animalists who resist the way of sparse ontology as a means of preserving **No Rival Thinker** have a friend in Substantial Priority.

Notes

1. What I am calling *the terminus argument* is a close relative to the argument offered by Schaffer (2010) in favor of Monism from the metaphysical possibility of gunky worlds. Following, Tallant (2013), I extend the argument to include the possibility of both gunk and junk.
2. I have adapted Tallant's Gunk Argument and Junk Argument for the sake of simplicity. If one worries whether worlds that are both gunky *and* junky are possible, one can offer two independent arguments here, one against Monism from the possibility of junky worlds, and one against Atomism from the possibility of gunky worlds, the conjunction of which aims to undermine the project of fundamental mereology per se.
3. Hudson (2001: 84–90), for instance, relies on both the truth of the Doctrine of Arbitrary Undetached Parts as well as the exclusive disjunction that either the Pointy View or MaxCon is the correct answer to the Simple Question—i.e., what are the necessary and jointly sufficient conditions for which an object is a material simple. And Schaffer's (2010:64–65) arguments in favor of the impossibility of junky worlds hinge on the axiom of Unrestricted Composition and a modal ontology where "worlds are understood as possible concrete cosmoi."
4. See Bohn (2009). Coitner (2013) points out that there are models of extensional mereology that are both non-junky and junky, that is, that contain both a maximal element as well as infinite upward parthood relations. Commenting on Whitehead's non-classical extensional mereology, Simons (1987) notes, "That the world is 'open' both above and below seems to have been something which Whitehead found self-evident, for he gives no argument for it" (83) and "It is worth nothing also that Whitehead rejects U [the maximal sum of classical mereology], since he has an axiom to the effect that every individual is a proper part of some individual" (35). If formal models of non-classical-extensional mereology represent metaphysical possibilities, then junky worlds are possible. See Simons (1987: Chapter 2) for more on non-classical mereologies and their bearing on junky worlds.

5. Schaffer (2010) himself has argued along these lines. See also Sider (1993) and Zimmerman (1996) who argue in favor of gunk.
6. An object's being derivative entails that it is posterior to either (i) its proper parts, or (ii) to some fundamental object of which it is a proper part.
7. Thanks to an anonymous reviewer for this objection.
8. See Schaffer (2004).
9. And, as Lewis (1986a:60) states concerning the perfectly natural properties, "there are only just enough of them to characterize things completely and without redundancy."
10. See Lewis (1999a:66) when he states "physics discovers which things and classes are the most elite of all."
11. In particular, see premise 1—*Leibnizian Substance*—of his argument from nomic integrity for Monism. Sider (2008) also interprets Monism to entail the view that "no natural features are had by any object other than the world-object."
12. It is important to underscore that *Tracking* has as its scope the fundamental or non-redundant causal properties in particular. Arguably there are many fundamental, i.e. ungrounded or unanalyzable, properties and relations that do not exclusively track the fundamental objects—e.g., identity, parthood, having some determinate mass, distance relations, earlier-than/later-on eternalism, etc. I do not think that these fundamental properties carve out non-redundant causal structure in the world.
13. The falsity of both micro-naturalism and cosmic-naturalism does not strictly entail the proposition that at least some perfectly natural properties reside at the intermediate level (i.e., the truth of T2), since one could outright reject the existence of perfectly natural properties altogether (or even an intermediate level entirely and endorse mereological nihilism). Since I am assuming that there are, in fact, fundamental properties as well as an intermediate mereological level, and that the atomic (x,y,z), intermediate (r,s,t), and the cosmic (U) levels are exhaustive, the assumption here seems unproblematic.
14. Here I remain neutral as to whether human persons are identical to mere animals (animalism), not wholly material animals, i.e. rational animals (hylomorphism), constituted by animals (constitutionalism), are temporal parts of animals, or are identical to spatial parts of an animals (i.e., the brain). What I say next about persons as fundamental intermediate composite objects can be appropriated by any of the earlier views about the human person. But since the overall context in the book is fundamental mereology and is restricted to the mereological hierarchy of concrete *material* beings, varieties of substance dualism that identify the person with a fundamental *immaterial* substance do not, strictly speaking, gloss human persons as intermediate composite objects in the sense that I mean here. I also assume, but will not argue for, the view that human persons have proper parts.
15. See also Steward (2012) for a defense of what she calls "agency incompatibilism," the view that agency or what she calls "settling" in general, which applies to both human and non-human agents by her lights, is incompatible with determinism for roughly similar reasons as discussed here.
16. Turner (2009) offers a thorough discussion of the "bottom-up" threat to free will, including the logical form of this close relative of the Consequence Argument. Also, Cover and Hawthorne (1996); Bishop (2003: esp. §VI and §VII); Loewer (1996); Unger (2002) offer arguments similar in kind to the one outlined here.
17. I have adapted the broad outline of the argument from Merricks (2001:156), but I have formulated the argument in terms of dependence and not

Getting Personal 229

supervenience as does Merricks, as well as generalized the argument to apply to both Atomism and Monism.
18. Schaffer (2014).
19. For reasons already outlined earlier, here I set aside the further option (d): accept the premises of the argument but deny that the conclusion logically follows. I have already noted that I am assuming in this discussion that the Consequence Argument is both valid and sound, which includes the validity of a suitable closure principle linking C2 with the argument's conclusion. The relevant closure principle or what some label as the "Transfer of Powerlessness Principle" that has received the most attention is van Inwagen's (1983: 94) "Beta Principle". Where "Np" denotes "p and no one has, ever had, or will have a choice about p": Np and N($p \rightarrow q$), entails Nq. In light of objections to the Beta Principle, defenders of the Consequence Argument such as Finch and Warfield (1998: 521–2) and Widerker (1987: 41) have offered the following in its place, where "$\square$" represents broad logical necessity: Np and $\square(p \rightarrow q)$, entails Nq.
20. See Turner (2009).
21. It is not entirely clear to me how this is supposed to go for the Monist in the case of ensuring the falsity of global facts about the cosmos.
22. See Moreland (2013) for an argument along these general lines.
23. See also Barnett (2008, 2010).
24. Where van Inwagen (1990: 118) focuses more on the activity of thinking *per se* as essentially unitary, and Merricks (2001) on the essentially unitary nature of non-redundant causal action.
25. For discussion on these cases as well as the wider implications for mereological metaphysics see Bailey (2016).
26. Bailey (2016).
27. This point is underscored by Hasker (1999: 140–144).
28. But note that some defend versions of animalism—namely, hylomorphic animalism, that claim that while human persons are indeed material beings, they have as one of their proper parts or constituents an immaterial soul. See Toner (2011).
29. There are Thinking Parts Arguments against compound dualism and hylomorphism as well. I think the argument can be extended to those who think that human persons are *constituted* by (and thereby distinct from) human animals as well.
30. Note that P states only a sufficient condition for consciousness. Though vague, the qualifier "appropriately integrated" is geared toward mereological universalists who would prefer to deny that the fusion of a desk lamp, a coffee mug, and a human person, would thereby be conscious. In the case of arbitrary mereological sums that have human persons (and ipso fact brains and/or souls as proper parts as per the transitivity of parthood), the brain and/or the soul would fail to be appropriately integrated with the other parts of the sum (lamp, mug); mere existence nor spatiotemporal relatedness between brains/souls and the disjoint parts of a sum are sufficient to produce conscious states in the whole.
31. Sider (2003), Hudson (2001), and Merricks (2003) all endorse **C-Maximality**, although not all make the application here to TPA. In fact, as we will see, Merricks favors the eliminative route in response to TPA.
32. Here some might argue that if Substantial Priority entails that the mereological boundaries of objects are determinate, then so much the worse for Substantial Priority; a straightforward *reductio* of Substantial Priority, one might say. While I myself don't share the intuition about mereological indeterminacy,

this is a fair point nevertheless. But of course the way in which metaphysical models derive (or diminish in) their epistemic justification concerns matters much broader in scope than a single point like this—e.g., overall explanatory power, scope, integrity with the empirical sciences, etc.
33. See Merricks (2001: 53), Olson (2007: 211–232), and van Inwagen (1981, 1990).
34. See Toner (2011) for a similar move here, although Toner doesn't explicitly draw on what I am calling "*SUB-Thinker.*"

8 Substantial Priority
Counting the Cost

Having offered several arguments in favor of Substantial Priority, in this chapter and the next I want to consider the merits of a range of objections to fundamental intermediates, in the order of what I take to be the least to the most worrisome. Any package of metaphysical views about the fundamental structure of the world ought to be able to carry its weight in light of impending objections. And Substantial Priority is no exception here. If the advantages of Substantial Priority highlighted in the previous chapter are far outweighed by its drawbacks, then we ought to abandon the view in favor of an alternative fundamental mereology. In the next chapter I will unpack what I take to be the most serious objection to the view, that it is empirically inadequate in that it fails to save the phenomena regarding empirical data about the causal activity of the parts of composite substances.

While I do believe that Substantial Priority is in fact a fruitful theory about the mereological structure of composite substances, it is certainly not without its own problems and counterintuitive consequences. At the very least, then, my aim in this chapter is to argue that a fundamental mereologoy that ascribes metaphysical primacy to at least some intermediate composite objects if defensible despite recent opinion to the contrary. Despite its costs, Substantial Priority is a neo-Aristotelian mereology worth taking seriously and thus deserves a place at the table as a viable yet under appreciated fundamental mereology. I consider the objections in the next two chapters in the order of what I take to be the least to the most worrisome.

8.1 Substantivalism and Ubiquitous Mereological Overlap

The first objection to Substantial Priority is that the view is incompatible with substantivalism regarding the nature of spacetime. Like their material occupants, regions are said to exhibit mereological structure, whether such structure is atomic or gunky is beyond our concern here. If regions are substances as per spacetime substantivalism, and the substantial occupants of regions are not identical to those regions (denial of supersubstantivalism), then the substantial occupants of substantival regions will exhibit mereologically overlap with respect to another *to some degree or other*. But this violates **No Fundamental Parthood** and hence Substantial Priority for intermediate substances. Note, all that is needed here is the minimal claim that the occupant and its region are not mereologically disjoint, a single shared part between a substantial region and a substantial occupant of that region will suffice to undermine Substantial Priority. Given that substantivalism appears to be somewhat of a consensus among contemporary philosophers of physics, this spells trouble for Substantial Priority. As a result, the defender of Substantial Priority is forced to either *identify* substantial occupants with their occupying regions and thus endorse supersubstantivalism, or reject substantivalism outright, neither of which (in my opinion) are attractive options.

Let's assume the truth of spacetime substantivalism for the sake of argument.[1] The objection harbors both a fundamental confusion and a precarious assumption. Let's start with the confusion: ordinary material objects do not *mereologically* overlap their occupying regions, rather, they stand in the primitive *occupation* relation to them. My occupying my current region in no way means that I share my region's proper parts or vice versa—i.e., that *its* proper parts are *my* proper parts.

It is plausible to think that my proper parts do, however, *mirror* the proper parts of my occupying region to some degree or other. That is to say, there is a mereological harmony between the proper parts of my occupying region and my proper parts.[2] The region that is occupied by my hand, for instance, appears to be hand-shaped and thus perfectly mirrors one of my proper parts. This mereological harmony between me and my occupying region, as has been previously pointed out, need not be taken to be *isomorphic* such that I decompose into proper parts in *any* and *every* way in which my occupying region decomposes into proper parts.[3] The point remains: mereological overlap is one thing, region-occupation another. Since substances do not mereologically overlap their substantial regions, Substantial Priority remains unscathed.

But suppose the objector presses the following line in response:

> Granted, mereological overlap and region-occupation are two different relations. But is it not strange that a substance can exactly occupy a region and either perfectly or near-perfectly mirror the parts of that region and yet not share *any* of that region's mereological structure? What exactly *explains* the mereological harmony between my proper parts and the proper parts of my occupying region? Surely *something* must explain this fact. Some would take such correlation as reason to *identify* occupants with their underlying regions. But such an extreme move would be hasty. Suppose instead we explain mereological harmony in terms of the fact that material occupants inherit their mereological structure from their occupying regions, and hence possess such structure *extrinsically*. Only spacetime regions have their parts

intrinsically. On this view, the parts of material occupants of spacetime mirror the parts of their occupying regions precisely because they inherit one and the same compositional structure from them. Accordingly, the phenomena of mereological harmony offers reason to think that material objects not only occupy their regions, but also mereologically overlap their regions in sharing the same compositional structure.[4]

Suppose we grant for the sake of argument the highly controversial assumption that the material occupants of spacetime not only occupy but also inherit their mereological structure from their regions. What follows from this? In order for the objector here to infer the falsity of Substantial Priority from the mereological overlap between occupants and their regions they need to build in some rather precarious assumptions regarding the precise formulation of spacetime substantivalism.

For one, the substantivalist camp in the philosophy of physics is a rather diverse lot.[5] In particular, substantivalism per se is *neutral* as to the precise nature and structure of general relativistic spacetime—namely, between those that identify spacetime with the manifold alone ("manifold substantivalism") and those that take spacetime to be identical with the manifold together with the metric field ("metric field substantivalism"), the latter being essentially a set of points with a topological and differential structure.[6] On manifold substantivalism, the entire manifold exhausts the nature of physical spacetime and functions as a substantial substratum which supports fields, geometric, and topological properties. Metric field substantivalists, on the other hand, argue that spacetime itself cannot be identified as such in so far as a bare manifold alone—i.e., one devoid of metric structure, is unable to possess crucial properties such as distance, the difference between spatial and temporal intervals, and light-cone structure that make it distinctively *spatiotemporal*.

More importantly, contemporary substantivalists are sharply divided as to whether the manifold (or the manifold together with the metric field) is a *single* substantial whole or whether each individual sub-region (or point) of the manifold is itself a substance (i.e. spacetime being an aggregate or collection of regions *qua* basic substances). Maudlin (1988: 86) has argued that a general-relativistic reconstruction of Newton's conception of absolute space and time would yield a single substantial metrical whole, such that "spacetime is an essentially metrical object and that the points of space-time bear their metrical relations essentially."

Two formidable contemporary variations of such a view are *moderate structural realism* as defended by Esfeld and Lam (2008) and *metric essentialism* as put forward by Maudlin (1988) and Hoefer (1996), both of which hold that spacetime is a *single* substance whose structure is defined by the metric field and whose sub-regions (whether zero-dimensional points or extended regions) are individuated in terms of their place within the metric.[7] In fact, these two versions of substantivalism have a particular advantage over others in so far as they advertise a straightforward solution to *the hole argument*—one of the most pressing objections to standard variations of substantivalism. As such, moderate structural realism and metric essentialism are well-motivated ontologies of spacetime.

The view that substantival spacetime (or space *per se* regarding the first quote that follows) is viewed as a single, unitary substance along the lines of a grounding whole is not uncommon in the literature. Consider the following representative samples:

> In describing space as being, on this view, "unitary" or "singular," I mean that it is conceived as a whole which has ontological priority over its parts–that is, as a whole which, while it undoubtedly *possesses* parts (at least, the three-dimensional parts that are its "regions"), is not in any sense *composed* of those parts, since its parts cannot exist independently of space as a whole. Thus, for the absolutist, space is no mere aggregate or plurality of entities, in the way that a heap of sand is an aggregate or plurality of grains, something whose existence and identity depend on the existence and identity of the things which constitute its parts. This is because, according to the absolutist, the parts of space are necessarily related to one another in an unchangeable order or arrangement, unlike the grains in a heap of sand—and the very identity of each part of space depends upon its position in this order or arrangement of all the parts, rather in the way in which the very identity of a natural number depends upon its position in the entire series of natural numbers. In sum, for the absolutist, space is a substance, in one technical metaphysical sense of the term in which it denotes an entity which does not depend for its existence or identity upon the existence or identity of any other entity. Hence, the absolutist conception of space may also—and perhaps more perspicuously—be called a *substantivalist* conception of space.
>
> (Lowe 2002: 271–272)

Healey (1995: 300) remarks, "The serious spacetime substantivalist believes not only that spacetime exists, but also that it is a substance," he then goes on to add the following regarding the structure of spacetime as a single substantial whole:

> The substantivalist needs to realize that even if spacetime is a substance composed of parts (spacetime points and/or regions), it does not follow that these parts are equally substantial. The parts of spacetime are not like classical atoms, which retain their individuality no matter how they are arranged to compose material substances. They are rather to be individuated by means of their properties, their relations to the rest of spacetime, and their relations to the material contents of spacetime.
>
> (Healey 1995: 300)

Nerlich (2005: 13), in addition, asks us to

> [a]ssume that space itself is real, but it is not *made up* of its parts, nor yet *analysable into* parts with any kind of ontic *independence*. Perhaps, even, that spatial parts and their relations are, ontologically, *supervenient* on the structure of space. Space, not its parts, is the foundation of spatial relations.[8]

And lastly, after highlighting the virtues of metric essentialism regarding its ability to sidestep the hole argument, Dainton (2010) remarks,

> The important point is that metrical essentialism, however the fine print is formulated, seems a clear and well-motivated form of substantivalism. There is a cost. Spacetime points lose the ontological autonomy they have in manifold substantivalism and, to this extent, the substantialist's position might be thought weakened: an attribute of traditional "substances" is their ability to exist independently of all other entities. It is not clear, however, that the loss is to be regretted. *The doctrine that spacetime is a real entity does not in itself entail the view that this entity has component parts that are capable of independent existence.*[9]

The issue as to whether spacetime as a whole is a single substance is not orthogonal to the objection from ubiquitous mereological overlap against Substantial Priority. If the entire manifold (or manifold plus the metric field) is a substance in its own right, then it is, according to Substantial Priority, a grounding whole as per the nature of fundamental substances in general. As such, each of its proper sub-regions (extended or unextended) are inseparable parts of it and thereby not fundamental substances in their own right (**No Fundamental Parthood**). If so, then the regions that you, I, and every other intermediate composite substance occupy will be rendered non-substantial and thus the problem of ubiquitous mereological overlap between distinct substances disappears.

The objection from ubiquitous mereological overlap ultimately equates substantivalism per se regarding spacetime with a particular *interpretation* of substantival spacetime—namely, one that denies that the manifold (or manifold plus metric field) is a single substantial whole in its own right. But the defender of Substantial Priority who is inclined toward substantivalism is free to endorse an interpretation of substantivalism that is in accord with their wider metaphysical views concerning the nature and structure of fundamental substances in general, such as moderate structural realism or metric essentialism.

As it turns out, it is rather interesting to note that what appear to be the most well-motivated versions spacetime substantivalism are those that construe substantival spacetime along the very lines I have defended in this work for fundamental substances as grounding wholes. This point deserves underscoring. Many philosophers of physics who are inclined toward substantivalism about spacetime *already* explicate substantival spacetime in terms of the grounding description captured by Substantial Priority; the identities of each of the proper parts of spacetime—*what* they are and *which* parts they are in the structure—are grounded in spacetime as a whole.

This is significant for two reasons. First, this shows that the core commitments of Substantial Priority as a fundamental mereology are not without precedent in the contemporary literature in philosophy of physics and metaphysics. Second, it provides motivation for those who are inclined to accept ordinary composite substances in addition to a substantival spacetime to utilize a *single* notion of *substance* in order to preserve ideological economy in fundamental metaphysics. If one is inclined to think that both spacetime as a whole and an elite subset of its intermediate occupants are substances, then why *not* think that the very same Whole-Priority grounding description applies to each?[10]

8.2 Mereological Mooreanism Revisited

A second objection to Substantial Priority proceeds in the form of a question: "Isn't the fact that intermediate composite substances have *substantial* proper parts a Moorean fact, only to be denied at the expense of common sense?" We have already examined this line of thinking in our discussion of the various reasons offered in favor of Part-Priority and Priority Microphysicalism (PM) (see §4.2). But perhaps there are worries here that remain unresolved.

For, one might argue, it is possible to construct plausible scenarios where one and the same proper part of a substance survives (*as such*) minute compositional alteration. It is not uncommon to hear the following objection to Substantial Priority along these lines:

> Do you mean to tell me that the microscopic skin cell that was once a proper part of me is therefore a numerically distinct entity when it is no longer included in my compositional base? How can facts about the mereological structure of fundamental wholes be so sensitive to such minute differences? Surely the skin cell is able to retain its identity upon ceasing to be a proper part of me!

The intuition-pump is a powerful one, I admit. But as I emphasized in chapter 4, while it is plausible to think that we are able to observe some degree of continuity or other between material objects over time, experience alone doesn't deliver the further thesis that what we observe is strict *numerical identity* through time. In this sense, the proponent of Substantial Priority is in the same general position as those who deny that material objects in general maintain strict numerical sameness through time, particularly stage theory and mereological essentialism (although Substantial Priority restricts this denial to the proper parts of substances only). Most philosophers who reject these views do not rest their case on strictly empirical or observational grounds: "We can just *see* that material objects survive part replacement!" or "Isn't it empirically obvious that I am strictly one and the same person that you greeted this morning? One thing's clear from experience: I am no instantaneous stage!" Rather, most would admit that metaphysical theses regarding the nature and persistence of material objects aim to capture fine-grained structural features of the world and thereby fall outside the immediate purview of ordinary perceptual experience.

Robert Pasnau (2011: 24–25) emphasizes this point nicely with respect to whether observation alone can settle whether there is one and the same subject that exists throughout an instance of change:

> In fact, however, this is surely a case where observation offers no help at all. What we *see* occurring, through substantial change, is some amount of sensible continuity: more-or-less the same bulk, with more-or-less the same sensible qualities, seems to endure. But it is a further substantive step, a step that requires metaphysical rather than empirical argument, to show that these constant appearances are supported by some ongoing substratum. An enduring subject of change is simply never observed . . . Questions of identity over time—whether a thing endures, or is succeeded in time by something new and perhaps qualitatively quite similar—are metaphysical questions that can never be decisively settled by observation.
> (Pasnau 2011: 24–25)

Here I'm in complete agreement with Pasnau: whether the skin cell that was once a proper part of me at one time is *numerically* identical to the object now lying in a petri dish is beyond the ken of experience; one must resort to philosophical considerations concerning the nature and persistence of material objects to settle the score. And, according to Substantial Priority, what it means for a substance to be metaphysically fundamental is that it is not composed of further fundamental entities and that it serves to ground each of its respective proper parts. From this particular conception of substantiality, it follows that even the smallest material parts of composite substances, in this case one of my skin cells, is such that it is grounded in the substantial whole of which it is a part.

I have offered philosophical considerations (as well as empirical suggestions) that aim to show how thinking of certain ordinary composite substances as matching this particular grounding description yields a unified solution to a host of puzzles in material objects. Given that numerical identity is arguably not a datum of experience or empirical observation, and since the very issue at hand is a *metaphysical* thesis regarding whether the proper parts of fundamental substances are best construed as separable or inseparable, the earlier intuition that it is *one and the same* skin cell that survives removal carries little weight in the absence of supporting philosophical considerations in favor of a Part-Priority fundamental mereology.

In addition to the earlier reply, the defender of Substantial Priority can emphasize that while the deep ontological story about the identity of the object in the petri dish does not, strictly speaking, involve strict numerical continuity with the skin cell that was once a proper part of me, this does not mean that absolutely *nothing* remains strictly the same throughout the process. Recall once again our formulation of a grounding whole in §3.4 as a whole that serves to ground the identity of each of its *individual* or *objectual* proper parts. As such, it is perfectly consistent to maintain that while the skin cell that was once a part of me is not one and the same *object* that now occupies the petri dish, there is one and the same *portion of matter or stuff* that underlies or composes each numerically distinct object. While I will not argue for the fundamental distinction between objects or individuals and portions of non-individual stuff here, the distinction allows the proponent of Substantial Priority to maintain, in good Aristotelian fashion, the strict numerical continuity of something or other (but not some individual *thing* or *object*, see §3.4.1)—namely portions of stuff—in cases involving compositional alteration as noted earlier.[11]

But perhaps I am being uncharitable to my interlocutor here. Perhaps the Moorean objection is more of a *conceptual* worry—"I just can't *conceive* of how the skin cell could fail to survive removal; how *could* facts about the decompositional structure of fundamental substances be so sensitive to such minute differences?" This is indeed a different objection than the one above, but one that I think carries little force in the end. The inconceivability in question would equally apply to a non-transferable trope's, *F-ness*, ceasing to exist upon its bearer ceasing to be F (where F might refer to *being uniformly red*), a spatial boundary's ceasing to exist upon the slightest topological change in its host, or a material object's ceasing to exist upon the loss of one of its minute proper parts (a carbon atom) as per mereological essentialism. In all three cases, we have grounded entities (tropes, boundaries, and composite objects) whose existence is highly sensitive to minute alterations in their grounds. In so far as these cases are clearly conceivable as evidenced by their being widely discussed in the literature (particularly the case involving mereological essentialism), I fail to see the conceptual difficulty in endorsing the view that a minuscule inseparable part of a fundamental substance ceases to exist upon ceasing to be a proper part of that substance.[12]

Moreover, the conceptual worry neglects the fact that skin cells and the epidermis in which they are embedded play a vital functional role in sustaining and regulating the life of the biological organism. For example, the epidermis and individual skin cells act as a barrier that protects the organism from the invasion of pathogens, provides insulation and helps with overall temperature regulation, aids in the production of vitamin D, and prevents unregulated loss of water and solutes.[13] I surmise that the deep intuitions driving this Moorean objection stems more from conceiving of the generation of composite substances more along the lines of the summation of tiny Democritean atoms or Lewisian point-sized masses that are ontologically *separable* and independent from one another (and the sum of which they are parts), rather than any inherent conceptual problem with Substantial Priority.

Suppose at this point that the objector grants Substantial Priority for composite entangled wholes at the quantum level, "Sure" they might argue, "Substantial Priority may very well apply to the structure of entangled quantum wholes, but why think such grounding structure applies to plausible medium-sized substance-candidates like trees, people, and poodles?"

This is a rather unstable move in my opinion, for two reasons. One, Substantial Priority aims to explicate "the laws of metaphysics" concerning the nature and structure of substances—i.e., what necessarily follows from the nature of a substance as a metaphysically fundamental entity: necessarily, for any x, if x is a composite substance, then x is metaphysically prior to its proper parts. If so, then the objector's rejoinder amounts to saying that either the only existing substances are quantum entangled systems or that there are multiple and distinct sets of metaphysical laws that govern the existence and identity conditions for substances, those that apply to entangled quantum wholes and those that apply to higher-level (non-quantum) substantial wholes. The former route faces the foregoing objections in Chapter 4 to Priority Microphysicalism for higher-level wholes (viz. the failure of whole-part supervenience). The latter route forfeits an important theoretical unity to the category of *substance*.

To illustrate, consider two substances x and y, where x is an entangled quantum whole and y is Schrödinger's cat. If x is a grounding whole and thus metaphysically prior to its proper parts, and y is a grounded whole (on objector's assumption) and thus metaphysically posterior to its proper parts (and thereby metaphysically derivative), in what sense are x and y entities of the *same* ontological category?[14] If x and y have such distinct existence and identity conditions, then it seems as if we lose all grounds for affirming that they belong to the very same category—i.e., substance. As a result, bifurcating the existence and identity conditions of substances forfeits a crucial theoretical unity concerning the existence and identity conditions that belong to the category of *substance*.

But doesn't the same charge apply to the proponent of Substantial Priority in so far as they admit both simple and composite substances? No. Recall that the definition of a substance employed by Substantial Priority (see **Substance**, Chapter 3, §4.1) is such that it captures the existence and identity conditions of both simple and composite substances. According to **Substance**, x is a substance only if (a) there is no y such that (i) y is concrete, (ii) y is not identical with x, (iii) x is grounded in y and (b) x is unified in the right kind of way, where the unity ascribed in clause (b) is such that a substance lacks separable parts. It was pointed out that there were two distinct ways a substance might lack separable parts, either by lacking parts altogether or having only inseparable parts. Simple substances (if there are any) lack separable parts in the first sense, complex substances in the second. Hence, **Substance** offers a unified account of the nature of substances, both simple and complex. But the objector is in no similar position regarding the unity of the category of *substance*.

Moreover, arguing that Substantial Priority applies exclusively to quantum systems places a great deal of weight on the divide between the small objects of quantum mechanics and the medium-sized objects of ordinary experience, one that some might think unwarranted. Lowe's (2008: 66) remarks are insightful along these lines:

> All we can say with any confidence, indeed, is that quantum physics aspires to offer a general explanatory framework for all physical phenomena, not just physical phenomena which occur on the very small scale. Any attempt to segregate physical phenomena in a principled way into those that are "small-scale" and submit to the principles of quantum physics and those that are "large-scale" and do not submit to those principles is doomed to failure, as the very example of Schrödinger's cat demonstrates: for, by any standard, a radium atom is a "small-scale" phenomenon and a cat is a "large-scale" phenomenon, and yet in this case we have a single physical system embracing them both and subject to the principles of quantum physics.

If there is good reason to think, as the objector grants, that Substantial Priority governs certain small microphysical systems, then what principled reason is there to think that the grounding structure it ascribes to very small physical systems fails to obtain for larger physical systems such as trees, people, and poodles (a principled reason other than the fact that there are no such substances)? To maintain that Substantial Priority applies exclusively to small composite objects or systems is to neglect the *metaphysical* import of the view as concerning the grounding structure of composite intermediate substances per se, whether small, medium or very large indeed.

8.3 No Principled Objection to Priority Monism

In response to ascribing fundamentality to intermediates, Jonathan Schaffer (2010: 63–64) writes,

> Further the use of basic molecules [fundamental intermediates] is already quasi-monistic. Given the tiling constraint (§1.3), no proper parts of any basic molecules can themselves be basic. Hence the use

of basic molecules involves treating the whole as prior to its parts, with respect to the basic molecules and their derivative parts. So it is hard to see how the molecular pluralist could have any principled objection to monism. For instance, if the objection to monism was the "commonsense" objection that parts are prior to their wholes, then the molecular pluralist is equally open to the objection. Or if the objection to monism was from heterogeneity, then given that the basic molecules can be heterogeneous—as is needed to cover the case of heterogeneous gunk—then the molecular pluralist is equally open to the objection.

As I understand it, Schaffer's primary worry here is that if one opts for the view that (at least some) intermediate wholes are prior to their parts, and every objection leveled against Priority Monism likewise counts against fundamental intermediates, then one is left without a principled way to rule out the fundamentality or priority of the cosmos.

Regarding Schaffer's introductory claim that assigning fundamentality to intermediate composites is "quasi-monistic," it needs to be reiterated that the Priority Monist has no right to stake out the thesis of the priority of wholes *per se* over their parts as a piece of monistic metaphysics (see Chapter 3, §3.2.2). The general thesis that wholes *per se* are prior to their parts is independent of the further question of *which* wholes in particular we ought to be ontologically committed to, including the cosmos, as well as which class of composite objects are best suited to qualify as fundamental.

I think Schaffer's overarching worry here is misguided. For one, the objection conflates (a) being subject to the same (or highly similar) objections to the priority of wholes per se to their parts with (b) not having a reason to reject Priority Monism, a specific application of this classical piece of metaphysics to a particular whole, the maximal sum of classical mereology. These are quite different claims. As two individual species of a fundamental mereology that is committed to the priority of wholes per se over their parts, Priority Monism and Substantial Priority share a common fate and thus stand or fall together; any objection against the priority of wholes per se over their parts counts equally against both views in so far as each are minimally committed to this general thesis for at least some composite objects.

But this in no way suggests that the friend of Substantial Priority is bereft of principled reasons to reject the fundamentality of the cosmos *in particular*. There are, on the one hand, plausible reasons *not* to ascribe fundamentality to the cosmos as the maximal mereological sum of classical mereology. Even more, however, is the fact that even *if* one grants both the existence and fundamentality of Schaffer's cosmos in particular, this *on its own* in no way undermines Substantial Priority. Let's turn to the positive reasons against ascribing metaphysical fundamentality to the cosmos.

First, full-strength classical mereology with its axiom of Unrestricted Composition and commitment to the Universe (U) as the unique maximal sum, carries a high ontological price tag. As Simons (1987: 15) has noted, the Universe of classical mereology is only "slightly less controversial than the existence of arbitrary sums." And if controversy surrounds the very *existence* of the maximal sum, how much more so its *fundamentality*?[15] As far as I can tell, Schaffer (2010) assumes classical mereology in its full-strength with its axiom of Unrestricted Composition, which "guarantees the existence of the cosmos as the fusion of all actual concrete objects" (34). Yet for those who remain unconvinced that composition obeys the axioms of classical mereology in the first place and thus opt instead for a non-classical mereology, the existence (let alone the fundamentality) of the cosmos is certainly not beyond dispute.

Second, the existence and identity conditions that are commonly thought to govern the sums or fusions of classical mereology preclude them from being fundamental and prior to their parts. The standard gloss on the existence and identity conditions of sums involves reference to all and only the proper parts of sums; sums exist and are what they are in virtue of the existence and identity of their proper parts.[16] In this way, sums share the same existence and identity conditions as sets, which is no surprise given that classical mereology was originally offered by the Polish logician Stanisław Leśniewski as a more parsimonious alternative to set theory (see Simons 1987: Chapter 1). Along these very lines, Crawford Elder (2011: 139–140) makes this point as follows:

> It is natural . . . to suppose that the identity of this mereological object is given by the identity of its parts—that this object could not have had different parts from its actual ones, and that necessarily this object exists exactly where and when its actual parts exist . . . It is these objects that most philosophers have in mind when they speak of "mereological sums," and these objects that most philosophers take the thesis of UMC [Unrestricted Composition] to affirm.

It is precisely because they display this particular one-many grounding structure that classical sums—and by extension the cosmos as the maximal (concrete) sum—appear to be ill-suited to be fundamental and prior to their proper parts.

But *must* the proponent of Priority Monism ascribe to the existence and identity conditions for sums that naturally follow on the heels of full-strength classical mereology (especially the axioms of Unrestricted Composition and Uniqueness) and thereby gloss the cosmos as a sum with the aforementioned existence and identity conditions? There is, of course, nothing that prevents the Monist from rejecting classical mereology and opting instead for a non-classical view. Yet once one leaves behind full-strength classical mereology with its commitment to Unrestricted Composition, it is not at all clear that any compelling grounds remain in favor of the existence of the cosmos qua maximal concrete sum. Schaffer (2010: 34) offers two quick considerations apart from the fact that classical mereology "guarantees the existence of the cosmos": natural language provides a singular term for such an entity ("the cosmos"), and the cosmos is the primary subject of empirical inquiry in cosmology. While English does indeed include the term "the cosmos," natural language on its own is silent as to whether or not such a term is a singular or a plural referring term; one's underlying metaphysic will determine whether "the cosmos" picks out a single individual or a plurality of individuals. Natural language *on its own*, then, does not offer a compelling independent consideration in favor of the existence of the cosmos.

A similar line can be taken with respect to the cosmos being the primary subject matter of cosmology. Whether cosmology has within its empirical purview a *single* composite object is inextricably bound up with one's views about composition in general. Mereological nihilists, for instance, might replace Schaffer's cosmos as the primary subject of cosmology with the large-scale structure and distribution of pervading gravitational fields over spacetime points and set-theoretic constructions of these points.[17] Mereological moderates, on the other hand, might offer instead the large-scale structure and distribution of such fields over spacetime points and (restricted) mereological sums of these points as the principle target of cosmological inquiry. What one takes to be the primary subject of cosmology will no doubt hinge on what one takes the referent of "the cosmos" to be, whether such a term picks out a *one* or a *many*, and, surely, there is room even for mereological nihilists and moderates in the theoretical physics departments at Cal Tech and MIT.

Third, the defender of Substantial Priority might argue, in true Chisholmian fashion, that we have stronger grounds for thinking that at least one kind of intermediate composite object—namely, human persons, is fundamental than for thinking that the cosmos is fundamental. Given the implications of fundamental mereology for the metaphysics of free will, mind, and human persons as noted in Chapter 7, the defender of Substantial Priority is well-within her epistemic rights to take her own basic awareness of herself as an irreducibly conscious and causal agent as prima facie evidence in favor of her being a fundamental substance in her own right. Suppose she thinks these features of human persons are deeply intuitive and part of the package of pre-philosophical beliefs she brings to her metaphysical theorizing (see the Introduction). If, as we have seen, Priority Monism threatens to undermine these well-entrenched beliefs, and there are no compelling reasons to think that these beliefs are mistaken, she has good grounds for rejecting Priority Monism. Consequently, if one has reasonably good independent grounds for thinking that human persons are fundamental, then by **No Fundamental Parthood**, one has good grounds for thinking that the cosmos is not fundamental (it's an open question whether the cosmos is a derivative aggregate, a plurality, or perhaps doesn't exist at all).

Lastly, I want to point out what I consider to be a dialectical weakness in Schaffer's own case for Priority Monism. Even *if* one grants Schaffer both the existence and fundamentality of the cosmos, this in no way *on its own* undermines the existence of fundamental intermediate composite objects. To see this, we must pry a bit deeper into what exactly Schaffer means by "the cosmos" in his own formulation and defense of Priority Monism.

Schaffer offers the following explications of what he means by "the cosmos": (i) "[w]hen I speak of the world—and defend the monistic thesis that the whole is prior to its parts—I am speaking of the material cosmos and its planets, pebbles, particles, and other proper parts" (2010: 33) and (ii) "By 'the cosmos' I mean the whole material universe, the total system, the sum of all concrete things" (2013: 74). We are offered a more detailed account of the exact nature of Schaffer's cosmos in his defense (Schaffer 2009) of a version of a substantivalist view of spacetime he dubs "monistic sustantivalism." Monistic substantivalism says that there is only one substance—the general-relativistic spacetime manifold itself—where the material contents of spacetime such as planets, pebbles, and particles are to be identified with their occupying regions. People and pebbles *are* spacetime regions on this view.[18]

In the course of defending monistic substantivalism, Schaffer (2009) argues that such a view entails Priority Monism that "the whole material cosmos is ontologically prior to any of its parts" (2009: 135). His reasoning, in his own words, is as follows: "Given the priority of the whole for spacetime, and the monistic identification of material objects with spacetime regions, the priority of the whole for material objects follows immediately" (ibid.: 136) He sums up his defense of monistic substantivalism as follows: "So I conclude that there is one and only one substance, and that substance is spacetime. To make the world, God only needed to create spacetime, and pin the fundamental fields directly to it" (ibid.: 146). From this it is clear that Schaffer takes the spacetime manifold and the cosmos to be *one and the same thing.*

But Schaffer's identification of the cosmos with the spacetime manifold itself raises the following worry that threatens to severely weaken the independent plausibility of Priority Monism as a fundamental mereology. In order for Schaffer to infer from the fundamentality of the cosmos that sub-world objects are not fundamental substances in their own right (as per the application of **No Fundamental Parthood**), he must first show that sub-world objects are, strictly speaking, proper parts of the cosmos. This is precisely because **No Fundamental Parthood** is a thesis about the *mereological* ordering of substances, that no substance has another substance as a proper part. But if the cosmos *just is* the entire spacetime manifold (2009: 135), then it follows that the cosmos has the same mereological structure as the manifold itself. But the proper parts of the manifold are commonly thought to be *regions* (whether extended or unextended), not the *occupants* of those regions. For many (perhaps most) metaphysicians, there is a fundamental difference between regions and region-occupiers, between the container and that which is contained. Thus for any view that holds to the non-identity of material objects and their occupying regions, it follows that the ordinary material occupants of spacetime such as people, pebbles and particles are *not*, strictly speaking, proper parts of the cosmos. While material objects stand in the primitive occupation relation to spacetime regions which are themselves proper parts of the manifold, such objects are not included among the compositional base of the manifold itself.

If one rejects the identification of material objects with substantival regions (as most do), then Schaffer's arguments in favor of the cosmos being a fundamental substance in no way undermine the existence of sub-cosmic fundamental substances, including intermediate substances as per Substantial Priority. If intermediate fundamental substances are not strictly speaking proper parts of the cosmos, then they fail to fall within the purview of **No Fundamental Parthood** and are in no way rendered non-fundamental by Schaffer's arguments for the fundamentality of the cosmos. One could straightforwardly grant to Schaffer that the cosmos, understood as the spacetime manifold itself as on substantivalism, is a fundamental substance, and yet still maintain Substantial Priority.

Consequently, *unless we assume the truth of supersubstantivalism*—a deeply counterintuitive view that even Schaffer calls "a revisionary and unpopular view" (2009: 133)—Substantial Priority (as well as every other fundamental mereology) remains untouched by Schaffer's arguments for Priority Monism. This, I think, leaves Schaffer in a rather untoward dialectical position. By building monistic substantivalism (supersubstantivalism) into his fundamental mereology, his arguments for the priority of the cosmos in no way establish Priority Monism over and above of rivals like PM and Substantial Priority. While the Priority Monist need not follow Schaffer in endorsing monistic substantivalism, there nevertheless remains a tension in Schaffer's own defense of the view.

8.4 Substantial Priority is UnAristotelian

Robert Koons (2014) has argued that a view like Substantial Priority (what he, following Koslicki (2008), calls "Reverse Mereological Essentialism" (RME)) runs counter to the following *Substrate Principle* that is part and parcel of Aristotle's conception of change (whether substantial or accidental):

> *Substrate Principle:* "All natural change requires a substratum that endures through the change."[19]

Koons (2014: 162–163) formulates the Aristotelian charge as follows:

> Aristotle's Substrate Principle demands that something, the substrate, exists both before every kind of change, including substantial change.

Reverse Mereological Essentialism is inconsistent with the Substrate Principle, since RME entails that both the substance and all of its material parts begin to exist at the same moment. Just because the pre-existing elements and the new substance contain the same quantity of material stuff (e.g., mass, charge, and so on) is not sufficient, since what Aristotle requires is some substrate that is numerically one and the same before and after substantial change.

If all of the material (proper) parts of a composite substance are grounded in the substantial whole as on Substantial Priority, then none of them can serve as the requisite enduring (and pre-existing) subtratum underlying the substantial change in question. This is a weighty charge for any view that claims some degree of continuity with aspects of Aristotle's metaphysics like Substantial Priority.

Let me first of all say that the *Substrate Principle* is not essential to Substantial Priority as such. Substantial Priority is a view about the mereological and grounding structure of substances, it says nothing about the precise ontological assay of substance (constituent vs. relational ontology, bare particularism, hylomorphism, etc.). Nor does the view require any particular view of persistence and change through time. But since I endorse the *Substrate Principle*, let me say a few words about how the defender of Substantial Priority might respond to this important Aristotelian objection.

As we've pointed out in §8.2, one might agree that in every instance of change there must be something that retains numerical identity through time, yet disagree with Koons that "there must be some *one thing* that endures through the change as its ultimate subject" (163). Recall that my formulation of the grounding structure of the parts of grounding and grounded wholes (§3.4) was restricted to *objectual* or *individual* proper parts. Each of the proper parts of composite substances belonging to the category of *object* or *individual* are grounded in the wholes of which they are a part. Following Lowe (2006), I consider entities in the category of *object* to have determinate synchronic and diachronic identity conditions, in addition to determinate countability. Objects have determinate identity conditions in that there is a fact of the matter regarding statements of the form "x at t_1 is numerically the same y at t_2."

Quantities or portions of stuff, by contrast, have determinate identity conditions yet lack determinate countability. Portions or quantities of stuff lack the intrinsic unity to be counted as *one* and are not objects or individuals for this very reason. But if quantities or portions of stuff have determinate identity conditions, as Koons recognizes, then there is a fact of the matter as to whether some portion is numerically the same before and after the substantial change. So, while the pre-existing *objects* or *individuals* no longer exist as proper parts of the newly generated substance, there nevertheless remains numerically one and the same quantity or portion of stuff as before.

It seems to me entirely consistent with the *Substrate Principle* to claim that all of the objectual proper parts of a composite substance were generated at the same moment as when the substantial whole was generated. The objectual parts are intrinsically "structure-laden" and are what they are in virtue of the whole. The enduring substratum of change, one might say, is not an object or individual, but a (non-individual) portion of stuff, the same portion of stuff that existed prior to the generation of the composite substance.[20] And it is no part of Substantial Priority that the very same "structure-ladenness" that applies to the objects or individuals as parts also applies to the (non-individual) portion of matter *from which* the substance is generated.

8.5 Fundamental Intermediates are Objectionably Arbitrary

A more promising line against Substantial Priority turns on the alleged arbitrariness of assigning fundamentality to some particular class of intermediate composite objects. Call this *the Argument from Objectionable Arbitrariness*. The objection was originally outlined in Schaffer (2010) and has been reaffirmed by Tallant (2013). Consider Schaffer's (2010: 63) original remarks:

> Finally, the pluralist might reject *Atomism*, maintaining that what is basic is mereologically intermediate. But this seems objectionably *arbitrary*, especially in cases where there is no natural joint in the mereological structure. For instance, in the case of a homogeneously pink sphere of gunk, all the levels of mereological structure (save for the top) are intermediate, and all are homogeneously pink. No layer of decomposition seems privileged. Homogeneous gunk thus emerges as especially problematic for the pluralist since (i) there are no atoms for the atomist, and (ii) there are no privileged molecules for the molecularist. The only privileged level of structure is at the top.

Tallant (2013: 436) reiterates the worry in terms of fixing on the molecules in particular as fundamental:

> First, that, as noted in the set-up to the case, we fixed upon the molecular level *entirely* at random. There is no principled reason to think that molecules *are* fundamental. The problem will generalize: for any level, L, why should we think *that* level is fundamental? Why not the atoms? Why not the electrons?

I must admit that the precise nub of the concern is not entirely clear to me. On the one hand, the objection as stated by Schaffer in particular suggests that the *natural* or *privileged* mereological joints in non-gunky and non-junky worlds *just are* the relevant termini of the mereological hierarchy as represented by the three atom model of classical mereology (Figure 3.1)—i.e., the top (U) and bottom (x,y,z) levels. Since decomposition fails to terminate in atomic minima in gunky worlds, there are therefore no natural or privileged mereological joints left on which to hang the fundamental entities other than the top level. In Schaffer's words, "The only privileged level of structure is at the top."

But to gloss the naturalness or privileged status of a mereological joint in terms of its serving as a *terminus* on the three-atom model disqualifies the intermediate joints from attaining this status from the outset. And, surely, this victory by exclusion is not what Schaffer has in mind. We may grant that the objection has force on the assumption that a joint's being privileged or natural is determined by purely *formal* considerations like being one of the relevant termini of the three-atom model of classical mereology. But the prospects for constructing a non-question begging argument against fundamental intermediates on the basis of such an assumption is rather dim.

But perhaps I've misunderstood the way in which Schaffer glosses a mereological joint as natural or privileged. Perhaps, as Schaffer's example of the homogeneously pink sphere of gunk suggests, a mereological joint's being privileged or non-arbitrary has something to do with the qualitative features instantiated at that joint. Since each intermediate object from which the pink sphere of gunk is composed is qualitatively uniform and is homogenous with every other intermediate object (all the way down), no such level is uniquely suited to host the metaphysically fundamental entities save the top level.

The example seems "cooked up," as they say, to suit Schaffer's point. Even granting the possibility of qualitatively homogenous worlds given the assumptions that drive fundamental mereology, if all the mereological levels of Schaffer's sphere of gunk are homogeneously pink, then this would include the top level as well (as Schaffer admits). If both the intermediate and the topmost level of the sphere of gunk are uniformly pink (and only pink), then what grounds are there for claiming that the topmost level is privileged over and above the intermediate level? If the intermediate and the top mereological levels are qualitatively indiscernible, what makes it the case that "[t]he only privileged level of structure is at the top" in such a scenario? The lack of qualitative variation between the two levels makes such a difference in privilege ungrounded. I can think of only one reason for privileging the top over the intermediate level of the sphere in spite of their qualitative indiscernibility: the top level alone serves as the mereological terminus for the parthood ordering in a gunky world. But as we noted earlier, to gloss the privileged or natural status of a mereological joint in this particular way is a rather hollow victory in so far the cosmos and the atoms alone serve as the termini of the three-atom model; the intermediates are rendered arbitrary from the start.

The thrust of Tallant's statement of the Argument from Objectionable Arbitrariness noted earlier, on the other hand, is that the defender of fundamental intermediates is bereft of non-arbitrary grounds for determining *which* intermediate objects in particular are fundamental. Here I think the defender of fundamental intermediates has at least two candidate diagnostics at hand to assuage the worry.

Suppose the defender of fundamental intermediates endorses the earlier line of reasoning outlined in the tracking argument (§6.2.1), in particular the premise I referred to as *Tracking*: necessarily, the fundamental causal properties exclusively track the fundamental bearers of properties. If so, then we have a candidate diagnostic as to which intermediate objects are metaphysically privileged in terms of the instantiation of certain fundamental or perfectly natural properties, in particular those natural properties that carve out non-redundant causal structure in the world. The question as to *which* intermediate level hosts a fundamental substance with non-redundant causal properties in this sense is, I take it, a question to be decided on wider philosophical and empirical grounds.

Additionally, if we sign-on to Schaffer's tiling constraint for fundamental mereologies (in particular **No Fundamental Parthood**) we have an additional diagnostic for fundamentality in that whether or not a particular intermediate object is fundamental will also be determined by whether it is itself a proper part of a higher-level fundamental intermediate.[21] If an intermediate composite is a proper part of a larger fundamental substance in particular, then the intermediate composite is derivative as dictated by the tiling constraint (and likewise if it has fundamental substances as proper parts).

So, for any intermediate composite x we can ask the following two diagnostic questions regarding whether or not x is fundamental or metaphysically elite, (a) does x carve out fundamental or non-redundant causal structure in the world?, and (b) does x fail to be proper part of a higher level intermediate substance, one that carves out non-redundant structure in its own right? If *both* (a) and (b) are true of x, then we can plausibly infer that x is a fundamental substance in its own right. Contra Tallant, the earlier diagnostics afford the proponent of fundamental intermediates principled grounds for determining which intermediate composites are metaphysically elite.

8.6 Failure to Meet the Tiling Constraint

The next objection is, I believe, one of the most serious for proponents of Substantial Priority. The worry stems from Schaffer's tiling constraint over the fundamental entities. Recall from our explication of fundamental mereology (§3.1) that the main thrust of Schaffer's **Covering** constraint is that the fundamental entities must be complete in that their collective duplication, together with the fundamental relations between them, suffices to duplicate the entire cosmos. As was noted in §1, the notion of "completeness" is understood in terms of an exhaustive ontological base for a domain; the fundamentals must ultimately ground the existence of every distinct entity in the target domain, *without remainder*. And according to **No Fundamental Parthood**, the fundamental entities must not stand in part-whole relations to one another.

Assuming the tiling constraint, Jonathan Tallant (2013) argues that locating the fundamental entities at an intermediate level would leave large portions of reality ungrounded; no intermediate level would suffice to cover the entire cosmos without standing in part-whole relations to one another. In his own words:

> The advantage of fixing upon *either* the whole world or the very smallest entities in reality is obvious. Both of these candidates for being a fundamental level *do* cover the whole cosmos without overlapping. It is hard to see that anything at any level in between can manage that trick. There are gaps between the macroscopic into which the microscopic sometimes fall. A bottom level or a top level will generate total coverage; it's hard to see that can be achieved by anything in between.
>
> (2013: 436)

First of all, whether or not a particular fundamental mereology is successful in meeting the demands of the tiling constraint as defined depends, of course, on what one takes to be within the most inclusive domain of the existential quantifier. For instance, if a proponent of a fundamental mereology denied the existence of Schaffer's cosmos, then it would be much too quick to object that their preferred account failed to meet the tiling constraint in so far as it failed to cover the cosmos itself; if there is no maximal sum of classical mereology then the collective duplication of the fundamental entities need not collectively ground it.

Moreover, recall that the view I am defending in no way entails that *all* intermediate composite objects are fundamental; the fundamentals need not uniformly occupy one and the same mereological level as on Intermediate (§3.2.1.). Nor do I see any requirement that all fundamental entities be properly classified as "macrophysical." One might argue that the inclusive set of fundamental entities on the mereological hierarchy consists of a mixture of both microphysical and macrophysical substances, each occupying distinct mereological levels (the atomic and intermediate levels, respectively), and collectively suffice to duplicate the entirety of the mereological hierarchy without overlapping as per **No Fundamental Parthood**.

For illustrative purposes, suppose the defender of fundamental intermediates with neo-Aristotelian sympathies held to the view that living organisms are among the fundamental intermediates that instantiate non-redundant causal properties.[22] Hence living organisms, on this view, would be among the fundamental intermediate objects that are prior to their proper parts and governed by **No Fundamental Parthood**.

The advocate of such a view need not assume that *all* intermediate composite objects fit this particular description. As was hinted at earlier, arguably not all composite objects carve reality at its joints as closely as others. Perhaps certain non-living intermediate composites such as tables, automobiles, bicycles, and the like are derivative intermediates in so far as they, along with their distinctive qualitative profile, are totally grounded in their metaphysically fundamental microphysical parts and the relations between them. On the mixed fundamental mereology on offer, the fundamental substances that collectively provide an exhaustive ontological base for the hierarchy of composition include a subclass of macrophysical intermediates, including living organisms, as well as a subclass of microphysical atoms (or microphysical composites if a gunky scenario obtains). If Tallant (2013: 436) is willing to grant that the duplication of all the fundamental entities at the atomic level suffices to cover the cosmos, then I don't see why the duplication of all the fundamental macrophysical intermediates, *together* with all the microphysical atoms save those that compose the fundamental macrophysical intermediates (including living organisms), wouldn't likewise do the trick.

Nevertheless, one might argue that such a view fails to satisfy the **No Fundamental Parthood** constraint in so far as the fundamental macrophysical intermediates will inevitably be composed of the fundamental microphysical atoms on this view.

But how exactly does the mixed view on offer here violate **No Fundamental Parthood**? It is one thing to say that living organisms have atomic or microphysical parts, and it is another altogether to say that those microphysical parts are *fundamental in their own right*. While the former is beyond dispute, the latter is a much stronger thesis that needs to be argued for; in fact, it is the very question under dispute between proponents of Priority Monism, Atomism, and Intermediate or a variant thereof. No Priority Monist would be persuaded by the line that their view fails to satisfy the **No Fundamental Parthood** constraint in so far as the cosmos—as the sum of all concreta—is inevitably composed of atomic parts that are fundamental in their own right. Monism *just is* the view that no part of the cosmos is fundamental! In the same way, no proponent of the mixed view on offer here will grant the failure of **No Fundamental Parthood** on the grounds that fundamental intermediates have as parts microphysical atoms that are fundamental in their own right; to do so would be to abandon the fundamentality of intermediates in the first place.

The objector replies,

> But doesn't this mixed view have the untoward consequence that, at best, the fundamental atoms change their status from fundamental to derivative upon becoming a part of a living organism as per the tiling

constraint; or, at worst, fundamental microphysical atoms cease to exist altogether upon becoming a part of a living organism qua fundamental intermediate?

It is true that the defender of a mixed view needs to tell a story as to *how* the fundamentals can reside at both the atomic and the intermediate levels without violating **No Fundamental Parthood**. But the friend of fundamental intermediates can arguably take either route outlined by the objector, and attempt to mitigate the counterintuitive consequences that result.

First, they might broadly follow Schaffer (2013:81) in taking fundamentality to be a *contingent* feature of an object; while the atoms that are now parts of the living organism were once fundamental in their own right, they are now derivative in so far as they are functionally defined in terms of their place within the organism as a whole.[23] On this view, organisms are what Alicia Juarrero (2000: 31) has called "dissipative structures" such that

> [b]y delimiting the parts' initial repertoire of behavior, the structured whole in which the elements are suddenly embedded also redefines them. They are now something they were not before, nodes in a network, components of a system. As such, they are unable to access states that might have been available to them as independent entities.

The unappealing consequence of this route is that it cuts against the intuition that the status of being metaphysically fundamental is a non-contingent affair.[24]

Alternatively, the defender of the mixed account might opt instead for the view that the fundamental atoms literally cease to exist when they compose a fundamental intermediate, in this case a living organism. Upon becoming a proper part of a fundamental intermediate that is prior to its parts, the atoms go out of existence and are replaced by numerically distinct yet qualitatively similar items, each of which are grounded in the fundamental intermediates of which they are a part (I will discuss this notion more in §9.1.7).

Borrowing the terminology put forward by Koslicki (2008), this second route has the consequence that RME is true of fundamental or substantial wholes in particular. In general, RME stands the thesis of Mereological Essentialism on its head: *parts have their wholes essentially*. In her discussion of Plato's mereology in particular, Koslicki (2008: 114) underscores the implications of RME for wholes per se (without endorsing the view), although our discussion here is restricted to RME as it applies to fundamental intermediates in particular:

> Reverse mereological essentialism asserts that one and the same part cannot survive gaining or losing its whole, so to speak, i.e., the whole of which it is part. In other words, according to this thesis, no

single object could survive, for example, *becoming* a part of a whole of which it is not already part or *ceasing* to be part of a whole of which it is part; any such change would involve the coming-into-existence and going-out-of-existence of numerically distinct, qualitatively similar objects.[25]

Since the modal profile of each part of a fundamental intermediate involves reference to the whole, a fundamental atom's becoming a part of a living organism results in the atom's ceasing to exist as such (assuming the atom's status as fundamental is non-contingent and thus part of its modal profile).[26]

Again, the objector retorts,

> But don't these replies serve as a *reductio* against your mixed fundamental mereology as well as the prospects of admitting fundamental intermediates in the first place? Isn't it evident that fundamentality is non-contingent? Moreover isn't it obvious, nay, empirically manifest, that the lonely, fundamental atom at t is *numerically identical* to the derivative object that is now a part of an organism at t_1?

I do admit that these are substantive metaphysical commitments, but arguably no more substantive than other views in material-object metaphysics currently on the market. I do not think, however, that it is at all obvious that the earlier routes constitute a *reductio* against my mixed view in particular as well as fundamental intermediates in general. It would be overly simplistic to maintain that substantive metaphysical questions such as the categorial classification of concrete objects (i.e., whether fundamental or derivative) and whether the parts of substances persist by maintaining strict numerical identity over time, can be decisively settled by lone appeals to the dictates of common sense or empirical observation. Most philosophers who reject mereological essentialism or a stage-theoretic view of persistence, for instance, do not do so solely on the basis of the following speeches: "We can just *see* that material objects survive part replacement!" or "It is obvious that I am the very same person that you greeted this morning? One thing's clear from experience: I am no instantaneous stage!" Rather, the task of theorizing about the nature, persistence, and identity of material objects aims at sufficiently general features of the world that fall outside the *immediate* purview of commonsense opinion and ordinary empirical observation.

While pre-philosophical beliefs and empirical observation ought to guide and constrain our metaphysical theorizing in important respects (see the Introduction), few are inclined to think that such considerations are able to single-handedly settle the score on such matters. As a result, I don't think it at all obvious or empirically evident that RME is false for fundamental intermediates, and that the lonely, fundamental atom at t is *numerically* as opposed to *qualitatively* identical to the derivative object that is a proper part of an organism at t_1. In the absence of an argument against the tenability of the contingency of fundamentality or RME for fundamental intermediates, the objector's stand-alone appeal to the alleged implausibility of such views carries little dialectical force in my estimation.

One notable cost of *any* fundamental mereology that adheres to the tiling constraint, not just the mixed view on offer here, is that a great many of the objects that play an integral role in reconstructing our ordinary and scientific discourse about the world are not, in fact, fundamental in their own right. To illustrate, John Heil's (2012) preferred atomistic fundamental mereology, which is outlined explicitly in terms of **No Fundamental Parthood**, renders *all* ordinary intermediate objects like tomatoes, people, trees, and molecules as derivative (he calls them "quasi-substances," which bear "quasi-properties") in so far as they are composed of simple, microphysical substances. Likewise, Schaffer claims that Priority Monism renders *all* sub-world objects derivative in so far as they are all proper parts of the cosmos as the single fundamental substance.

My point here is that whether one assigns metaphysical fundamentality to the atomic, intermediate, or cosmic level (or a combination of the first two), fundamental mereologies that sign-on to the tiling constraint are committed to the view that certain classes of objects that appear to be fundamental and the bearers of fundamental causal properties—whether particles or people—are not fundamental in their own right. Thus I do not think the proponent of a mixed view of fundamental intermediates and fundamental atoms (atoms that are not proper parts of fundamental intermediates), in suggesting that the parts of fundamental intermediates such as living organisms are not fundamental in their own right, is faced with any unique worry that doesn't likewise threaten Monism or Atomism.

Notes

1. For reasons John Earman (1989, p. 173) has summed up nicely: "The absolutist can point to three reasons for accepting a substratum of spacetime points: the need to support the structures that define absolute motion, the need to support fields, and the need to ground the right/left distinction when parity conservation fails."
2. See Schaffer (2009b) and Uzquiano (2011) for more on the notion of mereological harmony.
3. This principle is called *arbitrary partition* in Uzquiano (2011) and bears a resemblance to DAUP.
4. This speech is inspired by Schaffer (2009: 138–139) but has been adapted to the present context. For the claim that material occupants inherit their geometrical, topological, and metrical features from their occupying regions, see Hudson (2006: 111).
5. For an excellent introduction to the metaphysics of spacetime see Dainton (2010).

6. Earman (1989) and Norton (2011) defend manifold substantivalism, while (Maudlin (1993) and Hoefer (1996) defend the metric field variety. Healey (1995: 288) suggests that such views are united under the label "minimal substantivalism," the view that spacetime exists over and above any material objects or events which exist within it.
7. Interestingly enough, the particular understanding of spacetime as per moderate structural realism and metric essentialism resembles the nature of what I have been calling a grounding whole. For instance, Esfield and Lam (2008: 38) state: "The bare manifold points (or rather the sets of manifold points) only get their—structural—physical identity and meaning through the specification of the metric tensor field (turning them into space-time points) . . . any attempt to identify and to individuate the space-time points independently of the space-time structure provided by the metric tensor field has no physical meaning."
8. Emphasis in original.
9. Emphasis mine.
10. As I pointed out in the previous chapter, this does not collapse into Priority Monism in so far as Substantial Priority retains the fundamental distinction between the relations of parthood and occupation; while spacetime qua singular substance has its dependent sub-regions as proper parts, the occupants of those sub-regions are not proper parts of spacetime. The only way to move from substantivalism to Priority Monism is to adopt supersubstantivalism and thus *identify* the occupants of spacetime and their underlying regions. You and I, on this view, *are* identical to regions of spacetime. This is precisely the route taken by Schaffer (2009).
11. See Scaltsas (1994) for an excellent discussion of Aristotle's thinking on this particular matter, as well as Kronen et al. (2000: 879) where such a view is attributed explicitly to Aquinas (under the guise of what the authors refer to as "gamma").
12. This is precisely the reverse of what the mereological essentialist holds: instead of the whole ceasing to exist upon losing one of its parts, the part ceases to exist upon being separated from its whole.
13. See for instance Proksch et al. (2008).
14. This point has been made by Toner (2010) and discussed in Koslicki (2013).
15. Yet another reason some have been suspect of the existence of the cosmos stems from thinking of "the cosmos" as a plural term; the cosmos is a plurality and not a single, unified entity. "The universe is not an individual: monism is false. It is a multiplicity" (Simons (2003: 249)).
16. For more on the standard gloss on the existence and identity conditions of sums see Koslicki (2008: 28), Baker (2007: 184), Sider (2001: 135), Lewis (1991: 85).
17. See Sider (2013) for example.
18. This particular part of monistic substantivalism is known as "supersubstantivalism."
19. This is Robert Pasnau's formulation of what he calls the "substratum thesis" endorsed by Aristotle and medieval Aristotelians. See his (2011: 18) for a survey of this principle in medieval Aristotelianism.
20. See Brower (2014) for a fuller development of the application of a mixed ontology of thing and stuff to a Aristotelian ontology of material objects. For an interpretation of Aristotle along these very lines see Scaltsas (1994).
21. Although this appears to have the rather counterintuitive consequence that an entity's status as fundamental is extrinsic. Yet this may well be a bullet any friend of the tiling constraint will need to bite.
22. Of course one need not endorse such a view to defend the fundamentality of intermediates.

23. One might argue that while it may be necessary that at least some intermediate is fundamental, it is contingent which intermediate is, in fact, fundamental in any given world.
24. Toner (2010) claims that an object's status as a substance is a contingent affair. Moreover, Koons (2014) suggests another route whereby the natures of the atoms remain essentially unchanged, they nevertheless have one set of (non-essential) causal powers when they are proper parts of higher-level substances of a certain kind, and a distinct set of causal powers when they fail to be proper parts of a substance—i.e., when they are "lonely." Since on this account the natures of the atoms remain unchanged when they become parts of the whole, the connection between grounding, parthood, and essence explicated in Chapters 2 and 3 must be severed.
25. Rob Koons (2014) follows suite in his use of the same terms in his classification of various brands of Aristotelian hylomorphism. Both Theodore Scaltsas (1994) and Anna Marmodoro (2013) have argued for an interpretation of Aristotle's view of substance along the lines of what we are calling RME. Also, Kit Fine (2010: §IX,X) offers a general mereological framework that admits of "generative operations"—i.e., "an operation—taking objects into objects—and the identity of a given object will be explained to be the result of applying this operation to certain other objects" that proceed from *both* part-to-whole as well as from whole-to-part.
26. I say "as such" in so far as one might still say that the matter or stuff that once composed or constituted the atom nevertheless survives becoming a part of the fundamental intermediate.

9 Substantial Priority and Empirical Inadequacy

9.1 Substantial Priority is Empirically Inadequate

Perhaps the most problematic objection to Substantial Priority stems from the empirical worry that the view fails to capture the fundamental causal activity of what appear to be substantial proper parts of composite substances. If Substantial Priority is true and no composite substance has substantial proper parts, and substances are the sole bearers of non-redundant causal properties, then *none* of the proper parts of such wholes instantiate such properties. But is it not true that some of our best empirical theories involve reference to fundamental or irreducible causal properties of the proper parts of composite substances? That is, does not the truth of scientific explanations require the existence of substantial proper parts of substances qua bearers of causally fundamental properties? Biological explanation, for example, is replete with the attribution of seemingly irreducible causal powers and dispositions to the proper parts of substances.

Take the example of gene transcription. Many would see DNA as being the fundamental unit of life in that there is a correspondence between the genotypic and phenotypic traits of a living organism, with the direction of determination proceeding from the former to the latter. Strands of DNA, together with their constituent genomic sequences, are the primary units of inheritance and thus play the primary causal role in the growth and genetic adaptation and variation of living organisms. Surely if *any* causal powers are perfectly natural or non-redundant it would be the dispositional properties of genes. And since DNA molecules and their genomic sequences are, strictly speaking, proper parts of substantial living organisms, this would appear to call into question the grounding structure attributed to composite substances as per Substantial Priority.

This is a formidable objection indeed, one that has no doubt helped foster the widespread acceptance of a Part-Priority fundamental mereology in contemporary metaphysics. At the very least, the objection presses those who espouse Substantial Priority to offer a story as to how it's *as-if* the proper parts of substantial wholes are themselves substantial and instantiate perfectly natural properties. If the class of *fundamental* facts are those that specify which objects possess the perfectly natural properties, and this role belongs exclusively to substances qua metaphysically basic entities, then the defender of Substantial Priority needs to explain how facts about substances and their qualities can ground what appear to be metaphysically fundamental facts about their proper parts. And surely the proponent of such a view must tell some story or other if they want to avoid the charge of espousing an ontology that is detached from well-entrenched empirical theory. I surmise that given how entrenched Part-Priority and Priority Microphysicalism (PM) are among contemporary metaphysicians, no such strategy aimed at reconstructing scientific and ordinary discourse will move the objector to over to the side of Substantial Priority. In what follows, then, my aim is to offer Substantial Priority a defense before the tribunal of empirical adequacy.

Here I offer four different strategies available to the defender of Substantial Priority in explaining its being *as-if* the proper parts of substantial wholes are basic in their own right and instantiate non-redundant causal properties. The phenomenon to be saved here is that the causal powers of the proper parts of substances–hydrogen atoms, electrons, and genes, for instance—appear to be fundamental or basic in virtue of their playing an integral causal role in our best empirical theories. The task before us here is to say why, on Substantial Priority, things *seem* this way.

The first four strategies in responding to the objection from empirical inadequacy grant that the causal powers at work in alleged bottom-up scientific explanations—such as the *power of gene transcription* in our earlier example—are indeed *perfectly* natural or non-redundant causal properties, while the fifth argues that the naturalness of such properties per se suffices for their playing an important causal and explanatory role in scientific explanation.

In order to better grasp the first four options, some stage setting is in order. There has been a rather lively and interesting discussion in the contemporary literature as to whether extended mereological simples— non-point-sized material objects devoid of proper parts—are metaphysically possible.[1] One major obstacle for friends of extended simples involves solving *the problem of spatial intrinsics*: explaining how extended simples can exhibit qualitative heterogeneity given their lack of proper parts. We often think of an object's having spatial qualitative variation, such as being blue on one side and red on the other, in terms of its having distinct proper parts that instantiate different intrinsic qualities. The critic of extended simples, then, rightly demands a story as to how material simples can be anything but qualitatively homogenous.

Defenders of extended simples have answered the charge by offering a host of ways to ground the variation of an object's intrinsic properties without pinning such properties to its proper parts (since it has none). As it turns out, many of these accounts can be wielded by the proponent of Substantial Priority in response to the objection at hand. Of course, the parallel here between extended simples and complex substances as per

Substantial Priority is not precise in that the objects under consideration are not mereologically simple; unlike the defender of extended simples, Substantial Priority has at least *some* decompositional structure (albeit non-fundamental) to work with in attempting to reconstruct appearances. On Substantial Priority, composite substances have proper parts, just not ones that are metaphysically basic or fundamental.

9.1.1 Power-Distributions

Once again, our aim is to reconstruct what appears to be a datum of science and experience: that there are *fundamental* causal properties possessed by the parts of composite substances. The first approach to solving the problem of spatial intrinsics I want to explore here, with the aim of applying it to the objection to Substantial Priority at hand, borrows some machinery from Josh Parsons (2004) and appeals to what he calls "distributional properties." As an informal gloss on distributional properties, Parsons notes, "Intuitively, though, a distributional property is like a way of painting, or filling in, a spatially extended object with some property such as colour, or heat, or density." Roughly, distributional properties are fundamental or basic in that an object's instantiating such a property does not obtain in virtue of its instantiating any distinct feature or quality.

Distributional properties can be either *uniform* or *non-uniform*. Examples of uniform distributional properties include *having a uniform density of 1 kg/m throughout* (a density-distributional property) and *being uniformly gunky* (a gunk-distributional property). Examples of non-uniform distributional properties are *being polka dotted* (a color-distributional property) and *being hot at one end and cold at the other* (a heat-distributional property). What's more, distributional properties admit of a determinate-determinable ordering such that *having a color distribution* is a determinable, *being polka dotted* or *being uniformly red all over* being several of its determinates. In addition, there can be further determinates of determinate distributional properties: *having red polka dots on a white background* and *being uniformly scarlet all over* being determinates of the former determinates.

In addition, it is important to note that distributional properties are *monadic*, they are not polyadic or relational. They are basic intrinsic monadic properties that involve reference to both intrinsic properties and regions of space. On this view, a metal rod's instantiating *being hot at one end and cold at the other* is not a polyadic *relation* that holds between the rod and the hot-region and the rod and the cold-region (that is, the regions where *hotness* and *coldness* are located) with the logical form "$rRh \wedge rRc$" such that the distributional property *just is* the conjunction of two dyadic relations. Instead, the form of statements involving the instantiation of distributional properties is "x is F."

For an extended simple to be qualitatively heterogeneous, on this view, is for it to instantiate a *non-uniform* distributional property. To illustrate, suppose that an object x is exactly located at a non-point-sized region R, where x is simple and thus lacking proper parts. Take further the fact of x's being qualitatively heterogeneous: that x is both *hot* and *cold*. Such intrinsic variation cannot be attributed to x's having proper parts, each of which occupy distinct proper sub-regions of x, the one being hot and the other being cold. We can, however, say that x instantiates the non-uniform temperature-distributional property *being hot at r_1 and cold at* r_2, where r_1 and r_2 are disjoint proper sub-regions of R. Due to the primacy of distributional properties in accounting for qualitative variation, it is *in virtue of* x's instantiating the earlier temperature-distributional property that it has the spatially indexed properties of *being hot at r_1* and *being cold at* r_2.

In fact, Parsons goes on to *define* spatially indexed properties like *being hot at r_1* and *being cold at r_2* as disjunctions of temperature-distributional properties, particularly those whose instantiation results in the distribution of *hotness* over r_1 as well as *coldness* over r_2, respectively.[2] The spatially indexed property *being hot at r_1*, for example, can be defined as the disjunction of the following temperature-distributional properties whose instantiation suffices for the distribution of *hotness* to r_1: *being hot at r_1 and cold at r_2*, $\vee$ *being uniformly hot* $\vee$ *being hot at r_1 r_4* $\vee$, . . .[3] Since these spatially indexed properties are disjunctions of (intrinsic) distributional properties, they too are intrinsic (non-relational) by Parson's lights. In this way, the intrinsic qualities of x that account for its heterogeneity can be distributed over its proper sub-regions in virtue of instantiating non-uniform distributional properties, yet without attributing such qualities to any proper parts occupying r_1 and r_2 (as there are none). The proponent of this route can generalize this line of reasoning such that any qualitative variation in some property F of an extended simple can be accounted for in terms of the object instantiating a non-uniform *F-distribution*. Distributional properties, in sum, can be put to work in offering a solution to the problem of spatial intrinsics.

How might we appropriate the earlier machinery to the objection leveled against Substantial Priority? Note first the fact that the use of distributional properties in responding to the earlier objection grants that the causal properties that are commonly attributed to the proper parts of substances are perfectly natural or causally fundamental. However, this route goes on to claim that while these properties are distributed over a substance's proper sub-regions, they are instantiated not by the proper parts that occupy those proper sub-regions but by the composite substance itself. Second, since the objector demands a grounding story concerning the appearance of fundamental causal activity among the proper parts of fundamental substances, the distributional properties at work in this response would need to be irreducibly *powerful* and capable of grounding irreducible scientific facts about the world.

Hence, adopting this first route involves ascribing *perfectly natural* distributional properties to the substantial whole—i.e., ones that distribute non-redundant causal powers over its proper sub-regions. Call these perfectly natural distributional properties: *power-distributions*. The instantiation of a particular power-distribution by a substance guarantees that the substance will have a certain distribution of causal powers among its proper sub-regions, whether biological (*power for gene transcription*), chemical (*being disposed to form covalent bonds*), physical (*power to repel like charges*), or perhaps psychological (power for intentional action). The important thing to point out here is that a non-redundant causal power's being located at a particular sub-region obtains *in virtue of* the substance instantiating a certain power-distribution.

Return again to our original example involving scientific experience: *the power for gene transcription* is instantiated by a DNA sequence, a proper part of a living organism. The sequence's having the *power for gene transcription* (what I am assuming to be a perfectly natural property) can be recast in terms of its higher-level substance, a cell, instantiating a distinctively *biological power-distribution* such as *having the power for gene transcription at* $r_1 \ldots r_n$ or perhaps *having the power for gene transcription at* r_1 *and having the power for neurotransmission at* r_4 (where $r_1 \ldots r_n$ and r_4 are disjoint proper sub-regions of the cell). The instantiation of each of the earlier biological power-distributions individually suffices to distribute the *power for gene transcription* to one of the cell's proper sub-regions, namely r_1. The thought is that by instantiating a power-distribution, a complex substance can have perfectly natural properties distributed over its proper sub-regions $r_1 \ldots r_n$ without having *substantial* or *fundamental* proper parts that occupy $r_1 \ldots r_n$ and instantiate such properties. This route is generalizable in that for any perfectly natural property F, appearances involving the proper part of a substance instantiating F can be accounted for in terms of the instantiation of a power-distribution by the substantial whole—namely, one whose instantiation suffices to locate F to one of the substance's proper sub-regions. It's *as-if* living organisms have proper parts that bear perfectly natural properties precisely because of their having power-distributions which assign such properties to their respective proper sub-regions.

9.1.2 Localized Powers

A second line of response to the objection at hand would be to agree that the exclusive bearer of the perfectly natural properties is the substantial whole, but assign a much greater explanatory role to the properties located at the whole's occupying sub-regions. Where this route differs from the first is in its denial of the claim that the region-indexed properties are instantiated solely in virtue of the whole's instantiating distributional properties.

McDaniel (2009) endorses this route as a unified solution to both the problem of temporal and spatial intrinsics.[4] Properties such as *being F*, on this view, are maximal fusions of exactly resembling tropes. Tropes, according to McDaniel, are intrinsically *regionalized* and thereby located at the various sub-regions that make up the underlying spatiotemporal structure of the substantial whole (are intrinsically *localized* in that they are defined in terms of the region at which they are located).[5] In contrast to the distributional route which analyzes spatially indexed properties in terms of disjunctions of distributional properties, this route assigns pride of place to the localized tropes themselves.[6] As a solution to the problem of spatial intrinsics, an extended simple is qualitatively heterogeneous in virtue of instantiating non-resembling localized tropes at distinct proper sub-regions. More precisely: *x* is *F-at-r* just in case *x* exemplifies an *F*-trope existing at *r*.

Here we must proceed with caution. In claiming that localized tropes are defined in terms of their occupying regions (what is commonly symbolized as *F-at-r*), proponents of this view do not mean to introduce an extra argument place to stand between localized tropes and their occupying regions (where F bears the *located-at* relation to a region of spacetime: *located-at(F,r)*). Localized tropes are not relations. They are, rather, *regionalized monadic properties* whose logical form, like that of distributional properties, involves a single argument place. As Ehring (1997) points out, building region-location into the nature of properties (or temporal-location in his case) does not, by itself, convert properties into relations.[7] If it did, then the appeal to localized tropes would, as is familiar, have the untoward consequence of turning all intrinsic properties into relations and hence *extrinsic*.[8] But just as the temporal part of a perduring spacetime worm can be time-indexed (or better, *temporalized*) without itself being a two-place relation that links the worm to a particular time, so too a localized trope can be region-indexed (or better, *regionalized*) without itself being a two-place relation that relates its bearer to a region.[9] In light of this, perhaps it would be better to symbolize localized tropes as F_r instead of *F-at-r* to avoid confusing them with relations to regions (where *r* is the region that enters into the real definition of *F*).

Again, the application of localized tropes to the objection against Substantial Priority is straightforward. This move allows the defender of Substantial Priority to attribute all of the fundamental joint-carving causal properties to the substance as a whole without relying on the machinery of distributional properties. It is in virtue of a substance instantiating a localized perfectly natural property that it's *as-if* a proper part that occupies one its sub-regions instantiates that property.

Consider, once again, our example of the *power for gene transcription*, a perfectly natural property that, by all appearances, is instantiated by a proper part of a living organism (a gene). This datum of scientific experience can be reconstructed in terms of the substantial whole possessing a fundamental causal property that is located at one of its occupying sub-regions. In the same way that an extended simple may instantiate a localized trope F at one of its proper sub-regions without a proper part at that region instantiating F, so too a substantial whole may instantiate a localized irreducible causal power P at one of its proper sub-regions without having a *substantial* proper part that occupies the sub-region where P is localized and that bears P. By invoking localized perfectly natural properties, the defender of Substantial Priority has a way of grounding scientific appearances.

9.1.3 Regionalized Instantiation

A third alternative would be to shift our focus from the perfectly natural properties themselves to the *having* of such properties, that is, indexing the *instantiation relation* (copula) to regions of space: x *is-at-r* F. This route has been labeled "spatial adverbialism" (McDaniel 2007b) and is, of course, the spatial analogue of the adverbialist solution to the problem of temporary intrinsics. On this view, the instantiation relation itself is region-indexed in that it is a three-place relation between an object, a property, and a region of spacetime; regions are built right into the copula itself. This route allows the friend of Substantial Priority to reconstruct science and common sense by the use of spatially indexed adverbs regarding a substance's being modified *F-ly* at one of its particular sub-regions. For instance, we might say that while it is, strictly speaking, false that the properties *being negatively charged* and *being positively charged* are instantiated by *substantial* proper parts of a HCl molecule (viz. chlorine and hydrogen, respectively), it is true however that "HCl is r_1-*ly negatively charged*" and "HCl is r_2-*ly positively charged*" (where r_1 and r_2 are disjoint regions).

9.1.4 Stuff-Occupants

Lastly, Markosian (2004) has proposed a solution to the problem of spatial intrinsics that turns on there being two irreducible kinds of entities that occupy regions of space. There are two fundamental kinds of region-fillers on this view: *objects* and *stuff*. Generally, objects or things are referred to using count nouns such as "tree," "mouse," and "gene" while the latter are picked out using mass nouns such as "wood," "steel," and "bronze." While stuff comes in portions or quantities, it is argued that objects have an intrinsic unity that makes them *individual* and hence *countable*.[10] Material objects such as trees, turnips, and tyrants are constituted by their portions of material stuff and are non-identical to such portions.

According to this response to the problem of spatial intrinsics, while an extended simple may be lacking proper parts entirely, the portion of stuff that constitutes the object may exhibit a complex mereological structure in that it decomposes into further sub-portions of stuff.[11] If so, even if we cannot directly pin the distinct intrinsic properties to the proper parts of the simple (as there are none), we can pin them directly to the sub-portions of stuff that constitute the simple. Markosian (2004: 406) puts it as follows:

> But I said that we can capture what is literally true in the intuitive claim that the statue has a right arm that is made of a different type of matter from the rest of it by talking about the arm-shaped sub-region of the region occupied by the statue, and the fact that the matter occupying this sub-region differs from the matter occupying the rest of the region occupied by the statue. Thus my reply to the statue objection committed me to saying that, at least in some cases, talk about matter, or *stuff*, is not reducible to talk about *things*. And I think it is clear that anyone who believes in the possibility of extended simples must also take a similar line.

Markosian's solution will find favor with those friends of Substantial Priority who are apt to endorse a mixed ontology of objects and stuff as well as the *constitution* relation that obtains between the two region-occupiers. On this approach, while no proper part *per se* of the substantial whole instantiates perfectly natural properties, we can say that the stuff that constitutes its parts are the bearers of fundamental causal powers. It is precisely because portions and sub-portions of stuff are not *proper parts* of substances (rather they constitute them) that they are capable of bearing perfectly natural properties *simpliciter*. As a result, it is not the substantial whole *itself* (i.e. qua entity that is non-identical to its stuff) that instantiates the perfectly natural properties that are thought to be distributed among its proper parts. Rather, such properties are pinned directly to the distinct sub-portions of its constituting material stuff.

One worry with this line of response is that it runs contrary to our initial claim that individual substances are the exclusive bearers of the perfectly natural properties (see §7.2). This is a steep price that I think the friend of Substantial Priority should avoid paying, if possible. Of course, in order to remain consistent with **No Fundamental Parthood** and Substantial Priority in general, a great deal of weight has to be placed on the *irreducibility* of constitution to the relation of composition. That is, a portion of stuff's constituting its object *cannot* be analyzed in mereological terms (even a partial mereological overlap between substantial stuff and a substantial whole would violate **No Fundamental**). The defender of Substantial Priority may find this burden too heavy to bear in so far as a mereological gloss on constitution is both natural and straightforward.[12] Others will remain undeterred given that constitution is best construed as either primitive (Markosian 2004) or as capable of being analyzed in *non-mereological* terms (Baker 2007: 161). Whether the relation is taken as primitive or analyzable in non-mereological terms, those congenial to constitutionalism will see the appeal to a mixed ontology of objects and stuff as no additional cost to the defender of Substantial Priority in responding to the foregoing objection from material inadequacy.

In adopting a mixed ontology of objects and stuff, this solution, in contrast to the earlier three, makes no reference to either individual occupants of regions or proper sub-regions occupied by the substantial whole in accounting for the distribution of perfectly natural properties among its proper parts. Rather, the fundamental causal properties that are distributed among the proper parts of a substance are instantiated by one of the *stuff-occupants* of those regions, occupants that lack the intrinsic unity and countability that constitute objects or individuals.[13]

We have, at this point, examined four different routes available to the defender of Substantial Priority in response to the objection from material inadequacy. All begin by granting the objector that the properties distributed among the proper parts of a substance (those that factor into "bottom-up" scientific explanations) are indeed *perfectly* natural. What unites the earlier responses is their common denial of the following principle that undergirds the objection at hand:

> **Property-Part Distribution:** If a composite substance has fundamental causal properties distributed among either its non-overlapping proper sub-regions or the stuff-occupants of those regions, then it has non-overlapping fundamental proper parts that occupy or are constituted by the stuff of those regions that instantiate the properties in question.

The first three responses to the charge of material inadequacy–power-distributions, localized tropes, regionalized instantiation–are alike in that they all attribute the fundamental causal properties directly to the substance *as a whole* yet go on to tell a further story as to *how* these elite joint-carving properties of the whole can be located at or distributed among its proper sub-regions. They are all specific versions of what Rob Koons (2014) calls "the Upward Power Migration account" where the fundamental causal properties of the parts migrate to the whole. The aforementioned routes are strong forms of the Upward Power Migration Account in so far as they maintain that all of the fundamental causal properties of the parts belong to the substantial whole (in so far I'm working on the assumption that only fundamental substances bear fundamental causal properties). The final appeal to a mixed ontology of objects and stuff predicates the perfectly natural properties directly to the sub-portions of stuff that constitute the substance, where portions (and sub-portions) of stuff and their occupying regions are numerically distinct.

In short, all of the earlier responses to the charge of material inadequacy are of the opinion that a substantial whole x or its constituting portion of stuff S can instantiate an irreducible causal power P at either (i) one of its sub-regions r or (ii) at one of its sub-portions of stuff s, without having a *substantial* proper part y either located at r or constituted by s such that y instantiates F.

9.1.5 Comparative Naturalness

There is, however, one last response to the objection from material inadequacy that I'd like to consider. Recall that the charge in question is that Substantial Priority is empirically inadequate due to its inability to reconstruct the phenomena of science and common sense. What's more, recall that we have been granting the objector the fact that the causal powers at work in bottom-up scientific explanations—such as the *power of gene transcription* in the original formulation of the objection—are indeed *perfectly* natural properties. This last route denies that such properties need be perfectly natural in order to play a causal and explanatory role in our best empirical theories.

For one, it is entirely consistent with Substantial Priority that the proper parts of substances instantiate *natural properties*, that is, causal powers that genuinely carve the causal structure of the world and factor into scientific explanations. The objection seems to harbor the following dilemma: either the causal powers of the proper parts of composite substances are not causally relevant in our best scientific theories or they are causally *fundamental*. But the dilemma is a false one. Why think that we ought to attribute perfect naturalness to the powers and dispositions at work among the parts of composite substances in order for such dispositions to carve the causal structure of the world? It seems like the only pressure to ascribe causal fundamentality or perfect naturalness to lower-level causal mechanisms (and hence metaphysical fundamentality to the bearers of such mechanisms) stems from the lure of Part-Priority and PM, in particular the thesis of *micro-causation* (MC).

Surely, the objector retorts, the lower-level causal mechanisms are perfectly natural, how could they *not* be given that mereological wholes are built up out of ontologically prior parts?

Given the grounding structure that characterizes mereological wholes on Part-Priority and PM, the worry would hit its mark. But of course the objector is not *given* Part-Priority and PM. If the objector wants to avoid begging the question against the proponent of Substantial Priority, then they need to offer some *independent* reason for thinking that the lower-level causal mechanisms at work in bottom-up explanations are fundamental or perfectly natural.

Recall that naturalness is commonly thought to be a degreed notion in that certain causal properties are *more natural* than others. But a causal power's failing to be perfectly natural in no way undermines its naturalness *per se*—i.e., its ability to play a causal and explanatory role in carving nature's joints (that is, just because they don't carve nature at her *fundamental* causal joints in no way means that they are not joint-carving at all). Now, it is certainly true that one often (always) finds properties such as *velocity*, *energy-mass*, and *charge* as topping the list of perfectly natural properties. And indeed this "*fundamental* conception of sparse properties," as Schaffer (2004: 92) calls it, is by far the predominant view among philosophers working closely with the notion of naturalness in the wake of Lewis (1986, 1999), most notably Sider (2005).[14] For Lewisian-inspired metaphysicians, the total class of *causally* fundamental properties—i.e., perfectly natural, and the class of *(micro) physically* fundamental properties (i.e., those in the domain of microphysics) are coextensional.

It is, however, difficult to succumb to the widespread temptation of locating the elite causal properties at the level of fundamental physics apart from a commitment to the *metaphysical* primacy of physics in the first place. Apart from endorsing PM, as does Lewis (1999:66) when he states "physics discovers which things and classes are the most elite of all," we are offered little reason to side with the presumption that all chains of naturalness terminate in the highly elite and metaphysically privileged properties of microphysics.[16]

Not all, however, share this penchant for the metaphysical fundamentality of physics when it comes to the causal properties that carve nature at its joints. John Hawthorne (2006: 205) states,

> Sider, like many of us, believes in some objective ranking of properties on a scale of naturalness, with perfectly natural properties at one end and utterly gerrymandered properties at another. But he also tacitly accepts another commitment—namely that a property's naturalness is given by its ease of definability in terms of fundamental microphysics. This is far from obvious.

Hawthorne goes on to contrast two fundamentally different views as to the naturalness ordering we find in the world, what he calls "austere physicalism" and "emergentism:"[16]

> Which are the natural properties? Even supposing that we think that everything supervenes on physics, the issue is not settled. For if we accept a natural property framework, we must choose between an austere physicalism on the one hand and what might be called an "emergentist" framework on the other . . . According to the austere physicalist, the perfectly natural properties will only be found at the

microphysical groundfloor, relative naturalness being a matter of definitional distance from the perfectly natural properties . . . The "emergentist" by contrast, believes that naturalness is not a matter of mere definitional distance from the microphysical groundfloor . . . Perhaps being a cat is far more natural than certain properties far more easily definable in Lewis's canonical language. On the emergentist conception of things, there is no algorithm available for calibrating naturalness in terms of a perfect microphysical language.

(2006: 206)

This conception of naturalness comports nicely with what Schaffer (2004: 92) calls "the *scientific* conception of sparse properties," which are "drawn from all the levels of nature—they are those involved in the scientific understanding of the world." At the very least, then, the question as to whether the causal powers at work in bottom-up scientific explanations need be *perfectly* natural is by no means independent of the question of fundamental mereology.[17]

But not only are we offered little reason to think that the causal properties possessed by the proper parts of substances are perfectly natural apart from the truth of Part-Priority and PM, the objector's own example in terms of DNA and its constituent genomic sequences acting as the primary causal agent in the growth and genetic adaptation of living organisms suggests otherwise.

There has been a great deal of work in developmental biology that supports the thesis that the living organism as a whole, together with its causal powers and dispositions, is the primary causal factor in activating and regulating gene expression and morphogenesis.[18] While genes are the fundamental units of life in the sense that they are the suppliers of the materials required for transcription and organismal development,

> the protein and cell machinery works to stimulate and control transcription and all the post-transcriptional modifications. This is what "plays" the genes . . . clearly, then, the expression of a gene (in the rather misleading jargon) will involve levels of activity that are determined by the system as a whole.[19]

Along similar lines, Noble (2006: 51) notes that while

> the genome is sometimes described as a program that directs the creation and behaviour of all other biological processes in an organism. But this is not a fact. It is a metaphor. It is also an unrealistic and unhelpful one.

All of the earlier reconstructions are intended to help the proponent of Substantial Priority assuage some of the untoward consequences of affirming **No Fundamental Parthood** with respect to fundamental intermediates.

Substantial Priority and Empirical Inadequacy

The strategies aim to reconstruct the appearances regarding both ordinary as well as scientific discourse concerning the causal powers and fundamentality of the proper parts of substances. My aim has been simply to show that *there are* such strategies, and that while some are more defensible than others, they nevertheless go some way toward dissolving the objection that Substantial Priority is in direct conflict with scientific appearances.

9.1.6 Scientific Appearances Once More

At this juncture, the objector from empirical inadequacy might press further:

> Alright, you've highlighted a few strategies to save the scientific and common sense phenomena, fair enough. I grant that there is at least *some* way to plausibly reconstruct its being *as-if* the proper parts of substances are substantial bearers of non-redundant causal properties. But in so far as Substantial Priority entails that statements like "Human beings have H$_2$O molecules among their substantial proper parts" and "A sodium atom is a substantial proper part of Sodium Chloride" are literally false in the case of substances and their proper parts (assuming that all the objects in question are substances), it is simply too radical a departure from what we know from science to be taken seriously.

By way of response, let's take the following datum as our target statement:

DATUM: Cells have genes as substantial proper parts.

The objector is correct in pointing out that if cells are fundamental substances then, strictly speaking, DATUM is false on Substantial Priority. Note that DATUM is false on Substantial Priority in precisely the same way that "(composite) genes encode (composite) proteins" is false on mereological nihilism (or eliminitivism), and "genes are non-instantaneous" is false on stage theory, and "genes survive the removal of introns in the splicing process" is false on mereological essentialism. All four of the aforementioned ontologies must engage in the project of reconstructing scientific appearances; Substantial Priority is not alone in this regard.

The mereological nihilist or elimintivist (van Inwagen 1990: 109) offers the following paraphrase in place of the empirical claim that "(composite) genes encode (composite) proteins": "there exist xs and ys such that the xs are arranged gene-wise, the ys are also arranged protein-wise, and the xs encode for the ys." The stage theorist (Sider 2006; Hawley 2006), a bit less clumsily, offers the following paraphrase in the place of "genes are non-instantaneous:" "there are distinct instantaneous gene-stages that are related by temporal counterpart relations." Finally, in the place of "genes survive the removal of introns in the splicing process" the mereological essentialist (Chisholm 1976: 99–103) holds that "there exist successions of numerically distinct, but appropriately related, genes with different proper parts throughout the splicing process."

First of all, why follow the objector in thinking that DATUM is a deliverance of science in the first place? If the earlier strategies for reconstruction cut any ice at all, then DATUM cannot simply be "read-off" of our knowledge of molecular biology. As stated, DATUM is a *philosophical* claim regarding the *ontological category* of one of the proper parts of a cellular whole. Questions of high-level categorial classification have traditionally fallen within the purview of metaphysics. While one's view concerning the composition, structure, and persistence of material objects ought to be informed and constrained by the content of our best empirical theories (see the Introduction), they do not "fall out" of such theories. Mereological nihilism, for example, is not directly refuted by the empirical claim that "genes encode proteins" precisely because the question of whether atoms arranged gene-wise compose a gene and whether atoms arranged protein-wise compose a protein is not straightforwardly empirical. This is to repeat the familiar maxim that metaphysics, in our case the question of the ontological category of the proper parts of substances in general, is underdetermined by the empirical data; molecular biology doesn't wear specific metaphysical commitments on its sleeve.[20]

If the earlier strategies for reconstructing scientific appearances carry any weight whatsoever, the evidence that would lead the objector (as well as any metaphysically inclined molecular biologists) to posit genes as *substantial* proper parts of cells can be adequately accounted for by the strategies that follow. Any one of the following reconstructions of DATUM would be available to the proponent of Substantial Priority (recall from §1.2.3.1 that the *causal profile* of x is the range of causal properties and powers x has in every world in which it exists):

Power-Distribution: For every power $p_1 \ldots p_n$ included among the causal profile of a gene, there is a power-distribution D (or class of power-distributions) that assigns $p_1 \ldots p_n$ to at least one proper sub-region of the cell C's occupying region R, and D is instantiated by C.

Localized Powers: For every power $p_1 \ldots p_n$ included in the causal profile of a gene, there are localized powers $f_1 \ldots f_n$ that are instantiated by a cell C located at region R, and $f_1 \ldots f_n$ exactly occupy at least one of R's proper sub-regions.[21]

Regionalized Instantiation: For every power $p_1 \ldots p_n$ included in the causal profile of a gene, there is a cell C located at region R such that for at least one proper sub-region r of R, C is r-ly $p_1 \ldots p_n$.

Stuff-Occupants: For every power $p_1 \ldots p_n$ included in the causal profile of a gene, there is a portion of stuff S located at region R such that S constitutes a cell C, and $p_1 \ldots p_n$ are instantiated by least one sub-portion s of S.

Comparative Naturalness: For every power $p_1 \ldots p_n$ included in the causal profile of a gene, $p_1 \ldots p_n$ are natural properties and there is at least one proper part y of a cell C such that y instantiates $p_1 \ldots p_n$.

With these reconstruction strategies in place, even if we *were* (contra my proposal earlier) to follow the objector's lead in taking DATUM as a deliverance of molecular biology, the defender of Substantial Priority (like the proponents of nihilism, stage theory, and mereological essentialism) might argue that while DATUM is strictly speaking false, it is nevertheless "correct" in so far as it satisfies the semantic standards for ordinary and scientific discourse. On this view, the *correctness* of ordinary and scientific assertions (in contrast to those uttered in the ontology room we might say) are insensitive to the truth of particular metaphysical positions in fundamental mereology.

To illustrate, we might say that the *correctness* of the common, everyday existence assertion "There are prime numbers" is insensitive to the truth of Platonism or nominalism in the philosophy of mathematics; we normally would not (should not) press the school-teacher in her maths lesson or the theoretical physicist in their mathematical modeling of the physical world for uttering such a statement. Yet when uttered in the ontology room as a distinctively metaphysical assertion, the *truth* of "There are prime numbers" is indeed sensitive to the truth of Platonism and nominalism; on nominalism, for instance, such a statement is false. The precise boundary separating correctness-conditions from truth-conditions is a difficult question in metasemantics that need not be settled here.[22] The underlying point here is that it may well be the case that various types of discourse and contexts are governed by different semantic standards. The defender of Substantial Priority might argue that even if DATUM were in fact part and parcel of our ordinary scientific discourse, such a statement is "correct" if and only if one of the foregoing strategies obtains in the world (i.e. **Power-Distribution, Localized Powers, Regionalized Instantiation, Stuff-Occupants,** and **Comparative Naturalness**), even if DATUM is not strictly true.[23]

9.1.7 A Lingering Worry

But a lingering worry remains. If the causal profile of a gene $p_1 \ldots p_n$ is located within the boundaries of the cell, whether the bearer of this profile be the substantial whole itself, a sub-portion of its constituting stuff, or one of its proper parts, why not think that *there is*, in fact, a gene qua fundamental substance within the boundaries of the cell? All of the foregoing reconstructions assume that the accompanying necessary properties and dispositions of a substance o can be instantiated in a sub-region without a substance o being in that sub-region.[24] But is this not absurd?

Well, it depends. If you think that being a particular substantial kind of entity K is nothing more than possessing all the properties that particular Ks have in every world in which they exist, then it is absurd indeed to think that a region can contain $p_1 \ldots p_n$ without containing a substance of kind K; being a member of substantial kind K *just is* having $p_1 \ldots p_n$! We have examined this package of views in detail in Chapter 1 under the guise of modal essentialism (in particular ME1 and ME2), the theses that x is essentially Φ if and only if it is necessarily the case that if x exists then it is Φ (ME1), and that the essence of x is identical to the sum or collection of x's essential properties (ME2). There, I offered the now familiar line that the mere possession of properties satisfying Φ is not sufficient to capture x's fundamental identity. There must be something more, then, to being a tiger than having the properties that accompany individual tigers in every world in which they exist. As was pointed out, the "something more" is being something whose fundamental nature (as stated by its real definition) involves reference to the kind *tiger*. While the *Kind-Power Connection* (see Chapter 1, §2.3.1) requires that $\Box(Kx \rightarrow \Phi x)$, the denial of ME2 entails that the converse $\Box(\Phi x \rightarrow Kx)$ does not hold.

In addition, I argued that fundamental natures are *irreducible* to properties *per se* in that if a substance's nature were reducible to mere collections of powers and properties we would be left without an explanation as to why such powers and properties systematically cluster to form an integral unity and not a mere accidental grouping of features (recall CLUSTER). Without appealing to gold's being an irreducible *kind* of substance, for example, one is hard pressed to explain what grounds the uniform and systematic possession of the properties of *being malleable* and *having high luster* by distinct items of gold.

But we have seen reason to think that both tenets of modal essentialism are ill-suited to capture the modal structure of the world. If we resist the temptation to identify a thing's essence or kind with the sum of properties that it modally requires for its existence, as I think we should, then there is no absurdity in claiming that the causal profile of a gene can be instantiated within the boundaries of a cell and yet those boundaries fail to contain an object whose fundamental identity (as stated by its real definition) involves reference to the substantial kind *gene*.

As noted by Toner (2007) in his defense of a view that is similar to Substantial Priority, the particular machinery required to make sense of such a claim is already present in the literature on material constitution and discussed in §5.1.2.[26] Recall that the defender of spatiotemporal coincidence maintains that while both the statue and the lump are non-identical, their qualitative profiles are nevertheless empirically indistinguishable during their time of spatiotemporal overlap. But while the lump of bronze and the statue are *qualitative* duplicates at the time of overlap, they are not *classificatory* duplicates in that one is a member of the kind *lump of bronze* and the other is a member of the kind *statue* given their distinct persistence conditions. Here we have exact qualitative resemblance and yet what appears to be a difference in classificatory kind-membership.

As was noted in §5.1.2., Michael Rea (2000a) proposes a solution that distinguishes between two fundamental ways of satisfying a sortal or kind:

> Thus, proponents of the standard account might hold that there are two ways of satisfying a sortal. They might say that an object satisfies a sortal in the *classificatory way* just in case that sortal gives the metaphysically best answer to the "What is it?" question for that object, and an object satisfies a sortal in the *nominal way* just in case the object exemplifies the distinctive qualitative features of those things that satisfy the sortal in the classificatory way.
>
> (Rea 2000a: 172)

At the heart of the distinction between satisfying a substantial kind (sortal) in a *classificatory* versus a *nominal* way is that the latter involves possessing all of the properties that accompany entities whose fundamental nature (as stated by their real definition) involves reference to the substantial kind in question. Note that this route entails that the instantiation of the necessary properties that characterize the members of a particular substantial kind is not sufficient *to be* a classificatory member of that substantial kind (i.e., a substantial member of that substantial kind), "Having one's matter arranged in such a way as to exemplify the distinctive qualitative features of the members of a kind is not sufficient."[26]

We have seen that Rea's own solution to the problem of material constitution involves identifying the statue and lump of bronze, arguing that the proponent of coincidence mistakenly assumes that a difference in kind-membership between the statue and the lump of bronze entails a difference in *classificatory* kind-membership. It is possible to be a *K* nominally without being a *K* in the classificatory sense (although the converse does not hold as we will see). By Rea's lights, there is a *single* material object occupying the region in question, albeit one that satisfies the kind *statue* in a classificatory way and one that satisfies the kind *lump of bronze* in a nominal way given its possessing all of the qualitative properties that characterize things that belong to the kind *lump of bronze* in the classificatory way. Since the real definition of the object in question is best picked out by the kind *statue*, it inherits the persistence conditions of the members of the kind *statue*. Rea (2000a: 169) notes,

> I ... deny that in saying that there is a lump of bronze in the region we are committed to the claim that there is something in the region that has the essential properties associated with the kind *lump of bronze*.

In addition to the literature on material constitution, just about all of the predominant species concepts at play in the philosophy of biology—biological, ecological, cladistic, etc.—are committed *in principle* to the idea of sameness of qualitative properties without sameness of biological classification. Since all of the earlier species concepts characterize biological species as purely relational and extrinsic, whether or not two members of a species are intrinsic qualitative duplicates is irrelevant to whether or not they belong to the same biological species. Samir Okasha (2002: 201), for instance, maintains that the purely relational nature of biological species (whether determined by interbreeding, occupying a particular ecological niche, or being a member of a segment of the genealogical nexus, respectively) entails the denial of the principle that sameness of qualitative properties equals sameness of species-membership: "Two molecule-for-molecule identical organisms could in principle be members of different species, on all of these species concepts." Sober (1993: 148) makes the very same point, albeit in terms of life forms that (hypothetically) originated independently of life on earth (and thus independently of the global genealogical nexus according to cladism):

> [I]f we discovered that other planets possess life forms that arose independently of life on earth, those alien organisms would be placed into new species, *regardless of how closely they resembled terrestrial forms*. Martian tigers would not be tigers, even if they were striped and carnivorous. Similarities and differences among organisms are *evidence* about whether they are conspecific, but a species is not defined by a set of traits.[27]

If we apply this machinery to our example of a gene within the boundaries of a cell, we might say that if the substantial kind *gene* enters into the real definition of an object o (where, as per §1.2.3, *gene* is a constitutive predicable of o), then o satisfies the substantial kind *gene* in a classificatory way and is what we might call a *classifiable gene*. As per the *Kind-Power Connection* espoused in Chapter 1, an object's belonging to the substantial kind *gene* in a classificatory sense *necessitates* its having a particular range of causal properties and dispositions; there is, in other words, a direct explanatory relation linking its fundamental substance nature with its characteristic operations as specified by $p_1 \ldots p_n$. Classifiable genes, *in virtue of what they are*, are disposed to behave in a particular manner in every world in which they exist.

Alternatively, if the substantial kind *gene* fails to enter into the real definition of o (i.e., does not answer the "What is it fundamentally?" question for o) yet o is characterized by the properties included in $p_1 \ldots p_n$ (among others), then o satisfies the substantial kind *gene* in a nominal way and is what we might call a *nominal gene*, an instance of the substantial kind *gene* "in name only."[28] A nominal gene's instantiating $p_1 \ldots p_n$ is not a consequence of what it is fundamentally. While nominal genes are qualitatively similar enough to classifiable genes to be called "genes," they nevertheless lack the relevant explanatory connection between *what* they are fundamentally and their possessing $p_1 \ldots p_n$ to be properly classified as instances of the substantial kind *gene*.

We can illustrate the notion of a nominal gene within the boundaries of a cell in terms of the localized powers strategy earlier. On this route, $p_1 \ldots p_n$ are localized tropes that are instantiated by the cell and occupy at least one of the cell's proper sub-regions, call it r.[29] Since the powers that make up the causal profile of a gene are integral to cellular functioning, it is plausible to think that the region r which hosts $p_1 \ldots p_n$ is occupied by a proper part y of the cell.[30] We can refer to the proper part (y) which occupies the region where $p_1 \ldots p_n$ are located as a "gene" in so far as it is qualitatively similar to a classifiable gene (in the same way that we can refer to the statue of Goliath as a "lump of bronze" in so far as it is qualitatively indiscernible from a classifiable lump of bronze).

Consequently, while DICTUM is strictly speaking false in that classifiable genes are not proper parts of cells (assuming that it is part of the essence of classifiable genes and classifiable cells to belong to the category of *substance* if they exist), it is true that cells have nominal genes as parts at some level of decomposition. Scientific explanations in molecular biology that appeal to the causal powers of genes are entirely compatible with Substantial Priority, in so far as we don't build into such explanations the *metaphysical* assumption that the irreducible causal work is being done by *substantial*, classifiable genes that are proper parts of the cell.[31] It is open to the defender of Substantial Priority to say that a cell can undergo gene regulation in virtue of having a nominal gene as a proper part, or perhaps, in virtue of being *nominally gened-at-r_1*, *nominally-gened-at-r_2*, etc (where r_1 and r_2 are distinct regions of spacetime).[32] And, one might argue, statements in molecular biology that apparently involve quantification over classifiable genes can instead be reformulated into statements that quantify over nominal genes only.

Consequently, in light of the earlier strategies available to the proponent of Substantial Priority, I take the view to withstand the objection of empirical inadequacy; science in no way renders Substantial Priority empirically defective. While some of the foregoing ways to save the scientific phenomena are more or less plausible than others, they go some way, at the very least, toward offering a story as to why it's *as-if* the causal activity of the parts of substances is fundamental assuming the truth of Substantial Priority.

Notes

1. For discussion see Simons (2004), Zimmerman (1996b), and Schaffer (2007a). The debate has centered around both the maximally small (extended fundamental particles with no proper parts) and the maximally large (monistic ontologies which say the cosmos has no proper parts).

2. Parson (2004) argues that distributional properties cannot be reduced to non-distributional properties as follows: suppose gunk is metaphysically possible. If so, suppose we attribute a distributional property P to a hunk of gunk x. On this scenario, it is metaphysically possible that every proper part of x instantiates a distributional property such that there is no non-distributional reductive base for which P to be defined in terms of. Since there is a possible world where there is no non-distributional reductive base for distributional properties, then the latter cannot be reduced to or be "nothing over and above" the former.
3. In his own words, Parsons notes (albeit with respect to temporally indexed properties): "To generalize: wherever we have a temporally indexed property of being X-at-t, we have a number of corresponding permanent distributional properties: the X-ness distributions. X-at-t is a disjunction of some of those X-ness distributions, the ones that are compatible with being X-at-t."
4. McDaniel follows Ehring (1997) here.
5. This of course implies that all particularized properties have a spatiotemporal location, a thesis some may not be ready to accept.
6. This is not to say that this route excludes the machinery of distributional properties tout court. As McDaniel points out, the proponent of this route may define distributional properties as sums of localized tropes.
7. Consider the similarity here between McDaniel's localized tropes with what Davidson (2003) calls "relational properties." Davidson offers the following as examples of relational properties *being taller than Tom* or *being meaner than Leroy* and goes on to state: "Relational properties aren't relations. They're possessed by a single individual in the same sort of way as non-relational properties like *being blue* are possessed. They don't 'hold between' individuals in the way that relations do; rather, they're exemplified by a single individual—they're monadic."
8. Well, not all intrinsic properties would turn out intrinsic on this line. One might think that there are *relational intrinsic* properties such as *having a proper part that is F*.
9. Again, see Ehring (1997) for more on this line.
10. See Laycock (2006: 95) and Lowe (1998: Chapter 3) for more on the connection between individuality, unity, and countability. Consider Laycock: "Since the concept of an object is the concept of a unit or a unity, the concept of a physical object is the concept of a physical or spatiotemporal unity; and the loss of a physical object's unity is thus the loss of its physical objecthood. To possess a physical unity is precisely to possess a physical form or spatiotemporal structure ('however scattered or diffused,' as Quine might say); hence formlessness is not to be distinguished from disunity." Also, Lowe (1998: 77), "It is the formlessness of parts of matter which deprives them of individuality and makes them uncountable as such."
11. Whether such decomposition is endless will, of course, depend on whether material stuff is gunky or non-gunky.
12. See in particular Sider (2002), Zimmerman (2002).
13. This is not to say that all natural properties per se must be attributed to the stuff that constitutes the proper parts of substance and the not the proper parts themselves. Here we are only dealing with the fundamental or perfectly natural properties.
14. See also Sider (2012). For a nice discussion on the distinction between the fundamental and scientific conception of sparse (natural) properties see Schaffer (2004).
15. See also Lewis (1986: 60–61): "Physics has its short list of 'fundamental physical properties': the charges and masses of particles, also their so called 'spins'

and 'colours' and 'flavours,' and maybe a few more that have yet to be discovered . . . What physics has undertaken, whether or not ours is a world where the undertaking will succeed, is an inventory of the sparse properties of this-worldly things."
16. Note the qualifier "austere" in Hawthorne's characterization of a framework which locates the perfectly natural properties at the microphysical groundfloor of reality. As I argued in Chapter 4, a "non-austere" physicalism is a variety of physicalism nonetheless.
17. The recent work by Anjum and Mumford (2011) on the metaphysics of causation has been a welcome corrective to the tacit commitment to the ontological primacy of physics in the literature on causation. They take causation in the biological domain as their base for developing a theory of causation that accords with total science. They state, "To take all our examples from physics, or disproportionately so, is thus to prejudge as to the sole importance of physics to causation. Causation in psychology or sociology may be just as important to us and their neglect seems justified only if physical fundamentalism [the claim that all other sciences are ultimately reducible to physics] is true. We have no strong reason yet to believe that it is. In fact, its the very issue in question."
18. As a sample, consider Moss (2003: 3) on the widespread causal primacy ascribed to genes in contemporary molecular biology (which he rigorously argues against), "as an entity, its existence is now widely believed to be somehow temporally, ontologically, and causally antecedent to organismic becoming. The gene (or genetic program) envisaged as context-independent information for how to make an organism appears to have become the new heir to the mainstream of western metaphysics." For defenses of the centrality of the biological organism in morphogenesis see Moss (2003), Wilson (2005), and Noble (2006).
19. Noble (2006: 45).
20. For an excellent treatment of this see French (1998). Note that this is not to say that empirical data cannot serve as either a potential defeater or as positive warrant in favor of a metaphysical theory. Rather, the claim here is that empirical considerations cannot *force* one to either endorse or abandon a particular metaphysical model; there is no one model that is consistent with the observable data. In fact, I have tried to show in Chapter 4 that there are good empirical considerations which suggest that Part-Priority and PM fail to adequately capture portions the mereological structure we find in the world. I also noted that there are empirical reasons that point in the direction of (albeit not conclusively) a Substantial Priority fundamental mereology.
21. Where $(p_1 \ldots p_n = f_1 \ldots f_n)$.
22. For an interesting discussion here on the difference between correctness and truth see Chalmers (2009).
23. For a similar line see van Inwagen (1990) and Horgan & Potrč (2000).
24. To say that o is not the possessor of the causal profile is not to say that it has no possessor at all.
25. In what follows I am heavily indebted to Toner's (2007) application of the following nominal/classificatory kind distinction to the fundamentality of substances. For the distinction at work in material constitution see Burke (1994a and 1994b) and Rea (2000a) in particular.
26. See Rea (2000b). Along the same lines, consider Rheins (2011: 257), "Yet the realist claims that what makes all instances of gold really gold is not that they satisfy the formula, 'soft, shiny, yellow metal,' but rather that the atoms of such samples share the common essential property of having atomic number 79. If, say, pyrite has all other outward properties in common with

real gold, but its atomic or molecular microstructure is different, then realists (at least the modern Putnamian sort) deny that it is real gold."
27. Emphasis mine.
28. Compare with van Inwagen's (1990: 112) notion of a "virtual object" and a "virtual part." Although I, in contrast to van Inwagen, think that nominal objects exist.
29. Of course, there will be a vast number of the cell's sub-regions that each host a class of tropes that resemble $p_1 \ldots p_n$.
30. If not every occupiable sub-region of a substance corresponds to a proper part of that substance (rejection of DAUP), then this route offers a nice way to distinguish between those occupiable sub-regions of a substance that do in fact host a proper part and those that do not. Philosopher of biology William Bechtel (2007) puts it as follows: "the component parts of a mechanism are the entities that perform the operations which together realize the phenomena of interest. A structure within the mechanism may be well delineated (it has boundaries, continues to exist over time, is differentiated from the things around it, etc.). However, if it does not perform an operation that contributes to the realization of the phenomena, it is not a working part of that mechanism. For example, while the gyri and sulei of the brain are well delineated, they are not working parts of the brain but byproducts of the way brains fold to conserve the length of axons."
31. Here again I am indebted to Toner (2007) for this insight.
32. Here I illustrate scientific explanations involving the causal powers of genes in terms of the localized powers strategy. However, the approach can be easily generalized to any of the earlier reconstruction strategies as well as any higher-level substantial whole.

Conclusion

My general aim in this book has been to explore the topic of fundamental mereology, the question of how mereological and metaphysical structure come together in the domain of concrete material beings. In particular, I've taken up the task of defending a view I call Substantial Priority, a heretofore widely neglected fundamental mereology that assigns metaphysical fundamentality to ordinary, intermediate composite objects in the category of *substance*. Against the contemporary tide that ascribes fundamentality exclusively to either the maximally small (microphysics) or the maximally large (the cosmos), I've argued for the tenability of including within the domain of fundamental beings at least some intermediate, composite objects, living organisms and human persons being prime candidates.

On Substantial Priority, it is not the case that all grounding chains run *through* ordinary, intermediate objects without ever terminating *in* them. Rather, in good-old Aristotelian fashion, at least some of the fundamental substances reside among the ordinary and familiar. Yet not *all* intermediate composites are metaphysically elite and carve nature at its most fundamental joints in this sense (and are what I've called "grounding wholes"); some ordinary composites are aggregates (what I've called "grounded wholes"), derivative or non-fundamental objects that are totally grounded in their proper parts and the basic arrangements between them (artifacts, heaps, and the like). Substantial Priority carves out space for a mixed view which includes among the class of fundamental substances certain intermediate composites (living organisms and human persons) as well as the micro-entities that compose all composite objects save the intermediate substances.

I've argued that Substantial Priority is a fundamental mereology that is worthy of consideration by those with neo-Aristotelian sympathies. Let's rehearse the overall costs and benefits of Substantial Priority. To start, Substantial Priority preserves many of our pre-philosophical beliefs about material objects commended by empirical theory and common sense. First, Substantial Priority retains the existence of both living and non-living composite material objects like molecules, biological organisms, statues, lumps of bronze, human persons, heads, and brains (etc.); the various puzzles in material objects (as well as the Thinking Parts Argument in personal ontology) are not solved at the expense of the existence of such objects (contra nihilism, eliminativism, and the way of sparse ontology). Second, the view also retains our intuitive notion of identity as transitive and absolute (contra versions of relative identity). Third, ordinary composite substances like cats and human persons persist through change and survive the loss or replacement of some of their proper parts (contra mereological essentialism). Fourth, the view (at least on its monistic variant) has the resources to retain our commonsense belief that two distinct material objects of different kinds cannot exist in the same place at the same time (contra constitutionalism). Fifth, Substantial Priority offers principled grounds for preserving the deeply intuitive notions that (i) there is exactly one substance-candidate within the boundaries of any ordinary composite substance (Problem of the Many), and (ii) that (for materialists) nothing that is not strictly me thinks my thoughts. Lastly, the view preserves the belief that ordinary composite substances are non-redundant contributors to the causal dynamics at work in the world.

Some will argue here that Substantial Priority incurs a significant cost in the category of intuitive fit in its maintaining that composite substances fail to have other substances as proper parts (**No Fundamental Parthood**). I've already noted in §4.2.3. and §9.1.6. why I'm less optimistic about the prospects of common sense registering such a heavyweight metaphysical beliefs about the *ontological category* to which the proper parts of substances belong (at least on its own). But even if we did grant that this is a significant intuitive strike against Substantial Priority, it does not decisively settle the score against the view (in precisely the same way that failure to fit with pre-philosophical beliefs about strict numerical identity through time does not conclusively refute stage theory or mereological essentialism).

In addition to preserving many of our pre-philosophical beliefs about the existence, identity, and causal activity of ordinary material objects, Substantial Priority is theoretically fruitful. In Chapters 5 and 6 I argued that Substantial Priority affords a unified solution to a host of puzzles in mereological metaphysics. The view has broad explanatory scope as its basic machinery lends a theoretically simple and elegant solution to a range of conundrums such as Tib and Tibbles, Goliath and Lumpl, the Vagueness Argument (against restricted composition), the Problem of the Many, and Causal Overdetermination. And even despite the perceived cost of applying **No Fundamental Parthood** to ordinary composite substances, Substantial Priority has significant explanatory power over many rival views in the metaphysics of material objects.

Many will no doubt note that a significant cost of Substantial Priority in the area of theoretical utility is that it is shot-through with heavyweight metaphysical commitments concerning the nature and structure of grounding, metaphysical fundamentality, non-redundant causal properties, the denial of Part-Priority as a global fundamental mereology, and the view that fundamental composite beings have determinate mereological boundaries. Indeed, the staunch defender of neo-Humeanism will find little in Substantial Priority worthy of praise. But for neo-Aristotelians who already incline toward a robust fundamental ontology that includes essence, grounding, fundamentality, substance, and causal powers, Substantial Priority offers a fruitful neo-Aristotelian mereology that deserves a place at the table.

Lastly, Substantial Priority is empirically adequate with respect to *total* science. On the one hand, I have argued that the view is not straightforwardly in tension with what we know from our best empirical theories. Empirical inquiry on its own cannot tell us, for instance, that cells have genes as *substantial* or *fundamental* proper parts (in precisely the same sense that Priority Monism cannot be cast aside by the claim that empirical theory alone tells us that some sub-cosmic composites are fundamental in their own right). Arguably, the question of the ontological category of the proper parts of composite substances falls within the purview of fundamental metaphysics.

Nevertheless, one might think that the charge of empirical inadequacy hits its mark in that the view cannot save the scientific appearances that the causal properties of the proper parts of fundamental composites (e.g., hydrogen atoms, electrons, genes) appear to play a fundamental causal and explanatory role in our best empirical theories. By way of response, in Chapter 9 I outlined five different strategies that aim to reconstruct scientific appearances (Power-Distributions, Localized Powers, Regionalized Instantiation, Stuff-Occupants, and Comparative Naturalness); if one or more of these strategies is successful in reconstructing scientific appearances, then Substantial Priority remains empirically adequate. If nihilism/eliminitivism, stage-theory, and mereological essentialism can survive the charge of empirical inadequacy by offering reconstruction strategies, so too can Substantial Priority (see §9.6). Not only is Substantial Priority empirically adequate, I have argued that the view is scientifically serious in that it accords with what are plausible instances of Whole-Priority structure in quantum, chemical, and biological systems.

All in all, Substantial Priority is defensible and is, by standard measures for evaluating metaphysical models, worth taking seriously. It deserves a place at the table as a viable yet under appreciated fundamental mereology.

Bibliography

Adams, Robert. (1979). "Primitive Thisness and Primitive Identity." *Journal of Philosophy* 76, pp. 5–26.
Adams, Robert. (1994). *Leibniz: Determinist, Theist, Idealist*. Oxford: Oxford University Press.
Aquinas, Thomas. (1947). *Summa Theologica*. Trans. by Fathers of the English Dominican Province, in three volumes. New York: Benziger Bros.
Aquinas, Thomas. (1949). *On Spiritual Creatures*. Trans. and Eds. Mary C. Fitzpatrick and John J. Wellmuth. Mediaeval Philosophical Texts in Translation, 5. Milwaukee: Marquette University Press.
Aquinas, Thomas. (1975). *Summa Contra Gentiles*. Trans. and Ed. A. C. Pegis. Notre Dame: University of Notre Dame Press.
Aquinas, Thomas. (1984). *Questions on the Soul (De anima.)*. Trans. James H. Robb. Milwaukee: Marquette University Press.
Aquinas, Thomas. (1999). *Commentary on Aristotle's De anima*. Trans. Robert C. Pasnau. New Haven: Yale University Press.
Aristotle. (1984a). "On the Soul." In Jonathan Barnes (Ed.), *The Complete Works of Aristotle*. Vol. 1. Princeton: Princeton University Press.
Aristotle. (1984b). "Metaphysics." In Jonathan Barnes (Ed.), *The Complete Works of Aristotle*. Vol. 2. Princeton: Princeton University Press.
Arlig, Andrew. (2015). "Medieval Mereology." In Edward N. Zalta (Ed.), *The Stanford Encyclopedia of Philosophy* (Fall 2015 Edition), URL = <https://plato.stanford.edu/archives/fall2015/entries/mereology-medieval/>.
Armstrong, David. (1978). *A Theory of Universals*, volume 2 of *Universals and Scientific Realism*. Cambridge: Cambridge University Press.
Armstrong, David. (1983). *What Is a Law of Nature?* Cambridge: Cambridge University Press.
Armstrong, David. (1997). *A World of States of Affairs*. Cambridge: Cambridge University Press.
Audi, Paul. (2012). "A Clarification and Defense of the Notion of Grounding." In Fabrice Correia and Benjamin Schnieder (Eds.), *Metaphysical Grounding: Understanding the Structure of Reality*. Cambridge, UK: Cambridge University Press.
Bailey, Andrew. (2014). "You Needn't Be Simple." *Philosophical Papers* 43 (2), pp. 145–160.
Bailey, Andrew. (2015). "The Priority Principle." *Journal of the American Philosophical Association* 1 (1), pp. 163–174.
Bailey, Andrew. (2016). "Composition and the Cases." *Inquiry* 59 (5), pp. 453–470.
Baker, Lynne Rudder. (2002). "Precis of Persons and Bodies." *Philosophy and Phenomenological Research* 64, pp. 593–98.

Baker, Lynne Rudder. (2007). *The Metaphysics of Everyday Life*. Cambridge: Cambridge University Press.
Barnes, Elizabeth. Forthcoming. "Symmetric Dependence." In Ricki Bliss and Graham Priest (Eds.), *Reality and Its Structure*. Oxford: Oxford University Press.
Barnett, David. (2008). "The Simplicity Intuition and Its Hidden Influence on Philosophy of Mind." *Noûs* 42 (2), pp. 308–335.
Barnett, David. (2010). "You Are Simple." In Robert C. Koons and George Bealer (Eds.), *The Waning of Materialism* (pp. 161–174). Oxford University Press.
Baxter, Donald. (1988). "Identity in the Loose and Popular Sense." *Mind* 97, pp. 575–82.
Bechtel, William. (2007). "Reducing Psychology While Maintaining its Autonomy via Mechanistic Explanation." In Maurice Schouten and Huib Looren de Jong (Eds.), *The Matter of the Mind: Philosophical Essays on Psychology, Neuroscience and Reduction* (pp. 172–198). Oxford: Basil Blackwell.
Bennett, Karen. (2004). "Spatio-Temporal Coincidence and the Grounding Problem." *Philosophical Studies* 118 (3), pp. 339–371.
Bennett, Karen. (2011). "Construction Area (No Hardhat Required)." *Philosophical Studies* 154, pp. 79–104.
Bennett, Karen. (2017). *Making Things Up*. Oxford: Oxford University Press.
Bird, Alexander. (1998). *Philosophy of Science*. Montreal: McGill-Queen's University Press.
Bird, Alexander. (2007). *Nature's Metaphysics: Laws and Properties*. New York: Oxford University Press.
Bird, Alexander. (2012). "Are Any Kinds Ontologically Fundamental?" In Tuomas Tahko (Ed.), *Contemporary Aristotelian Metaphysics* (pp. 94–104). New York: Cambridge University Press.
Bishop, Robert. (2005). "Patching Physics and Chemistry Together." *Philosophy of Science* 72, pp. 710–722.
Bishop, John. (2003). "Prospects for a Naturalist Libertarianism: O'Connor's Persons and Causes." *Philosophy and Phenomenological Research* 66(1), pp. 228–43.
Block, Ned. (1978). "Troubles with Functionalism." In Ned Block (Ed.), *Readings in Philosophy of Psychology 1980* (pp. 268–305). Cambridge: Harvard University Press.
Bobik, Joseph. (1988). *Aquinas on Being and Essence: A Translation and Interpretation*. Notre Dame, IN: University of Notre Dame Press.
Bohn, Duenger Einar. (2009). "Must There be a Top Level?" *The Philosophical Quarterly* 59 (235), pp. 193–201.
Boyd, Richard. (1999). "Homeostasis, Species, and Higher Tax." In Robert Wilson (Ed.), *Species: New Interdisciplinary Essays* (pp. 141–185.). Cambridge: Cambridge University Press.
Boyle, Robert. (1991). *Selected Philosophical Papers of Robert Boyle*. Trans. M. A. Stewart. Indianapolis: Hackett Publishing Company.
Bricker, P. (2006). "The Relation Between the General and the Particular: Entailment vs. Supervenience." In Dean Zimmerman (Ed.), *Oxford Studies in Metaphysics*, Vol. 2 (pp. 251–287). Oxford: Oxford University Press.
Broackes, Justin. (2006). "Substance." *Proceedings of the Aristotelian Society*, pp. 131–166.
Brower, Jeffrey. (2004). "Abelard on the Trinity." In Jeffrey E. Brower and Kevin Guilfoy (Eds.), *The Cambridge Companion to Abelard* (pp. 223–257). Cambridge University Press."
Brower, Jeffrey. (2010). "Aristotelian Endurantism: A New Solution to the Problem of Temporary Intrinsics." *Mind* 119 (476), pp. 883–905.

Brower, Jeffrey. (2014). *Aquinas's Ontology of the Material World*. Oxford: Oxford University Press.
Brown, Christopher M. (2005). *Aquinas and the Ship of Theseus: Solving Puzzles about Material Objects*. New York: Continuum.
Buridan, John. "Quaestiones in Aristotelis De anima liber tertius." In John Zupko (Ed.), "John Buridan's Philosophy of Mind: An Edition and Translation of Book III of his 'Questions on Aristotle's De Anima' (Third Redaction)" (Ph.D. dissertation, Cornell University, 1989).
Burke, Michael. (1994a). "Preserving the Principle of One Object to a Place: A Novel Account of the Relations among Objects, Sorts, Sortals, and Persistence Conditions." In Michael Rea (Ed.), *Material Constitution: A Reader* (pp. 236–273.). Lanham: Rowman & Littlefield.
Burke, Michael. (1994b). "Dion and Theon: An Essentialist Solution to an Ancient Puzzle." *Journal of Philosophy* 91, pp. 129–139.
Butler, Jospeh. (1726). *Fifteen Sermons Preached at the Rolls Chapel*. London: J. and J. Knapton.
Cameron, Ross. (2008). "Turtles All the Way Down: Regress, Priority and Fundamentality." *The Philosophical Quarterly* 58 (230), pp. 1–14.
Cameron, Ross. (2010a). "From Humean Truthmaker Theory to Priority Monism." *Nous* 44 (1), pp. 178–198.
Cameron, Ross. (2010b). "Quantification, Naturalness and Ontology." In Allan Hazlett (Ed.), *New Waves in Metaphysics*. Basingstoke: Palgrave Macmillan.
Campbell, Neil A. (1996). *Biology*, 4th edition., Benjamin/Cummings Publishing Company.
Cartwright, Nancy. (1992). "Aristotelian Natures and the Modern Experimental Method." In John Earman (Ed.), *Inference, Explanation, and Other Frustrations: Essays in the Philosophy of Science*. Berkeley: University of California Press.
Chalmers, David. (2009). "Ontological Anti-Realism." In David J. Chalmers, David Manley, and Ryan Wasserman (Eds.), *Metametaphysics: New Essays on the Foundations of Ontology* (pp. 77–129). Oxford: Oxford University Press.
Chisholm, Roderick. (1976). *Person and Object*. London: George Allen and Unwin Ltd.
Chisholm, Roderick. (1989). *On Metaphysics*. Minneapolis: University of Minnesota Press.
Chisholm, Roderick. (1991). "On the Simplicity of the Soul." *Philosophical Perspectives* 5, pp. 167–181.
Clayton, Phillip. (2004). *Mind and Emergence: From Quantum to Consciousness*. New York: Oxford University Press.
Correia, Fabrice. (2005). *Existential Dependence and Cognate Notions*. Munich: Philosophia Verlag.
Correia, Fabrice. (2008). "Ontological Dependence." *Philosophy Compass* 3 (5), pp. 1013–1032.
Correia, Fabrice. (2010). "Grounding and Truth-Functions." *Logique et Analyse* 53 (211), pp. 251–279.
Correia, Fabrice and Benjamin Schieder (Eds). (2012). *Metaphysical Grounding: Understanding the Structure of Reality*. Cambridge: Cambridge University Press.
Corry, Richard. (2012). "Emerging from the Causal Drain." *Philosophical Studies* 160, pp. 1–19.
Cover, J. A. and John (O'Leary) Hawthorne. (1996). "Free Agency and Materialism." In Jeff Jordan and Daniel Howard-Snyder (Eds.), *Faith, Freedom, and Rationality* (pp. 47–71). Lanham, Md: Rowman & Littlefield.
Cowling, Sam. (2013). "The Modal View of Essence." *Canadian Journal of Philosophy* 43 (2), pp. 248–266.

Daintith, John. (2000). *The Oxford Dictionary of Physics*, 4th ed. Oxford: Oxford University Press.
Dainton, Barry. (2010). *Time and Space* (3rd edition). Durham: Acumen.
Dasgupta, Shamik. (2009). "Individuals: An Essay in Revisionary Metaphysics." *Philosophical Studies* 145, pp. 35–67.
Davidson, Matthew. (2003). "Presentism and the Non-Present." *Philosophical Studies* 113, pp. 77–92.
Dehmelt, Hans. (1989). "Triton, . . . Electron, . . . Cosmon . . . : An Infinite Regression?" *Proceedings of the National Academy of Sciences* 86, pp. 8618–8619.
Della Roca, Michael. (1996). "Essentialism: Parts 1 & 2." *Philosophical Books* 37, pp. 1–20; 81–9.
Denkel, Arda. (1996). *Object and Property*. Cambridge: Cambridge University Press.
deRosset, Louis. (2010). "Getting Priority Straight." *Philosophical Studies* 149 (1), pp. 73–97.
Descartes, Rene. (1988). *The Philosophical Writings Of Descartes* (3 vols.). Trans. by John Cottingham, Robert Stoothoff, and Dugald Murdoch (Volume 3 including Anthony Kenny). Cambridge: Cambridge University Press.
Descartes, Rene. (2008). *Meditations on First Philosophy: With Selections from the Objections and Replies*. Trans. by Michael Moriarty. Oxford: Oxford University Press.
Des Chene, Dennis. (1996). *Physiologia: Natural Philosophy in Late Aristotelian and Cartesian Thought*. Ithaca: Cornell University Press.
Des Chene, Dennis. (2006). "From Natural Philosophy to Natural Science." In Donald Rutherford (Ed.), *The Cambridge Companion to Early Modern Philosophy*. New York: Cambridge University Press.
Devitt, Michael. (2008). "Resurrecting Biological Essentialism." *Philosophy of Science* 75, pp. 344–382.
Dorr, Cian. (2005). "What We Disagree About When We Disagree About Ontology." In Mark Kalderon (Ed.), *Fictionalism in Metaphysics* (pp. 234–286). Oxford: Oxford University Press.
Dumsday, Travis. (2012). "A New Argument for Intrinsic Biological Essentialism." *Philosophical Quarterly* 62 (248), pp. 486–504.
Dupré, John. (2010). "It Is Not Possible to Reduce Biological Explanations to Explanations in Chemistry and/or Physics." In Francisco Jose Ayala & Robert Arp (Eds.), *Contemporary Debates in Philosophy of Biology*. Malden, MA: Wiley-Blackwell Publishing.
Earley, Joseph. (2003). "How Dynamic Aggregates May Achieve Effective Integration." *Advances in Complex Systems* 6, pp. 115–126.
Earley, Joseph. (2005). "Why There is No Salt in the Sea." *Foundations of Chemistry* 7, pp. 85–102.
Earman, John. (1989). *World Enough and Spacetime*. Cambridge: MIT Press.
Ehring, D. (1997). "Lewis, Temporary Intrinsics, and Momentary Tropes." *Analysis* 57 (4), pp. 254–258.
Elder, Crawford. (2004). *Real Natures and Familiar Objects*. Cambridge, MA: MIT Press.
Elder, Crawford. (2007). "On the Phenomenon of Dog-Wise Arrangement." *Philosophy and Phenomenological Research* 74, pp. 132–155.
Elder, Crawford. (2011). *Familiar Objects and their Shadows*. New York: Cambridge University Press.
Ellis, Brian. (2001). *Scientific Essentialism*. Cambridge: Cambridge University Press.
Ellis, George F. R. (2001). "Quantum Theory and the Macroscopic World." In Robert J. Russell et al. (Eds.), *Quantum Mechanics: Scientific Perspectives on Divine Action* (pp. 259–291). Vatican City State and Berkeley: Vatican Observatory and Center for Theology and the Natural Sciences.

Erefsheski, Marc. (1992). "Eliminative Pluralism." *Philosophy of Science* 59, pp. 671–690.
Esfeld, Michael and Vincent Lam. (2008). "Moderate Structural Realism about Space-Time." *Synthese* 160 (1), pp. 27–46.
Fine, Kit. (1981). "Acts, Events and Things." In Werner Leinfellner, Eric Kramer, and Jeffrey Schank (Eds.), *Language and Ontology: Proceedings of the Sixth International Wittgenstein Symposium 23rd to 30th August 1981*. Kirchberg am Wechsel, Austria: Holder-Pichler-Tempsky.
Fine, Kit. (1991). "The Study of Ontology." *Nous* 25, pp. 263–94.
Fine, Kit. (1994a). "Essence and Modality." *Philosophical Perspectives* 8, pp. 1–16.
Fine, Kit. (1994b). "Ontological Dependence." *Proceedings of the Aristotelian Society* 95, pp. 269–290.
Fine, Kit. (1994c). "Compounds and Aggregates." *Nous* XXVIII, 2, pp. 137–158.
Fine, Kit. (1995). "Senses of Essence." In Walter Sinnott-Armstrong, Diana Raffman, and Nicholas Asher (Eds.), *Modality, Morality, and Belief*. Cambridge: Cambridge University Press.
Fine, Kit. (1999). "Things and Their Parts." *Midwest Studies in Philosophy* 23, pp. 61–74.
Fine, Kit. (2001). "The Question of Realism." *Philosophers Imprint*, 1(1), pp. 1–30.
Fine, Kit. (2002). "The Varieties of Necessity." In Tamar Gendler and John Hawthorne (Eds.), *Conceivability and Possibility* (pp. 253–281). Oxford: Oxford University Press).
Fine, Kit. (2003). "The non-identity of a material thing and its matter." *Mind* 112 (446), pp. 195–234.
Fine, Kit. (2010). "Towards a Theory of Part." *Journal of Philosophy* 107 (11), pp. 559–589.
Fine, K. (2012). "A Guide to Ground." In Fabrice Correia and Brian Schnieder (Eds.), *Grounding and Explanation*. Cambridge: Cambridge University Press.
Freddoso, Alfred. (1986). "The Necessity of Nature." *Midwest Studies in Philosophy* 11 (1), pp. 215–242.
French, Steven. (1998). "On the Withering Away of Physical Objects." In Elena Castellani (Ed.), *Interpreting Bodies: Classical and Quantum Objects in Modern Physics* (pp. 93–113). Guildford, UK: Princeton University Press.
Geach, P.T. (1967). "Identity." *Review of Metaphysics* 21, pp. 3–12.
Gelman, Susan A. (2003). *The Essential Child: Origins of Essentialism in Everyday Thought*. New York: Oxford University Press.
Gelman, Susan A. (2004). "Psychological Essentialism in Children." *Trends in Cognitive Sciences* 8 (9), pp. 404–409.
Gelman, Susan A. (2009). "Boys Will Be Boys; Cows Will Be Cows: Children's Essentialist Reasoning About Gender Categories and Animal Species." *Child Development* 80 (2), pp. 461–481.
Georgi, Howard. (1989). "Effective Quantum Field Theories." In Paul Davies (Ed.), *The New Physics* (pp. 446–57). Cambridge: Cambridge University Press.
Gibbard, Allan. (1975). "Contingent Identity." In Michael Rea (Ed.), *Material Constitution: A Reader* (pp. 93–126). Lanham: Rowman & Littlefield.
Gilmore, Cody. (2014). "Location and Mereology." In Edward N. Zalta (Ed.), *The Stanford Encyclopedia of Philosophy* (Spring 2014 Edition), URL = <http://plato.stanford.edu/archives/spr2014/entries/location-mereology/>
Ginsberg, Allen. (1984). "On a Paradox in Quantum Mechanics." *Synthese* 61, pp. 325–349.
Goetz, Stewart. (2001). "Modal dualism: A Critique." In Kevin J. Corcoran (Ed.), *Soul, Body, and Survival: Essays on the Metaphysics of Human Persons*. Ithaca: Cornell University Press.

288 Bibliography

Goodman, Nelson and Leonard, Henry S. (1940). "The Calculus of Individuals and Its Uses." *Journal of Symbolic Logic*, 5, pp. 45–55.
Gorman, Michael. (1993). "Ontological Priority and John Duns Scotus." *The Philosophical Quarterly* 43(173), pp. 460–471.
Gorman, Michael. (2005). "The Essential and the Accidental." *Ratio* 18 (3), pp. 276–289.
Gorman, Michael. (2006). "Substance and Identity-Dependence." *Philosophical Papers* 35, pp. 103–11.
Greene, Brian. (1999). *The Elegant Universe: Superstrings, Hidden Dimensions, and the Quest for the Ultimate Theory*. New York: Random House.
Harré, Rom. (1970). "Powers." *The British Journal for the Philosophy of Science* 21 (1), pp. 81–101.
Harré, Rom and Madden, E. H. (1975). *Causal Powers: A Theory of Natural Necessity*. Oxford: Blackwell.
Harré, Rom. (2005). "Chemical Kinds and Essences Revisited." *Foundations of Chemistry* 7, pp. 7–30.
Harré, Rom and Jean-Pierre Llored. (2011). "Mereologies as the Grammars of Chemical Discourses." *Foundations of Chemistry* 13, pp. 63–76.
Harte, Verity. (2002). *Plato on Parts and Wholes: The Metaphysics of Structure*. Oxford: Clarendon Press.
Hasker, William. 1999. *The Emergent Self*. Ithaca, New York: Cornell University Press.
Hasker, William. 2010. "Persons and the Unity of Consciousness." In Robert Koons and George Bealer (Eds.), *The Waning of Materialism*. New York: Oxford University Press.
Hawley, Katherin. (2001). *How Things Persist*. Oxford: Oxford University Press.
Hawley, Katherin. (2006). "Selections from *How Things Persist*." In Sally Haslanger and Roxanne Marie Kurtz (Eds.), *Persistence: Contemporary Readings*. Cambridge: MIT Press.
Hawthorne, John and Andrew Cortens. (1995). "Towards Ontological Nihilism." *Philosophical Studies* 79, pp. 143–165.
Hawthorne, John. (2006). *Metaphysical Essays*. Oxford: Oxford University Press.
Healey, Richard. (1995). "Substance, Modality, and Spacetime." *Erkenntnis* 42 (3), pp. 287–316.
Heil, John. (1998). "Supervenience Deconstructed." *European Journal of Philosophy* 6 (2), pp. 146–155.
Heil, John. (2003). *From an Ontological Point of View*. New York: Oxford University Press.
Heil, John. (2005). "Kinds and Essence." *Ratio* 18 (4), pp. 405–419.
Heil, John. (2012). *The Universe as We Find It*. Oxford: Oxford University Press.
Heller, Mark. (1990). *The Ontology of Physical Objects: Four-Dimensional Hunks of Matter*. New York: Cambridge University Press.
Hendry, Robin. (2006). "Is There Downward Causation in Chemistry?" In Davis Baird, Lee McIntyre and Eric Scerri (Eds.), *Philosophy of Chemistry: Synthesis of a New Discipline* (pp. 173–189), Boston Studies in the Philosophy of Science Volume 242. Dordrecht: Springer.
Hendry, Robin. (2010). "Ontological Reduction and Molecular Structure." *Studies in History and Philosophy of Modern Physics* 41, pp. 183–191.
Hendry, Robin. Forthcoming. *The Metaphysics of Chemistry*. Oxford: Oxford University Press.
Hoefer, Carl. (1996). "The Metaphysics of Space-Time Substantivalism." *The Journal of Philosophy* 93 (1), pp. 5–27.

Hoefer, Carl. (2003). "For Fundamentalism." *Philosophy of Science* 70, pp. 1401–1412.
Hoffman, Joshua and Gary Rosenkrantz. (1997). *Substance: Its Nature and Existence.* New York: Routledge.
Hofweber, Thomas. (2009). "Ambitious, Yet Modest, Metaphysics." In David Chalmers, David Manley, and Ryan Wasserman (Eds.), *Metametaphysics* (pp. 347–83). Oxford: Oxford University Press.
Holden, Thomas. (2004). *The Architecture of Matter: Galileo to Kant.* New York: Oxford University Press.
Horgan, Terence. (1982). "Supervenience and Microphysics." *Pacific Philosophical Quarterly* 63, pp. 29–43.
Horgan, Terence and Matjaz Potrč. (2000)."Blobjectivism and Indirect Correspondence." *Facta Philosophica* 2, pp. 249–270.
Howard, D. (1989). "Holism, Separability and the Metaphysical Implications of the Bell experiments." In James Cushing and Ernan McMullin (Eds.), *Philosophical Consequences of Quantum Theory: Reflections on Bell's Theorem* (pp. 224–253). Notre Dame: University of Notre Dame Press.
Hudson, Hud. (2001). *A Materialist Metaphysics of the Human Person.* Ithaca: Cornell University Press.
Hudson, Hud. (2006). *The Metaphysics of Hyperspace.* New York: Oxford University Press.
Hull, David. (1965). "The Effect of Essentialism on Taxonomy: 2000 Years of Stasis." *British Journal for the Philosophy of Science* 15, 314–326. (Reprinted in Ereshefsky (1992)).
Humphreys, Paul. (1997). "How Properties Emerge." *Philosophy of Science*, 64, pp. 1–17.
Hütteman, Andreas. (2004). *What's Wrong with Microphysicalism?* London: Routledge.
Hütteman, Andreas and David Papineau. (2005). "Physicalism Decomposed." *Analysis* 65, pp. 33–39.
Hütteman, Andreas. (2005). "Explanation, Emergence, and Quantum Entanglement." *Philosophy of Science* 72, pp. 114–127.
Hütteman, Andreas and Alan C. Love. (2011). "Aspects of Reductive Explanation in Biological Science: Intrinsicality, Fundamentality, and Temporality." *The British Journal for Philosophy of Science* 62, pp. 519–549.
Huxley, Thomas Henry. (1866). *Lessons in Elementary Physiology.*
Inman, Ross. (2012). "Essential Dependence, Truthmaking, and Mereology: Then and Now." In Lukas Novak, Daniel D. Novotny, Prokop Sousedik and David Svoboda (Eds.), *Metaphysics: Aristotelian, Scholastic, Analytic* (pp. 73–90). Ontos Verlag.
Inman, Ross. (2014). "Neo-Aristotelian Plenitude." *Philosophical Studies* 168 (3), pp. 583–597.
Inman, Ross. (2018). "Against Constitutionalism." In Jonathan Loose, Angus Menuge, and J.P. Moreland (Eds.), *The Blackwell Companion to Substance Dualism.* Oxford, UK: Wiley Blackwell.
Jacobs, Jonathan D. (2010). "A Powers Theory of Modality: Or, How I Learned to Stop Worrying and Reject Possible Worlds." *Philosophical Studies* 151, pp. 227–248.
Johnston, Mark. (1992). "Constitution Is Not Identity." In Michael Rea (Ed.), *Material Constitution: A Reader* (pp. 44–63). Lanham: Rowman & Littlefield.
Johnston, Mark. (2006). "Hylomorphism." *Journal of Philosophy* 103 (12), pp. 652–698.
Juarrero, Alicia. (2000). "Dynamics in Action: Intentional Behavior as a Complex System." *Emergence* 2(2), pp. 24–57.

Kant, Immanuel. (1965). *Critique of Pure Reason.* Trans. N. Kemp Smith. New York: St. Martin's.
Kaplan, David. (1978). "Transworld Heir Lines." In Michael J. Loux (Ed.), Reprinted in *The Actual and the Possible: Readings in the Metaphysics of Modality* (pp. 88–109.). Ithaca: Cornel University Press.
Karakostas, Vassilios. (2007). "Nonseparability, Potentiality, and the Context-Dependence of Quantum Objects." *Journal for General Philosophy of Science* 38, pp. 279–297.
Karakostas, Vassilios. (2009). "Humean Supervenience in the Light of Contemporary Science." *Metaphysica* 10, pp. 1–26.
Keil, Frank C. (1989). *Concepts, Kinds, and Cognitive Development.* Cambridge, MA: MIT Press.
Keller, Evelyn Fox. (2010). "It Is Possible to Reduce Biological Explanations to Explanations in Chemistry and/or Physics." In Francisco Jose Ayala and Robert Arp (Eds.), *Contemporary Debates in Philosophy of Biology.* Wiley-Blackwell Publishing.
Kim, Jaegwon. (1978). "Supervenience and Nomological Incommensurable." *American Philosophical Quarterly* 15, pp. 149–156.
Kim, Jaegwon. (1988). "Explanatory Realism, Causal Realism, and Explanatory Exclusion." *Midwest Studies in Philosophy* 12, pp. 225–240.
Kim, Jaegwon. (1993). "Supervenience for Multiple Domains" Reprinted in *Supervenience and Mind: Selected Philosophical Essays* (pp. 109–130). New York: Cambridge.
Kim, Jaegwon. (1998). *Mind in a Physical World: An Essay on the Mind-Body Problem and Mental Causation.* Cambridge, MA: MIT Press.
Kim, Jaegwon. (1999). "Making Sense of Emergence." *Philosophical Studies* 95, pp. 3–36.
King, Peter. (2004). "Metaphysics." In Jeff Brower and Kevin Guilfoy (Eds.), *The Cambridge Companion to Peter Abelard* (pp. 65–125). New York: Cambridge University Press.
Klima, Gyula. (2002). "Contemporary 'Essentialism' vs. Aristotelian Essentialism." In John Haldane (Ed.), *Mind, Metaphysics, and Value in the Thomistic and Analytical Traditions* (pp. 175–194). Notre Dame, IN: University of Notre Dame Press.
Kment, Boris. (2014). *Modality and Explanatory Reasoning.* New York: Oxford University Press.
Knuutitila, Simo. (1993). *Modalities in Medieval Philosophy.* New York: Routledge.
Knuuttila, Simo. (2011). "Medieval Theories of Modality." In Edward N. Zalta (Ed.), *The Stanford Encyclopedia of Philosophy* (Summer 2011 Edition), Edward N. Zalta (Ed.), URL = <http://plato.stanford.edu/archives/sum2011/entries/modality-medieval/>.
Koons, Robert. (2010). "Epistemological Objections to Materialism." In Robert Koons and George Bealer (Eds.), *The Waning of Materialism* (pp. 281–306). New York: Oxford University Press.
Koons, Robert. (2014). "Staunch vs. Faint-hearted Hylomorphism: Toward an Aristotelian Account of Composition." *Res Philosophica* 91 (2), pp. 151–177.
Koons, Robert and Timothy Pickavance. (2015). *Metaphysics: The Fundamentals.* Malden, MA: Wiley-Blackwell.
Koons, Robert and Timothy Pickavance. (2017). *The Atlas of Reality: A Comprehensive Guide to Metaphysics.* Malden, MA: Wiley-Blackwell.
Korman, Daniel. (2010). "Strange Kinds, Familiar Kinds, and the Charge of Arbitrariness." In Dean Zimmerman (Ed.), *Oxford Studies in Metaphysics*, Volume 5. Oxford: Oxford University Press.

Korman, Daniel Z. (2011). "Ordinary Objects." In Edward N. Zalta (Ed.), *The Stanford Encyclopedia of Philosophy* (Winter 2011 Edition), URL = <http://plato.stanford.edu/archives/win2011/entries/ordinary-objects/>.
Korman, Daniel Z. (2015a). *Objects: Nothing Out of the Ordinary*. Oxford: Oxford University Press.
Korman, Daniel Z. (2015b). Review of *The Double Lives of Objects*, Notre Dame Philosophical Reviews, http://ndpr.nd.edu/
Koslicki, Kathrin. (2007). "Towards a Neo-Aristotelian Mereology." *Dialectica*, 61 (1), pp. 127–159.
Koslicki, Kathrin. (2008). *The Structure of Objects*. Oxford: Oxford University Press.
Koslicki, Kathrin. (2013a). "Ontological Dependence: An Opinionated Survey." In Benjamin Schnieder, Miguel Hoeltje and Alex Steinberg (Eds.), *Varieties of Dependence: Ontological Dependence, Grounding, Supervenience, Response-Dependence* (pp. 31–64). Philosophia Verlag.
Koslicki, Kathrin. (2013b). "Substance, Independence, and Unity." In Edward Feser (Ed.), *Aristotle on Method and Metaphysics* (pp. 169–195). Palgrave Macmillan.
Kronen, John D., Sandra Menssen, and Thomas D. Sullivan. (2000). "The Problem of the Continuant: Aquinas and Suarez on Prime Matter and Substantial Generation." *The Review of Metaphysics* 53, pp. 863–885.
Kronz, Fredrick M., Tiehen, Justin T. (2002). "Emergence and Quantum Mechanics." *Philosophy of Science* 69, pp. 324–347.
Ladyman, J. and Ross, D. (2007). *Every Thing Must Go: Metaphysics Naturalized*. Oxford: Oxford University Press.
Laubichler, Manfred and Günter Wagner. (2000). "Character Identification in Evolutionary Biology: The Role of the Organism." *Theory Bioscience* 119, pp. 20–40.
Laubichler, Manfred and Günter Wagner. (2001). "How Molecular is Molecular Developmental Biology? A Reply to Alex Rosenberg's Reductionism Redux." *Biology and Philosophy* 16, pp. 53–68.
Lavine, Shaughan. (1991). "Is Quantum Mechanics an Atomistic Theory?" *Synthese* 89 (2), pp. 253–271.
Laycock, Henry. (2006). *Words Without Objects: Semantics, Ontology and Logic for Non-Singularity*. Oxford: Clarendon Press.
Leibniz, Gottfried Wilhelm. (1969). *Philosophical Papers and Letters*. Trans. and Ed. by L. E. Loemker. Dordrecht: Reidel.
Leibniz, Gottfried Wilhelm. (1951). *Monadology*. In Philip Weiner (Ed.), *Leibniz Selections*. New York: Charles Scribner's Sons.
Lewis, David. (1968). "Counterpart Theory and Quantified Modal Logic." *Journal of Philosophy*, 65, pp. 113–126. Reprinted in Michael J. Loux (Ed.), *The Actual and the Possible: Readings in the Metaphysics of Modality*. Ithaca: Cornel University Press, 1979, pp. 110–128.
Lewis, David. (1973). *Counterfactuals*. Cambridge, MA: Harvard University Press.
Lewis, David. (1983). *Philosophical Papers*, Vol. 1. Oxford: Oxford University Press.
Lewis, David. (1986a). *On the Plurality of Worlds*. Oxford: Basil Blackwell.
Lewis, David. (1986b). "Introduction." In *Philosophical Papers*, Vol. 2, ix–xvii. Oxford: Oxford University Press.
Lewis, David. (1991). *Parts of Classes*. Oxford: Blackwell.
Lewis, David. (1999). *Papers in Metaphysics and Epistemology*. Cambridge: Cambridge University Press.
Lewis, David. (1999a). "New Work for a Theory of Universals." In *Papers in Metaphysics and Epistemology* (pp. 8–55). Cambridge: Cambridge University Press.
Lewis, David. (1999b). "Reduction of Mind." In *Papers in Metaphysics and Epistemology* (pp. 291–324). Cambridge: Cambridge University Press.

Lewis, David. (1999c). "Humean Supervenience Debugged." In *Papers in Metaphysics and Epistemology* (pp. 224–247). Cambridge: Cambridge University Press.
Lewis, David. (1999d). "Putnam's Paradox." In *Papers in Metaphysics and Epistemology* (pp. 56–77). Cambridge: Cambridge University Press.
Lewis, David. (1999e). "Many, But Almost One." In *Papers in Metaphysics and Epistemology* (pp. 164–183). Cambridge: Cambridge University Press.
Lewis, David. (1999f). "Defining 'Intrinsic' (with Rae Langton)." In *Papers in Metaphysics and Epistemology* (pp. 116–133). Cambridge: Cambridge University Press.
Lewis, Peter J. (2006). "GRW: A Case Study in Quantum Ontology." *Philosophy Compass* 1 (2), pp. 224–244.
Llored, Jean-Pierre. (2010). "Mereology and Quantum Chemistry: The Approximation of Molecular Orbital." *Foundations of Chemistry* 12, pp. 203–221.
Locke, John. (1975). *An Essay Concerning Human Understanding*. Ed. Peter H. Nidditch. Oxford: Clarendon.
Loewer, Barry. (1996). "Quantum Mechanics and Free Will." *Philosophical Topics* 24 (2), pp. 91–112.
Loewer, Barry. (2001). "From Physics to Physicalism." In Carl Gillet and Barry Loewer (Eds.), *Physicalism and its Discontents* (pp. 37–56). Cambridge: Cambridge University Press.
Loux, Michael. (1974). "Kinds and the Dilemma of Individuation." *The Review of Metaphysics* 27 (4), pp. 773–784.
Loux, Michael. (1978). *Substance and Attribute*. Dordrecht: Reidel.
Loux, Michael. (2006). *Metaphysics: A Contemporary Introduction*. New York: Routledge.
Lowe, E. J. (1983). "On the Identity of Artifacts." *The Journal of Philosophy* 80, pp. 220–31.
Lowe, E. J. (1998). *The Possibility of Metaphysics: Substance, Identity, and Time*. Oxford: Clarendon Press.
Lowe, E. J. (2002). *A Survey of Metaphysics*. Oxford: Oxford University Press.
Lowe, E. J. (2005a). "How are Ordinary Objects Possible?" *The Monist* 88, pp. 510–533.
Lowe, E. J. (2005b). "Ontological Dependence." In Edward N. Zalta (Ed.), *The Stanford Encyclopedia of Philosophy*. URL = <http://plato.stanford.edu/entries/dependence-ontological/>.
Lowe, E. J. (2006). *The Four-Category Ontology. A Metaphysical Foundation for Natural Science*, Oxford University Press: Oxford.
Lowe, E. J. (2008a). "New Directions in Metaphysics and Ontology." *Axiomathes* (2008) 18, pp. 273–288.
Lowe, E. J. (2008b). "Two Notions of Being: Entity and Essence." *Philosophy* 83 (62), pp. 23–48.
Lowe, E. J. (2009a). *More Kinds of Being: A Further Study of Individuation, Identity, and the Logic of Sortal Terms*. Oxford: Wiley-Blackwell.
Lowe, E. J. (2009b). "An Essentialist Approach to Truthmaking." In E.J. Lowe and A. Rami (Eds.), *Truth and Truth-making* (pp. 201–216). Durham: Acumen.
Lowe, E. J. (2010). "Ontological Dependence." In Edward N. Zalta (Ed.), *The Stanford Encyclopedia of Philosophy* (Spring 2010 Edition), URL = <http://plato.stanford.edu/archives/spr2010/entries/dependence-ontological/>.
Lowe, E. J. (2011). "The Rationality of Metaphysics." *Synthese* 178, pp. 99–109.
Lowe, E. J. (2012a). "Against Monism." In Philip Goff (Ed.), *Spinoza on Monism* (pp. 92–112). London: Palgrave.
Lowe, E. J. (2012b). "Asymmetrical Dependence in Individuation." In Fabrice Correia and Benjamin Schnieder (Eds.), *Metaphysical Grounding: Understanding the Structure of Reality* (pp. 214–233). Cambridge University Press.

Lowe, E. J. (2012c). "What is the Source of our Knowledge of Modal Truths?" *Mind*, 121 (484), pp. 919–950.
Lowe, E. J. (2012d). "A Neo-Aristotelian Substance Ontology: Neither Relational Nor Constituent." In Tuomas Tahko (Ed.), *Contemporary Aristotelian Metaphysics* (pp. 229–248). New York: Oxford University Press.
Lowe, Jonathan and Tuomas Tahko. (2005). "Ontological Dependence." In Edward N. Zalta (Ed.), *The Stanford Encyclopedia of Philosophy*, URL = <https://plato.stanford.edu/archives/win2016/entries/dependence-ontological/>.
Mackie, J.L. (1976). *Problems from Locke*. Oxford: Oxford University Press.
Mackie, Penelope. (2006). *How Things Might Have Been*. Oxford: Oxford University Press.
Markosian, Ned. (2004). "Simples, Stuff, and Simple People." *Monist* 87 (3), pp. 405–428.
Markosian, Ned. (2005). "Against Ontological Fundamentalism." *Facta Philosophica* 7, pp. 69–84.
Marmodoro, Anna. (2013). "Aristotle's Hylomorphism Without Reconditioning." *Philosophical Inquiry* 37 (1–2), pp. 5–22.
Martin, Elizabeth A. (2010). *Oxford Dictionary of Science*. Oxford: Oxford University Press.
Maudlin, Tim. (1988). "The Essence of Spacetime." *Proceedings of the Biennial Meeting of the Philosophy of Science Association*, Vol. 1988, Volume Two: Symposia and Invited Papers, pp. 82–91.
Maudlin, Tim. (1993). "Buckets of Water and Waves of Space: Why Space-Time Is Probably a Substance." *Philosophy of Science* 60, pp. 183–203.
Maudlin, Tim. (1998). "Part and Whole in Quantum Mechanics." In Elena Castellani (Ed.), *Interpreting Bodies: Classical and Quantum Objects in Modern Physics* (pp. 46–60). Princeton, NJ: Princeton University Press.
Maudlin, Tim. (2003). "Distilling Metaphysics from Quantum Physics." In Michael J. Loux and Dean W. Zimmerman (Eds.), *The Oxford Handbook of Metaphysics* (pp. 461–487). Oxford: Oxford University Press.
Maudlin, Tim. (2007). *The Metaphysics Within Physics*. Oxford: Oxford University Press.
McDaniel, Kris. (2003)."Against MaxCon Simples." *Australasian Journal of Philosophy*, 81 (2), pp. 265–275.
McDaniel, Kris. (2006). "Gunky Objects in a Simple World." *Philo* 9 (1), pp. 39–46.
McDaniel, Kris. (2007a). "Brutal Simples." In Dean Zimmerman (Ed.), *Oxford Studies in Metaphysics*, Volume 3 (pp. 233–265). Oxford: Oxford University Press.
McDaniel, Kris. (2007b). "Extended Simples." *Philosophical Studies* 133, pp. 131–141.
McDaniel, Kris. (2008). "Against Composition as Identity." *Analysis* 68 (2), pp. 128–133.
McDaniel, Kris. (2009). "Extended Simples and Qualitative Heterogeneity." *The Philosophical Quarterly* 59 (235), pp. 325–331.
McTaggart, J.M.E. (1927). *The Nature of Existence*, Volume 2. Cambridge: Cambridge University Press.
Mellor, D.H. (1998). *Real Time II*. London: Routledge.
Melnyk, Andrew. (2003). *A Physicalist Manifesto*. Cambridge: Cambridge University Press.
Merricks, Trenton. (2001). *Objects and Persons*. Oxford: Oxford University Press.
Merricks, Trenton. (2003). "The End of Counterpart Theory." *The Journal of Philosophy* 100(10), pp. 521–549.
Merricks, Trenton. (2005). "Composition and Vagueness." *Mind* 114, pp. 615–637.

Molnar, George. (2003). *Powers: A Study in Metaphysics*. Oxford: Oxford University Press.
Moreland, J.P. (2001). *Universals*. Chesham: Acumen.
Moreland, J.P. (2009). *The Recalcitrant Imago Dei: Human Persons and the Failure of Naturalism*. London: SCM Press.
Moreland, J.P. (2013). "Mental vs. Top-Down Causation: *Sic et Non*: Why Top-Down Causation Does Not Support Mental Causation." *Philosophia Christi* 15 (1), pp. 133–148.
Morganti, Matteo. (2009). "Ontological Priority, Fundamentality and Monism." *dialectica* 63 (3), pp. 271–288.
Morrison, Donald R. (2006). "Socrates." In Mary Louise Gill and Pierre Pellegrin (Eds.), *A Companion to Ancient Philosophy* (pp. 101–118). Oxford: Blackwell Publishing.
Moss, Lenny. (2003). *What Genes Can't Do*. Cambridge, MA: MIT Press.
Mulliken, R.S. (1932). "Electronic Structures of Polyatomic Molecules and Valence Iii. Quantum Theory of the Double Bond." *Physical Review* 41, pp. 751–758.
Mulliken, R.S. (1981).*Life of a Scientist*. Springer-Verlag, Berlin and London.
Mumford, Stephen and Anjum, Rani Lill. (2011). *Getting Causes from Powers*. New York: Oxford University Press.
Murphy, Nancy. (2007). "Reductionism: How Did We Fall Into It and Can We Emerge From It?" In Nancy Murphy and William R. Stoeger, SJ (Eds.), *Evolution and Emergence: Systems, Organisms and Persons* (pp. 19–39). New York: Oxford University Press.
Myro, G. (1997). "Identity and Time." In Michael Rea (Ed.), *Material Constitution: A Reader* (pp. 148–172). Lanham: Rowman & Littlefield.
Nerlich, Graham. (2005). "Can Parts of Space Move? On Paragraph Six of Newton's Scholium." *Erkenntnis* 62, pp. 119–135.
Noble, Denis. (2006. *The Music of Life: Biology Beyond the Genome*. New York: Oxford University Press.
Normore, Calvin. (2006). "Ockham's Metaphysics of Parts." *Journal of Philosophy* 103 (12), pp. 737–754.
Norton, John D. (2011). "The Hole Argument." In Edward N. Zalta (Ed.), *The Stanford Encyclopedia of Philosophy* (Fall 2011 Edition), URL = <http://plato.stanford.edu/archives/fall2011/entries/spacetime-holearg/>.
Novák, Lukáš, Daniel Novotný, Prokop Sousedík, David Svoboda (Eds.). (2012). *Metaphysics: Aristotelian, Scholastic, Analytic*. Ontos Verlag.
Oderberg, David. (2004). "Temporal Parts and the Possibility of Change." *Philosophy and Phenomenological Research* 69 (3), pp. 686–708.
Oderberg, David. (2007). *Real Essentialism*. New York, NY: Routledge.
Oderberg, David. (2011). "Essence and Properties." *Erkenntnis* 75, pp. 85–111.
Okasha, Samir. (2002). "Darwinian Metaphysics: Species and the Question of Essentialism." *Synthese* 131 (2), pp. 191–213.
Olson, Eric T. (2001). "Material Coincidence and the Indiscernibility Problem." *The Philosophical Quarterly* 51 (204), pp. 337–55.
Olson, Eric T. (2007). *What Are We?*. Oxford: Oxford University Press.
Oppenheim, Paul, and Hilary Putnam. (1958). "Unity of Science as a Working Hypothesis." In Herbert Feigl et al. (Eds.), *Minnesota Studies in the Philosophy of Science*, Volume 2 (pp. 3–36). Minneapolis: Minnesota University Press.
Oppy, Graham. (2000). "Humean Supervenience?" *Philosophical Studies* 101, pp. 77–105.
Papineau, David. (2008). "Must a Physicalist be a Microphysicalist?" In Jakob Hohwy and Jesper Kallestrup (Eds.), *Being Reduced: New Essays on Reduction, Explanation, and Causation* (pp. 126–148). Oxford: Oxford University Press.

Parsons, Josh. (2004). "Distributional Properties." In Frank Jackson and Graham Priest (Eds.), *Lewisian Themes: The Philosophy of David K. Lewis* (pp. 173–80). Oxford: Oxford University Press.
Parsons, Josh. (Unpublished). "Entension, or How It Could Happen That an Object Is Wholly Located in Each of Many Places."
Paseau, Alexander. (2010). "Defining Ultimate Ontological Basis and the Fundamental Layer" *The Philosophical Quarterly* 60, (238), pp. 169–175.
Pasnau, Robert. (2011). *Metaphysical Themes 1274–1671*. New York: Oxford University Press.
Pasnau, Robert. (2012). "Mind and Hylomorphism." In John Marenbon (Ed.), *The Oxford Handbook of Medieval Philosophy* (pp. 486–504). Oxford: Oxford University Press.
Paul, L.A. (2006). "Coincidence as Overlap." *Nous* 40, pp. 623–59.
Paul, L.A. (2012a). "Building the World from its Fundamental Constituents." *Philosophical Studies* 158, pp. 221–256.
Paul, L.A. (2012b). "Metaphysics as Modeling: The Handmaiden's Tale." *Philosophical Studies* 160 (1), pp. 1–29.
Pearce, Kenneth. (Forthcoming). "Foundational Grounding and the Argument From Contingency." *Oxford Studies in Philosophy of Religion*, Volume 8. Oxford: Oxford University Press.
Plantinga, Alvin. (1974). *The Nature of Necessity*, Oxford: Clarendon Press.
Pettit, Philip. (1993). "A Definition of Physicalism." *Analysis* 53 (4), pp. 213–23.
Proksch E, Brandner and JM Jensen. (2008). "The Skin: An Indispensable Barrier." *Experimental Dermatology* 12, pp. 1063–72.
Putnam, Hilary. (1967). "The Nature of Mental States." In Ned Block (Ed.), *Readings in Philosophy of Psychology 1980* (pp. 223–31). Cambridge: Harvard University Press.
Raven, Michael. (2013). "Is Ground A Strict Partial Order?" *American Philosophical Quarterly* 50 (2), pp. 191–199.
Rea, Michael. (1998). "Sameness Without Identity: An Aristotelian Solution to the Problem of Material Constitution." *Ratio* 11 (3), pp. 316–328.
Rea, Michael. (2000a). "Constitution and Kind Membership." *Philosophical Studies* 97, pp. 169–93.
Rea, Michael. (2000b). "Naturalism and Material Objects." In William Lane Craig and J.P. Moreland (Eds.), *Naturalism: A Critical Analysis* (pp. 133–155). London: Routledge.
Readhead, Michael. (1988). "A Philosopher Looks at Quantum Field Theory." In Harvey Brown and Rom Harré (Eds.), *Philosophical Foundations of Quantum Field Theory*. New York: Oxford University Press.
Reid, Thomas. (1994). *The Works of Thomas Reid*. W. Hamilton (Ed.), 2 vols. 6th Edition. Edinburgh: MacLachlan and Stewart.
Rettler, Bradley. (2017). "Grounds and 'Grounds'." *Canadian Journal of Philosophy* 47 (5), pp. 631–655.
Rheins, Jason. 2001. "Similarity and Species Concepts. In Joseph Keim Campbell, Michael O'Rourke, Matthew H. Slater (Eds.), *Carving Nature at Its Joints: Natural Kinds in Metaphysics and Science* (pp. 253–289). Cambridge, MA: MIT Press.
Robb, David. (2009). "Substance." In Robin Le Poidevin, Peter Simons, Andrew McGonigal, Ross Cameron (Eds.), *Routledge Companion to Metaphysics* (pp. 256–264). New York: Routledge.
Rodriguez-Pereyra, Gonzalo. (2015). "Grounding Is Not a Strict Order." *Journal of the American Philosophical Association* 1 (3), pp. 517–534.

Rosen, Gideon. (2010). "Metaphysical Dependence, Grounding and Reduction." In Bob Hale and Aviv Hoffmann (Eds.), *Modality: Metaphysics, Logic, and Epistemology* (pp. 109–36). Oxford University Press.
Rosen, Gideon. (2015). "Real Definition." *Analytic Philosophy* 56 (3), pp. 189–209.
Rosenkrantz, Gary. (1993). *Haecceity: An Ontological Essay*. Dordrecht: Kluwer.
Ross, James F. (1989). "The Crash of Modal Metaphysics." *Review of Metaphysics* 43, pp. 251–279.
Ross, James. (2008). *Thought and World: The Hidden Necessities*. Notre Dame, IN: University of Notre Dame Press.
Russell, Bertrand. (1945). *History of Western Philosophy*. London: George Allen & Unwin.
Saenz, Noël B. (2015). "A Grounding Solution to the Grounding Problem." *Philosophical Studies* 172 (8), pp. 2193–2214.
Sattig, Thomas. (2015). *The Double Lives of Objects*. Oxford: Oxford University Press.
Scaltsas, Theodore. (1994). *Substances and Universals in Aristotle's* Metaphysics. Ithaca: Cornell University Press.
Schaffer, Jonathan. (2003a). "Is There a Fundamental Level?" *Nous* 37, pp. 498–517.
Schaffer, Jonathan. (2003b). "The Problem of Free Mass: Must Properties Cluster?" *Philosophy and Phenomenological Research* 66, pp. 125–38.
Schaffer, Jonathan. (2004). "Two Conceptions of Sparse Properties." *Pacific Philosophical Quarterly* 85, pp. 92–102.
Schaffer, Jonathan. (2007). "From Nihilism to Monism." *Australasian Journal of Philosophy* 85, pp. 175–91.
Schaffer, Jonathan. (2009a). "On What Grounds What." In David J. Chalmers, David Manley, and Ryan Wasserman (Eds.), *Metametaphysics: New Essays on the Foundations of Ontology* (pp. 347–83). Oxford: Oxford University Press.
Schaffer, Jonathan. (2009b). "Spacetime the One Substance." *Philosophical Studies* 145, pp. 131–148.
Schaffer, Jonathan. (2010a). "The Internal Relatedness of All Things." *Mind* 474, pp. 341–376.
Schaffer, Jonathan. (2010b). "Monism: The Priority of the Whole." *Philosophical Review* 119, pp. 31–76.
Schaffer, Jonathan. (2012). "Grounding, Transitivity, and Contrastivity." In Fabrice Correia and Brian Schnieder (Eds.), *Metaphysical Grounding: Understanding the Structure of Reality* (pp. 122–138). Cambridge, UK: Cambridge University Press.
Schaffer, Jonathan. (2014). "Monism." In Edward N. Zalta (Ed.), *Stanford Encyclopedia of Philosophy* (Spring 2014 edition). URL = http://plato.stanford.edu/archives/spr2007/entries/monism/.
Schaffer, Jonathan. (2016). "Grounding in the Image of Causation." *Philosophical Studies* 173 (1), pp. 49–100.
Scotus, Duns. (1949). "*De Primo Principio*." In Evan Roche (Ed.), *The De Primo Principio of John Duns Scotus*. (A Revised Text and Translation). St Bonaventure, N.Y.: Franciscan Institute.
Scotus, Duns. (1975). *Quaestiones Quodlibetales*. In Allan Wolter and Felix Alluntis (Eds.), *God and Creatures: The Quodlibetal Questions*. Princeton: Princeton University Press.
Scotus, Duns. (1997). *Quaestiones super libros Metaphysicorum Aristotelis*. In Girard J. Etzkorn and Allan B. Wolter OFM (Eds.), *Questions on the Metaphysics of Aristotle by John Duns Scotus*. St. Bonaventure, NY: The Franciscan Institute.
Searle, John. (1980). "Minds, Brains, and Programs." *The Behavioral and Brain Sciences* 3, pp. 417–424.

Sider, Theodore. (1997). "Four-Dimensionalism." *The Philosophical Review* 106 (2), pp. 197–231.
Sider, Theodore. (2001). *Four-Dimensionalism: An Ontology of Persistence and Time*. Oxford: Clarendon Press.
Sider, Theodore. (2002). "Review of Persons and Bodies: A Constitution View." *Journal of Philosophy* 99, pp. 45–48.
Sider, Theodore. (2003). "Maximality and Microphysical Supervenience." *Philosophy and Phenomenological Research* 66 (1), pp. 139–149.
Sider, Theodore. (2005). "Sparseness, Immanence, and Naturalness." *Nous* 29, pp. 360–377.
Sider, Theodore. (2006). "All the World's a Stage." In Sally Haslanger and Roxanne Marie Kurtz (Eds.), *Persistence: Contemporary Readings* (pp. 267–284). Cambridge: MIT Press.
Sider, Theodore. (2007). "Against Monism." *Analysis* 67, pp. 1–7.
Sider, Theodore. (2008). "Monism and Statespace Structure." In Robin Le Poidevin (Ed.), *Being: Developments in Contemporary Metaphysics* (pp. 129–150). New York: Cambridge University Press.
Sider, Theodore. (2012). *Writing the Book on the World*. Oxford: Oxford University Press.
Sider, Theodore. (2013). "Against Parthood." In Karen Bennett and Dean W. Zimmerman (Eds.), *Oxford Studies in Metaphysics*, Volume 8 (pp. 237–293). Oxford: Oxford University Press.
Silberstein, Michael and John McGeever. (1999). "In Search for Ontological Emergence." *The Philosophical Quarterly* 49, (195), pp. 182–200.
Simons, Peter. (1987). *Parts: A Study in Ontology*. Oxford: Oxford University Press.
Simons, Peter. (1994). "Particulars in Particular Clothing: Three Trope Theories of Substance." *Philosophy and Phenomenological Research* 54, pp. 553–576.
Simons, Peter. (1998). "Farewell to Substance: A Differentiated Leave Taking." *Ratio* 11(3), pp. 235–252.
Simons, Peter. (2003). "The Universe." *Ratio* 16, pp. 237–250.
Simons, Peter. (2004). "Extended Simples: A Third Way Between Atoms and Gunk." *The Monist* 87 (3), pp. 371–384.
Simons, Peter. (2006). "Real Wholes, Real Parts, Mereology Without Algebra." *Journal of Philosophy* 103 (12), pp. 597–613.
Sober, Elliot. (1993). *Philosophy of Biology*. Boulder, CO: Westview.
Spinoza, Benedict de. (1955). *On the Improvement of the Understanding, Ethics, Correspondence*. Trans. by R.H.M. Elwes. New York: Dover.
Spinoza, Benedict de. (1985). *Ethics*. Trans. by Edwin Curley, in *The Collected Writings of Spinoza*, Volume 1. Princeton: Princeton University Press.
Suarez, Francisco. (2000). *On the Formal Cause of Substance: Metaphysical Disputation XV*. Trans. by John Kronen and Jeremiah Reedy. Milwaukee: Marquette University Press.
Symons, J. (2008). "A Computational Modeling Strategy for Levels." *Philosophy of Science* 75, pp. 608–620.
Tahko, Tuomas (Ed). (2012). *Contemporary Aristotelian Metaphysics*. Cambridge: Cambridge University Press.
Taylor, Barry. (1993). "On Natural Properties in Metaphysics." *Mind* 102 (405), pp. 81–100.
Thomasson, Amie. (2006). "Metaphysical Arguments Against Ordinary Objects." *Philosophical Quarterly* 56, pp. 340–359.
Thompson, Naomi. (2016). "Metaphysical Interdependence." In Mark Jago (Ed.), *Reality Making* (pp. 38–56). New York: Oxford University Press.

298 Bibliography

Thomson, Judith Jarvis. (1999). "Parthood and Identity across Time." In Jaegwon Kim and Ernest Sosa (Eds.), *Metaphysics: An Anthology* (pp. 301–311). Oxford: Basil Blackwell.

Toner, Patrick. 2006. "Metaontology and Accidental Unity." *Philosophical Quarterly* 56 (225), pp. 550–561.

Toner, Patrick. (2007). "Emergent Substance." *Philosophical Studies* 141 (3), pp. 281–297.

Toner, Patrick. (2010). "On Substance." *American Catholic Philosophical Quarterly* 84 (1), pp. 25–48.

Toner, Patrick. (2011). "Hylemorphic Animalism." *Philosophical Studies* 155 (1), pp. 65–81.

Trogdon, Kelly. (2013). "An Introduction to Grounding." In Miguel Hoeltje, Benjamin Schnieder and Alex Steinberg (Eds.), *Varieties of Dependence: Ontological Dependence, Grounding, Supervenience, Response-Dependence* (pp. 97–122). Philosophia Verlag.

Unger, Peter. (1980). "The Problem of the Many." *Midwest Studies in Philosophy* 5, pp. 411–467.

Unger, Peter. (2002). "Free Will and Scientiphicalism." *Philosophy and Phenomenological Research* 65 (1), pp. 1–25.

Unger, Peter. (2006). *All The Power in the World*. Oxford: Oxford University Press.

Uzquiano, Gabriel. (2011). "Mereological Harmony." In Karen Bennett and Dean Zimmerman (Eds.), *Oxford Studies in Metaphysics*. Oxford: Oxford University Press.

Uzquiano, Gabriel. (2014). "Mereology and Modality." In Shieva Kleinschmidt (Ed.), *Mereology and Location* (pp. 199–224). New York: Oxford University Press.

van Inwagen, Peter. (1968). "Two Conceptions of Possible Worlds." *Midwest Studies in Philosophy* 9 (pp. 35–56). Reprinted in van Inwagen, *Ontology, Identity, and Modality*. New York: Cambridge University Press.

van Inwagen, Peter. (1981). "The Doctrine of Arbitrary Undetached Parts." *Pacific Philosophical Quarterly* 62 (2), pp. 123–37.

van Inwagen, Peter. (1990). *Material Beings*. Ithaca, NY: Cornell University Press.

Walsh, Denis. (2006). "Evolutionary Essentialism." *British Journal for the Philosophy of Science* 57, pp. 425–448.

Wasserman, Ryan. 2002. "The Standard Objection to the Standard Account." *Philosophical Studies* 111, pp. 197–216.

Wiggins, David. (1968). "On Being in the Same Place at the Same Time." In Michael Rea (Ed.), *Material Constitution: A Reader* (pp. 3–10). Lanham: Rowman & Littlefield.

Wildman, Nathan. (2013). "Modality, Sparsity, and Essence." *Philosophical Quarterly* 63 (253), pp. 760–782.

Wildman, Nathan. (2016). "How (Not) to Be a Modalist about Essence." In Mark Jago (Ed.), *Reality Making*. New York: Oxford University Press.

Wilson, Jessica. (2014). "No Work for a Theory of Grounding." *Inquiry* 57 (5–6), pp. 535–579.

Wilson, Robert A. (2004). *Boundaries of the Mind: The Individual in the Fragile Sciences: Cognition*. New York: Cambridge University Press.

Wilson, Robert A. (1999). "Realism, Essence, and Kind: Resuscitating Species Essentialsim?" In Robert A. Wilson (Ed.), *Species: New Interdisciplinary Essays* (pp. 187–207). Cambridge: Cambridge University Press.

Wilson, Robert A. (2005). *Genes and the Agents of Life: The Individual in the Fragile Sciences: Biology*. Cambridge: Cambridge University Press.

Witmer, D. G., B. Butchard, and K. Trogdon. (2005). "Intrinsicality without Naturalness." *Philosophy and Phenomenological Research* 70 (2), pp. 326–350.

Wolkenhauer, O. (2001). "Systems biology: the reincarnation of systems theory applied in biology?" *Briefings in Bioinformatics* 2, pp. 258–270.
Wong, Hong Yu. (2006). "Emergents from Fusion." *Philosophy of Science* 73, pp. 345–367.
Yablo, Stephen. (1987). "Identity, Essence, and Indiscernibility." *The Journal of Philosophy* 84 (6), pp. 293–314.
Zimmerman, Dean. (1996). "Indivisible Parts and Extended Objects: Some Philosophical Episodes from Topology's Prehistory." *Monist* 79 (1), pp. 148–180.
Zimmerman, Dean. (1996b). "Could Extended Objects Be Made Out Of Simple Parts? An Argument For 'Atomless Gunk'." *Philosophy and Phenomenological Research* 56, pp. 1–29.
Zimmerman, Dean. (1997). "Immanent Causation." *Philosophical Perspectives: Mind, Causation and World* 11 (s11), pp. 433–471.
Zimmerman, Dean. (2002). "Persons and Bodies: Constitution Without Mereology?" *Philosophy and Phenomenological Research* 64, pp. 599–606.
Zimmerman, Dean. (2010). "From Property Dualism to Substance Dualism." *Aristotelian Society Supplementary Volume* 84 (1), pp. 119–150.

Index

Abelard, Peter 189–190
aggregate: as derivative 97, 103; as grounded whole 102
Albert the Great 107
animalism 221–227
Anjum, Rani 50n70, 50n74, 277n17
Aquinas, Thomas 4, 23, 41, 48n37, 48n39, 54, 94, 104–105, 113n55
Argument from Causal Overdetermination, the 194–201
Argument from Objectionable Arbitrariness, the (against Substantial Priority) 247
Argument from Vagueness, the 183–188
Aristotle 17, 27, 47n15, 48n18, 54, 94, 104, 112n46, 226, 245–246, 255n19, 255n20, 256n25
Armstrong, David 30, 33–35, 41
atomism 78–79, 87
Audi, Paul 54

Bailey, Andrew 171, 222
bare particular 40
Barnett, David 216, 219
Bechtel, William 278n30
Bennett, Karen 113n65
Bird, Alexander 35–37, 51n87
Bishop, Robert 144
Boyd, Richard 31–33
Boyle, Robert 30, 49n45
Brower, Jeffrey 173–174, 180n26
Brown, Christopher 175, 179n1
Burke, Michael 167

Cameron, Ross 110n24, 134
causal overdetermination: Argument from 194–201; defined 196; and metaphysical fundamentality 197; objectionable vs. unobjectionable 196
causal pluralism 197–198
Chisholm, Roderick 7, 217, 220, 243, 269
Consequence Argument 209
constitutionalism 165
cosmic-naturalism 208

Dainton, Barry 235
Davidson, Matthew 276n7
Della Roca, Michael 15
Denkel, Arda 33
deRosset, Louis 111, 118
Doctrine of Arbitrary Undetached Parts (DAUP) 132–133
dominant kinds 162, 167
Dupre, John 146

Earley, Joseph 9n12, 149–150
Elder, Crawford 242
Ellis, Brian 29, 36, 116
Ellis, George 148
emergence: dynamic 148–149, 199; ontological 136

Fine, Kit 3, 11–29, 54, 66–67, 70–71, 94, 110n29, 181n30, 256n25
"four category ontology" 28
fundamentality: absolute and relative 80–81; compositional 78–79; metaphysical 81–82
fundamental mereology 82–109; covering 84–85; direction of mereological grounding 92–94; minimal fundamental mereology 94–96; no fundamental parthood 84–85, 101–109; reformulated

90–96; taxonomy of views 87; the tiling constraint 83–85

Gelman, Susan 50n80
Goliath and Lumpl: Monist solutions to 166–168; neo-Aristotelian solutions to 168–174; pluralist solutions to 164–165; stated 163; and Substantial Priority 175–179
Gorman, Michael 11, 26, 68, 98, 100, 112n47
Greene, Brian 153n7
grounding (indiscernibility) problem 165, 177–178
gunk (mereological) 130–135

Harre, Rom 39, 44, 150, 157n67, 150–151
Harte, Verity 101, 111n32, 111n38, 113n64
Hawthorne, John 208, 267
Healey, Richard 234, 255n6
Heil, John 29, 107–108, 140, 148, 157n63, 208, 219, 254
Hendry, Robin 143–144
Hoefer, Carl 126–127
Holden, Thomas 103
Hudson, Hud 131, 188
Humean Supervenience 2, 119–122
Humphreys, Paul 113n68, 202n28
hunk (mereological) 203–207
Hutteman, Andreas 117
hylomorphism: and human persons 220–221; and metaphysical fundamentality 100–101; perspectival 168–172

Inman, Ross 54, 74n38, 171, 180n13, 180n22

Johnston, Mark 71, 94
Juarrero, Alicia 151, 252
junk (mereological) 203–207

Karakostas, Vassilios 140, 147, 155n45
Keller, Evelyn Fox 151
Kim, Jaegwon 54, 57, 62, 75–76, 78, 92, 109n11, 116–117, 125, 136–138, 152, 155n39, 212
Kind-Power Connection (KPC) 38
Kment, Boris 50n77

Koons, Robert 9n1, 112n44, 112n51, 113n69, 202n30, 215, 245–247, 256n24, 265
Korman, Daniel 159, 172, 177, 193
Koslicki, Katherin 3, 70, 94, 110n26, 112n53, 172–173, 245, 252
Kronz, Fredrick 148–149, 199

Ladyman, James 78
Laubichler, Manfrid 145, 152
Laycock, Henry 276n10
Leibniz, G. W. 23, 54, 61, 134
Lewis, David 1, 42, 56, 79, 84, 119–122, 183, 190
Llored, Jean-Pierre 150, 157n67, 150–151
Locke, John 40
Loux, Michael 34, 39, 50n81
Lowe, E. J. 3, 11, 41, 54, 61, 67, 70–72, 98, 101, 105, 111nn39, 134, 234, 240

Mackie, Penelope 11
Markosian, Ned 81, 263–265
Marmodoro, Anna 256n25
Maudlin, Tim 140, 156nn49–50
maximality: and consciousness 224–225; and the problem of the many 191; and Substantial Priority 224–227; as unprincipled solution 192–194
McDaniel, Kris 132, 141, 155n30, 214, 262, 263
mereological Mooreanism 7, 127–130, 236–239
mereological structure: Doctrine of Arbitrary Undetached Parts 132–133; general 76–79; and generative operations 105–107; grounding and grounded wholes 102; gunk 79, 92–93, 111n36, 130–135; hunk 203–207; junk 203–207; separate/inseparable part 93–94
Merricks, Trenton 185, 195, 200, 209
metaphysical grounding: formal structure of 57–62; intelligibility 54–55; metaphysical explanation 42, 50n77, 55–56; modal consequences of 137–138; monistic multivocalism 55–56; and ontological commitment 55; and supervenience 56–57; varieties

of 62–73; well-foundedness 60–62, 134–135
metaphysical method 6–8
metaphysical structure 79–82
micro-causation 117, 142, 156n57
micro-determination 117
micro-government 117
micro-naturalism 208
modal essentialism 12–17
Moreland, J. P. 94, 217
Morrison, Donald 23, 48n27
Moss, Lenny 146, 277n18
Mulliken, Robert 150
Mumford, Stephen 50n70, 50n74, 277n17
Murphey, Nancy 117–118

naturalness: comparative 266; degreed 44–46; and essence 37–47; and explanatory structure 42–43; fundamental vs. scientific conceptions of 267–269; perfectly natural properties 136
neo-Aristotelianism 1–8
neo-Humeanism 1–8
Nerlich, Graham 235
No Fundamental Intermediates 91, 159
No Fundamental Parthood: arguments for 101–109; stated 84–85
Normore, Calvin 107
numerical sameness without identity 173–174

object (vs. "stuff") 102–103
Oderberg, David 11, 32, 94, 112n52
Okasha, Samir 274
Olson, Eric 215, 225–227
Oppenheim, Paul 75

Papineau, David 117–125, 143
Parsons, Josh 259, 276n2
Part-Priority: argument from the failure of whole-part supervenience against 135–141; argument from possibility of gunk against 130–135; stated 92–93
Pasnau, Robert 201n6, 202n18, 237, 255n19
Paul, Laurie 9n7, 113n65
perdurantism 164–167

personal ontology: and mereology 215–221; and the Thinking Parts Argument 221–227
Pettit, Philip 123
Pickavance, Timothy 9n1, 112n44, 215
Plantinga, Alvin 24, 47n3
Plato, and structure-based mereology 93, 101, 254
Plural Duplication Principle (PDP) 109n15, 137
Priority Microphysicalism (PM): arguments against 130–153; arguments for 122–130; stated 115–122
Priority Monism: considerations against 241–245; stated 85–90, 95
Priority Principle 171, 174
problem of spatial intrinsics 258
Problem of the Many 188–194
property: accidents (proper vs. extraneous) 27; clustering 29–37; distributional 259–261; essentially unitary 215–218; and "four category ontology" 28–29; localized tropes 261–263; non-redundant causal 136, 185, 207; perfectly natural 136, 207, 258; power-distributions 261; and truthmaking 29
property-part distribution 265
Putnam, Hilary 75

quantum chemistry 143
quantum entanglement 138–141

Raven, Michael 58
Rea, Michael 162, 167, 178, 273
real definition 17–23
Reid, Thomas 40
Rettler, Bradley 55–56
Reverse Mereological Essentialism 245, 252–254
Rheins, Jason 277n26
Robb, David 100
Ross, Don 78

Saenz, Noel 177
Sattig, Thomas 168–172
Scaltsas, Theodore 104

Index

Schaffer, Jonathan 54, 61, 62, 78, 82–96, 134–135, 176, 197, 210, 240–245, 267–268
Scotus, John Duns 54, 66–68
Separability Principle 138–141
serious essentialism: and irreducible substantial kinds 29–37; and real definition 17–23; stated 17–47
Sider, Theodore 116, 125–127, 162, 183–184, 206
Simons, Peter 9n12, 65, 79, 94, 100, 111n39, 112n41
singlet state 139
Sober, Elliot 274
spacetime substantivalism 231–236
sparse ontology 225
stage theory (exdurantism) 166
"stuff" (vs. object) 102–103, 238, 245–247, 263
Suarez, Fransisco 49n46
substance: as grounding whole 102; and metaphysical grounding 99–100; as metaphysically fundamental 96–109; and **Minimal Fundamental Mereology** 94; necessary conditions 98–109; and **No Fundamental Parthood** 97, 101–109; proper parts as structure laden 101–102, 111n38, 147, 247; and theism 99; and unity constraint 101–109
Substantial Priority: and the Argument from Causal Overdetermination 194–201; and the Argument from Vagueness 183–188; and Goliath and Lumpl 163–179; and human persons 215–227; a mixed view 97, 249–254; and the Problem of the Many 188–194; stated and explained 96–109; and Tib and Tibbles 161–163

Substrate Principle 245–247
supersubstantivalism 243–245

Tahko, Tuomas 71
Tallant, Jonathan 203, 247–251
terminus argument, the (for Substantial Priority) 203–207
Thinking Parts Argument, the 221–227
Thomasson, Amie 197
Thomistic Substratum Theory (TST) 173–174
Tib and Tibbles 161–163
Tiehen, Justin 148–149, 199
Toner, Patrick 98, 112n50, 178–179, 179n1, 181n35, 229n28, 230n34, 256n24, 265, 272
tracking argument, the (for Substantial Priority) 207–215
Turner, Jason 209–210

Unger, Peter 188
Uzquiano, Gabriel 113n66

van Inwagen, Peter 3, 164, 195, 209, 218, 278n28

Wagner, Gunter 145, 152
Wasserman, Ryan 180n29
Whole-Priority: and biology 151–153; and chemistry 149–151; and empirical adequacy 146–153; and Priority Monism 88–90; and quantum mechanics 147–149; stated 88–94
Wildman, Nathan 16

Zimmerman, Dean 214